Information and liberation

Writings on the politics of information and librarianship

Shiraz Durrani

Information and liberation

Writings on the politics of information and librarianship

Shiraz Durrani

Library Juice Press
Duluth, Minnesota

Copyright Shiraz Durrani, 1979-2008

Published in 2008

Library Juice Press
PO Box 3320
Duluth, MN 55803
http://libraryjuicepress.com/

Printed on acid-free paper

ISBN 978-0-9802004-0-9

Library of Congress Cataloging-in-Publication Data

Durrani, Shiraz.
 Information and liberation : writings on the politics of information and librarianship / Shiraz Durrani.
     p. cm.
 Includes bibliographical references and index.
 Summary: "A collection of the writings of Shiraz Durrani, British-Kenyan library science professor and political activist"--Provided by publisher.
 ISBN 978-0-9802004-0-9 (acid-free paper)
 1. Information policy--Kenya. 2. Information policy--Great Britain. 3. Library science--Political aspects--Kenya. 4. Library science--Political aspects--Great Britain. 5. Library science--Social aspects--Kenya. 6. Library science--Social aspects--Great Britain. 7. Information society--Political aspects. 8. Libraries and society. I. Title.
 ZA3159.K4D87 2008
 020.96762--dc22

2008042284

Go to the people

Go to the people
Live among them
Learn from them
Love them
Serve them
Plan with them
Start with what they know
Build on what they have

Kwame Nkrumah, father of Pan-Africanism and 1st Prime Minister of Ghana

Table of Contents

Contents	vii.
Acknowledgments	xi.
Foreword by Prof. John Gabriel	xiii.
Introduction by Tony Olden	xv.
To Inform is to Liberate	xxvii.
SOCIETY AND INFORMATION: A SOUTH PERSPECTIVE	1.
Setting the scene (1): Rocking the boat	3.
Veterinary Information in Kenya (1979)	4.
Lessons in Kenyan librarianship: leadership, management and the library worker (1984)	7.
Rural information in Kenya (1985)	10.
Agricultural information services in Kenya and Third World needs (1987)	19.
Libraries, communication & development in Kenya: the missing political factor (1990)	27.
Human rights and information in Kenya: a question of political power (1994)	35.
The mirage of democracy in Kenya (1994)	43.
Independence in Kenya and the lost opportunity (1998)	55.
Information relevance, equality and material security—the Kenyan experience (1998)	60.
Politics of information, information for politics	67.
Setting the scene (2): A mere librarian doing research	67.
The politics of food (1983)	68.
The other Kenya: underground and alternative literature (1997)	71.
Information in Kenyan liberation struggle—facts and fiction (2000)	73.
Voices of resistance: underground publishing in Kenya, 1963-1998	74.
THE BATTLE CONTINUES IN COLDER CLIMATE	81.
Setting the scene (3): No equality of conditions	83.
The search for social justice	83.
Black communities and information workers in search of social justice (1999)	85.

Combating racism in library and information services (2000)	92.
Struggle against racial exclusion in public libraries (2000)	94.
Equality: a service development approach (2000 – SD, PJ)	110.
Mainstreaming equality, meeting needs (2003 – SD/ES)	113.
Create a people-orientated public library service (2004)	123.
Creating a new library, creating a new library manager (2005)	126.
Comments on "New direction in social policy" (2005)	131.
The challenge for libraries in a multicultural society (2007)	134.

Politics of information and resistance .... 141.

Capitalism and socialism – has the contradiction been resolved? (1992)	141.
Returning a stare; people's struggles for political and social inclusion (2000)	143.
The professional is political: redefining the social role of public libraries (2004, SD-ES)	157.
The role of the Library Association (2007)	171.
Never be silent – launch, Nairobi (2006)	185.
Communications for liberation: launch of *Never be silent*, London (2006)	189.
Trade union movement in Kenya & their communications system (2006)	193.
Politics of information & knowledge in Africa (2007)	196.

TAKING A STAND .... 213.

Setting the scene (4): Need for active involvement	215.
Explaining the stand	216.
Three questions from *bis* (2001)	216.
Interview with Shiraz Durrani 11th May 2004 (Anna Goulding)	218.
Breaking the culture of silence (2006)	224.
Three questions from bis (2006)	226.

Information activism	231.
Library Association Motions on race and class (1996)	231.
Comprehensive and Efficient: Standards for modern public libraries, a response (2000)	232.
Progressive librarians & activists campaign to save CRE library (2004)	235.

Study, teaching and learning	236.
The educational role of public libraries in combating racism and xenophobia (1999)	236.
Incorporating reflective learning ... in information management (2007)	252.
Learning by doing: lifelong learning through innovations projects at DASS (2007)	255.
Changing course content to meet changing needs (2007)	269.
Ideas into action	272.
The facts behind the Three Continents Liberation Collection (1993)	272.
The Black and Minority Ethnic Stock Group in Hackney Libraries (1999)	274.
Young people in control (SD-DB, 2004)	282.
Quality Leaders Project — Youth: a search for a relevant information service (2005-06)	289.
Progressive librarianship in Africa: The PALIAct story (2006)	294.
Quality Leaders Project (Youth): Report 4 to PHF (2006)	299.
QLP-Y on a journey of a thousand kilometres (2007)	301.
Filling the youth shaped hole (2007)	308.
BOOK REVIEWS	311.
Sturges, Paul and Neill, Richard (1990): The quiet struggle. London: Mansell. (1991)	313.
Foreword to Kinyatti, Maina wa: Mother Kenya (1995)	314.
Libraries for all — A tool for change? (1999)	318.
Stop talking, start doing! (2000)	322.
Black perspective on history of libraries; a review article (2000)	332.
Review: Framework of lost opportunities (2003)	338.
ORGANISE, DO NOT AGONISE	340.
INDEX	343.
About Shiraz Durrani	345.

Acknowlegments

The activities that have inspired the articles in this book could not have taken place without the active involvement of a large number of library workers in Kenya and in Britain. Ideas and projects remain in the academic domain unless given life by people active in the process of implementing these ideas to develop innovative services that meet people's needs. The very process of putting these ideas into practice involved many debates and discussions among participants. These in turn generated more ideas for further implementation. These articles are a testament to the enthusiasm and commitment of these activists who chose to move out of their comfort zones and instead put into practice the African saying that "paths are made by walking". But we did not do the walking on our own. We were taught lessons by community members, workers and peasants who helped us learn the real meaning of what relevant librarianship is all about.

I would like to dedicate this book to these library workers and community members without whose active involvement and support this book could not have been written.

I would also like to thank the coauthors of jointly written articles included in this book — not only for permission to reproduce the articles, but also for the opportunity they provided me in learning from their ideas and experiences during the process of writing the articles.

Finally, I would like to thank Rory Litwin for seeing the need for publishing this book and for his support and encouragement during its preparation.

Shiraz Durrani
18 July 2008

Foreword

Professor John Gabriel

This is a remarkable collection of articles, reports, extracts which represents a fitting testimony to Shiraz Durrani's lifelong struggle for justice and equality as a theorist, activist and professional working in public libraries and the academic field of information services. As an archival record dating back almost thirty years it also records both an analysis of library provision in Kenya as well as Shriaz's role as part of a diasporan community struggling for social justice in the UK.

There are a number of very important themes running through this collection. One is that information is never neutral either in terms of its content or the form in which it is communicated (or not). One such example is that of the needs of rural workers in Kenya whose livelihoods are dependent on technical information about climate, rainfall, irrigation, innovative use of available resources, better agricultural practices, etc as well as a wider analysis of food scarcity. However, information, as the author points out, is not organised around the needs of the rural population, despite the fact that they are in the majority. Information that resides in public libraries in Kenya has been organised on firm (British) colonial foundations and has traditionally served the needs and interests of the colonial and post-colonial elite rather than the population at large. It is not just about the information either but how it is communicated, particularly given the high rates of illiteracy and practical difficulties with access to public libraries. Policies should be built on the principle of information rights for all and strategies adopted that entail innovative ways of communicating information e.g. radio, and now, of course, web-based materials.

His work as a library professional and academic in the UK is reflected in a variety of forms of intervention from resolutions to the National Library Association to policy documents produced for local purposes. Again, the driving force behind these is the commitment to making public libraries 'public' in practice as well as in theory and to ensure that all groups particularly those hitherto effectively excluded are motivated to use and contribute to the development of their services.

One of the major projects credited to the author is the Quality Leaders Project, which aimed at increasing participation of young people in libraries through their involvement in a series of cultural and media initiatives.

Inevitably outreach work with socially excluded communities has featured prominently in his calls for a library service that has traditionally had difficulty attracting diverse service users. At the same time he has argued against the ghettoisation of provision and the importance of influencing mainstream of service delivery. There is a strong sense that organisational policies do make a difference. Decisions about where to locate libraries, opening hours, purchasing priorities, and personnel decisions combine to affect both staffing profiles and responsibilities as well as the take up of services by different groups. At a national level Shiraz has also played an active role in the Chartered Institute of Library and Information Professionals, where he has campaigned for greater equality and justice including support for black librarians.

The baseline data that has acted as a continual source of inspiration for the author confirms that 70 percent of the world's population cannot read, that 1 percent own 40 percent of global assets and the bottom 50 percent of the world's population own 1 percent. Shiraz has worked and campaigned tirelessly against the conditions behind such statistics, with the emphasis on information and knowledge as both an entitlement and source of empowerment. This collection stands as a tribute to his achievements.

Prof. John Gabriel
Head of Department
Department of Applied Social Sciences
London Metropolitan University
Profile available at: http://www.londonmet.ac.uk/depts/dass/staff/johngabriel/

21 May 2007

Introduction

Anthony Olden

For thirty years Shiraz Durrani has specialised in writing about sensitive subjects, and ones by no means restricted to librarianship, first in his native Kenya and then in the United Kingdom. While a librarian at the University of Nairobi his research on Pio Gama Pinto got him into serious trouble. Pinto was a journalist and publisher whose involvement in the *Mau Mau* liberation movement in the 1950s led to five years detention without trial by the colonial authorities. Although by 1965 a Member of Parliament, Pinto was equally distasteful to the post-independence government headed by Jomo Kenyatta, and he was gunned down in a politically-motivated assassination. Nor was taking an interest in such activists appreciated by the regime of Kenyatta's successor, Daniel arap Moi, and Durrani's article in *The Standard* in 1984 led to interrogation by the Special Branch in Nairobi and ultimately to political asylum in Britain.

After he graduated from the University of East Africa Durrani had studied librarianship in the small campus town of Aberystwyth in Wales. Now a refugee, he became a public librarian in a very different part of the UK: Hackney, one of London's inner boroughs and one of its most multicultural. Hackney had been home to Huguenots fleeing religious persecution in 17th century France and Jewish immigrants fleeing pogroms in Tsarist Russia. In the 1980s it had immigrants from the Caribbean, Africa, and many other parts of the world. The books in Hackney Library Service, however, bore little or no relation to this diversity, and Durrani was determined that the stock should be made relevant to the community in which it was located. Although some papers in this volume concentrate on Kenya and Africa and others on the UK, there is a unity throughout. Just as Hackney Library Service was irrelevant to many local residents and their children, the Agricultural Library of the University of Nairobi was of no value to the many Kenyans who strove to make a living by growing crops and keeping chickens on tiny plots of land.

Durrani reminds us that libraries exist in a political, economic and social context. He says they are institutions that "primarily serve the needs of the class in power...serving the needs of one race or class, while a myth is maintained that the needs of all are served" ("Information Relevance, Equality and Material Security...," 1998). This was certainly true of colonial Kenya. It is not widely known that the Carnegie Corporation of New York helped to finance library services that charged subscriptions and restricted their services on a racial basis, but this is what it did in Kenya in the 1930s (Olden, 1995). The McMillan Memorial Library in Nairobi and the Kenya (Carnegie) Circulating Libraries were for Europeans only, although a 1963 Carnegie publication engaged in retrospective white-washing by listing its grants of US $40,000 as "Government of Kenya: public library development, 1930-35" (Anderson, 1963, p. 99). As Rosenberg (1984, p. ii) points out, "public libraries are a part of the ideological apparatus of the state". It was class rather than race that became the discriminating factor in Nigeria. The Carnegie-supported subscription library in Lagos was open to blacks as well as whites because the colony was settler-free and because Alan Burns, the administrator who secured the grant, came to realise that the Westernised African elite were the natural allies of the Europeans.

The links between the colonial and the post-colonial world are easy to illustrate, the visit of the former governor of Kenya, Sir Evelyn Baring, to President Jomo Kenyatta in 1965 being a classic political example. In the words of Elkins (2005), what can you possibly say to someone whose trial you rigged and whom you had banished to a remote outpost for years? Kenyatta was sitting at Baring's old desk, and Baring pointed out to him that it was there that he signed the order to have him detained. Kenyatta told him he knew that, that had he been in Baring's place he would have done exactly the same — and that he himself had since signed detention orders while sitting at that same desk.

Reaching the Masses

According to Durrani, the official information services in Kenya and other Third World countries only reach 10 percent or thereabouts of the population. These people mainly live in urban areas — although as he says by no means all urban dwellers are reached — and are literate in English or another European language. As for such libraries as exist in rural areas, they should stop circulating English and American fiction, and "irrelevant material from all over the world, and concentrate on what is relevant to the peasants" ("Agricultural Information Services in Kenya...," 1987). In fact rural areas in most of Africa are still largely unserved by the public library services set up around the time of independence. Public libraries in Nigeria operated first on a regional level and then on a state level after states replaced regions. Although the country was awash with oil money in the 1970s, the public libraries that had been set up in the 1950s served very few people indeed (Olden, 1985). The norm in Nigeria and in countries such as Tanzania (where public libraries were set up under a board with a remit for the whole nation) was to start by establishing service points in the main urban areas (Olden, 2005). Years later the rural population still waits for library books, as for more fundamental needs: as Durrani says, "the basic need in Kenya today is the provision of adequate food, clothing, and shelter for all the people" ("Libraries, Communication and Development in Kenya...," 1990).

Durrani advocates a translation programme into African languages and from one African language to another. He mentions the success of the Kenya Land and Freedom Army in publishing news in Kiswahili, Gikuyu and other languages, and he provides examples of this in his book *Never Be Silent* (Durrani, 2006). One could link this with examples from other parts of the world, for example Hawaii in the 19th century. The New England missionaries who arrived in 1820 came at a time of great change and assumed a significance that they could hardly have anticipated. Kamehameha the Great had died and the old religion had been overthrown. The missionaries introduced literacy and printing in both the Hawaiian language and English (Day and Loomis, 1972). In the opinion of one modern critic they then went on to control the power of the printed word on the islands for the next forty years, and they did this "not just to save souls but to assist in the progress of plantation/colonial capitalism, to control public education, to mold government into Western forms and to control it, and to domesticate *Kanaka* [Hawaiian] women" (Silva, 2004, p. 55). Then in 1861 a group of Hawaiians started a newspaper in their own language that began a tradition of nationalist resistance.

Durrani tells how the Kenya Land and Freedom Army combined oral experience with print in the 1950s, and later on how during the Moi regime (1978-2002) songs critical of the government were played on cassette by *matatu* (public taxicab) drivers, some of whom were arrested as a result. These Kenyan examples bring to mind the use of poetry as a weapon by the Somali nationalist, Sayyid Muhammad 'Abdille Hassan. Although they disparaged him as the "Mad Mullah of Somaliland", it took the British from 1900 to 1920 to put down his revolt. The poems he composed were memorised and recited by his followers throughout British Somaliland, an ideal method of communicating his message of defiance to a non-literate population that placed much value on oratory. According to Samatar (1982), poetry is a form of broadcasting for nomadic Somalis: it is equivalent to the radio and newspapers in industrial societies.

Radios and newspapers are found in food kiosks in Kenya, described by Durrani as the best places to find out about anything important that is happening in the country. Illiteracy is no barrier because someone else can always be found to read aloud. *Matatu* and bus drivers exchange news over their meals, and women bringing agricultural produce to sell help to bridge the gap between town and country. The walls are covered in pictures and news cuttings of popular heroes, from Dedan Kimaathi (the *Mau Mau* fighter executed by the colonial authorities in 1957) to contemporary footballers.

Durrani's description of English as a language that many are compelled to use because it is the language of the former colonial power is largely true, but there are exceptions. Although possessing a rich oral tradition the Somali language was hardly used in written-down form until 1972, and only then on the insistence of Muhammad Siyad Barre, the ruler who had taken power in the Somali Republic (a merger of the former British and Italian territories) in a coup in 1969. Whereas Kenya was an important colony British Somaliland had been the "Cinderella of Empire". Partly because of the twenty year struggle to defeat Sayyid Muhammad and its legacy, it was not until 1938 that the colonial authorities opened the first government school for boys. The new director of education, R.E. Ellison, wanted to use written Somali in preference to Arabic, but was forced to abandon his plan in the face of intense criticism from local religious leaders. They maintained that the proper language for Muslim boys to write in was Arabic, the language of the Koran. But they were also using the issue as a way to maintain their own position as men of learning and position, as well as to attack the government. Antagonism to Ellison and his school in Berbera led to a riot in the town of Burao in 1939 in which three people were killed. In parts of the British Empire such as 19th century Ireland and 20th century Kenya children could get into trouble for conversing in their native language instead of English. In Somaliland they were prevented from learning to write in Somali by their own religious leaders, backed up by the British governor ("Education to an empty belly breeds sedition only or at its highest paranoiacs like Hitler, Stalin and Mussolini") and by the Colonial Office in London, which wanted no more religion-linked upheaval in that troublesome and unrewarding corner of the empire (Olden, 2008).

Local or International?

In one of the earliest papers in this collection Durrani urges the University of Nairobi and other national institutions in Kenya to encourage their staff to publish locally, and to publish in Kiswahili as well as in English. He says that publishing overseas works against building up a local readership. However many of his academic colleagues in Kenya appeared to consider local publications inferior. Zeleza (1998, p. 30) ascribes the yearning to publish overseas on the part of African academics as "insecure provincialism", although he does list the drawbacks of many African journals, especially those started by individuals anxious to get their own papers into print and their careers established. Anyone familiar with journal publishing in Africa over a period of time will know that some new academic and professional journals never get much further than volume 1 issue number 1, or at any rate volume 1 issue number 2. But few would be as dismissive as Smart (2007, p. 311), who finds it "very difficult to see how the low visibility and respect (national as well as international) for the majority of journals from this continent could ever be improved".

Ngugi wa Thiong'o (1986) famously said that African writers were bound to do for their languages what Shakespeare had done for English and Tolstoy for Russian. He believes in writing in African languages and publishing his work in Africa. Academics in much of Africa and elsewhere are constrained by the ever-increasing dominance of English in the international world of scholarship. Most want to publish abroad as well as at home, and are likely to do so whenever they have the opportunity.

Imperialism and Africa

One thing that quickly becomes obvious in Durrani's writing is his visceral hatred of Western imperialism. This is understandable in a Kenyan with an interest in the colonial era and a strong sense of justice. He refers to the colonial policy of divide and rule, which set one group against another in Kenya. In his account of the long decline of the British Empire, Brendon (2007, p. 382) cites Winston Churchill, who said he "regarded the Hindu-Moslem feud as a bulwark of British rule in India". Brendon goes on to say that Britain made use of differences between the Greek and Turkish communities in Cyprus in the 1950s in just the same way that it had done earlier in India.

Durrani maintains that the disappearance of discrimination on a racial basis towards the end of the colonial era led to the consolidation of two classes: workers and peasants on the one hand and the bourgeoisie on the other. He says that this has influenced every aspect of life in Kenya, including the work of those who provide information: "they fall into one or the other class and their views, professional or otherwise, and actions are decided by their class interests" ("Libraries, Communication and Development in Kenya...," 1990). Writing about the exercise of indirect domination, Howe (2002, p. 116) says that one has to work through local people: "one needs, bluntly, to be able to buy such people, offering direct subsidies, or links of trade, aid, and investment, that will woo them to one's side, or access to cultural capital that confers local prestige...or at the very least the weapons that will keep them in power when all else fails". Durrani expresses disappointment with the Kenyan library staff sent to the UK for professional education with a view to ultimately taking over from the expatriates. He says that after their return they did not take up the challenge, and little changed. One understands his point, but perhaps it is a little harsh. It takes originality and strength of character well above the norm to make a fundamental change of direction in most organisations and professions.

Durrani says that the West replaced colonialism with neo-colonialism in order to continue with the exploitation of Africa, and that the "Soviet Union had nothing to do with this unequal relationship. Indeed it provided valuable material and moral support to the African liberation movements" ("The Mirage of Democracy in Kenya," 1994). In fact Soviet weaponry and advisers were used all the time by the Ethiopian dictator Mengistu Haile Mariam in his attacks on Eritrean liberation fighters. The background is as follows. Eritrea was an Italian colony until Britain invaded during World War II. After the war Britain controlled the territory under United Nations mandate until it was joined in federation with Ethiopia. In 1961 the federation was terminated and Eritrea was made a province of Ethiopia, starting a struggle for independence that was to last for thirty years. Under the Emperor Haile Selassie, Ethiopia was an ally of the United States, and adept at securing arms and other forms of support. At the same time the Soviet Union was arming Ethiopia's neighbour, Somalia, which laid claim to the Somali-speaking Ogaden region inside Ethiopian borders. Then the elderly Haile Selassie was overthrown. The army and ultimately Mengistu Haile Mariam came to power. The two Cold War superpowers now switched sides, the Soviet Union supporting Ethiopia while the United States backed Somalia, although not nearly to the same extent. Meanwhile China, sympathetic to the Somalis and the Eritreans, was denouncing Russian imperialism (Issa-Salwe, 2000; Lewis, 2002; Wrong, 2005).

On China, Durrani feels that Africa has a lot to gain from developing relations with this particular rising world power "which seeks no colonies nor to enslave or colonise people" ("Politics of Information and Knowledge in Africa...," 2007). This is not a view of China shared by the German historian, Osterhammel (1995, English edition 2005, p. 118). He maintains that, in Tibet, China practices "virtually flawless colonial politics right down to invasions by settlers and a justification of a 'civilising mission' on the basis of historically dubious claims".

According to figures cited by Wrong, over fourteen years the Soviet Union gave $9 billion US dollars worth of military hardware to Ethiopia, equivalent to $5,400 for each Ethiopian adult and child. Bizarre is the word Hill (2004, p. 51) uses to describe "Marxist rebels fighting a Marxist government supported by the USSR". But by the late 1980s the fast-changing Soviet Union was no longer willing to waste vast sums of money on a far-away and seemingly endless war. The United States came back into the picture. Israel supplied cluster bombs and other weaponry in exchange for permission from Mengistu to airlift the Falashas (Ethiopian Jews) out of the country (Wrong, 2005). Durrani complains that the arms and torture weapons supplied by Britain, the United States and Israel were all used against Kenyans by the regime of President Moi. They were not used against anyone else because Kenya has no external enemies. Ethiopia had an external enemy — Somalia — on occasion, but the arms used by Mengistu against his own people as well as against the Eritreans and Somalis came mainly from the Soviet Union (Wrong, 2005).

Although little known outside the Horn of Africa, the Eritrean struggle was a genuine people's movement, supported financially by members of the world-wide Eritrean Diaspora. The Eritreans arranged schooling for their fighters and for the civilian population in the liberated areas. Similarly in the detention camps of 1950s Kenya alleged *Mau Mau* activists and sympathizers organized literacy and other classes for fellow inmates. Both Eritreans and Kenyans were good at communicating their message and publicising their cause. Durrani says that "the first demand of the people in Africa is to be left alone by the Western countries to find their own solutions" ("The Politics of Food," 1983). This is unrealistic, given the way the world is ever more bound together, and given the links that stretch back over the centuries and their repercussions. But the Eritreans succeeded without aid from the West or anywhere else, and in the face of great odds, although the dream was to turn sour in the years after independence. The Kenyan struggle did not succeed, but it brought the end of colonial rule nearer. Both struggles offer lessons in the value of self-sufficiency.

The Public Library Service in the United Kingdom

The critic of the British public library as a model for Kenya found himself working for a public library service in Britain itself from the mid-1980s onwards. His reservations about the stock in the London Borough of Hackney have already been mentioned. In collaboration with other staff Durrani developed the Three Continents Liberation Collection. This illustrates not just the importance he placed on library collections being relevant to their local communities but also the importance of recognising the contribution that staff at all levels are capable of making. In Kenya he had noticed that professional staff looked down on the typists, book carriers, messengers, security men and women, cleaners and others who did so much to keep libraries functioning. Why were such people considered "small"? In his opinion they were "small only in terms of their salaries and in the estimation they receive" ("Lessons in Kenyan Librarianship...," 1984). In practice they were often more stimulating and open to ideas than more senior staff. In Hackney he was happy to work with anyone within the library service and outside it who took an interest in the Three Continents Liberation project. Durrani criticises the fact that there are so few staff from African, Asian and Caribbean backgrounds in British libraries, and that hardly any of these are in senior positions. His Quality Leaders Project aimed to do something about this.

Durrani moved from Hackney to the London Borough of Merton. With financial support from the Paul Hamlyn Foundation he went on to the second stage of the Quality Leaders Project, this time with an emphasis on Youth. The aim was to "refocus public library services so that young people themselves decide on the services they need" ("Diversity Matters 3," 2003). Durrani feels that libraries have not captured the imagination of the young, who want more involvement with Information and Communications Technology, media, publishing, drama, film-making and music. Library staff would develop their managerial skills through service development, and they would be assisted by mentors.

The future of British public libraries—or indeed whether they have a future—has been under debate for years, a debate in which Durrani has actively participated. The number of books borrowed declined by 38% between 1994/95 and 2004/05 (Chartered Institute of Library and Information Professionals [CILIP], 2007). A drop in the amount of adult fiction borrowed is the main reason for this according to Grindlay and Morris (2004a; 2004b), who conducted an extensive literature review and analysis of the statistics. The drop in the amount of adult non-fiction borrowed also plays a role. An increase in the amount of disposable income from the early 1980s onwards is suggested as one possible cause, given that book sales have been going up while borrowing from public libraries has been going down. Reductions in book budgets and cuts to opening hours are suggested as other possible reasons for the decline, as is a possible reduction in the amount of time people spend reading. In tandem with this, the number of visits to public libraries was also on the decline until a few years ago, when visits started to increase again, the likely reason being the popularity of free Internet access. Under the People's Network scheme, financed by Britain's national lottery, public libraries were connected to the Internet and staff trained to European Computer Driving Licence standard (CILIP, 2007). However the statistics for 2006/07 showed a decline in both visits and book borrowing according to the Chartered Institute of Public Finance & Accountancy (Page, 2008).

It is Durrani's view that:

> "Some White petty bourgeois groups can be extremely articulate in demanding—and getting—the lion's share of library resources at the expense of Black communities, and the working class as a whole" ("Black Communities and Information Workers...," 1999).

> "Those who have benefited from library services for generations are not likely to give up some of the services in the interest of the 'socially excluded' without a fight" ("Libraries for All...," 1999)

This is debatable. The huge investment in computers in libraries largely benefits those who do not have a computer at home or ready access to one at work. Such people are generally less well off. The cuts in book budgets certainly do not impress many of those who have benefited from libraries for generations. But rather than fighting against this it is likely that some simply give up on a service that they no longer see as having much to offer, a service that has not kept pace with the times. This leaching away of support can hardly benefit public libraries in the long run. According to the government's agency for museums, galleries, libraries and archives, the MLA Partnership, one of the challenges for public library improvement is "to counter the continuing decline in spend on books and other resources and secure sustained investment to provide current and comprehensive stocks to meet demand and need" (*A Blueprint for Excellence*, 2007, p. 7).

Durrani complains about the continual purchase of romantic fiction and "mindless fiction": "Is it always good for people to read more of what they always read while the rest of the population gets nothing?" ("Interview with Shiraz Durrani...," 2004). One can link this with his earlier comment that Kenyan libraries should stop circulating British and American fiction ("Agricultural Information Services in Kenya...," 1987). But reading for recreation is part of Western culture, whereas reading for education and information is the norm in Kenya and other parts of the Developing World. It is indeed anomalous that recreational reading should be free in the UK (or rather free at point of service, because someone has to pay for it, and of course the taxpayer does), when one has to pay to watch comedy and other programmes on television. (Every household must purchase an annual television licence, the cost in 2008 being £135.50—approximately $272). But the commitment of British public libraries to leisure reading is unlikely to change.

Durrani's term "mindless fiction" brings to mind the stance of certain librarians and library committee members a century ago and more. They saw the upholding of standards as part of their job. They wanted the users of their libraries to benefit from the works of Charles Dickens and other great 19th century novelists. They did not want to supply fiction they considered to be of low quality, no matter how popular it was. Yet romantic fiction is mainly read by women, and women made up 58% of public library users in 2004/05. In the same year 37.4% of public library users were retired (LISU, accessed April 12, 2008), and the financial means of retired people are often limited. A visit to a public library for an older reader can be more than just an opportunity to borrow books. It can provide a focus to a morning or afternoon and an opportunity for social contact.

Black communities are no more homogenous than White communities. Blacks and Asians in the United Kingdom are by no means all disadvantaged, and many would be unhappy to be typecast in such a way. To take just one example, the Ugandans of Asian background who were expelled by the government of Idi Amin in the early 1970s were forced to leave everything behind them. They were admitted to the UK, where some eventually became very successful in business, despite having arrived with nothing beyond their own ability, capacity for work, and determination to build a new life. One might well ask what the contemporary British public library has to offer successful Black and Asian—and White—businessmen and women.

Black Librarianship

Durrani defines Black as everyone from Africa, Asia and the Caribbean and everyone who considers himself or herself to be Black. He maintains that "Black Librarianship" is necessary in order to fight racism, that adding on marginal policies to a Eurocentric library system will not do much, nor will the provision of a token service solve real information needs. Hackney Library Service had a Black Stock Group. Few would argue against fighting racism or providing a genuine service, but the term Black Librarianship is open to question. What about White Librarianship? It brings to mind the British National Party, the small far-right group that wants to put the interests of "white Britons" first, stop immigration to the United Kingdom, introduce a scheme of voluntary repatriation for immigrants who are already here legally, link foreign aid to countries that take immigrants back, and ban asylum seekers. Durrani is critical of the library profession—"a sanitised profession that wants to keep away from getting involved in people's struggles" ("Returning a Stare...," 2000)—and often rightly so, but it would hardly countenance the notion of White Librarianship.

In the 1960s Wilfred Plumbe came up with the term "tropical librarianship". He had served as director of new university libraries in Nigeria, Malaysia, Malawi and Guyana, and was to go on to Fiji and Papua New Guinea. He understood the importance of designing new buildings in such a way as to maximise the free flow of air. He was familiar with bookworms, cockroaches, silverfish, termites, mildew, and other hazards to stock. He knew all about training staff and starting and building up national library associations. But the term "tropical librarianship" never caught on, although Plumbe published a collection of his articles under that title in 1987, and Evelyn Evans had published *A Tropical Library Service: The Story of Ghana's Libraries* in 1964. Why tropical librarianship, asked critics? What about temperate librarianship?

Léopold Senghor and other Francophone intellectuals from Africa and the Caribbean devised the term *négritude* in the 1930s, partly in reaction to the racism of the times. Senghor went on to become President of Senegal and a member of the *Académie française*. But early in his career the Nobel Prize-winning Nigerian author Wole Soyinka made fun of the concept of *négritude*. He pointed out that the tiger does not go on about its tigritude, it acts.

"Organise, Do Not Agonise"

To be fair, it has always been Durrani's view that when a situation is unjust one must act: "organise, do not agonise". An example of this is his involvement in the setting up of the Progressive African Librarian and Information Activists' Group (PALIAct), which attempts to develop "people-oriented information services decided upon by workers, peasants, pastoralists, fisher people and other marginalised groups whose information needs have not been met" ("Progressive Librarianship in Africa...," 2006). Durrani was described as a "mere librarian" by the Kenya Special Branch officers who queried his temerity to write about Pio Gama Pinto. How many other "mere librarians" have written so much over the course of thirty years? It is possible to disagree with Shiraz Durrani's views, but at least they are worth disagreeing with, and it is essential to take them seriously. His contribution has been a very considerable one.

> Anthony Olden
> Thames Valley University
> St Mary's Road
> Ealing
> London W5 5RF
> tony.olden@tvu.ac.uk

References

Anderson, Florence. *Carnegie Corporation: Library Program 1911-1961.* New York: Carnegie Corporation of New York, 1963.

A Blueprint for Excellence: Public Libraries 2008-2011. MLA Partnership, 2007. Blueprint for Excellence: Public Libraries 2008-2011 (PDF 62KB) (accessed April 10, 2008).

Brendon, Piers. *The Decline and Fall of the British Empire 1781-1997.* London: Jonathan Cape, 2007.

Chartered Institute of Library and Information Professionals. "Evidence Submitted [to the] Library Review [Conducted by] Hampshire Culture and Communities Policy Review Committee". 2007.

http://www.cilip.org.uk/policyadvocacy/responses/consultations2007/evidence.htm (accessed April 10, 2008).

Day, A. Grove, and Albertine Loomis. *Ka Pa'I Palapala: Early Printing in Hawaii.* Honolulu: Printing Industries of Hawaii, 1972.

"Diversity Matters 3: The Quality Leaders Project—Youth Programme." *Library Management* 24 (2003): 362-66.

Durrani, Shiraz. *Never Be Silent: Publishing & Imperialism in Kenya 1884-1963.* London: Vita Books, 2006.

Elkins, Caroline. *Britain's Gulag: The Brutal End of Empire in Kenya.* London: Pimlico, 2005.

Grindlay, Douglas J.C., and Anne Morris. "The Decline in Adult Book Lending in UK Public Libraries and Its Possible Causes. I. Literature Review." *Journal of Documentation* 60 (2004): 609-31.

Grindlay, Douglas J.C., and Anne Morris. "The Decline in Adult Book Lending in UK Public Libraries and Its Possible Causes. II. Statistical Analysis." *Journal of Documentation* 60 (2004): 632-57.

Hill, Justin. *Ciao Asmara: A Classic Account of Contemporary Africa.* London: Abacus, 2004.

Howe, Stephen. *Empire: A Very Short Introduction.* Oxford: Oxford University Press, 2002.

Issa-Salwe, Abdisalam M. *Cold War Fallout: Boundary Politics and Conflict in the Horn of Africa.* London: HAAN, 2000.

Lewis, I.M. *A Modern History of the Somali: Nation and State in the Horn of Africa.* 4th ed. Oxford: James Currey, 2002.

LISU, Loughborough University. Libraries, Archives, Museums and Publishing Online Statistics Tables.

http://www.lboro.ac.uk/departments/ls/lisu/lampost06/users06.html#plustatgr (accessed April 12, 2008).

Ngugi wa Thiong'o. *Decolonising the Mind: The Politics of Language in African Literature.* Nairobi: Heinemann Kenya, 1986.

Olden, Anthony. "Constraints on the Development of Library Service in Nigeria." *Library Quarterly* 55 (1985): 398-423.

Olden, Anthony. *Libraries in Africa: Pioneers, Policies, Problems.* Lanham, Md.: Scarecrow Press, 1995.

Olden, Anthony. "'For Poor Nations a Library Service Is Vital': Establishing a National Public Library Service in Tanzania in the 1960s." *Library Quarterly* 75 (2005): 421-45.

Olden, Anthony. "Somali Opposition to Government Education: R.E. Ellison and the Berbera School Affair, 1938-1940." *History of Education* 37 (2008): 71-90.

Osterhammel, Jürgen. *Colonialism: A Theoretical Overview.* Princeton: Markus Wiener Publishers, 2005.

Page, Benedicte. "There's More to Libraries than Lending." *The Bookseller*, February 11, 2008. http://www.thebookseller.com/in-depth/feature/52901-theres-more-to-libraries-than-lending.html (accessed April 11, 2008).

Rosenberg, Diana Bryant. "The Colonial State and the Development of Public Libraries in Kenya Prior to 1965." Fellowship thesis, The Library Association, London, 1984.

Samatar, Said S. *Oral Poetry and Somali Nationalism: The Case of Sayyid Mahammad 'Abdile Hasan.* Cambridge: Cambridge University Press, 1982.

Silva, Noenoe K. *Aloha Betrayed: Native Hawaiian Resistance to American Colonialism.* Durham, N.C.: Duke University Press, 2004.

Smart, Pippa. "Journals—The Wrong Model for Africa." *Learned Publishing* 20 (2007): 311-13.

Wrong, Michela. *I Didn't Do It for You: How the World Betrayed a Small African Nation.* London: Fourth Estate, 2005.

Zeleza, Paul Tiyambe. "The Challenges of Editing Scholarly Journals in Africa." In *Knowledge Dissemination in Africa: The Role of Scholarly Journals,* ed. Philip G. Altbach and Damtew Teferra, 13-38. Chestnut Hill, Mass.: Bellagio Publishing Network, 1998.

To Inform is to Liberate

The last 25 years have seen momentous changes in all aspects of people's lives in almost every part of the world. One factor influencing these changes is advances in information and communication technologies (ICT), which have created networked societies. Many economies have moved from industrial to service and now to information-based economies, although strong manufacturing sectors in China and India—as in Japan and Germany—are still the engines for their unprecedented growth.

The growth of the Internet and World Wide Web marks the transition to the Networked Society. Information and knowledge have played an important part in the growth of major older industrialised countries. These revolutionary changes are visible throughout the world. While these are more clearly apparent in industrialised countries, their impact is also felt in the less industrialised, agriculture-based countries. These technological developments have created new tools that manage information at great speed and efficiency. Their potential for growth and development has still not been fully exploited. A lot of attention is therefore given to the technologies associated with these global changes.

The changes are better understood in the context of the development of capitalism and imperialism which gained additional power with what Milne[1] calls the "demise of communist rule in the Soviet Union and eastern Europe", thus leaving capitalist USA and its Western European allies as the dominant world economic and political power. It is here that the technology-driven changes have had the greatest impact. Globalised capitalism has sought to take over natural and human resources of the whole world through an aggressive use of its key instruments—the IMF and the World Bank, now joined by the World Trade Organisation, but backed by the largest military hardware the world has ever seen.

Globalised capitalism survives on fast and efficient control over information without which it cannot retain control over the world. Information is at the very core of its activities. Equally, those threatened by the negative impact of globalised capitalism have asserted their own genre of control over the information sector as a means of resisting transnational assault on their lives and to survive as individuals, countries, communities and nations.

Against this backdrop, major confrontation is evolving between the two opposing forces of globalised capitalism and people's resistance movements. Both these forces struggle at the information level in order to control content as well as forms of information communication and its associated technologies. But whereas in the past capitalist exploitation was always "global" and resistance to it was usually local, now resistance to capitalism is increasingly global. While the battle has been rather uneven between these two contending forces in the past, the people's movements have learnt lessons and are fast taking control of information technologies to organise and gather their forces under a global agenda. Examples of this are the world-wide anti-capitalist/globalisation movement, the World Social Forum as well as electronic international solidarity links between people engaged in struggles at local levels, resulting in the linking of local with global struggles.

---

[1] Milne, Seumas (2007): Movement of the people (Review of: Service, Robert (2007): Comrades; a world history of communism. London: Macmillan). Guardian. 12 May 2007.

This struggle places information and its home institutions—libraries—at the forefront of information wars of the 21st century. Control over information can enable globalised capitalism to control lives and resources of the world; similarly control over it by people's forces through alternative media can give them power to liberate themselves from corporate strangulation and create a new, more just world.

In this war, it is in the interest of corporate power holders to influence people's thinking and world outlook, to ensure that no alternative ideas, visions and information gets through their tightly controlled information world. They seek to emphasise the technological aspects in people's thinking and divert attention from the all-important social aspects. This lead is followed through in teaching and learning institutions, in the mass media, as well as in the all-important cultural field. It is further reinforced by market forces, which emphasise the need for technical skills as the key requirements for employment.

It is this rather neglected social aspect of the "information revolution" that this book addresses. It documents the search for relevant information policies and practices over a period of almost 30 years—covering two countries: Kenya and Britain and reflects differing needs in two continents—as well as globally. In essence, this search is for an information system, which meets the needs of the majority of people, not those of corporate capitalism, which turns information into a commodity for profit. If this search is to be met, information workers and professionals have, of necessity, to move out of their libraries into the streets of their wider society and join the struggles of the people for a society based on the principles of equality, democracy, social and economic justice and human rights. This book is a record of one such rather long search.

That this volume starts with the struggle in Kenya is not accidental. Long before the spectre of "globalization" hit the consciousness of progressive people in the industrialised countries in a big way, people of the South have had to contend with the devastation created by various waves of capitalist globalization, which hit them over centuries. The current phase of globalisation uses new technologies to accelerate and reinforce the earlier damage done to humanity.

Vision of a fair and just society

The hope after independence in Sub-Saharan Africa was to realise the vision of a fair and just society that was the battle cry of anti-colonial movements—symbolised in Kenya by the demand made by Mau Mau for "land and freedom". When people realised that political independence was a hollow shell without economic liberation, their struggle became one against imperialism and their local political allies who had taken over power from the departing colonialists thus marginalizing the liberation forces.

These wider social and political struggles were inevitably reflected in the information field. The articles from Kenya during this period bear witness to this information struggle. What is not included in this book is the underlying political struggle, which was the background against which the information struggle was waged. In this sense, it provides rather an incomplete picture—to be completed perhaps at a future date by a companion political record.

The first article reproduced is from 1979. The 1980s saw important developments in global terms as well as in Kenya. At the international level, a new phase of capitalism can be said to have begun. The demise of the Soviet Union saw the emergence of USA as the sole super-power in the world. The 1990s were also the period when the wider world became fully aware of the growth of the power and presence of China, India and Brazil. This growth, in turn, led to the gradual development of a multi-polar world where economic—and thus political—power began to shift from USA and Western Europe to China, India and countries of East Asia and South America, as well as a remodelled Russia. At the same time, an increasingly powerful global movement of people's power, made possible by ICT, was growing and expanding.

The articles in this book reflect the attempts to develop new visions and practices of using information for development of peoples and countries. This theme runs throughout the articles. A theme not of tradition and stagnation but one which represented a new way of thinking, a new way of doing, indeed a new approach which sought to use information as a tool for social development and to practice it as a basic right of working people—something which traditional information and librarianship had often ignored. Some aspects of this search for change are considered below.

Putting politics into information

"Professionalism" in librarianship has too often been understood as developing and delivering a service exclusively by "professional" librarians whose role is seen to be like that of, say for example, doctors. But while doctors are guided by a set of scientific principles, librarians do not have any such principles to guide them. Librarianship, by its very nature of being a service provider, is more akin to *social science* and it is necessary for the profession to understand the social, political and economic forces that affect societies. At the same time librarians themselves are part of their societies and follow the social and political rules set by their class and social position within these societies. Yet, for the library profession as a whole, the study of societies often takes a second place, not only in the teaching of librarianship, but also in practice. These articles—and the experience that underpins them—seek to reconnect librarianship with their social, political and economic context.

In Kenya, as well as in Britain, a key aspect of "professional" library work has been the de-politicization of information, both in the academic as well as in the practical spheres. This can be illustrated by examining the case of Kenya. At the time of independence in Kenya, a new generation of professional librarians took charge of public and academic libraries. Many of them replaced expatriate librarians; others filled the new posts created after independence. While some of them were trained in the East African region (many at the Makerere's East African School of Librarianship in Uganda), a good number were trained in Britain and the USA. Some went to East Germany and USSR, but, in keeping with the marginalisation of politicians and activists with a socialist bend, the latter were usually marginalised.

This first generation of Kenyan librarians reflected the general situation of all professionals in the Kenyan society at that time: their outlook was influenced by their class position, their de-politicised "professional" training and often by the "traditional" outlook of the old colonial practice. The process of de-politicization of social life was the key weapon used against progressive people and their organisations after independence. An important example was the trade union movement, which had stood firm as a bulwark for liberation from imperialism before independence and had become the backbone of the Mau Mau movement. It had always fought not only for workers' economic rights but also their political rights in the belief that the former could not be achieved without the latter. However, as part of the departing colonialist legacy to depoliticize trade unions, laws were used to suppress progressive trade unions, their leaders arrested or marginalised. At the same time, a new trade union structure was set up with Western support—but this time severing links with the political aspects. In effect, the new political administration became an arm of the neo-colonial state and suppressed progressive ideas in all areas, emphasising the technical areas and this extended to librarianship as well.

Under the new legislation introduced by the "independent" Kenyan Government, all organisations had to become apolitical in order to get registered as legal entities. Librarians were no exceptions. They became even further removed from the reality of the lives of the majority of people through using the British Library Association—now called CILIP—as a "professional" model. The latter, with its "Royal Charter", was—and remains—even more averse to linking its work with anything political.

Two decades of independence (1963 to 1980s) saw the sharpening of contradictions in Kenyan society as a whole. This climaxed in late 1970s and early 1980s. By this time, there were a large number of strikes by rank and file workers (the official Trade Union movement having been made ineffective by legislation); peasants everywhere took up arms against injustices they faced. The strikes and protests reached professional people as well, with lawyers, lecturers, teachers, architects, and doctors all joining in the demand for change. Students were often at the forefront of the struggle for change with the main Universities (University of Nairobi and Kenyatta University) being closed regularly every year as a result of student strikes. This resistance is well documented by Mwakenya's underground publications, such as *Register of Resistance, 1986*.[2]

By late 1970s a new generation of librarians was getting increasingly influenced by the on-going social action by various groups, including many underground political organisations whose literature talked about creating a new society to replace the neo-colonial one. However, such librarians were mostly at the lower levels in their libraries, with little power to influence policies at the organisational level. It is this group of library workers who were to challenge the status quo and start debates about the social role of libraries, and discuss which relevant library services could meet the needs of the working people in Kenya. They sought to re-establish the links between information and politics, but because of the on-going Government repression, they had to find acceptable methods to discuss their ideas and progress their vision. Their activities are recorded in some of the articles in this book.

Uniting theory with practice

The articles had two inter-linking aims. The first aim was to provide alternative ideas, views, and interpretations to those of the "mainstream" which, generally speaking, served the interests of the elite. The articles are influenced by the vision of a just society, which serves the needs of the majority of people—the working people. They were published in local as well as international publications; in newly started newsletters (such as *Sauti ya Wakutubi*) as well as in peer-reviewed journals; they also featured as talks given to small group of librarians (such as the University of Nairobi Workshops) as well as in presentations made at international conferences.

The focus throughout has been on conceptualising ideas for developing a relevant information service, which serves the needs of the majority of people. Thus one of the

---

[2] Mwakenya (Nairobi) 1986: Underground publication.

earliest articles reproduced is entitled *Relevant library service* (1980)[3]. This search for relevance informs the whole collection.

The second aim of these articles was to put these ideas into practice. There has always been an emphasis on implementation, on making innovations, change and movement. This is in recognition of the fact that ideas in themselves do not change the situation on the ground. They have to be put into practice and lessons learnt and in the process, provide living examples of their validity and workability.

Connected with the above aims was a belief that it was necessary to develop information workers themselves if the changes were going to be successful and sustainable. The need for a cultural revolution among librarians was a key requirement for change. This would ensure that the workers were empowered to decide and deliver a relevant service. This could only be achieved by widening their perspectives and expanding their horizons. But they also needed to be given practical experience in implementing a new agenda.

Barbarians at the Gates

A number of recent publications highlight many of the issues that are addressed in this book. These issues are gradually taking centre stage in the literature on social and political context of information and public libraries in the 21st century. A brief look at two recent publications illustrates this.

According to D'Angelo[4] the most important function of a public library is "to promote and sustain the knowledge and values necessary for a democratic civilization". "Postmodern consumer capitalism", he continues, "transforms discourse into private consumer product and as such reduces knowledge to mere information or entertainment". Libraries are not immune to the increasing move towards marketisation and privatization of services, driven by various rules coming from WTO. As D'Angelo[5] says, the public library is "uniquely positioned to feel the effects of a declining democratic civilization; and it is the first to go when knowledge gets reduced to information and entertainment".

This trend has been evident in British libraries driven increasingly by managerialism divorced from social responsibility. The ability to make savings by cutting staff costs is seen as a more important attribute of Heads of libraries than their ability to meet the information needs of their communities. Furthermore, their "professional" competence is measured by how well they spin their "successes" rather than whether they deliver a relevant information service to meet user needs in a rapidly changing world. With their eyes firmly on these monetary targets, they become mini dictators reluctant to share decision-making powers with their staff or their communities. This also explains the lack of a policy and performance management approach to running libraries. This democracy deficit in the information sector is perhaps the greatest challenge facing the sector today. The current situation is a reflection of the approach taken at the highest political levels by Bush and Blair in their blind passion to wage wars on Iraq and other countries, without any concern

---

[3] University of Nairobi. Library Magazine. No. 3 (1980) Editorial. Also published in Quarterly Bulletin, IAALD. XXVI (1) 1981(12-20).
[4] D'Angelo, Ed (2006): Barbarians at the gates of the public library; how postmodern consumer capitalism threatens democracy, civil education and the public good. Duluth, Minnesota: Library Juice Press.
[5] Ibid.

about moral and legal issues of such illegal wars, not to mention massive loss of life and millions of displaced people the wars continue to create. The possible emergence of a more democratic Britain and USA will perhaps help in spreading democracy, accountability and transparency in the information and other sectors too. At present, a lack of effective leadership is indeed a key shortage in the information sector.

But the questions posed by D'Angelo are getting increasingly urgent: "How did we get to the point of having libraries without librarians? How did we lose the 'public' in 'public library'?" he asks. With the on-going "restructuring" of public libraries in Britain, a new model of public libraries is fast emerging—based on the models of supermarkets and driven by a need to save and downsize services. In this process, little thought is given to the social impact of this loss. All declining civilizations start their decline by attacking the free flow of information and reducing free information services. The process of USA and Europe being overtaken by India, China, Brazil and other countries is having an impact on these Western societies, which for generations have been the "leaders of the world".

The question raised by this book, "why is information so important in today's world?" is answered in brief by Civallero[6]:

> Information means power; economic power as well as social, political and human. This great power has always been seized by a few and it is not often shared.

Roy[7] highlights the danger posed by "neo-liberal capitalism" to our freedoms, including freedom of free speech and information:

> Neo-liberalism isn't just about the accumulation of capital (for some). It's also about the accumulation of capital (for some), it's also about the accumulation of power (for some), the accumulation of freedom (for some). Conversely, for the rest of the world, the people who are excluded from neo-liberalism's governing body, it's about the *erosion* of power, the *erosion* of freedom. In the 'free' market, free speech has become a commodity like everything else—justice, human rights, drinking water, clean air. It's available only to those who can afford it. And naturally, those who can afford it use free speech to manufacture the kind of product, confect the kind of public opinion, that suits their purpose. (News they can use).

The key issue then is who has the power and what it is used for. The central plank of this book is the need for librarians to empower themselves to decide on information and library policies and practices from a progressive, people's perspective. It is only on the basis of such activism among librarians that it will be possible to reconnect to the central values of librarianship—sustaining democratic societies based on the principles of social justice and human rights.

There is no "neutrality" in this struggle

However, some recent trends provide emerging grounds for optimism about the future direction of information and libraries. Progressive librarian groups are active in a number of countries, working with other progressive communities.[8] Prominent

---

[6] Civallero (2007): Foreword to Samek, Toni (2007): Librarianship and human rights: a twenty-first century guide. Oxford: Chandos.
[7] Roy, Arundhati (2004): The ordinary person's guide to empire. London: Harper Perennial.
[8] See for example the list in "Communities of change and resistance" (2007)—Communities of change and resistance (2007). Study guide prepared by the author from whom copies are available. It is also available at: "Information and Social Exclusion" page at:
http://www.londonmet.ac.uk/depts/dass/research/informationsocialexclusion/.

among them is the Progressive Librarians Guild in the USA. New publications such as Samek[9] take on issues of human rights as basic to the theory and practice of librarianship. Issues of progressive librarianship are now more widely available, for example Litwin[10].

Perhaps the most important developments in this area are two key documents, the "Ten point Program"[11] and "A declaration of cultural human rights"[12]. They point to a new approach to the roles and responsibilities for librarians and the services they run.

The challenge to librarians is to use information to liberate all those exploited and oppressed by rules of capitalist globalisation. They need to pay attention to sources of power in our societies as indicated by Jones, Branwen, Bujra, and Love[13]:

> ... we need to recognise that post-colonial and feminist analysis has taught us to pay far more attention to the spaces, opportunities and sources of power and how they are used by the oppressed, whether these be the self-defined 'poor', women, ethnic groups or all of these together (though without discarding the class element), than many Western influenced academic thinkers and analytical paradigms have previously allowed.

This challenge is perhaps taken up more seriously by progressive librarians in USA, than in Britain. But a younger generation of information activists everywhere is beginning to question their current practices and starting to search for a model that meets the needs of working people. The articles reproduced in this book will, it is hoped, help in making this crucial shift in mindsets if we are to succeed in using information as a tool of liberation. Such liberation requires active engagement with ideas, policies, and experiences generated globally. It requires a committed understanding of our social, political and cultural reality. It requires active participation in the struggle on behalf of those marginalised and excluded from the "mainstream" society. There is no "neutrality" in this struggle—we all are participants, on one side or the other.

Milne's assessment that "radical movements will emerge—and already are [emerging]—to challenge the world's grotesque and growing inequality and its domination by a handful of great powers" provides a picture of the reality of our world in the 21st century. However, such radical movements need to learn appropriate lessons from historical and current struggles if they are to guide people towards a society based on principles of social justice and equality. In the absence of such alternative information, "cold warriors" inspired by the neo-conservative

---

[9] Samek, Toni (2007): Librarianship and human rights: a twenty-first century guide
[10] Litwin, Rory (2006): Library Juice concentrate. Duluth, Minnesota: Library Juice Press.
[11] Ten Point Program developed by Mark Rosenzweig for the groups which met at the Vienna Conference of progressive librarians sponsored by KRIBIBIE in 2000. Progressive Librarians Guild, 2000. http://www.libr.org/PLG/
[12] A Declaration of Cultural Human Rights – as it appeared in Progressive Librarian. No. 4.38-45 Winter 1991/1992. Available at http://libr.org/plg/chr.php [Accessed: 13 May 2007].
[13] Jones, Branwen Gruffydd; Bujra, Janet; Love, Roy. Love (2007): Review of African Political Economy. Vol. 34(111). http://0-www.informaworld.com.emu.londonmet.ac.uk/smpp/title%7Econtent=t713443496%7Edb=all%7Etab=issueslist%7Ebranches=34—v34March, pp. 5 – 10.

movements will "have a largely open field — and their highly coloured views become received historical wisdom by default"[14].

It is the aim of this book to challenge that "received historical wisdom". The ruling classes in the world today have taken over the control of information as a way of enslaving people. They have built barriers to prevent the free flow of alternative information. Information about people's resistance, about their leadership, their organisations, and their ideologies are all covered up as if they do not exist. The only information freely available is that which sees capitalism and the "freedom" to exploit and be exploited as the norm. But progressive people everywhere are asserting their right "never to be silent", to use appropriate information as a tool of liberation. It is a long, hard and an uphill task which calls for continual struggle and sacrifices. But it is a battle worth waging. For without this battle, survival itself is under threat.

Anthony Olden makes some important points in his introduction to this book. In a way, he addresses one of its aims, which is to encourage debate about the issues discussed here. It is essential if democracy is to be meaningful that there is space, environment and opportunity for free exchanges of ideas, for debate, and for discussion on the basis of which ideas can be clarified for appropriate policies to be developed and implemented. It is hoped that readers will similarly engage with issues and viewpoints raised in this collection. It needs to be noted, however, that the articles in this book are not the same as chapters in a "unified" book. They were written at different times, in response to particular contradictions and "situations on the ground." They were also written with a particular audience in mind. They seek to understand principles and theories in the context of dynamic, specific situations.

In many situations, the very existence of a problem is not even recognized. "Where do correct ideas come from?" asks Mao. They come from actual practice, and these articles are all based on concrete experiences. They seek to understand the opposing forces in a specific social and organisational situation, to make sense of them within a larger social context and to draw lessons from what actually happens. They seek to develop new ideas and theories which *may* be applicable to other situations. Thus the perspective and views on a specific topic in an article written in 1980 will not necessarily be the same as in 2008 — although the world outlook remains essentially the same. In particilar situations, one aspect may be more important than others. Thus, for example, in Hackney the issue of race became important and the various articles written at the time took on this as the key aspect. This did not mean that other aspects, such as gender or class, became less important. Similarly, when developing a new staffing structure and new services in Merton, a different approach to racism was required, and this resulted in the development of a model based on needs of people of all races and classes. Again, this does not imply that race was not an important issue in Merton. Olden raises some other issues and points of view which need further discussion. Thus, how one sees the role of USSR and China in Africa, the need for "White Librarianship," the role of "mindless fiction," etc., are all issues that need further responses; but perhaps in another forum. Otherwise this book would become a "never-ending" book...

---

[14] Milne. op.cit.

Society and Information:
A South Perspective

Setting the scene (1): Rocking the Boat

The year is 1979. The place is Kabete Campus housing the Faculties of Agriculture and Veterinary Science of the University of Nairobi. A peaceful, quiet academic atmosphere reigns in the campus and its library. It is about 15 kilometres from the City Centre. The University farm is a few miles away. Research and scholarship are evident everywhere. The library is perhaps the best agricultural and veterinary library in the region. Lecturers come from all parts of the world creating a research environment that aims to train the next generation of scientists who will hold the future of their country in their hands and minds.

But this peace and quiet of academic life is shattered. A number of activities, which challenge the "normal" academic life on and off the Campus take place here. The first is the showing of three films in the well-equipped lecture theatres. Nothing unusual about this—a common enough occurrence on any Campus. But two features distinguish this scene. The first is the audience. While there were many students among the house-full auditorium, the majority were peasants and workers who lived around the campus on their small *mashamba*[15], among them women who walked all the way to sell fruit and vegetables to homes in Nairobi. There were workers from local farms, the Government's Veterinary Department, and local schools and shopping centres. There were workers employed in formal and "informal" sectors in the City in the Sun, barely managing to earn enough to get by. There were children and young people full of hope for a bright new future, but also full of despair at the reality of their lives.

For most of these people, this was the very first time they had entered the University Campus. The University did all sorts of research—for a national and international readership; it taught a new generation of scientists so that they could look after and develop vast farms owned by multinationals. But the research and training did not meet the needs of the vast majority of workers and peasants, many of whom had lost their land to foreign landowners during the colonial period. The vast resources in the library included vast amounts on export cash crops, but little on food and agriculture that could feed local populations. Relevant local material on social aspects of agriculture was conspicuous by its absence. Missing also was information from countries such as China and Cuba, which were making rapid advances in agriculture and science in general which could have greatly benefited Kenyans. There was almost nothing on or about oral agricultural information collected by the Kenyan peasants over generations.

So what was it that brought all these people to the Campus? They were driven by a deep thirst to learn, to know their own history, to understand a world that had no place for them—and to enjoy a social evening with family and friends. They had come to see a series of films on the Mau Mau struggle for liberation in Kenya. Such subjects were not part of the mainstream thought in the independent Kenya where the message from above was to forgive and forget—forget their very history, forget their loss of land and freedom even after gaining independence; forget that they ever had

---

[15] Shamba, pl mashamba { English: farm , pl farms } – Source: The Kamusi Project. Available at: <http://www.yale.edu/swahili/>. [Accessed: 03 June 2007].

land, that their family members were massacred—and forgive those responsible for these atrocities, and those others who had usurped their place at the big table.

The crucial point in this story is that it was the library service that brought the working people of Kabete to their local *Chuo Kikuu*.[16] The library was the one trying to find its social role, to find a connection between people's information and learning needs and the vast resources it held. Thus workers and peasants teach the first lesson to librarians: connect with the people, meet their needs and work with them. A lesson few professional librarians learnt during their years of professional training.

The second activity that shatters the placid library environment is a series of workshops for library workers held at the Kabete Campus. Again, not anything unusual in this, in a "normal" University. But it is the composition of participants and what they are talking about that sets a new standard in library work. The participants, from all over Kenya, are not the professional librarians who prefer to go to all expense-paid national and international conferences. No, these are library assistants, library attendants, library cleaners, binders, accountants and other library staff who are giving talks and participating actively in deciding the future role of libraries. And they are talking about a subject, which has not yet seriously reached the "professional" horizon: the role of libraries in rural development. The Workshop deliberations and recommendations form the content of a Newsletter[17] produced by them. It is the library workers responding to the needs and demands of the working people of Kenya. They are teaching a lesson on how to run libraries.

It is against this background that some of the earliest articles reproduced below need to be read. The questions they pose and the solutions they offer to social and political questions relate to a particular society at a particular historical moment, in a particular situation of social and political contradictions. Yet they have a strange universality, as a librarian from Leicester pointed out in response to one of the articles. Some of the articles were reproduced and distributed by Zambia Library Association. Many others were reproduced a number of times in Kenyan and international journals.

Veterinary Information in Kenya (1979)[18]

Dear Editor,

It is with great pride and satisfaction that we welcome the publication of *Kenya Veterinarian, the journal of Kenya Veterinary Association*. In order to understand the special significance of this publication, one needs to go back a little in the history of Kenya and that of the development of veterinary services in Kenya in particular.

Veterinary science is one of the subjects on which Kenyan nationalities have developed much knowledge over many generations. Let us take two examples:

---

[16] Chuo Kikuu—Kiswahili for "University".
[17] Newsletter. University of Nairobi Library. 4 issues were published in all. Later renamed "Sauti ya Wakutubi" – "Voice of librarians".
[18] Letter to the Editor, The Kenya Veterinarian. Published in Vol. 3 (2) pp. 27-28.

Fratkin[19] gives a very detailed account of the use of human and veterinary medicine by the Samburu. Here we see the development of scientific knowledge based on theory and practice of veterinary science. For example, he discusses many livestock diseases and how the Samburu cure them. He also mentions other achievements:

> Samburu recognise 135 species of trees and shrubs of medicinal value, as well as several hundred other botanical species relevant to their culture, such as livestock, foods and poisons (p.5).
>
> A Samburu is always selectively breeding his livestock — improvements in nutrition and health that yield superior calves.

In the second example, Ogenga[20] mentions examples of the development of veterinary medicine among the Luo nationality of Kenya. He mentions the development of drugs to cure East Coast Fever. He also mentions the use of sisal leaves to cure the chicken disease *ajujo* and the use of *Cactus Ogaka* to cure a wound from a mad dog's bite to prevent rabies.

As we see from the above examples, together with veterinary knowledge, Kenyan nationalities have also developed their languages so that all animal diseases and their treatments known to modern science had their names in Kenyan languages.

This knowledge was developed before Kenya was colonised. This reflected the mode of production of pre-colonial Kenya. Kenyan nationalities were agriculturalists and pastoralists. Products from cattle, goats, sheep, camels and chicken satisfied some of the basic material needs of the people. It thus became necessary to develop the science of animal husbandry to ensure the survival of a healthy herd as a primary need and of the development of animal products as secondary.

The colonization of Kenya brought about major changes in every aspect of life. When the nationalists took up arms to defend their land and material wealth, the development of animal production and knowledge was also affected.

The main reason why British imperialism sought to control Kenya was for its rich land and natural resources. The foreign settlers thus confiscated land and turned peasant farmers into cheap wage labourers on their farms. They then tried to instil a sense of uselessness in the people and suppress their confidence in their own ability to control their own lives. They tried to make Kenyan people believe that they had no knowledge in the fields of human and animal medicine.

At the same time, the European settlers exploited the veterinary science of Kenyan peasants to develop their meat and dairy farms. It was the knowledge and labour of Kenyan "herdsboys" which developed settler cattle from dawn to dusk, and then again at night. It is a well-known fact that the cattle, which the Boers came with, all died because of the settlers' lack of knowledge and skill in cattle keeping and that they had to learn how to breed and keep cattle from Kenyan peasants and pastoralists. The case of the Maasai people developing Lord Delamere's estates is one concrete example.

The colonialists also attempted to suppress the knowledge of the peasantry and establish their own institutions to provide veterinary services and to undertake

---

[19] Fratkin, Elliot M. (1975): Herbal medicine and concepts of disease in Samburu. Institute of African Studies. University of Nairobi. Seminar Paper no. 65.
[20] Ogenga, J, M. (1979): University of Nairobi Library Magazine. No. 2. Special issue on Agri-Vet information. p. 54.

research which was to serve their own interest versus the interests of the Kenyan masses: the agricultural and veterinary services "developed" as market research branches of Western multinationals dealing with agricultural and veterinary products. Kenya became an experimental ground for foreigners. As early as 1903 we see the establishment of Veterinary Department under the Ministry of Agriculture and Animal Husbandry, and the establishment of The East African Veterinary Research Organisation in 1948 and the Faculty of Veterinary Science at Makerere College in Kampala in 1930s with the Kabete Campus to serve clinical courses.

The Kenyan agriculturalists and pastoralists never identified themselves with the British imperialist research and scientific experiments in Kenya. The masses understood that all the imperialist "developments" were directed towards the interests of the oppressors: the colonialists and the foreign settlers in Kenya. Thus in our history we have the resistance of the nationalities against foreign agricultural and veterinary services serving foreign interests. We mention just a few examples of such resistance.

1. In 1947 in Murang'a during the time of D.C. Coutts ("Ithe wa Kamau"), the peasants refused to dig terraces as a means of struggle against foreign occupation of their land and forced labour. The following year saw a women's revolt.
2. In 1951, again in Murang'a peasants objected to rinderpest inoculation and backed this up by burning cattle crushes.
3. The above incident was not an isolated one in one area only. In the same year (1951) peasants in Kirinyaga also objected to rinderpest inoculation and also resorted to burning cattle crushes.[21]

These were not isolated incidents, but covered large areas and were in direct response to attempts by the settlers and the colonial government to deprive the peasants of their means of livelihood. Thus the struggles against foreign science became an aspect of the total struggle against British imperialism.

When the long struggles against foreign occupation ended in victory and independence was achieved in 1963, direct control over Kenyan resources by the British came to an end. It was then felt that gradually, even the foreign veterinarians in Kenya, would soon be replaced by national ones and all research and science would serve national interests. It was also hoped that then at last the nationality veterinary practices so long suppressed by imperialism would be placed in its proper place to serve the needs of the peasantry; and that the profession would re-examine its practice.

This of course has hardly happened to the extent that one would call significant. Therefore, today much more remains to be done. For example, although much research is undertaken, the application of this research still needs to be seen.

Take for example the case of the milk industry in Kenya. Research indicates that resources are not fully utilised for the benefit of the nation. It has been estimated by one expert[22] that milk production techniques available in the country can increase production by as much as four times the present figure. This, if implemented, would

---

[21] Republic of Kenya. Kenya population census (1979): Enumerator's instructions. Events calendar for Muranga (p.65) and Kirinyaga (p. 49).
[22] Dr. D. M. Mukunya, University of Nairobi: personal communications.

make available to a large majority of people a ready source of cheap, nutritious food. That this research has not been put into practice is not without reasons: the technologies and science in general are really being controlled by the multinationals directly, or through their control over "national" companies and institutions. Their profit motive does not allow for the application of science and technology for the benefit of the people.

It is in the practical application of scientific knowledge that we hope that the *Kenya Veterinarian* would go a long way by starting the communication process so that Kenyan researchers, scientists, field workers and ultimately the farmers could exchange ideas and information for the benefit of the country as a whole.

It would also go a long way to kill the prejudice in certain academic circles (especially at the University of Nairobi) against local publications. The view of many people at the University is that anything published locally is of an "inferior quality", while articles in foreign publications are "superior" and "more professional". This needs to be challenged. These views reflect the interests of foreigners rather than those of Kenyan nationals. Indeed, the University and all other national institutions should set an example by encouraging all publications by its staff to be locally published.

The result of this attitude, which is foreign-orientated is that there does not exist a Kenyan reading audience interested in agricultural and veterinary sciences. And as long as such attitude continues, there will never be such an audience.

It is with the hope that your journal will help to encourage Kenyans to publish in Kenya so as to address and build up a Kenyan audience that I welcome it. I would like to make one suggestion. It would be useful to accept articles not only in English, but also in Kiswahili so as to reach a wider national audience. This has also been the feeling of readers of our journals in the [Kabete] Library.

Lessons in Kenyan librarianship: Leadership, Management and the Library worker (1984)[23]

The second University of Nairobi Workshop was held in October 1980 and was - attended by over 70 participants and was representing 15 libraries from throughout the country, The University Library Services were also well represented; all Main Library sections and all sub libraries (except Kikuyu Library which was not represented because of staff shortage,) sent at least some of their workers. The full list of participants and their institutions is reproduced at the end of this issue.

Thus although it was not officially a national Workshop, in practice it became national. In the absence of any really nationally organized workshops in the field of librarianship, this Workshop acquired even more importance. The organization, the presentation of papers and the discussions and recommendations of the Workshop

---

[23] Editorial in Sauti ya Wakutubi ["Voice of librarians"] – (formerly University of Nairobi. Library Magazine). No. 4. September 1984, pp. iii-viii.

therefore achieve Kenya--wide relevance and are necessary reading for anyone interested in librarianship in the Republic.

The significance of the Workshop also comes from another level: while most discussions on librarianship have been dominated by high-level administrative staff of the large libraries in the country, now for the first-time the voice of the majority of staff at the service level is being heard on issues of national importance. These are the staff who are in direct contact with the public using the libraries. For the first time these librarians are exercising their constitutional right to hold free discussions by bringing forth their experiences from the grass-root level. We hope this will further encourage debate among librarians about Kenyan librarianship practices.

Let these discussions by the library service sector workers not be dismissed as insignificant views of "non-professionals", or, to use a derogatory term used by some, "para-professionals".

The outstanding quality of the participants of the workshop was their total commitment to their country. It is their fierce patriotism that is responsible for their attendance at the Workshop. The Expression of their views is a further reflection of the sincerity of their concern over the issue of librarianship in Kenya.

Theirs are not only the views of the librarians who attended the Workshop. They are representatives of the views of all their colleagues who could not attend. These are the views also of the vast majority of their parents, sisters, and brothers, friends and relatives and generally of all library users with whom they are directly in contact: in short these are the views of all the working people of Kenya, of the workers and peasants of Kenya.

These library-staff at service level, those who work at various technical jobs behind closed doors unobserved by users, and those who work hard at the so-called routine, "non-professional" jobs are in practice often considered by some professionals to be of marginal significance in the library field. Such workers are the typists, secretaries, binders, photographers, shelvers, carriers of books and boxes across libraries and campuses, filers and sorters of borrowers and public catalogue cards, messengers and cleaners, preventors of theft from libraries, spine markers, cataloguers who spend their lives looking to see if the American Library of Congress has catalogued books received by us, photocopying and other machine operators, stampers of books with due dates and Library stamps, issuers of books, those answering reference and other queries at issue desks, processors of book orders, library accountants, collectors and processors of information which make bibliographies and other reference tools, maintainers of interlibrary loans.... and many other such jobs. A library service cannot run without such workers.

Such workers are considered "small" by some "professionals". But they are small only in terms of their salaries and in the estimation they receive officially from some "professionals". In all other ways they are-big: their numbers, the amount of work they do, in the service they provide, and in the vast amount of initiative, creativity and knowledge they collectively possess.

What role do those library workers play in library services as a whole? Is there any contribution they can make towards providing a service that can be relevant in the Kenyan context? Can their experiences in librarianship be summed up and organized to form the basis of new theories on librarianship, which could truly be called Kenyan librarianship? Answers to these questions will help us understand how great the contribution of the library workers is. The proceedings of this workshop are one example of their contribution.

In any free, democratic society, it is essential that all members of the society should be actively involved in discussion, implementing and in re-discussing and re-implementing policies aimed at the general welfare of members of that society. This is what should be happening in Kenya as a whole, and it should also be happening in the field of librarianship as among other fields.

It is in the course of discussing and formulating policies and implementing them that new and relevant Kenyan librarianship practices and theories can evolve, not in isolation from the society but in a unified action of all patriotic people for the welfare of the majority.

But what do we find in the actual practice of librarianship in Kenya? The librarians are divided into bureaucratic and service groups. This has resulted from foreign academic and professional training, foreign advice from 'experts' from foreign countries, foreign technical and financial "aid", all of which seek to control the development of information science in Kenya.

This next stage was capitalism where again capital sought to appropriate to themselves the products of the worker. Capitalism gradually changed into imperialism, which sought to make the people of the whole world into physical workers to serve the needs of the mental 'master' who has taken upon itself the tasks of the 'mind' in opposition to the muscle of the workers of the world. True to their historical traditions, the workers of the world have intensified their struggles to change the situation and in the process, to reunite their physical and mental aspects in order to serve their own material and cultural needs.

Thus present conditions in Kenya as a whole and in Kenyan libraries in particular are not something accidental nor should they be seen in isolation from their national and international links.

An examination of our colonial history can explain the background to many of our current librarianship practices. The case of the divisions in our libraries between the administrators and the service sectors continue the colonial librarianship practices in Kenya and follows from the necessity of the colonial power to divide Kenyans so as to more easily rule over them. In political, economic, military, social and cultural fields the colonialists sought to divide a Kenyan from another Kenyan. In every field these emerged under British patronage, leaders and the led. The colonial authorities did their best to give all legal, moral, economic and military backing that its colonial rule commanded to the leaders who really were leaders only in the sense of being imposed on the people. What of those who were led? They rejected their false leaders and in continuing their struggle created their own leaders.

What lessons do we learn from history? The main lesson is that leadership does not consist of giving orders which the "led" have to follow. The relationship of leaders and the led is not that of the slave and the slave owner, where one does the physical work to produce wealth and the other does the thinking on how this wealth is to be divided up.

The real leaders are those who follow the commands of those they lead. The leadership's role is that of organizing the resources so as to fulfil the wishes of the people. When leaders fail to obey the people and begin to impose their will on the people, there emerges dictatorship.

How much dictatorship and how much democracy, is there in the library field in Kenya? True answers can be given after examining some of the following: Who gives orders and who carries them out? Who decides what orders are to be given? On what basis are such decisions taken? Is there a proper consultation with all librarians before decisions are taken? Each one of us needs to answer these questions.

A correct decision can be taken only on the basis of an examination of concrete information. What is a correct decision? A correct decision is one that, in the final analysis, answers a concrete information need the people of Kenya, one that will help them in their struggles against nature and their social struggles for the production and protection of material wealth.

Can a correct decision, then be taken by the leaders without taking guidance from the majority of library workers who are in direct contact with the people whose information needs the decision seeks to satisfy? It is not possible.

It is in this that the significance of the Workshop lies. The views expressed at the workshop represented the point of view of those who have become used to receiving instructions only. Through the forum of the Workshop, Kenyan librarians are again pointing the way our library and information services should go. They are providing a basic lesson in Kenyan librarianship. This is the challenge to all in the information field in Kenya today. The challenge is contained in the contents of this publication, which is a testimony of what the staff in the lower grades can contribute.

Rural information in Kenya (1985)[24]

The Kenyan reality today

The information scene in Kenya resembles that in many independent third world countries: the official information services reach no more than about 10 percent of the people in the country. Most of these people live in the towns, although not all town dwellers are reached. Again, most of those reached have to be proficient in the English language, which is not understood by the country's peasants.

Information dissemination in Kenya shows an over-reliance on the printed word, which, at present, is not accessible to the majority in the countryside. Most of the newspapers, for example, are aimed at the educated elite, mostly in the towns. Moreover, their high cost means that the poor rural peasants and pastoralists cannot afford to buy them, even in areas where there are good roads to enable newspapers to be brought in regularly. In any case, even the agricultural articles in the newspapers are aimed at the comparatively well off peasants. The same applies to the few agricultural periodicals.

An experiment that holds some hope for the future is the rural press project of the Ministry of Information with assistance from UNESCO[25]. This produces weekly or monthly newspapers in Kiswahili or the national languages using mobile printing presses, which visit rural centres. Although technically successful, this project still faces the problem of making the peasants accept these newspapers as really theirs. Not only will the content have to be reviewed, but the peasants will have to be

---

[24] Information Development Vol. 1, no 3, July 1985 pp. 149-157.
[25] See footnote 27, below.

involved enough so that they themselves would come to run the project. Only then will they accept this press as their own.

Kenya National Library Service

As far as library services are concerned, the Kenya National Library Service has a legal obligation to look after the information needs of the whole country. An ambitious plan has been drawn up to provide public library services to all Districts in the country. But not much research seems to have gone into what information is required in different parts of the country, and how best to provide it. At present, a large number of publications from British and American publishers are purchased in multiple sets and kept in all branch libraries. These include a large quantity of fiction. No acquisition policy seems to be in operation to decide on the relevance of the material acquired, especially in the context of the needs of the rural users. Providing reading for entertainment seems to be a major preoccupation of this national service. The significance of this is apparent when one considers the present food shortages facing the country, where as many as two million peasants are facing starvation today. The national library service makes no attempt to collect and document information, which is available within the country in the collective memory of millions of peasants. This information is highly relevant as it has been tested and proved in the particular local conditions over generations of farming practice. Such information has been passed from generation to generation through the oral medium. But in an age when libraries are rushing to install computers and other sophisticated technologies, they cannot, it seems, make use of simple tape recorders to document the wealth of oral agricultural information preserved by the peasants.

No other library in Kenya even attempts to reach the rural people. The academic libraries restrict their service to the academic community. Although a case has been made to extend some services to the rural, non-academic people,[26] this has not met with the approval of the controllers of such services. There is a large number of libraries, both large and small, all over the country, run by the various government ministries. The Ministry of Agriculture, for example, runs over 200 libraries in every part of the country. But these are only for Ministry staff, and a peasant has no hope of ever getting any information from them.

The Ministry of Agriculture runs a useful information service, which could be further adapted to meet local needs. This comprises the Agricultural Information Centre and the Kenya Agricultural Documentation Centre. These two centres contain much relevant information and also have long experience in dissemination work. However, they are at present, mainly used by Ministry officials and extension workers who have not always succeeded in passing on the information to the peasants. Attempts will have to be made to reach the peasants directly.

---

[26] For example, at the Second University of Nairobi Library Workshop on Libraries and Rural Development (Maktaba na Maendeleo ya Sehemu za Mashambani), held in Nairobi from 2 to 3 October 1980. The Proceedings of the Workshop are published in: University of Nairobi Library Magazine, no.4, May 1985. See, in particular, in the Proceedings, the Discussions and Recommendations of the Workshop and also the paper 'The role of the University library in rural development' by Mwangi.

Radio and Other Media

The vast potential of radio, television, and the well-established oral media is not used to enable needed information to reach its potential users. Indeed, there are very few programmes for the peasants in the national radio broadcasts, which have the potential to reach the large rural population very easily.

The content of radio broadcasts is in many ways similar to the contents of libraries. There are two main channels broadcasting to the whole country. One is exclusively in the English language and so, even if it reaches rural areas, it is largely ignored by the peasants. The other service is in Kiswahili, which is spoken widely by workers in towns when in contact with people of different Kenyan nationalities. Only a few peasants speak Kiswahili, and these include those who live near urban centres.

Even if the language barrier were to be overcome, the content of most radio broadcasts leaves much to be desired. The emphasis is once again on entertainment for the educated elite in the towns. A certain number of hours are devoted to educational broadcasts for adults and schools, but the content of these is also far removed from the struggles of the peasants. The only broadcasts that cater to farmers are those prepared by the Agricultural Information Centre. These, however, are not sufficiently frequent to have any real impact. Again, they do not allow for regional variations, as they are broadcast nationally to areas with totally different climates, land use and agricultural practices. In addition, there is a tendency for such broadcasts to encourage the use of the so-called 'modern' technologies, without considering their appropriateness in the local situation. Peasants have rejected many of these methods as being unsuitable for them, having suffered large losses in the past. In order to win back the confidence of peasants, such broadcasts will have to promote only those technologies which have been proved useful for the peasants in their *shambas*, not in the Ministry's classrooms and laboratories.

A third broadcasting service offers valuable lessons in how to reach the peasants. This broadcasts in the national languages of the peasants and is extremely popular. It is easy for peasants to identify with broadcasts in their own languages. But the potential of this medium is not used for rural development. There are only a few hours of broadcasting on weekdays in each language and very few, if any, programmes aim to communicate with the peasants on agricultural issues that have any meaning for them. Indeed, these broadcasts have been gradually reduced over the years and many regional broadcasting stations have been closed down. There is pressure from some sections of the government to close down this service completely.[27] Used imaginatively, this service is capable of proving a powerful, effective medium of relevant communication for rural development.

Another fact that has not been accepted by the present information services is that the majority of peasants are women who are faced with the dual oppression both of the economic system and of the male-dominated and oriented society. The lives and problems of peasant women were vividly described at a recent Workshop on 'Libraries and Rural Development' and many suggestions were made as to the type of

---

[27] This indeed was the fate of one of the most promising broadcasting experiments in the Third World. Financed and organised by UNESCO, this was the Homa Bay Community Radio Station, located in Homa Bay, Nyanza Province, Kenya. It was closed down by the Government in 1984. For a good account of this experiment see Africa Events, April 1985, p. 6.

information service they need.[28] The issue of women's liberation is quite different in peasant neo-colonies when compared with Western industrialised countries. There is a need to undertake more research on this to allow the real voice of the women peasants to emerge, on the basis of which an appropriate information service can be provided.

We can sum up the reality today by saying that there are no information services which really satisfy the information needs of rural people: the peasants, the plantation workers, the squatters, as well as the workers in rural industries and students. Although there are token services, these do not provide relevant information. To do so, they need to undertake investigations to decide on the form and the content of the information needed by rural people. The only sector in the rural community whose information needs are satisfied is the plantation sector, which is linked to the multinational corporations, but their information needs do not concern us here.

Peasant Information System

All this, of course, does not mean that the peasants have no organised means of disseminating information to serve their needs. In the absence of any efficient formal service, they have developed their own informal systems based on their own oral traditions. It is through this system that useful agricultural information is passed from one generation to another. This system is also used to spread and popularise those new technologies that have proved beneficial, and to condemn those that have proved to be against the interests of peasant agriculture. This oral information system is a powerful medium, which has been developed through the initiative of the peasants themselves. No 'modern' information system will succeed in the rural areas unless it comes to terms with the existing oral system and with those who run it. There is no need to see this peasant information system as hostile and incompatible with the so-called modern information services, as it is seen by some 'professional' information workers. In fact, it should be viewed as an ally in the fight against poverty and ignorance. The foundation of an efficient, relevant information service in the rural areas already exists in these oral services. It remains for the 'modern' information services to build on this foundation. This is the challenge of information work in Kenya, and in many other developing countries today.

Another feature of the current rural information scene is the lack of any national information plan to provide information to the peasants and rural workers. The information services that do reach these areas, function in isolation from each other without any attempt at a coordinated approach. Again, no attempts are made to investigate what kind of information is relevant for the people and to seek their views on the most appropriate ways of making the information available. Nor is it considered the work of any of the services to see information communication as a two-way process and to acquire information from the rural people as well. The history of the people is not taken into account and the experiences of generations of struggle for obtaining and protecting land and resources are ignored. It was during these struggles that the oral medium was advanced to a very high degree to satisfy the information needs of all rural people: young and old, peasants on the land and

---

[28] See, in particular, the papers by Wanjohi, M. M.: "Women and rural development: Can libraries help?" University of Nairobi Library Magazine, no.4, May 1985, pp. 6-7 and Inoti, V.1. and Weru, W. "The role of women in rural development and their need for library services". University of Nairobi Library Magazine, no. 4, May 1985, pp. 6.

craftsmen, metal, wood and other workers, as well as of the warriors. Even the struggle for independence showed the usefulness of the oral medium.

Only a major change in the theories and practices of rural information services can provide a service that is relevant to the needs of the people.

Some theoretical considerations

The practices of information services, like all areas of social sciences, are based on a body of theories, which provide guiding principles for such practices. These theories may be written and explicit, or unwritten and implicit. In the information field, it is these theories that determine the type of information services, how they are provided, the type of user they are aimed at and what will be the content and language of the information disseminated. Historically, every ruling class has established an information service that serves its own class interests. In contrast, those ruled have also established, often against the wishes of the rulers, their own information services which take into account their own particular information needs and social conditions. In general, the former have always been elite-oriented, and the latter have been people-oriented.

The present information services in Kenya are based on the theories established by British colonialism. These, in turn, were based on the concrete reality of British capitalist society at the beginning of this century. Over the years these theories were developed to satisfy the changing needs of the British situation. Thus, for example, the library services were based on the assumption of universal literacy in the English language, as well as of a certain minimum income level, a common culture and a unity based on similar economic interests.

There was certain logic in the colonial regime in Kenya applying these theories to Kenyan society. After all, such theories safeguarded the interests of the rulers. Thus, the early libraries catered for the information needs of the foreign settlers and the colonial government bureaucracy. Later on, the needs of the African educated elite were also catered for. The Asians, for the most part, had established their own communication and information systems.

As independence approached, more library services were started and the activities of the Ministry of Information and Broadcasting were expanded. All these changes did not, however, question the philosophy of information services, but accepted the British model as being universally applicable. No attempts were made to look at the particularity of the situation in Kenya and to develop appropriate theories and practices to suit the needs of a newly independent country.

A programme was started to train young Kenyans as librarians to take over from the British librarians. This training was mostly in Britain. But these newly trained librarians did not take up the challenge to reorient library services, which continued on the same lines as during colonialism.

The post-independence library services have thus not changed qualitatively from the colonial ones. True, there has been a quantitative growth, with more libraries, more books, and more librarians being made available. But the service still remains urban and elite-orientated without any coordinated plan to bring together a relevant service. The information needs of the rural communities have not really been even considered. Over the years the younger generations of librarians have questioned the basis of library services, but their views and creativity have been suppressed as being 'non-professional'.

While the colonial and post-independence library services were being planned and run along elitist lines, the peoples' own information services were also developing. Based on the oral information and education systems of the peasants and pastoralists, these services were undergoing major qualitative changes in the face the new contradictions facing society.

The demands made on the informal information system changed as the main conflict in society changed from the struggle against nature, so as to satisfy basic material needs of food, clothing, and shelter, to the social struggle against foreign occupation of land and against forced labour. This changed the *content* of the information collected, stored and disseminated. Accelerated capitalist development had also established factory and plantation workers as a class, which saw peasants as its allies. It was these important social changes that induced changes in informal information services.

To begin with, the user community expanded to include both urban and rural workers. This in itself extended the scope of these services, which had to be confined in the past to specific nationalities. Thus, for example, the Gikuyu nationality had its own system, as did every other Kenyan nationality. When workers from different nationalities began to come together in factories and plantations, the information system that evolved helped to make it possible to form a united front in their common struggles.

The people's information services proved capable of accepting and adapting new technologies to serve the information needs of their users. The developments in the society had brought new literacy as well as print technologies. Oral traditions and print mediums were skilfully combined to transmit the people's anti-colonial ideology and to boost the morale of people active in the struggle, as well as to carry messages from people to active combatants and from the High Command of the armed forces to the people. The importance of songs and oral tradition as a system of communication during the struggle for independence has been well documented.[29] These songs now began to be printed by the Land and Freedom Army (Mau Mau) as booklets and handbills as well as in some fifty newspapers, which were being published by the liberation movement before independence.

There thus developed a relevant information service run by the people to satisfy their own information needs. It is doubtful whether the struggle for independence would have been successful without the development of a powerful information system. This system had proved itself capable in an earlier age of satisfying the information needs of peasant societies; in a new age it had again proved successful in fulfilling the needs of a people's movement for national independence. There is no doubt that it has the capacity to provide a relevant people-oriented service in the rural areas of Kenya today. It was a loss to information science that this system was not incorporated into the post-independence information service. However, the system never died and has continued to grow and develop among the rural and urban poor of today.

This informal information system provides a number of lessons, which can be applied in improving the practices of information services in their attempts to support rural development.

---

[29] Perhaps the best source is Kinyatti, M. wa (1980): Thunder from the mountains: Mau Mau patriotic songs. London: Zed Press.

The first lesson to be learnt is that it is necessary to reorientate information services from being aimed at only a small section of the population (i.e. the government officials, the educated) to providing a service to the 90 percent of the country's people (most of whom are peasants) who have not had any service up to now. This would call for a major overhaul of the present services.

There are various policy matters, which will have to be solved before such a change can be put into practice. First of all, a language policy will have to be worked out. It is essential that a service aimed at peasants should be in the language of the peasants. This implies that a major role of the central, national library will be to translate material from within Kenya as well as relevant material from overseas into the various national languages spoken by the peasants.

A people-oriented information service will also have to examine closely the content of the information supplied. This will have to deal with the real information needs of peasants, not what an official sitting in an office in Nairobi thinks the peasants should know. The major struggle of both the rural and urban people in Kenya is the satisfaction of basic material needs. Their everyday struggles are waged to ensure their rights to their land and to getting a fair return for their labour. Only an information service which becomes their ally in achieving these rights can be considered people-oriented. Those involved in planning information services will need to work out the practical implications of such a policy.

Another feature of a people-oriented information service is that it should be a democratic service. This, again, has various implications. First of all, it means that the information service will not be imposed from the top by officials, or from the capital. It should be a service initiated, planned and run by the people themselves. There is an unlimited source of ideas, initiative, and creative and management abilities in the people to help evolve an information system suitable for local needs. The role of a national information centre should be to coordinate and support these different local initiatives and to give them national guidance. It will also need to train local information workers at national institutes.

Democracy in information services implies that it will be the people themselves who will decide what kind of information will be collected and disseminated, how this will be done, in which languages and by whom. They will also be involved in the financial aspects of running an information service.

A people-oriented information service will ensure that communication is seen as a two-way process. Its responsibilities are not only to supply rural people with information from outside the community, but also to document the information existing within the community, reproduce it in print, visual and other media and make it available to other communities. It will need to organise conferences and workshops and undertake investigations to work out in practice what information is available in the community, what information it needs, how this can be supplied and other professional matters.

A relevant, people-oriented service should, in practice, be a *service* and not end up as a number of stone buildings called libraries, which have some books in them. Those selected to serve in this service should have proved their commitment to serving the people. A service is not something like a bar of soap available in shops. It should make information available where the people are. All available media should be used in such an information service so that everybody in the community can be reached. Thus radio broadcasts, television, video, sound recordings and cameras should all be tools of the information service.

The two aspects of information work, namely, technical and social, should each be accorded their appropriate places in the system. Technical aspects such as cataloguing, accessions, processing, classifying, etc., are important in assuring that the social aspects are looked after. They should not become the primary activity, as happens in many libraries. The social aspects are the ones that place people first, never forgetting that the primary duty of a service is to provide information to the people, and that the service is there because the people are primary in any social set-up.

The concept of a professional librarian removed from the struggles of the people around them also needs to be changed if a people-oriented information system is to emerge. A librarian, especially in the rural context, should be a fully committed member of the community and become involved in its productive activities. Only then will the users place full confidence in their information workers and the information service; only thus will the information workers themselves understand the information needs of the community.

Information workers should be teachers as well as themselves learning from the peasants; they should combine the role of educators, mass media workers, historians, broadcasters, and workers on the cultural front. Information centres should be centres of dramatic and creative activities, which can release the creativity of the peasants. Such activities can also be a powerful means of communication. Only by assuming all these roles (which also implies that educators, mass media workers, historians, broadcasters, workers on the cultural front, as well as the peasants themselves, in turn become part-time information workers), only by such a creative interpretation of the role of information workers, will it be possible to give birth to people-oriented information services. Only then will information users cease to be mere spectators in a drama played out for their benefit by 'professional' librarians, and become fully integrated in the work of information provision, which is today recognised as a basic human right.

There are no well-defined practices, which can be created in offices for providing an "ideal" information service. These will emerge during the actual practice of information work among the people, and this calls for a total commitment to the people on the part of information workers.

Breaking the walls — the way ahead

Walls have been created around the vast reservoir of knowledge available in our libraries and information stores. There are strict regulations about which information can enter the reserve and which information can leave. This restrictive practice has meant that there is no meaningful information service available for millions of rural workers and peasants. The time has come when these walls should be broken down so as to build up new practices of information collection, documentation and dissemination.

Much has been written about adopting new approaches to information services. Among these have been ideas of community libraries and barefoot librarians.[30]

---

[30] The following two provide a good coverage of the subject: Luanda, M. C. (1978): Development of information systems: the humanistic approach. Paper presented at the Third International Standing Conference of Eastern, Central and Southern African Librarians, Nairobi. (Conference Document no. 9). Wijasuriya, D.E.K., Lim Huck-Tee and

Experiences from many countries are also available to show the successes of alternative approaches. The most successful have been those from countries waging revolutionary struggles, when battles can be lost if correct information is not available at the right time. In such conditions, information is clearly seen as a basic necessity and ways have to be found to organise an appropriate system. Such was the experience during the war for national liberation in Kenya, and in other countries. Perhaps we now need to look at the role of information in such dynamic terms, for the lack of the right information at the right time can kill in peace as well as in war. The recent famines in Africa show this clearly.

Information kiosks

Various ideas for providing a people-oriented rural information service have emerged in the course of fierce discussions by patriotic librarians in Kenya on ways of providing a relevant library service. Many of these have been put into practice on a small scale, which has, nevertheless, proved successful. An example may be found in the idea of 'information kiosks'.

A way has to be found out of the high-cost, high-technology library system which cannot function without expensive buildings and equally expensive importation of foreign books, many of them irrelevant to the information needs of rural people.

Over the years there has developed, in most Kenyan towns, a network of food kiosks, which provide cheap and nutritious food for the country's workers. These kiosks provide not only the basic food needed for survival, but have also become centres for the communication of information. Most kiosks have a transistor radio set which provides current news and cultural programmes; others have invested in tape recorders, which provide music in Kiswahili and other national languages; yet others have installed television sets, which are a major attraction. Thus, over a mug of *uji*, (maizemeal-based porridge), or a plate of *githeri* (a popular worker dish made of maize and beans, often enriched with vegetables and meat), one is exposed to the latest news on the radio and television. There often turn up, mysteriously, copies of the *Taifa Leo* (a Kiswahili daily published in Nairobi), which provides additional news and views. Lack of reading skills is no barrier, as enough readers can be found to read the news aloud.

While absorbing all this, one cannot fail to get additional information from yet another medium: the walls of the kiosks are full of pictures and news-cuttings about the owners' favourite football players, and national heroes — Kimaathi's pictures being the favourite. Then to all this is added perhaps the most active source of knowledge, the latest news, rumours, and whispered reports of the latest underground publications, and continuous talks, discussions and conversations. This is a continuation of the oral tradition, which is even today the main source of information for millions of people.

Without any 'professional' guidance, the workers have created a relevant information service, which at one stroke has solved the problem of finance for expensive buildings. They have also solved the problem of using a multi-media approach to information communication. The sources of information, while not as extensive as those of a modern library, are vast. In fact, the quickest way of getting any information about any important happening in any part of the country is from

---

Nadarajah, R. (1975): The barefoot librarian: library developments in Southeast Asia with special reference to Malaysia. London, Clive Bingley.

such kiosks, where *matatu* (private cars on hire), and bus drivers who have travelled far and wide come for their mug of *uji*, bringing with them distant news. Similarly, peasant women also bring their produce for sale to kiosks, stop for *uji*, and exchange news, thus bridging the gulf between towns and countryside.

This shows the obvious potential of the 'information kiosk' approach to information collection and dissemination. If such kiosks were backed by a well-stocked national library service with modern technological aids, their potential would be increased even further. Such kiosks would have to be manned by librarians who should be aware of local conditions and be accepted by the users as one of their own. There is no limit to the kinds of activities that could be undertaken by these information kiosks. They could become centres for recording the oral traditions and agricultural knowledge from the peasants, using duplicating machines to reproduce relevant information from these and disseminating this to a wider audience. There is no reason why these kiosks could not also become broadcasting stations for local community radio, so as to reach the peasants right in the fields. They would, of course, have to lend cheap portable radio sets as part of their services.

The information kiosks can also duplicate relevant material from national libraries for disseminating to local schools and social halls. In return they would make available to the national library, material from schools that is considered of wider significance, such as teachers' lecture notes and student essays, as well as records of peasants' experiences in the fields. They would thus become important publishers. Information kiosks could become social centres in their areas. They could be involved in creative and literary activities, using the media of films, drama, songs and story reading to communicate ideas and views.

Conclusion

There is no lack of ideas on how a people-oriented rural information service can operate. What is lacking at present is a commitment on the part of the society as a whole to implement any meaningful policy. This applies, not only in the information field, but in every other aspect of life in third world countries also. The information sector is, after all, not an isolated aspect life, but is linked to the political, social and economic conditions in a country. Until these conditions change, there cannot be any change in the information sector.

Agricultural information services in Kenya and Third World needs (1987)[31]

The past year has seen African peasants, pastoralists and workers facing mass malnutrition, starvation and death. In the face of this calamity, it would be reasonable to expect African information workers to disseminate information on the causes of and remedies for this suffering. But this has not happened to any significant level. It is not individual information workers who should shoulder the blame for this failure to spotlight the natural and, more important, social reasons for the failure of the

---

[31] Journal of Librarianship 19(2) April 1987. pp.108-120.

potentially rich lands to feed the people. Indeed, most of the rank-and-file information workers are hard working and totally committed to the cause of providing information for the people.

The failure to provide the people of Kenya with an appropriate information service is due to faults in the whole information system; after independence the system was not adapted to satisfy the information needs of the population as a whole. This is a reflection of the prevailing social, economic and political reality which has not only suppressed people's creativity, but has ensured real development only for the elite, leaving the majority of the people without even basic subsistence. One cannot see an information service in a vacuum; its failures need to be examined in the context of its social reality, and any improvements will also depend on a changed reality in society.

The information systems that exist today in the Third World have not dropped from the sky, but have evolved over many years in the course of social struggles. Thus, for example, two distinct agricultural information services have developed in Kenya. The first is the service which was developed by the peasants, based on word of mouth, and was used to pass on useful experiences and practices in agriculture to the next generation, as well as to inform everybody involved in productive work in the community about useful agricultural practices. The other information service is the 'official' one, which having been established by the British colonial authorities to serve its own economic interests, has always served the needs of the ruling classes. This 'official' library service ignored the information needs of Kenyan peasants. For example, information on export crops such as coffee and tea, on which the colonial settlers depended, was readily available, but the people's food crops such as beans, millet, sorghum, cassava and maize were all ignored.

Since independence, there has not been a significant qualitative change in the agricultural information system. Although there has been an increase in the quantity of book and periodical material, in the number of people working in information centres, and in the number of library buildings, there has not been a corresponding improvement in the quality and relevance of agricultural information services. That the potential is there is shown in the work of new institutions such as the Kenya Agricultural Information Service and the Kenya Agricultural Documentation Centre. These and other similar systems (e.g. the current awareness service provided by the Kenya Agricultural Research Institute) have found it difficult to function to their full potential given the prevailing socio-economic conditions.

We will examine below some aspects of information services that will have to change in order to meet the needs of the rural community in Kenya today.

The users of agricultural information

Kenya, in common with many other Third World countries, has not yet resolved this fundamental question: who are the users of agricultural information at whom services should be aimed? The colonial belief was that it was only the settlers, bureaucracy, research and educational staff and perhaps extension workers who needed agricultural information. This practice of looking only at these groups as potential users has not changed much, except perhaps the settlers have been replaced by local 'telephone farmers' living in Nairobi, and by large-scale plantations which are controlled by transnational agribusinesses which satisfy their own information needs. The secondary level agricultural extension staff are covered but they are not always able to pass on information to peasants. The main group of potential users who have been left out altogether as far as information needs are concerned is that of the peasants, who are the ones actually involved in the labour of cultivation. Thus, the largest number of potential agricultural information users, are denied the information, which should be theirs by right. Agriculture cannot develop fully if the peasants are not given relevant agricultural information.

What is needed is a totally new approach to agricultural information, which should put the peasants at the centre of such a system. The importance of land to the lives of the people is obvious: over 90 percent of Kenyans are peasants, pastoralists, fisher people or workers on land; and basic human needs such as food, clothing and shelter are satisfied directly or indirectly by people working on land. By ignoring the information needs of this sector, we are really ignoring agriculture itself and inviting famine. New rural-based libraries will have to be established to replace the present system where rural libraries are only branches of the urban library set-up, merely miniature urban libraries, without any thought given to the particular problems of rural information needs. Thus, rural libraries will have to stop circulating English and American fiction, and irrelevant material from all over the world on every conceivable topic, and concentrate on what is relevant to the peasants, the centuries-old irrigation system developed by the peasants of Marakwet.

Other important information needs that will have to be satisfied are those of the urban farmers. One can see their maize and vegetable *shambas* (plots) along every road in major towns, including Nairobi. The office workers, factory workers, domestic and 'informal sector' workers, the unemployed- in fact, most urban people- use every available piece of land to grow subsistence and cash crops and to keep poultry, pigs and goats. Yet no attempts have been made by our present library service to reach them.

Training of agricultural librarians and information workers

Perhaps one of the first steps to be taken in building up a relevant library service for rural needs will be the appropriate training of agricultural librarians and information workers. Only when a large number of people are given this type of training and are stationed in rural information centres can we hope to see a change in the situation.

All trainee rural librarians should be given a basic course in agriculture and a course in awareness about conditions in the countryside. It would be advantageous to allow students of librarianship to live and work among peasants so that they acquire practical knowledge about their lives and their information needs.

Rural librarians and information workers should be recruited from among the local peasants. Librarians who have grown up in the area and know the local conditions, language and people will obviously be trusted more by rural users and will be more effective in providing a relevant library service. Of course, this should not preclude the creation of a national consciousness and outlook, as librarians can be moved to urban as well as other rural libraries once they have served their own area for a specific period.

There is also a need to provide a refresher course in Kenyan agricultural librarianship for all librarians who have qualified in the past, locally or overseas, so as to reorient them to the widespread need for agricultural information and to rid the service of many 'senior' librarians' bureaucratic tendencies.

The student recruitment policy of institutions which train librarians will need to be changed so that the present overemphasis on academic qualifications is modified;

admission should be open to those who may not have full academic qualifications but who are committed and have capacity for hard work, and long practical experience.

All librarians, trained or untrained, should have the right to adopt and to experiment with new ideas on practical librarianship. There is a tendency at present on the part of the old, established librarians – who had often been promoted by the outgoing colonial administration in a process of 'localisation' – to suppress the initiative and enthusiasm of more resourceful librarians. Over the years, these older librarians have risen even higher in the profession and have become new 'experts' and have controlled the profession as exclusively their own, private business. They have seen any new ideas coming from a new generation of committed librarians as a personal challenge and have opposed them, good or bad, thus depriving the profession of new ideas which could have provided solutions in a changing situation. These new ideas have not come only from the rank-and-file librarians; they really express the voice of the people with whom they have close links.

The senior librarians, meanwhile, have been increasingly alienated from the majority of working people in the country, reflecting their rise in economic status. This has increased their isolation and they have sought to maintain their authority by being more repressive towards those they are supposed to lead.

The content of an agricultural information collection

The issue of the content of a library is central to any discussion on an information service. If the content of a collection does not reflect the information needs of its potential users, the service will never provide that information which will solve problems in society. It will then not matter whether the most modern technologies are used or the best features of the oral medium are employed. The use of a particular medium in itself does not ensure the success of a service and even the oral medium has been used to give wrong information. It is only the content of a library that will decide whether the information supplied is relevant or not. Although a large volume of agricultural information from all over the world is collected by agricultural libraries; this is often done without an overall acquisitions policy, which would recognise the central role of local collections. It is, of course, necessary to collect material from those parts of the world, which have similar climate, landforms, and agricultural, economic and social backgrounds. In fact, accounts of such experiences from other countries should be more readily available to peasants, but only in a balanced way. Clearly there is no need to collect a lot of detailed information on, say, farming in the USA with its totally different socio-economic conditions when no material is available on the experiences of Tanzanian peasants, not to mention those of the Boran pastoralists from within Kenya itself.

A large part of local agricultural information has never been collected in Third World libraries. This should be a priority activity. This is the information that is passed from generation to generation of peasants by word of mouth, which has continued to develop and change in keeping with changing needs in the society. It includes much useful information, which has been tested and proved correct over centuries of practice. It is in this area that the so-called 'traditional' and 'modern' practices of librarianship should join hands to make relevant information accessible through the use of modern technologies. The training of agricultural librarians should emphasise the collection, organisation, storage and dissemination of this information, not only in print, but also in non-print media such as sound and film tapes, radio and television broadcasts as well.

Material collected in agricultural libraries should reflect the information needs of peasants. Investigations should be held to ascertain what these needs are. Then abstracts should be prepared to show what information is available by districts and provinces, by crops, by climatic zones, as well as by names of the various nationalities who live in the country, such as the Bajun, the Giriama and the Somali. Ways should then be found to make the information available to the peasants.

Language of agricultural collections

All Third World countries are linguistically very rich, with a wide variety of languages used by the peasants. These languages are the countries' cultural wealth and should not be seen as factors which divide people. It is the cultural diversity of the various nationalities who inhabit Kenya that gives a deep and rich dimension to the culture of Kenya as a whole.

The languages spoken by peasants are especially rich in agricultural usage and vocabulary, the languages themselves having evolved in the course of their experiments on the land. There are more words describing agricultural activities, processes, crops and technology than are available in European languages. Yet most of the information in Third World agricultural libraries is in foreign languages like English and French. If the agricultural libraries wish to address their services to the people of their own countries (as opposed to an undefined international audience), they will need to collect and disseminate more information in their own languages. They will need to translate material from one national language of the country to another and also to translate from foreign languages into the national languages spoken by the peasants.

In the final analysis, whatever the personal views of librarians on the language issue, if they are to succeed professionally in acquiring, disseminating and storing knowledge and information, they will have to adopt the languages of the peasants. It is the library, which will have to accept the languages of the peasants who naturally have strong cultural and scientific attachments to them and not the other way around. If the content of a collection is the most important aspect of an 'information-for-life' service, then use of the languages of the peasants is the next most important aspect.

The medium of communication

The sad point about the agricultural information system in Kenya, and in many other Third World countries, is that it is a passive system, originally established during colonial times to serve an elite audience. The service makes certain assumptions about its users, which, however, do not fit the social reality of the country today. These assumptions include the following: that rural people have easy access to library buildings, that they have full proficiency in foreign languages, that they have free time in which to read, that whatever material they find in libraries will be relevant to them.

One telling aspect of the passive library system is the almost exclusive use of the print medium. Although it is more effective and cheaper to use non-print media to disseminate information, our libraries have stubbornly continued to use print. They are ready to use computer technologies for in-house activities, yet will not adopt the multi-senses media that have been developed by the peasants, and those made available by today's technologies.

Although occasional radio programmes are used to disseminate agricultural information, there is no national information dissemination policy which would make possible well-organised and coordinated radio and television broadcasts which could be combined with print material and extension staff activities so as to form a basis for a people-orientated information service. At present no attempt has been made in radio broadcasts to allow for particular differences in climatic conditions, land use, tenure and social customs, and transport difficulties in different areas of the country. It is assumed that agricultural theories are applicable universally; there is no consideration for particularities of application in specific areas. The same radio broadcasts are supposed to satisfy information needs both in fertile, well-watered areas and in very dry areas. Television is, of course, used almost exclusively for the entertainment of the urban rich, and its potential as a powerful medium of information dissemination is wasted.

Information transmission or information communication?

As before Independence, agricultural libraries see their role in terms of information transmission rather than information *communication,* which implies a two-way exchange of information. This arose from the belief that peasants have no useful agricultural information which can be collected by libraries, that they do not have views on any aspects of agriculture or on the information that reaches them on new methods of farming. They are considered as recipients of information only. Their failure to understand foreign languages is often taken to mean a lack of intelligence. Hence, the library services see no reason to seek their participation in the process of communication.

Libraries established under colonial influences collect information from all over the world, especially from the industrialised Western countries, and this is supposed to satisfy local needs. As we saw earlier, this affects the content of such libraries. In order to change this situation, the libraries will need to become, in *practice,* centres for the exchange of views, ideas, experiences and information between peasants and librarians; the latter bringing in relevant information from other peasants, scholars, government officials and other countries. In implementing this new concept of rural librarianship, our librarians will evolve new theories and new practices.

The oppression of technology

Third World agriculture and agricultural information systems are increasingly being seen by transnational corporations as fertile grounds for profit and plunder. Agriculture itself has become one of the largest items of world trade and wealth. 'Advanced' agricultural technologies are being pushed on Third World countries. These include 'improved' seeds, fertilisers, machinery, computers, marketing and distribution 'systems'-the list is almost endless. Although such things are not necessarily bad in themselves, the profit motive of those pushing them is very strong. Third World agriculture forms ties and inevitably becomes totally dependent on transnational agribusiness. The agribusiness in turn exploits its control in order to maximise profits.

Third World libraries often become tools in the hands of 'advanced technologies' when they one-sidedly collect and disseminate to peasants information on such technologies, without at the same time providing a similar input on the not so advanced technologies in use by peasants which may be more suitable to the particular needs in a country.

Information itself has become a commodity to be bought and sold, like agricultural commodities, on the market. When a few voices are raised questioning the relevance of all these technologies in the present conditions of Third World agriculture, new tactics are employed. 'Appropriate technologies' are brought in to reap yet another harvest of super profits for the 'appropriate technology industry'.

The information field itself has also been invaded by the super and 'appropriate' technologies. It is no longer possible for Third World librarians to remain 'neutral' and uncommitted in the face of this invasion of technologies. This is not to deny the usefulness of new technologies if used properly and under the control of the people themselves. For this to happen, such technologies have to be rationally examined in the light of local conditions, local existing technologies and the alternatives available. Foreign technologies can then be selectively used to supplement local ones, keeping in mind local conditions and needs. The question of priorities should also be considered. In view of the limited resources available, deep thought should be given to whether national resources would be best used to provide a cheap and reliable water supply for peasants using local resources, technologies and labour or to acquire the latest foreign technologies and computers (e.g. for our libraries) to do work which can be done by local people, who in the process will find employment and perhaps develop their own appropriate technologies.

It is often assumed that only those technologies that come from industrialised countries can be classified as 'real' technologies and those that are developed by peasants in the Third World cannot be so classified. In fact, peasant-developed technologies are more relevant and apropriate as they have been developed under local conditions. They can even provide a much stronger foundation for the development of local technical and industrial revolutions in conjunction with selected advanced technologies from other countries.

It should be the primary role of agricultural librarians to document such local technologies and to publish local technology indexes by agricultural zones so as to draw to the attention of other peasants existing technologies, which they can adopt and improve. In general, it should be the role of agricultural librarians to ensure that it is the people who are in command of technologies, not for profit but to improve production to satisfy their basic needs. They can do this by documenting and disseminating knowledge about appropriate technologies developed by peasants from different regions and countries. They should also be active in innovating appropriate technologies in their own profession.

Librarians have a crucial role to play in the whole field of development and application of technologies in society. By providing wrong or inappropriate information or no information at all, they can indirectly lead society to starvation; but by providing relevant information in a balanced way they can support and sustain life. Each of us is making a choice in this matter.

Why do agricultural libraries fail to communicate?

It is clear that Third World agricultural libraries have, in the main, failed to break out of the mould into which they were set during the colonial experience. Often librarians are passive disseminators of information in a one-sided way and do not give much thought to collecting the vast amount of information that is available in oral and other non-print forms.

Why is it that the libraries have remained classic examples of non-communication? In an age when it is possible to reach the moon, it is not technically difficult to devise an information service that can communicate life-giving information. Just as it is possible for every peasant house to have a nearby source of Coca-Cola but no ready source of water, so it is possible for every peasant household to receive a Coca-Cola advertisement but no information that can be useful in the productive activities on the land. This is a measure of the failure of today's information services. And the reasons for this failure are social and economic, not technical; the solutions will have to be found in the social and economic fields and not in an ever-increasing import of foreign high technology.

The real reasons for the failure are to be found in the world's social-economic-political set-up today. There is fierce rivalry over the control of Third World mineral, industrial, agricultural and human resources. In this rivalry, not only has information become an industry and a source of enormous profit, but its possession brings a great deal of strategic power. Knowledge of the availability of good soil, sources of water, minerals and oil in particular areas can give the possessor control of many aspects of life of a country. With the development of satellite scanning techniques, those countries, which control this technology, have more information about Third World resources than the Third World countries themselves. This gives them the power to use the information to suit their own needs, or to withhold it, as when information about the presence of underground oil resources is withheld from the country itself to benefit commercial interests.

Thus agricultural information has come to be monopolised by transnationals who control more information about a particular country than even the major agricultural libraries in that country. Third World agriculture, and its information system itself have been split into two contradictory systems.

The first has all the information on scientific farming at its disposal, as well as the vast resources needed to exploit Third World land and labour. This is the plantation sector, which is controlled by transnational agribusiness concerns whose annual profits are much higher than the incomes of several countries put together. With their enormous political and economic power these transnationals get the best land and best labour, as well as total control over their own pricing policy, profits, exports and imports.

In the information field, this sector of agriculture, which is really outside national control, commands the latest scientific information and initiates its own research projects. It even buys up the best and most experienced and skilled information workers, thus depriving the national sector of this vital element. But its interest in developing local agriculture is marginal. It usually produces non-food products for export. Even when food crops are grown they are not for local consumption but for export.

Thus the best land in the country produces for export, mostly to industrialised countries. This plantation sector sees its activities in the Third World only as a short-term profit-making activity. No attention is paid to preserving long-term productivity and fertility of soils. No attempts are made to integrate its activities with national agriculture or with the needs of peasants. Moreover, it encourages the peasants, in outgrower schemes, to grow cash crops for sale to the transnationals, which then export them. Some transnationals operating in Kenya are Del Monte, BAT (British American Tobacco), Brooke Bond, Lonrho, ICI (Imperial Chemical Industries), Unilever. There are hundreds of others, which have become involved in every aspect of agriculture and agriculture-based industries. Much information is now available on their activities.

The social-economic-political factors that supply the latest information to the plantation sector deny it to the other system of agriculture found in the Third World- the peasant agriculture. Here the land is poorer, is fragmented, with generally less rainfall, and lacking systematic irrigation. International finance corporations and foreign banks control a large part of the finance of these peasant holdings. Peasants are under an ever-present threat of being evicted from their small landholdings for non-repayment of generously given loans. They cannot afford the high-cost technologies (imported hybrid seeds, fertilisers, irrigation, machinery, etc.), yet given the present conditions in agriculture they cannot survive without them.

At the same time, the agricultural information available to this peasant sector is minimal. Information is another 'high' technology they cannot afford. The national information services need to devise a well thought out information system that can supply the peasants with basic, simple, socio-economic and technical information that can be utilised without expensive inputs and which can have practical results. This is the challenge to Third World agricultural librarians.

It is not accidental that agricultural information systems in the Third World have failed to provide relevant information for the agricultural community. The failure is caused by the whole system that uses Third World agricultural resources, not for the benefit of the working people, but for the satisfaction of the profit motive of transnationals. It will be possible to provide a people-orientated service only when the people themselves are directly involved in planning and implementing the service.

Conclusion

Agricultural libraries will be able to provide "information for life" only when the real needs of peasants are understood. These are the basic material needs for survival: food, clothing and shelter. The information service must be able to help peasants and other rural and urban working people to satisfy these needs. This is the criterion on which its success will be judged.

Libraries, communication & development in Kenya: the missing political factor (1990)[32]

The reality and the dream—setting the scene

The contradiction between what a library or information system should be doing and what it actually does in the Third World context is shown by these two scenes from Kenya:

---

[32] Information and Libraries in the Developing World, 1: Sub-Saharan Africa. Compiled and edited by Michael Wise and Anthony Olden. 1990. London; The Library Association. pp.159-170. Reproduced with permission of Sage Publications Ltd.

The Headquarters of the Kenya National Library Service is located on Ngong Road in Nairobi. But the majority of the potential users live nowhere near the Headquarters building. They survive in the slums of Mathere, Kawangaware, Uthiru or on the pavements of River Road. Not only is the library building physically far away from the majority of Nairobi residents — the public library service offers little information that has any relevance to the daily needs of the people.

The library of the University of Nairobi's College of Agriculture and Veterinary Science is appropriately set ten miles out of Nairobi at Kabete. It holds thousands of books and periodicals from around the world. A myriad of ideas and experiences on agriculture are to be found here. But the residents of Kabete, many of whom cultivate small plots of land or keep poultry, have no right to the knowledge in the library. They have no academic credentials.

The professional librarians are totally dedicated to their profession. There can be no deviations from the theories learnt in far away centres of knowledge. They dream of building up a library that can rival the best public library in Britain, the mother of modern librarianship which ironically has failed to provide a relevant service to its own diverse population. But that matters little to the Third World librarian, who has the power to alter the library to suit local needs. The voices of protest from a large number of library workers are dismissed as non-professional opinions, which interfere with the dream of reproducing the British library system in foreign lands.

The remoteness of libraries from the lives of working people in the Third World is no mere accident, nor should it be seen in isolation from other social means of communication such as newspapers, radio, TV and cinema. The point about these is not that they fail to communicate, for indeed they do, and quite, successfully at that, but that they give wrong signals to the majority of people whose material needs demand an entirely different message. In general the media in the Third World is controlled by those whose economic and political interests are opposed to those of the majority of the people. Hence the message usually carried is one of hope and prosperity, not for the people but for those who are in positions of power.

The historical setting

The present library and information structures in the Third World have evolved historically in the course of intense social and political struggles. They thus reflect the past and current realities in society as a whole. Let us examine briefly the development of information services in Kenya so as to understand better the present set-up. Although differing in detail, many of these experiences are shared with other Third World countries.

The struggles of the Kenyan people have been waged at two levels, both requiring an efficient and relevant information service. These are the struggle against *nature*, and *social* struggles. The contest with nature has ensured survival in face of hostile forces — wild animals, extremes of weather, and dangerous diseases, among others. At the same time food, both of animal and plant sources, had to be procured and was achieved by the production of appropriate housing, clothing, and food systems which catered to the different needs of societies throughout the country. The development of appropriate tools and technologies was essential in the process of producing these material needs. But these technologies could not have developed without a simultaneous development of an information system that could sustain and improve the productive process. Thus every nationality or group in Kenya developed an information system that answered its own particular needs. Many of these systems were based on the oral method of collection and dissemination of information.

Such information dealt with weather patterns, useful plants and herbs, irrigation practices and so on. All this information was then passed on to succeeding generations through the indigenous education systems, which made extensive use of accumulated knowledge and passed it on as part of active involvement in the process of production.[33]

At the social level there have been internal struggles among the peoples of Kenya, but the primary social struggle for over 500 years has been against foreign forces that were attracted by the wealth in the land, its natural resources and labour. Thus, for example, in the earlier age of the recorded contacts, response to intrusion was against the Portuguese, while towards the end of the last century it was against British colonialism. With capitalism came the dramatically different methods of production, which brought about fundamental changes in the Kenyan society and this in turn influenced the redevelopment of information systems.

The most outstanding opposition to colonialism was led by the Kenya Land and Freedom Army, which mobilised an active guerrilla army of over 35,000 combatants. These fighters were supported by the broad masses in major cities and towns as well as by peasants. Such an intense struggle, which finally brought independence, could not have been waged without a functioning information system, which could acquire intelligence on military matters and communicate with combatants and masses. One of the most important achievements of the Kenya Land and Freedom Army was the development of an effective information system which ably combined oral experiences of the people with the new media associated with print. Thus, while a large number of songs were produced to pass on important information and to raise political consciousness, at the same time the KLFA published its own newspapers (including its main organ, the KLFA *High Command*). At one time its groups were publishing over 50 newspapers in Kiswahili, Gikuyu and other Kenyan languages.

Other media were also used by KLFA. Thus a large number of sound recordings were produced that supported and advanced the struggle, and special printing presses were established to produce books. These should be seen in the context of the colonial state's control of much greater financial resources, and its total control over the mass media—radio, newspapers, and the publishing industry. That the KLFA succeeded is an indication of their ability to organise their own information systems.

Post-independence Kenya has seen the consolidation of a process set into motion during the earlier period. This was the clear division of society along class lines. The disappearance of apartheid-type social divisions led to the consolidation of the two main classes: workers and peasants on the one hand, and the bourgeoisie on the other. This fundamental social fact has influenced every aspect of life in Kenya, including the function of information providers. They fall into one or the other class and their views, professional or otherwise, and actions are decided through their class interests. This explains the sharp contradictions in the information field in Kenya today.

The present practices

---

[33] These points on production, storage, and dissemination of information in society are discussed further in the author's article Agri-Vet Information: Production, Organisation, Storage & Retrieval', University of Nairobi. Library Magazine (Nairobi) No.2, Oct.1979, 23-37.

The post-independence period saw a consolidation of the former official, colonial practices, which, were mostly retained by the new officials. The methods evolved by the Kenya Land and Freedom Army in the course of defining basic Kenyan needs were discarded. This reflected the new economic, political and social reality in the society as a whole. The activists of the independence struggle found themselves without power and a new class which had been strengthening its economic position while the anti-colonial war raged, now inherited power. Nurtured and sustained by powerful foreign economic interests, this new ruling class legalised practices that suited its own class interests, as opposed to the interests of the majority of working people whose interests had in the past been represented by KLFA.

The effects of this social reality on the information field were clear. The resources of the state created an information sector, which was catering to the interests of a small minority. The dominant ideology of the ruling class, represented by the governing party—KANU, was given full exposure on every media. The capitalist values that benefited those in power became the national values, while the socialist outlook of those who fought for independence began to be considered 'subversive'; and the short-lived opposition party—Kenya Peoples Union, could not find a democratic way to propagate its platform. The vast majority of the people who had rallied behind the call for land and freedom found their needs submerged in the official calls for free market dominance.

This new situation was well represented in the newspaper field. In the colonial period, newspapers had played a crucial role in mobilising and politicising people in the struggle for independence. As mentioned previously a large number of newspapers had been used by the KLFA Central Command to establish a communication link with its supporters and between the active combatants. The colonial authority had made many attempts to suppress this activity by banning newspapers and jailing reporters, printers and publishers. But no sooner was one newspaper banned and its editors and printers arrested, than another newspaper was started, to take its place with new editors, printers and reporters.

This lesson was not lost on the leaders and their advisers after independence. Now it became almost impossible for ordinary Kenyans to start new newspapers. A large deposit was required and, more important, stricter formal and informal censorship was enforced to prevent views different from those of the government from being published. The result was that in the first years after independence only two national newspapers were in circulation, one of them was the *Standard*, which had been established in the early days of the century and had represented the settler interests. Neither of the papers dared to challenge or report on anything that the government found objectionable. In later years, a few new newspapers and journals were started but this did not change the basic situation and indeed, in recent years there has been an increase in the harassment of the press.

The tremendous potential of radio and television was similarly used to reinforce the interests of a minority. Entertainment was given priority and education, which was the main need, was treated as of secondary importance. As for information, this consisted mainly of the speeches and movements of a few leaders. Television was similarly directed at a minority of viewers and the educational and information needs of the majority were ignored.

The other powerful instrument of social communication, i.e. libraries, reflected a similar development and did not really satisfy the information needs of the people. The whole process was caught in between two systems that should have been brought together in order to provide a relevant information system. On the one hand, there existed the system that had historically proved successful. This was the traditional oral method, reinforced by judicious use of relevant modern technology. On the other hand, there exists the latest information technology to provide an information system that answers people's real needs. But what has been developed in Kenya is efficient in neither of these. Basing itself on foreign models, the library system has rejected the lessons from history. It has been influenced by foreign 'experts', who over the years have imposed small doses of new technologies. In the process there is no single, integrated plan that can develop libraries throughout the country using available resources and avoiding wasteful duplication.

The public library system functions in isolation from other library systems, such as those serving education (universities, colleges, schools), government and research. Not only is there an artificial barrier between the 'librarians' and 'information workers', but even within library workers, the senior librarians have encouraged further divisions between the 'professional', 'non-professional' and 'paraprofessional' librarians. These divisions, in essence, reflect the class divisions in the country. The result has been a sharp division of opinion about the direction that library service should take. On one side stand the senior librarians who have sought to reproduce the library system that exists in Britain or in other countries of their training. This they have done, as they are in positions of power. On the other side stand the mass of library workers whose ideas about information work are more closely related to the needs of working people, with whom they are in daily contact. Although they lack power, they do not lack commitment to their profession. They have clear ideas about how and why our present library services do not respond to the needs of the people, and how they can be made to respond to it. It is to their voice that we should turn since they represent the future direction of information services. It is imperative we do this if the libraries are to have any relevance in the social setting in which they exist.

Sauti ya wakutubi — the voice of Kenyan library workers

It is significant that whereas the views of senior librarians can easily reach those Kenyans who can read in English, and indeed, reach the whole English-speaking world, those of the majority of library workers may remain unknown even to their colleagues in libraries in the same town. This is no accident. It shows that the senior librarians are in power and their voice is projected as the universal voice of Kenyan librarians.

It is in this context that one sees the significance of publications such as *Sauti ya Wakutubi* from the University of Nairobi library services. Short-lived as it was, it has made a lasting impression on the library scene not only in Kenya but in other parts of the world which have similar conditions. Its chief contribution was that it gave an outlet to the silent majority of library workers whose professional views have never before been considered worthy of publication or implementation. The significance of these views lies in the fact that they address local conditions and give local solutions in a situation where alien methods have too often held sway in the past. Their main contribution is that they unashamedly take sides in supporting the needs of the working people and do not disguise the need for change in the library and information field. The workshops organised by *Sauti ya wakutubi* sum up the lessons on information work:

> The need to reorient librarianship in Kenya to the requirements of the majority of Kenyans was emphasised ... Most of our libraries at present are copies from the Western libraries. We do not have libraries that suit our context at the moment. The mistake so far made in our library system is that we have confined and concentrated ourselves to small communities who are learned or rich, instead of extending our ideas to rural communities.[34]

The workshop also addressed the question of what it was possible to achieve and the reasons why there was a lack of achievement. It sums up the experience in library work: On the question of what is possible, what we can actually do, it was felt that anything was possible. There is no reason why we should not be able to implement all we wished to do. We have all the resources we need, especially human resources: But important obstacles remain. Obstacles, which in practice, have retarded the development of a relevant library service. The workshop mentions one such obstacle:

> But in order to achieve anything we shall have to get rid of the dependency mentality instilled into us by colonial and neo-colonial experiences ... We should accept in practice that we have the capacity to organise and run our own library services to suit our own particular needs ... Only then will we be able to provide a relevant library service to the people of Kenya that can have any meaning to the workers and peasants who form the majority and who produce all the wealth of the country.[35]

The library workers did not stop at organising workshops and discussing ways of providing a more relevant service. Many projects have also been started such as the one below.

The *Sehemu ya Utungaji* started initially as the creative wing of *Sauti ya Wakutubi*, to provide artwork for the magazine. Gradually, its scope expanded and it began experimenting with various ways of providing a relevant information service. One such was the School and College Library Project, which provided relevant articles on history, geography, and culture all from local research, to a large number of schools and colleges throughout the country. Part of the material sent was a package on organising a small library with instructions on simple cataloguing and classification, processing, borrowing systems, author and subject catalogues, and other basic practices. This was extremely popular with schools who had also started contributing their own documents in the system.

Another project of the Sehemu was to make the film medium available to the people. Thus film shows were organised where many who had not in the past been exposed to films were attracted particularly because the content was relevant to the lives of the people. Similarly Sehemu also joined hands with a city theatre group and produced a play with an historical theme. This also attracted a wide audience and much media coverage nationally, including the Kiswahili press. Such shows gave people a pride in their own indigenous history.

Yet another project involved producing a pictorial interpretation of Kenya's history. Entitled *Kuvunja Minyororo* ('Breaking the Chains'), this project encouraged members to draw pictures, undertake historical research and work out ways of interpreting this history for a larger audience.

These and other projects pointed the way to how a library service should make use of its resources (humans and books and materials) in order to provide a

---

[34] Sauti ya Wakutubi (Nairobi) 4, 1984, 144.
[35] Sauti ya Wakutubi (Nairobi) 4, 1984, 154.

communication link with the people in their own language and in an appropriate form. Here also the crucial point was the content of such communication.

Rocking the boat

Such projects, however appropriate and successful in their own right, can only have a limited impact as examples of what should be done. They cannot have total national relevance since they remain isolated activities, which find no official sanction. Their chief achievement can be to mobilise opinion within libraries, especially among the rank-and-file library workers, to convince them that there are alternate ways of practising librarianship which are possible not only on paper, but in reality as well. This is indeed an important achievement in an environment which discourages initiative and experimentation.

But development, in its widest sense, requires an altogether different approach, both in terms of quantity and quality. The basic need in Kenya today is the provision of adequate food, clothing, and shelter for all the people. Libraries have to find ways of providing information in the people's search for these basic material needs. New ways have to be found of collecting information for this. All sources have to be used, oral and written, local and foreign. All languages have to be included, especially the languages of all the nationalities of Kenya. Scientific and technological as well as social knowledge will have to be coordinated to provide an appropriate content. Information and knowledge can no longer be treated as commodities to be bought and sold in the open market to the highest bidder. New ways of disseminating the required information will have to be found. All media will have to be used, including radio, TV, newspapers, films. Most important, an overall information plan will have to be worked out so that individual components do not function in isolation, in a vacuum, but should be related to other components in an organic relationship.

The crucial factor in this new approach will be the involvement of the people for whom the information service is supposed to function. Their ideas will have to be incorporated into any plans, and the people themselves must not remain mere bystanders while "professionals" work out what information system they need. They should be the centre of any information system. And that is precisely the reason why a new style information system cannot function in the present socio-economic climate. For such a people-oriented system to emerge, an important aspect of our social life will have to be taken into consideration. This is the all-important *political aspect*, which has often been ignored in devising information provision. Where the whole political system has failed to provide the basic needs of the people, can it be expected to give birth to an information system that answers the real needs of the people?

A society such as Kenya's has apparently absorbed (possibly for lack of effective information) the death of over a million children, under the age of five, in the last ten years caused by lack of proper medical care and by malnutrition.[36] It can hardly be expected to work out effectively the information needs of the millions of children and their parents who have lost out on development altogether.

Librarians may find it convenient to 'play the ostrich' and close their minds to the social reality surrounding them. Convenient because it ensures their material well-

---

[36] "Each year more than 100,000 children under the age of five die as a result of poor food or lack of adequate medical care. In the ten years therefore, over a million children have thus died." UMOJA (Umoja wa Kupigania Demokrasia Kenya), Background Document No. 2, London: UMOJA, 1989, 12.

being in a society where millions go to bed without a meal, where a multitude of people have no bed or shelter to turn to at night, where there is no hope, no prospect for a better tomorrow. But convenience is not what libraries are all about. The UN International Women's Decade Conference in Nairobi in 1985 came up with this call to women:

> The hand that rocks the cradle
> Should also rock the boat.

It is only when the boat is rocked that a new solution to the information problems will also be found.

A search for alternatives

After 25 years of independence it is clear that no relevant information system has been developed within the present system. It is important, in fact a basic right, to allow different ideas on development to circulate freely among the people. A meaningful choice about which is the best way of promoting development can be made by the people only if they have access to information on all the alternatives and on whose interests are served by the various alternatives. This in fact is the first struggle for information workers in Kenya. It can be a matter of life and death in this society where police can walk into libraries to check who is reading what material. Anything that does not agree with official views is considered 'subversive' and people reading them can be jailed and imprisoned.

Various United Nations Conventions, which Kenya has signed, as well as Kenya's own constitution, guarantee the right to a free flow of information. But these rights are on paper only. In practice, people have to resort to underground publications to receive and pass on relevant development ideas. The two themes, how information is communicated, and what ideas of developments are relevant, are important issues that librarians need to consider. These are issues dealing with *content* of communication.

Kenya's history teaches the need for information workers to be fully integrated with the production process and to be fully involved in the contests with nature and in society. In the pre-colonial societies, the process of information acquisition and dissemination was skilfully linked to the education process and with social production. The same was true during the struggle for independence where the combatants were also actively involved in the struggle for information and knowledge. Kimaathi wa Wachiuri, the leader of Kenya Land and Freedom Army, together with other Mau Mau activists was involved equally in organising strategies and tactics for battle, and with distributing KLFA newspapers. In October 1952, for example, when the government declared a state of emergency and arrested thousands of people, Kimaathi was busy carrying thousands of KLFA newspapers in baskets and transporting them in buses to peasants and workers in the Rift Valley.

This lesson has not been lost on the major underground movements that have continued the struggle in recent years. Both the December Twelve Movement and now MWAKENYA have issued their own underground newspapers, which are being widely distributed throughout the country. These have carried regular articles on issues of development and on food, such as that in Pambana (no.2, July 1983) entitled 'The Politics of Food' in which it attacked the one-sidedness of official news about food shortages and drew important lessons from China, and other countries. Similarly MWAKENYA, in its Draft Minimum Programme (September 1987) addresses the question of land and sets down the demands of peasants for a society that gives priority to the need of food.

Such documents are not available in our libraries, although they are freely available in many British and US libraries. Librarians need to question their own practice, which collects all types of information from around the world, yet cannot acquire the most relevant information circulating widely in Kenya through the underground network.

If libraries are to have any relevance in a situation of intense class struggle, then librarians themselves will need to openly take a stand and declare their interests as to which side they support. Their actions should then reflect their stand. But it will not do to shout their commitment to providing information to all, but in practice to ignore the needs of the vast majority of the nation's peoples. This is the most important challenge to information workers in Kenya and in the Third World generally as we approach the twenty-first century.

Human rights and information in Kenya: a question of political power (1994)[37]

I do not intend to give a detailed report on human rights or the human rights information situation in Kenya. Rather I will raise some facts about violations of human rights in Kenya and give some examples of how human rights information is collected and disseminated. I hope this will raise some issues that can lead us to a meaningful discussion.

Government changes the people...

It may surprise some of you to hear that the human rights situation in Kenya is one of the worst in the world. The surprise is that *information* about human rights violations is so rarely available. It is easy to hear about such so-called violations in countries such as Cuba, North Korea, and Iran, which do not meet the "democratic" standards set by Western governments. But little is heard of the inhumane use of state power against the people by Western-backed regimes in Indonesia, Zaire and Kenya.

In Kenya, for instance, people do not have the right to a passport which is "government property"; a meeting of more than five people, even for a funeral, needs a government licence; opposition MPs do not have the right to hold public meetings without a licence from the unelected DCs (District Officers), government bureaucrats who are as powerful as they were during colonialism.

But these are "small" human rights violations. In truth, in Kenya today there is no right to the most basic human right of all — to life itself. But this basic fact is hardly known outside Kenya.

It serves the business and political interests of the Western governments to play down the significance of state terrorism in countries where they hope to make mega-

---

[37] Paper presented at Link One-Day Conference on Human Rights, Information and Censorship. Saturday 19th November 1994. Link-up 8(4) 6-15 (1996).

profits. So rather than finding ways of stopping the atrocities, *news* about repression is suppressed or its importance is minimised. Caroline Moorehead analyses the current human rights situation in the world:

> The 1990s, supposedly the decade of international cooperation, looks set to become one of the most repressive eras in post-war history. But the Western powers, which once claimed moral superiority and expressed outrage at human rights violations, now point to the constitution and shrug off uncomfortable facts...the West appears intent on playing into the hands of the oppressors. Lip service to the written canons of international human rights agreements is now apparently enough to mollify Western governments.[38]

"Killing the messenger" has become a common way of suppressing news about human rights violations. Kenya's example in this field is alarming. UKenya estimates that in the first ten years in power the Moi regime was responsible for the deaths of at least 6,000 people.[39] When faced with mass popular demonstration during the period of Saba Saba (July 7, 1990) when Moi lost power to the people for almost a week, the regime was forced to hold the so-called multi-party elections. Knowing that it would not be returned to power in any free elections, the regime changed the Constitution, and used legal and illegal methods to ensure that it retained power. It intensified human rights violations on a massive scale.

The worst atrocities were started in areas where Moi knew he had no chance of winning. In the Rift Valley, thugs armed and transported by the government massacred thousands, and created a mass exodus of refugees, emptying towns and villages of people who were then immediately replaced by Moi's supporters. Those who were driven from their homes could not even register to vote, as they were not able to prove residency. The question of election "victory" was thus solved by Moi in the classic way of all dictators—instead of the people changing the Government, the Government changed the people.

In the face of mounting opposition to these government-instigated massacres, the Moi-Kanu regime sought to impose a news blackout. It declared the affected areas of Rift Valley "security zones", which in effect meant that no reporter could visit the area. Those who dared to go were immediately arrested and imprisoned by a judiciary system, which does the dirty work of the regime.

Mwakenya records the human suffering inflicted by Moi in recent years:

> We estimate from reports by human rights organisations, church-based accounts, and augmented by our own networks, that since Moi initiated state terrorism in 1992 over 3,000 have been killed and over 500,000 displaced. Why has there been world silence? Because it is the ordinary Kenyans who are being shot with bows and arrows supplied to Moi's terror squads by the government. It is also because Moi is a darling of the West, particularly the British, who feel grateful for what he has done for them since 1954.[40]

Caroline Moorehead sums up the effects of the news blackout brought about by the declaration of "security zones":

---

[38] Moorehead, Caroline: Killing the messenger. The Observer April 17, 1994. p.52
[39] Moi's Reign of Terror; A decade of Nyayo crimes against the people of Kenya. London. Umoja[UKenya]. 1989.
[40] Stop Moi's state terrorism against the Kenyan people! The statement of Mwakenya at the 7th Pan-African Congress, Kampala, Uganda, 3-8 April, 1994.

"Security operation zones" have been set up, ostensibly to quell the violence. In fact the first to suffer have been journalists, visiting parliamentarians and human rights activists, who have not only been banned from the area, but imprisoned when they attempted to describe their experiences.

The news blackout has thus permitted the West to profess ignorance about what is happening. At the Paris meeting of the Consultative Group on Kenya in November, the World Bank and bilateral donors agreed to restore aid, which had been frozen two years earlier after atrocities committed by government forces were reported.[41]

There is also another type of information, which is kept secret from the people of Kenya. This is the information on the secret diplomacy of Western governments in manipulating politicians and opposition groups in Kenya. There is a 30-year blanket of silence, which prevents us from examining what the British leaders are up to. In the case of Kenya, the British Government, the CIA and the US Government have used money and propaganda to discredit progressive, popular leaders and to promote their favourites who then become ready tools to achieve their goals. The US Ambassador in Nairobi became a sudden champion of democracy after years of backing the dictatorship. People's action during the Saba Saba made it necessary for Britain and the US to play tactical games to ensure they retain close relations whichever side won in Kenya. Since Moi's "re-election", the US has once again become the regime's firm supporter. One no longer hears the shouts of "democracy" from the Embassy rooftops.

One case of secret diplomacy was hinted at in a recent press report. This showed the underhand efforts of the West to undermine the position of Oginga Odinga, the popular opposition leader. The West was worried that Odinga and the Ford opposition party were popular and were sure to defeat Moi and Kanu in any free elections. While Moi was using all legal and illegal methods to defeat his opponents at home, London was doing its best to ensure that Odinga did not come to power. Victoria Brittain records:

> the influence of Britain remained strong in the political class, and British officials continued the same open suspicion of Odinga's politics that they had always had. The fatal ethnic challenge to Odinga for the leadership of FORD [the opposition Party] was triggered in London. He never recovered from the shock and disappointment.[42]

What is also kept totally secret is the lucrative arms deals which the West has with the regime. Recent documents released to the foreign affairs select committee investigating the Pergau dam affair shows that Kenya is among the big beneficiaries of Britain's defence contracts. It is also one of the countries which receives a big share of £100 million-a-year aid for trade programme. Britain has more defence interests in Kenya than in any other African country. British army holds regular army exercises in Kenya and British navy regularly visits Kenya. In addition, Britain trains Kenyan navy, army and air force.[43]

The arms and advanced torture weapons and techniques supplied by Britain, USA and Israel are all used in the end by the Moi regime against the people of Kenya, as Kenya has no external enemy. They are used to suppress the human and political rights of Kenyans.

---

[41] Moorehead, Caroline (1994): op.cit.
[42] Brittain, Victoria: Appreciation: Oginga Odinga. The Guardian Jan.25, 1994. p.19.
[43] Hencke, David: Britain builds on military ties with countries in aid-for-trade programme. The Guardian February 26, 1994 p.5

T-Shirts win court's wrath

Two recent incidents relating to human rights will help us understand the reality of the human rights situation in Kenya today. The first incident was in October 1994 when twelve people were arrested in court during a human rights case. They were arrested because they were wearing T-shirts with the words "RPP". These are initials of a human rights campaigning group — Release Political Prisoners. They had committed no crimes, used no violence, or advocated any illegal methods for the overthrow of the government. Their "crime" was wearing shirts with the words RPP. The organisation — RPP — is not banned in Kenya. It has been operating peacefully for some years campaigning for the release of all political prisoners and supporting families of political prisoners. As it happened, one of their members was not in court that day and escaped arrest — until he went to the local police station asking for information about his colleagues. He too was then swiftly arrested.

The second incident takes place in September 1994 "at a hideout in a city suburb". A reporter of the Nairobi weekly *The People* gets a tip-off that a former radical lecturer was in town and the scene is set for a secret interview with an "exiled former University lecturer and ... political prisoner of the Moi regime, Maina wa Kinyatti." Maina, the foremost historian in Kenya, has written path-breaking accounts of the Mau Mau Movement setting right the historical record from the people's and the movement's own point of view. Its history had consistently been distorted by colonial historians and the Kanu regime who never sympathised with its message of a struggle for a just society. In fact Moi is on record as having banned not only any discussion of Mau Mau but the mention of its very name as well.

Maina has served a six-year jail term on a trumped up charge of sedition. He was adopted by the Amnesty International as a Prisoner of Conscience and by the International Pen. Yet he cannot go openly to Kenya today, nor can the press interview him freely. The article on Maina appeared as the lead article in *The People* in its issue of September 4-10, 1994 — after Maina was safely out of the country.

Punishing the Printing Press

In this situation of extreme suppression of the right to free flow of information, how do information workers operate? There are two levels at which information workers operate in Kenya — an open, democratic level and an underground level. Librarians are not supposed to get involved in matters of human rights and freedom of information. If they do, they end up in the torture chambers like Maina who suffered "concentrated torture" at the notorious Nyayo House Police Special Branch headquarters. Most librarians, who wish to retain their jobs, and possibly lives, end up as mere observers of human rights violations, unable to take any democratic action. In a country of high unemployment and an inflation rate of over 40 percent p.a., it does not make much sense to open your mouth and risk all means of livelihood. Those librarians who wish to play a part in the struggle for the freedom of information do so in the underground organisations.

This is not to deny that there have been some improvements in the years since the Saba Saba week of popular opposition to the government. As Maina says, "Some of the things we could only articulate through seditious pamphlets are now said openly. However, so long as Moi and Kanu are still in power, there is still a long long way to go." For example, even the interview with Maina could not have been published before Saba Saba. There are now many newspapers and magazines, some run by opposition parties and the Church that have managed to survive. Some daily and weekly papers have been very outspoken. There are many brave journalists, publishers, printers and other information workers who have managed to maintain a certain level of free flow of information. People in buses and *matatus* can openly express their disgust with the corruption and the excessive wealth of the few in power at the expense of millions whose daily lives are getting to be almost impossible. In the past, arrests would follow within minutes for such "outspokenness".

Yet the apparent liberalisation is a short-term phenomenon until Moi feels strong enough to suppress them again. Once the eyes of the world are off Kenya, the situation will deteriorate rapidly. Already it is common for police to dismantle printing machines piece by piece because the regime did not like the content of what was printed. Journalists regularly end up in courts on flimsy charges and newspapers and publishers are made to pay excessive fines on similar petty charges. The reasoning on the part of the regime seems to be to stop "censorship by the bullet" (as it is in the habit of doing) as being too crude. "Death threats are enough to ensure self-censorship," as Carolyn Moorehead says.

Given the fact that information workers face life-threatening risks, how is human rights information disseminated? As far as the internal information scene was concerned, much progress had been made. The pioneering role of the underground press in Kenya, which has been well documented elsewhere should not be forgotten. For example Mwakenya has published its *Draft Minimum Programme, The Kenya Democracy Plank, The Mwakenya Stand* as well as its regular publications such as *Mzalendo Mwakenya* (for mass circulation) and its various internal publications such as *Mpatanishi*. All such publications have played a crucial role in pointing out the direction for achieving political rights and in preparing public opinion for demanding meaningful changes in society.

Other such internal sources included the information supplied by Mwakenya and Upande Mwingine, an organisation allied to Mwakenya, through its regular publications, *Article 5* (referring to Article 5 of the Declaration of Human Rights on the freedom of information) and its well documented monthly records on human rights violations, entitled *Upande Mwingine* (Kiswahili for "the Other Side" of the information scene — referring to the information monopoly of the regime and to the fact of resistance of the Kenyan people which never gets reported.) It is noteworthy that among its underground members, there were several librarians. Another important source was Mwakenya's *Register of Resistance*, which provided a real class analysis of the struggle in Kenya.

It is important to recognise that it is not easy for the underground to collect and disseminate information in a very repressive society. A vast mechanism of information gathering, organising, and disseminating exists. Some sources are open and democratic while others are only through the underground, disseminated through diverse means, including word of mouth. Many scribbled messages on pieces of paper have had to be swallowed by activists on being surprised by special branch police. Such information has, however, been regularly collected.

Once such information has been collected, ways have to be found of storing it safely internally. At the same time ways have to be found to disseminate it internally as well as outside the country. Kenya has one of the best-trained special branch secret police and all means of communications are closely monitored to intercept messages. Telephones are routinely tapped and mail is intercepted as a matter of course. Even the use of photocopying machines and typewriters is closely observed by special informers who are planted everywhere. But the underground manages to keep one step ahead and manages to send regular reports outside.

Let us look at the experience of producing the UKenya book, *Moi's Reign of Terror* issued in 1989. Although published in London, the research for its content was done in Kenya. The book documents ten years of crimes of the regime against the people in Kenya.

In the early 1980s the Western world saw Kenya as a tourist paradise in Africa with political stability and rapid economic growth, perhaps with a few minor human rights abuses, but on the whole a "good model" for Africa. This image was projected and promoted by the US and British governments who saw its billions of pounds investment and its strategic interest more important than worrying about Kenya's poor human rights record. After all it was only African lives that were being lost. The regime consistently received political and economic — not to mention military — support from its Western backers. Indeed Margaret Thatcher, on a visit to Kenya, praised its human rights record as the best in Africa. The regime continued attacking and killing people even as Thatcher was busy praising the regime.

The problem now was how to inform the world about the real situation in Kenya. There was a need for working closely with an external body that could publish the local research. It was the London-based Committee for the Release of Political Prisoners in Kenya that did a pioneering work by bringing out its newsletters and other publications in the 1980s. For the first time the world became aware of human rights abuses in Kenya.

The turning point for changing world opinion on the human rights situation came in 1987 with the formation of Umoja Kenya subsequently called UKenya. This was an organisation of Kenyans in exile and had branches in the USA, Australia, Sweden, Norway, Denmark and some African countries. UKenya has well-established links with activists on the ground. These connections become useful in the important task of keeping the world informed about the real situation in Kenya. It could get first hand information about the situation in Kenya.

Using the information, which included photographs from all these underground sources, UKenya produced *Moi's Reign of Terror*. It would have been impossible to publish such a title in Kenya, but once published overseas, it circulated widely through the underground. It recorded the massacres, murders and other human rights violations of the regime, giving irrefutable evidence to back its analysis. It even listed names of people known to have been murdered or "disappeared" by the regime. Such evidence changed the tide for Moi, as he could not face any international organisation without having to answer questions raised in the book. UKenya branches throughout the world distributed the book and questions were raised at the UN, at the House of Representatives in the US, and by MPs in the House of Commons in Britain. This was a valuable experience for the underground in Kenya as well as forces outside the country in breaking the regime's embargo on the free flow of information.

UKenya publications were now widely distributed internally. The content of these publications, just as with the underground publications, gives courage to various groups who had been struggling in isolation. It showed that information is a powerful tool, which can be used to undermine the unpopular regime. There was a growth in the formation of underground and overground opposition activities. Taking the lead from various underground publications and from the UKenya books and other statements, the Church and professionals such as lecturers and lawyers found the courage to stand up and speak against the dictatorship in the open. Whereas as late as 1984, it was difficult to find a lawyer who would openly defend a political case, by the end of the 1980s there were several.

Conclusion: human rights don't grow on trees

Human rights cannot be acquired by plucking them from trees or from chapters of well-meaning Declarations of Human Rights. Genuine human rights have to be fought for and are won in the course of fierce struggles waged with those who are opposed to them. It should be remembered that in class societies, there are those—the minority in power—who deprive the majority of their rights. It is necessary to accept this social reality if a correct analysis is to be made regarding the reasons why many societies and people do not have basic human rights. Only from such an analysis will a way be found to ensure that everybody has equal access to it.

The question of power in society also explains why some people in a society have economic, cultural and social rights while others go without: the right to basic human needs of food, clothing, and shelter; rights of nationalities to their cultures, languages, land and economic resources; the right of women for equality with men. It is not true that *everyone* in a society lacks these rights. It is only some *classes* that lack these rights.

The achievement of human rights is, by necessity an integral part of political struggles of a people. If all people in society have equal access to economic and political power, they would inevitably have equal access to human rights as well. Once the people have political power, they will free themselves from all forms of social oppression and from economic exploitation. Thus the struggle for human rights is in the final analysis, a political struggle. That is why well-meaning human rights support organisations such as Amnesty International can only monitor and appeal to those in positions of power to give these rights to all. But it is the action of the people themselves, which will win them these rights.

The so-called "Cold War" may be over, but the struggle for these basic rights is by no means over. Dictators such as Moi are still in power and are still backed by the US and Britain as part of their strategy to rule the world. Until the West lets go of its policy of controlling the world, it will not be possible to eradicate dictatorships, and the struggle for political and human rights will continue.

It is therefore important for progressive people and organisations in *every* country to support people's struggle for their rights. It is the united action of all such people that can, in the final analysis, ensure these rights for the people. It is in this internationalist spirit that I would like us to take concrete steps to support the struggle of information workers around the world:

Resolutions

1. We take practical steps along the lines suggested below to support information workers in Africa, Asia, Latin America, the Caribbean, the Pacific and in Britain who are victimised for ensuring free flow of information in their societies.

There is no international professional organisation for librarians and information workers, which support their activities in their struggle for human rights and in the field of free flow of information. These aspects are as central to us in our profession as are issues dealing with our conditions of work. Journalists, trade unionists, lawyers all have organizations, which support them if they become victims of oppressive regimes. It is as if as a profession we are saying that the struggle for a free flow of information and for basic human rights is not the business of the profession.

Practical steps could include:

1. Maintaining a Register of victims of information suppression/censorship who are victimised for their professional work and social commitment. Practical offers of help and support for them should be made and organising campaigns for their rights to free expression, assembly etc.
2. Maintaining a Collection of suppressed material (publications, music, etc), publicising their contents and making such material widely available on request.
3. Providing paper, typewriters, computers, FAX machines, etc. to support the work of those struggling to maintain the free flow of information in oppressive conditions.
4. Inviting victims of information suppression to conferences. Institute an annual Award to an individual, a community, or organisation for furthering the cause of free flow of information and struggle against censorship.
5. Explore ways of breaking information embargoes (whether in countries like Cuba, Libya and Iraq which are victims of US policy, or so-called "free" countries like Kenya) by providing practical support to those struggling under difficult conditions.
6. Publish a Newsletter to report progress on the above projects and to provide a forum for the exchange of ideas, views, and information on issues related to free flow of information.
7. Ensure wider awareness in Britain about issues connected with suppression of information.

All of the above can be done in conjunction with other international bodies such as Amnesty International, PEN, Index on Censorship etc. Special funding should be sought from international bodies such as UNESCO and the European Union. It is also important to work closely with radical publishers and booksellers.

2. We build a system of international exchange of information in the field of human rights and the social struggles of information workers to build just societies.

The first problem facing information workers is to know what material is being published. The second problem is to acquire material published throughout the world, particularly because of the shortage of foreign exchange in many countries.

It is proposed that we maintain a register of progressive material relevant to the struggle for the establishment of just societies. Perhaps authors can be encouraged to deposit a copy of their articles at a central library, perhaps at a school of library & information science. These, would then, be reviewed by an editorial board for the suitability of the project. A list could then be produced, quarterly or monthly, to be circulated to all those who have registered to be on the mailing list. If any article is required from the list, photocopies can be supplied free, or on payment of charges in local currency — payment to be made in UNESCO coupons, which can be purchased in local currency.

Such a project will enable information workers throughout the world to be alerted to new material and to be able to acquire material.

Funding for such a project can be applied for from UNESCO, EU or other aid organisations. Employers should be encouraged to allow their staff to be involved in work associated with the free flow of information and the struggle against censorship.

3. We establish a mechanism for influencing the training of librarians and information workers in all countries.

Schools of library and information science must give equal importance to social as well as technical aspects of an information worker's work. The tendency today is perhaps to emphasise technical and business aspects of the profession sometimes to the exclusion of social aspects. While the former are essential, they should not be seen to be more important than the *social* aspect of their work. Seminars, workshops and competitions need to be organised to give such a correct balance in all training.

All of the above projects can be run in conjunction with progressive Schools of Library Science who could run practical courses along these lines.

The mirage of democracy in Kenya (1994)[44]

Dictatorship in the Garb of Democracy

The theme of this Conference — "Emerging Democracies" — is a challenging one because it seems to imply that democracy is emerging all over the world. A general impression has been created in the Western world that since the end of the Cold War, "democracy" was emerging in the world today. Nothing can be further from the truth. While we will not go into an analysis of what has happened in Eastern Europe and the U.S.S.R.[45], it should be remembered that the formation of a large number of

---

[44] A paper presented at the International Group of the Library Association's Residential Conference held at Oxford in September 1994 on the theme Emerging Democracies and Freedom of Information. Published as "Dictatorship in the garb of democracy. Emerging democracy and freedom of information". Proceedings of a Conference of the International Group of the Library Association (IGLA). Edited by Barbara Turfan, Kathleen Ladizesky and Inese A. Smith. 1995. London. Library Association Publishing. pp. 145-154.
Reproduced in: Alternative Library Literature 1994-95 a Biennial Anthology, edited by Sanford Berman and James P. Danky. 1996 Jefferson, NC (USA): McFarland & Co. pp. 234-244.

[45] John Pateman, for example, presents some interesting points about the damage done to book production, reading and libraries in the former U.S.S.R and Eastern Europe since the emergence of "democracy" in these countries. "There is no doubt that Communism kept the Soviet Union literate", he writes. "The sight of everyone reading books on the Metro made a deep impression on visitors. Thick journals... had a circulation of between one and five million copies each month. In cultural terms, reading in Russia has stopped overnight...The Russians were the greatest readers in the world under communism. Capitalism has ended all. " See Pateman's forthcoming article, Libraries Under Communism and Capitalism in Focus on International and Comparative Librarianship.

political parties, which may objectively represent the class interests of just one class, does not automatically imply that there is "democracy". Nor does the existence of a Parliament in itself signify that there is democracy. Kenya, for example, has had a Parliament for over 30 years, but there is no democracy there yet.

In Africa, the struggle for democracy has by no means been won, although it may have reached a new level of intensity. The reality of what is happening in Kenya and in many other parts of Africa today is that class dictatorship is putting on the garb of democracy in a conspiracy to make the people believe that there is no need to struggle any more. People are being told that since socialism "no longer exists" we have "arrived" at the ideal society. We seem to be victims of a massive confidence trick that shouts out ever so loud that "democracy" is suddenly emerging all over the world. It is as if somehow the Emperor will have his clothes on if only we shout out loud enough that he *does* have his clothes on. Alas, naked reality cannot be clothed so easily.

The call that "democracy has arrived" is no more than the propaganda of the ruling classes to disarm the activists of genuine democracy, to make them give up the struggle. It is yet another cunning tool used by those in power in the fierce class struggle going on everywhere. As such it is not likely to be heeded by the masses who know through their very life experiences that democracy cannot have arrived while they continue to be exploited.

It is very important for us working in the information field to question more closely why it is generally assumed by some intellectuals, particularly in Europe and the U.S.A., that "democracy" is emerging. If we, who are supposed to be aware of the way information, can — and is — manipulated by vested interests, if we can be fooled so easily, what example can we set to those who accept everything in print — and in the media — as the ultimate "truth". We have a particular duty to question and challenge views that make implicit assumptions about the reality around us. That is where our "professional" duty lies.

It is true that important changes have taken place in many African countries in the last few years. Prof. Ali Mazrui lists the achievements of the struggle for democracy in Africa of 1980s and 1990s: "...some 20 countries in Africa have legalised political opposition since 1990. Military regimes have sometimes been forced to go to the polls (as in Ghana); founding fathers have been defeated at the polls (as in Zambia and Malawi); one- party systems have been forced to become multi-party (as in Kenya, Tanzania, and Cote d'Ivoire)."[46] South Africa is also on the road to democracy. These changes have come about as a result of years of struggle by the people themselves and because of changes in international situation. But unless these changes are followed by basic economic and democratic freedoms for the masses of the people, they will remain mere cosmetic changes.

It is not possible for those who are suffering in Somalia, in Rwanda, or for the victims of Western-backed Renamo thugs in Mozambique and the Savimbi mobs in Angola to believe that the dawn of "democracy" has suddenly emerged over the continent exploited for centuries by Western imperialism. Mere propaganda that there is democracy will not bring back to life those who died through bullets supplied by the Western armaments industry. We should avoid the danger of judging the whole world from a Euro-centric perspective. It would be difficult, for example, for a

---

[46] Mazrui, Ali: Brave New World of Media Bias. Sunday Nation (Nairobi) July 17, 1994, p.7.

Conference in Mogadishu, Nairobi or Kigale to set as its theme "Democracy has arrived". The reality of the anti-democratic forces outside the Conference room would only mock the good intentions of the organisers. Indeed, an international Conference by the World Bar Association, which was to have been held in Nairobi some years ago, had to be called off because of Kenya's poor human rights record. A conference on law and order would indeed be ironic under a regime that has consistently manipulated national laws in order to serve its own class interests.

We should thus not be too eager to accept that "democracy" has arrived. We are victims of a vast propaganda offensive that seeks to convince us that socialism has died, that there is no democracy under socialism, that now there is freedom of information for "all". Admittedly CNN news broadcasts are now available all over the world, side by side with bottles of Coca Cola and its associated culture. But these manifestations of the Western world's "riches" are a far cry from freedoms and democratic rights which are the basic rights of the people. Fundamental questions about social reality remain unanswered. We are made to believe that international events in the last few years have fundamentally changed the situation to the extent that social conflicts no longer exist. *Mpatanishi*, the internal organ of the underground Mwakenya movement in Kenya addresses this question in one of its articles:

> ...these changes, however important they have been, have not resolved the basic contradiction [in society]. Classes have not been abolished, class struggle has not ceased. Mois and KANUs still exist and still are in power. Their major backer—U.S.-led imperialism—still exists, more powerful and ruthless than ever before. Social oppression has not vanished; economic exploitation still deprives our people of the fruits of their labour. Children still die in their thousands through malnutrition and their parents are even today massacred and shot by forces of oppression that is the hallmark of capitalism.[47]

Mwakenya explains the current world situation thus: "Today, the post-Cold War situation is one of intensified neo-colonialism. Neo-colonialism is not dead. It is precisely because it is not dead, that it now takes on features of re-colonisation."[48] The Kampala Declaration recognises the reality of lack of democratic freedoms in Africa when it talks of "The New Imperialism": "The end of the cold war ushered in a new period of domination. The Cold War has now been replaced by the unleashing of an intensified economic war against Africa spearheaded by the IMF and the World Bank. This war will lead to a new scramble for the recolonisation of Africa."[49] It is obvious that those struggling for democracy on the ground have found no evidence of any

---

[47] Capitalism and Socialism; Has the Contradiction been Resolved? Mpatanishi; Internal Organ of Mwakenya Vol.2 (1) 11-12. Sept. 1992. Mwakenya, Muungano wa Wazalendo wa Kuikomboa Kenya (Union of Patriots for the Liberation of Kenya), is the longest surviving and the most consistent underground movement in Kenya. It publishes a variety of publications, some for internal use of its members and others for public distribution. Moi has failed to suppress it in spite of jailings, detentions, exiling and even murder of many of its members.

[48] "Stop Moi's State of Terrorism Against the Kenyan People; The Statement of Mwakenya at the 7th Pan-African Congress, Kampala, Uganda, 3rd-8th April 1994, read on behalf of the Central Committee by the current spokesperson, Ngugi wa Thiong'o". p.1

[49] Kampala Declaration; Resist Recolonisation; Pan African Congress: General Declaration by the Delegates and Participants at the 7th Pan African Congress, April 3-8 1994, Kampala, Uganda. 1994. Kampala p.4.

"democracy" emerging, but here in Oxford, thousands of miles from Africa, we seem to have detected African democracy!

Democracy in Africa can only be achieved on the basis of "attacking and combating the *external forces* that now threaten re-colonisation; we must also as ferociously attack and combat those social *forces within us* that ally with intensified neo-colonialism," as Mwakenya has said. That is precisely what the liberation forces in Africa are doing today. The freedom of information for the masses can become a reality only when this larger war has been won.

Freedom Not To Be Exploited

If we accept that there are classes in society today—and perhaps only the British Prime Minister John Major maintains that there are no classes in society—then we must also accept that freedom and democracy for one class implies bondage and dictatorship for other classes. Let us not forget the words of Mao on this:

> ...Freedom and democracy do not exist in the abstract, only in the concrete. In a society rent by class struggle, if there is freedom for the exploiting classes to exploit the working people, there is no freedom for the working people not to be exploited; if there is democracy for the bourgeoisie, there is no democracy for the proletariat and other working people...Those who demand freedom and democracy in the abstract regard democracy as an end and not a means. Democracy sometimes seems to be an end, but it is in fact only a means.[50]

For the masses in Africa and elsewhere in the world, the fundamental question is this: is our society organised in such a way as to satisfy the basic material needs— food, clothing, shelter, medical care, education—of the majority of people? Democracy should be a means of ensuring that these basic needs of the people are met. For the Western business and hence government interests, democracy means the ability to exploit Africa freely for its own profits. Thus for them Barre, Idi Amin, Mobotu, Moi and Banda pass as "democrats" since they allow Western business to have a free hand in making mega-profits. They are accorded the seal of approval by the so-called World Bank, which is no more than the financial arm of the same forces that deny democracy to the people of the world. But the people can never see these tyrants as democrats.

The term "democracy" needs to be defined clearly. "Democracy" as seen by the U.S.A. government or the World Bank means that there is freedom for transnationals to plunder freely the resources of countries of Africa, Asia, and South America, the Caribbean and the Pacific. So long as they are able to extract profits from a country, they are satisfied to call it "democratic". Thus unpopular and dictatorial regimes of Mobutus and Mois are considered "democratic" because they allow their countries to be used by Western business interests. Africa today is in a situation where for every £ that comes in as aid or investment, over £9 are taken out. There cannot be democracy for African people while this level of exploitation is allowed to go on. The first requirement for the achievement of democracy is that the £9 that leave Africa are made available to African masses for their own development. No amount of pious pleading for democracy and "aid", can alter this basic fact.

---

[50] Mao Zedong (1957): On the Correct Handling of Contradictions Among the People. Selected Works of Mao Tse-tung, Foreign Languages Press Peking 1977 First Edition 1977. Vol. V, pp. 384-421. Available at: http://www.marx2mao.com/Mao/CHC57.html. . [Accessed: 19 August 2007].

Important questions that have thus to be answered include the all-important one, "democratic freedom for whom, to do what?" The freedom of a few to exploit the many does not imply that there is democracy. From the people's point of view democratic freedom means the easy availability of the basic requirements for survival: food, clothing, shelter, education, medical care, culture etc. To them, freedom for foreign businesses to exploit local labour and resources certainly does not qualify as "democracy".

Our role as information workers is not to obscure the facts of exploitation and lack of democracy in these societies. Rather it is to expose oppression and show theoretical and practical sources of information which will help people end exploitation and enable people to enjoy all democratic rights. It is in this sense that librarianship is a "social" discipline, which can play a leading role in providing relevant information to people.

The Tears & the Triumphs

Democracy does not just "emerge" in a vacuum. Events outside the country, however significant, will not, *on their own* give birth to democracy. Democracy is always achieved as a result of a struggle, often a violent struggle by the people themselves. It often demands the sacrifice of many lives.

The current struggle for democracy and freedom of information in Africa has demanded a heavy sacrifice from the people, including rape, jailings, detentions, exiling, disappearances, murders and massacres. The triumphs in the struggle for democracy, are inevitably accompanied by tears of the tragic loss of life. The loss in terms of missed development opportunities cannot even be measured.

A number of recent events highlight the achievements and the suffering as a result of the peoples' resolve to fight for liberation. The first incident is from Kenya: On March 16, 1994 four journalists including the Managing Editor and deputy Chief Sub-Editor working with the daily, The Standard (Nairobi) were charged with subversion for publishing an article reporting renewed political violence in Molo, Kenya. They were denied bail and were remanded in custody in Nakuru prison. Six other journalists had also been arrested earlier.

The four face a charge of subversion "for an act prejudicial to the security of the state" for writing a report on an incident which occurred in Molo on 12 and 13 of March 1994. Amnesty International records the incident: "Nine people were allegedly killed in the violence and hundreds fled their homes. The journalists' report named an eyewitness who said that her three children were killed...Molo is in a restricted area in the Rift Valley province—designated a "Security Operation Zone" in September 1993. Only residents, officials and police can visit the area, preventing information about political violence in the area from being reported or verified."[51] In a recent report Amnesty International says:

> Since January 1994 over 14 journalists have been intimidated, harassed, arrested, fined or imprisoned; whole editions of journals have been impounded and printing presses

---

[51] Amnesty International: Urgent Action. London. 24 March 1994 (AFR 32/05/94). Amnesty International estimates that since May 1991, "some 1,000 people have been killed and 300,000 displaced by ethnic-based political violence in the Rift Valley and Western Kenya in which government involvement has been alleged...This is the first time that the charge of subversion has been used, which suggests that the authorities are further restricting freedom of expression in order to prevent criticism of the government."

have been put out of action. These actions by the Kenyan authorities have seriously undermined the right to freedom of expression in Kenya.[52]

So much for democracy and the freedom of information in Kenya.

This one incident is merely an indication of the level of oppression in Kenya today and indicates the total disregard for human rights in Kenya. Yet the Kenyan Government passes the Western Governments' test of "democracy". Such poor standards would not be accepted in Europe—but Africa is another matter.

The second incident indicates the Western control of Africa's system of communication through its control over communications technology. The scene is the prestigious 7th Pan African Congress held in Kampala in April 1994. One delegate who could not attend was Col. Gaddafi of Libya. As an alternative, it was agreed that his message to the Congress would be beamed to Kampala through communication satellite. But this was sabotaged by the government of the U.S.A., which uses its control of communication technology to suppress the voice of those it dislikes. Undeterred by the U.S.A.'s show of strength, the delegates of the PAC passed a resolution condemning U.S. action and went on to show their solidarity with the people of Libya by accepting their invitation to host the 8th Pan African Congress in Tripoli in 1997.

Who are the Enemies of Democracy?

If we agree that there is no democracy in many parts of Africa who then is responsible for this lack of democracy? The Conference's theme that democracy is now emerging implies that it was the Soviet Union that was responsible for the lack of democracy.

Africa was colonised by the Western powers, starting with the infamous Berlin Conference of 1884. It was the search for cheap raw materials and labour and the availability of ready markets that drove the colonial powers to claim continents for their own use. Kenya, for example, has had to face over 400 years of plunder by European powers. It was the struggles of African peoples that brought about independence. But after independence, it was the same Western countries that brought in neo-colonialism in order to continue the exploitation of African people and resources. The Soviet Union had nothing to do with this unequal relationship. Indeed it provided valuable material and moral support to the African liberation movements.

There have been no changes in the West that would inspire them to give up their exploitation of Africa. The culture of exploitation is the very *basis* of capitalism and imperialism, which is still very much alive. The end of the Cold War has not changed the nature of imperialism. Indeed it now has a totally free hand to exploit and bully whoever it dislikes without the fear of being opposed by a principled socialist state. It then follows that no democracy will "emerge" in Africa through the goodwill of the Western exploitative forces. It is the active struggle by the people against imperialism that alone can liberate Africa and usher in a new democracy. And that is precisely what the masses in Africa are doing today. But it is not an easy struggle. Imperialism and its local allies will go to any length to preserve their positions of power and maintain dictatorship. Witness the devastation brought to the people of Somalia, Rwanda, Mozambique, and Angola as the price for struggling against a situation

---

[52] Kenya; the Imprisonment of Two Prisoners of Conscience. Amnesty International, July 27, 1994 (AFR 32/12/94) p.1.

created by neo-colonialism. In every case it is the forces supported by imperialism, which would rather wreck whole societies than allow democracy to prevail.

Kenya—"*Uhuru Bado*"[53]

Kenya is a very good example of a country where there is no democracy even after 30 years of independence. Fundamental changes are needed before democracy can emerge.

As Mwakenya has said:

> ...no meaningful changes would take place as long as Moism and KANUism—with or without Moi and KANU—are still in existence. Mwakenya has always believed that the Moi-KANU government could not be trusted to oversee the democratization of our society. For Moi and KANU are themselves the problem... Let us not be deceived that just because the opposition parties have their members in Parliament that they will be in a position to effect any fundamental changes. Because, in order to ensure that the representatives Kenyans elected do not achieve their objectives, the Moi-KANU government has manipulated the Parliament.[54]

We saw earlier that parts of Kenya are declared "Security Zone". This ensures that nobody is allowed to go there to bring back a report about the real situation. In effect it is an attempt by the Government to stop the free flow of information about the massacres being organised by those in power. Past massacres in Kenya have included the ones in Garissa (1980), and in Wajir (1984). Such massacres have continued, says Human Rights Watch/Africa:

> Political violence has continued to affect the rural areas of western Kenya. In November 1993, Human Rights Watch/Africa estimated that 1,500 people had died and 300,000 had been displaced since the "ethnic clashes" first broke out in late October 1991...even high-ranking members of the government [of Kenya] are involved in provoking violence.[55]

These have resulted in massive protests inside the country and externally. The unpopular government cannot survive in power without periodic massacres to silence people's protests. The "solution" that the regime has hit on is not to stop massacres, but to prevent the news of the massacre from reaching the country or the world. All this is happening after the so-called liberalization, which allowed "multi-party" elections to take place. This shows not only that there is no democracy "emerging" in Kenya, but that there is no freedom of information either.

The murder of Pinto in 1965 was a clear indication that the hopes of achieving a democratic society were dashed. Since then all effective opposition to the Western-backed regime has gone underground. The main one was the December Twelve Movement, which emerged in the mid-80s as Mwakenya. It was these underground movements that continued the struggle for democratic change throughout the period after independence.

---

[53] Uhuru Bado"—Kiswahili for: "No Independence Yet".
[54] Mzalendo Mwakenya pp. 1,4. Special Issue May 1, 1994 (Mzalendo Mwakenya is Mwakenya's underground publication).
[55] Kenya: Multipartyism Betrayed in Kenya; Continuing Rural Violence and Restrictions on Freedom of Speech and Assembly. Human Rights Watch/Africa Newsletter Vol. 6 (5) 1994 July 1994 p. 2, quoting from its own Report Divide and Rule: State Sponsored Ethnic Violence in Kenya (1993).

One of the methods that the underground movements have used to mobilise supporters and to communicate with them is through underground publications. No open publications could have been issued, as there is a strict censorship, which detains, exiles, "disappears" anybody considered to be behind these publications. Printers, journalists and publishers are particular targets of the regime. The underground movements thus resorted to organise underground presses and distribution networks. Thus in the early 80s the December Twelve Movement published *Pambana* which was distributed throughout the country using an underground network. Earlier, the organization, which preceded it, Cheche Kenya issued an underground book *InDependent Kenya* (later reissued in London by Zed Press). Similarly Mwakenya has been issuing its mass publication, *Mzalendo Mwakenya*. Mwakenya has also published its *Draft Minimum Programme* (1987), the *Democracy Plank* (1991), *The Mwakenya Stand on the Current Situation in Kenya* (1992) in English and Kiswahili — all published underground. Such publications could not have been issued overground. Even reading or possessing copies of these publications can lead to long jail terms or detention. There has been some improvement in the situation in recent years, and newspapers like *The Nation* publishes "Free opinion" columns. Yet there is a limit to such freedoms and certainly publications of underground organisations are still banned, in practice, if not in law. The Special Branch police remain as watchful as ever.

It was the vision and the programme carried in these underground publications that gave people guidance and courage to openly defy the Government in 1990. What came to be known as the events of Saba Saba ("Seven Seven" — seventh day of the seventh month — July 7, 1990), Kenyans throughout the country defied the regime's armed forces and organised mass demonstrations and meetings. The regime was shaken by the week's events. It made token gestures of change in order to prevent genuine change. The result was the amendment to the Constitution that allowed "multi-party" elections.

But this was no democracy. It was merely whitewashing the dictatorship to give it the *appearance* of democracy. Mwakenya warned against the danger of "Moism with or without Moi". The momentum for real change was diverted by the cunning tactic of giving democratic garb to a ruthless dictatorship. Democracy remains to be achieved — "Uhuru bado", as the popular Kiswahili saying goes.

The whole experience in Kenya since independence shows that it is not possible to disseminate any information, which is in any way critical of the ruling class and indeed of imperialism. Any suggestion of an alternate method of development is not tolerated. There are many cases of people sentenced to long jail terms for entries made in their *private diaries*. The only way that such information can be disseminated is through the use of underground press. The use of theatre, music, and other creative methods to disseminate progressive information is also widely practised but is also attacked. Thus the regime destroyed the largest peasant-built open-air theatre in Africa at Kamiriithu because it disagreed with the *content* of the plays put up there. But the struggle continues to be waged at various levels. The lesson of the whole struggle is that democracy will not emerge on its own. It needs a constant struggle to be waged. A crucial input for democracy to emerge is the dissemination of appropriate information that is relevant, in an appropriate *form* and *language*.

The various underground documents have now become basic texts on the history of Kenya. They form an authentic documentation of what is happening in Kenya today.

The so-called "democracy" in Kenya today with its multi-party elections, is exposed as a sham by Mwakenya in its statement at the 7th Pan African Congress:

> The registration of opposition parties under Moi's conditions has been more beneficial to the Moi-Kanu regime than to the people of Kenya, since it allows Moi to shout multiparty democracy to cover the sounds of gunfire and the cries of the tortured.[56]

Until there is a genuine democracy, there will not be freedom to write, publish, disseminate, or even to read information for the people. It is only the final liberation that will ensure these freedoms in Kenya, as in other countries.

The Uganda Experience

The experience in Uganda is instructive as it shows that a guerrilla army also needs its own media to popularise its struggle among the people as a way of achieving liberation. Indeed it is an essential ingredient for the success of a revolution. Uganda is unique in the region in that a guerrilla-based movement came to power to form the current government. Thus the experience of Uganda during the period when the National Resistance Army was waging guerrilla warfare is instructive. Just as in Kenya during the period of Mau Mau, it was found necessary to establish an underground press in order to keep in constant contact with the people. We shall briefly examine this experience.

President Yoweri Museveni of Uganda sets out the need for communication in the context of a people's struggle and also gives the practical steps taken by the guerrilla army in Uganda to ensure that relevant practices were followed:

> ...Our struggle was launched by a few patriots armed with a cause and a few guns, and the conviction that the cause was a just one.
>
> At the time of launching the armed struggle, many people in the country did not know what it was all about. Moreover the majority of Ugandans knew there was something drastically wrong in Uganda, but they did not know that anything could be done to remedy the situation.
>
> We knew therefore that people both within Uganda and outside Uganda might misunderstand us, might misconstrue our reasons for launching an armed struggle. Within the country, we started a programme of politicisation and education of the people, which our political cadres were able to carry out, especially through Resistance Committees, which we had set up in our areas of control.
>
> This programme, however, has its limitations because it could be carried out only in those areas under our control. For purposes of disseminating our message, we launched a paper, *Uganda Resistance News*.
>
> Through this paper, we hoped to spread our message, explain and publicise our cause, and reach more people than we could if we used the Resistance Committees alone. The purpose was furthermore to use the paper to keep people informed about what was taking place in Uganda in general and with regard to the resistance war. We also wanted to alert Ugandans and friends of Uganda about the seriousness of the degradation that was taking place in our country as a result of a corrupt system, which was being perpetuated by a bankrupt leadership.

---

[56] Mwakenya : Statement at 7th Pan African Congress, Kampala, April, 1994. Nairobi/Kampala.

The aim was to explain to the people that the armed struggle we had launched was inevitable if we were to rid Uganda of a corrupt system so that Ugandans could get a chance to lay a new foundation for the future.[57]

The National Resistance Movement began publishing the *Uganda Resistance News* underground. Its editor recalls the difficulties of producing underground:

Uganda Resistance News was edited, printed and circulated clandestinely except in foreign capitals and the bush where NRA was in control...The news, features and interviews that originated from the bush would be carried through very risky roadblocks of the Obote era to the places where the *News* was published.

Production of the *News* was carried out using an old manual typewriter and an old cyclostyling machine, which were donated to the Movement in 1981. Both items were later stolen in 1983 when the house in which the *News* was being produced was raided. After the raid, production was suspended for some time until it resumed later using borrowed machines.

Through all this time, the publication of the *News* depended on the commitment of a few volunteers who sacrificed a lot of their time, money and sometimes lives to ensure that it came out regularly.[58]

Since it was this guerrilla movement that came to power, Uganda's information policy today is very enlightened, allowing a high level of freedom that is available in few other African countries.

Information For Liberation or for Enslavement?

These examples from Kenya and Uganda highlight the fact that the only effective means of ensuring the free flow of information in many African countries is through the underground press. This is true for literary and creative works, songs, music and drama, as well as for political, social, economic and other works of non-fiction. Indeed resistance literature has been recognised as an important literary form. This is due to *internal* oppression from the Western-supported dictators. Ali Mazrui highlights the *international* aspect of information control:

The Western media not only inform the West about the rest of the world. They also inform the rest of the world about the rest of the world. For example, what Africa knows about China comes disproportionately from Western sources. ...Unfortunately, the West is a flawed go-between — a messenger with its own agenda, subject to its own special biases.

Pro-democracy movements in Eastern Europe from the late 1980s were heavily covered in the Western press. Western television screen allocated massive time to what was regarded as momentous historical events. Similar pro-democracy activism occurred in Africa...and yet these developments have received far less publicity in the Western media...[59]

Yet it is not entirely true to say that there is no freedom of information in Kenya. While news about the atrocities committed by government-funded gangs is not

---

[57] Musenvi, Yoweri: Foreword to Mission to Freedom Vol.1. Kampala, Uganda. NRM Publications (1990) pp.i-iii.
[58] Mission to Freedom [A compilation of articles from issues of Uganda Resistance News in 3 volumes] The quotation is taken from the Acknowledgement. NMR, Kampala. 1990.
[59] Mazrui, Ali: Sunday Nation (Nairobi) July 17, 1994.

readily available, information, which suits the interests of those in power, is easily available. Meaningful news and information about resistance, peoples' struggles, and achievements about relevant technologies that can improve productivity and the quality of life for the masses which at the same time lessen the burden of labour is either absent or distorted. But there is no lack of useless, sensation-creating information from around the world. In general, information about protest and resistance to *status quo*, about people-orientated development strategies, about the real causes and cures of exploitation is not easy to disseminate. Thus we must distinguish between information for liberation and information for slavery. The former is in short supply, the latter available in abundance.

It is only the information that encourages subservience and the acceptance of the role of the under-dog that is freely available. Information that can liberate people's minds and provide a way out of social oppression and economic exploitation is not tolerated by those who thereby stand to lose their power. This situation is a reflection of the class forces in Africa: the comprador rulers of Africa seek to keep the masses in a state of ignorance in order to remain in power. The interest of the working people, on the other hand, requires a free flow of information. In the absence of "official" information services that serve their needs, people develop their own oral, written, and visual forms to ensure communication as part of their social struggle. Thus their information activities are a direct threat to the ruling classes. Hence the total lack of tolerance in countries like Kenya for anyone "caught" disseminating information of interest to working people.

Free flow of information in such conditions can only be achieved when this antagonistic social contradiction between the masses and their imposed, non-democratic rulers is resolved. It can only come about when the class whose material need requires the free flow of information — i.e. working class, is in control of its own destiny.

The Struggle Continues

The Kampala Declaration sounded an ominous note:

> The control of Africa remains in foreign hands. In most African countries, imperialism has the cooperation and compliance of the ruling elite. The overall result is that Africa is being forced into dangerous levels of economic impoverishment, social decay, and chemical genocide.[60]

But the story does not end there. The Declaration recognises a redeeming feature in the present situation: "In Africa...mass uprisings are once again manifesting themselves from Cairo to Durban." It is the very lack of democracy that causes uprisings against corrupt regimes. It is this people's action, guided by correct ideology, party and strategy that will bring about true democracy and liberation. Only then will information flow freely throughout the society.

Resolution

It would be a positive achievement if this conference comes out with some practical suggestions, which are then implemented. It will then not have been another empty talking shop, but make a concrete contribution towards fulfilling our social

---

[60] Kampala Declaration. op.cit.

responsibility. I would like to suggest the following resolution for adoption by this Conference:

> The Library Association and IGLA should take practical steps along the lines suggested below to support information workers in Africa, Asia, Latin America, the Caribbean and the Pacific who are victimised for ensuring the free flow of information in their societies.

Practical steps should include:

> 1. Maintaining a register of the victims of information suppression who are victimised for their professional work and social commitment. Practical offers of help and support for them should be made, organising campaigns for their rights to free expression, assembly etc.
>
> 2. Maintaining a collection of suppressed material (publications, music, etc.), publicising their contents and making such material widely available on request.
>
> 3. Providing paper, typewriters, computers, FAX machines etc. to support the work of those struggling to maintain free flow of information in oppressive conditions.
>
> 4. Inviting victims of information suppression to conferences.
>
> 5. Exploring ways of breaking information embargoes (whether in countries like Cuba, Libya and Iraq, which are victims of U.S. policy, or so-called "free" countries like Kenya) by providing practical support to those struggling under difficult conditions.
>
> 6. Publishing a quarterly newsletter to report progress on the above projects and to provide a forum for the exchange of ideas, views, and information on issues related to the free flow of information.
>
> 7. Ensuring wider awareness in Britain about the issues connected with the suppression of information.

All the above can be done in conjunction with other international bodies such as Amnesty International, PEN, Index on Censorship etc. Special funding should be sought from LA as well as from international bodies such as UNESCO, and from European organisations.

Independence in Kenya and the lost opportunity (1998)[61]

Independence in Kenya and the lost opportunity to build a people orientated library service

Introduction

Patricia Larby records her experiences in several Eastern African countries in the 1950s and 60s.[62] The period she talks about was a crucial time when revolutionary changes were taking place in these societies. It was a time when foundations of the old colonial world were being destroyed and those of new free societies were being laid. This included the vision of a society where all would have free access to information and knowledge created by the work of all. It was a time of immense change and high hopes for a just, equitable future after decades of colonial suppression and exploitation.

Yet one misses in Larby's report the tremendous climate of change and the new optimism that was sweeping the East African countries at that time. It remains a very subjective view of events in that part of the world. The dynamic reality that was to play a key role in the future remains unexplored. Unless the whole, dynamic reality is explored there is a danger of historical records becoming Euro-centric interpretations of the history of African librarianship. Larby's report is given added weight by the respectability afforded by the SCOLMA umbrella as it was presented at its AGM. If not challenged, it can become the "standard" way of interpreting African history and will be used as set text in Library and Information courses. No right of reply exists for the African librarians, information workers and indeed African people to correct the partisan interpretation of their history.

It is essential that any account of this period should record the full reality of sharp contradictions and the real hopes of meaningful change following the years of colonialism. It is true that some expatriates lived in a vacuum, unaffected by the tremendous changes taking place in every field of social life, except in so far as they could win new contracts for jobs and sales of "modern" technologies. This reality has to be balanced by a look at the progressive aspect of local librarianship, which was seeking a meaningful, relevant library service.

It is also interesting that Patricia Larby finds only one example of a "qualified" librarian in East Africa — John Ndegwa. There is no mention here of other librarians who made a contribution to the developments in the information field. No mention of the person who the Uganda Government appointed as Librarian in 1964 to replace Larby. Again Larby does not refer to the old established institutions such as the East African Agriculture and Forestry Research Organisation/East African Veterinary Research Organisation in Muguga, the Departments of Agriculture and Veterinary Services in Kenya where Kenyan librarians had been working for long periods. And of course there is no mention of the Seif Bin Salim Library in Mombasa, or the Desai Memorial Library in Nairobi as if there were no librarians there. But then these were not part of the British library tradition. It seems Larby sees only those librarians trained and promoted by the British Council and USIS as "qualified" librarians, and of course only Ndegwa qualifies.

---

[61] Library Review . Vol. 47 (8) 388-394 (1998).
[62] Larby, P.M.: People, Places and African Studies. African Research & Documentation. No.62 (17-24) 1993

Nor does Larby mention the wealth of experience and information work carried on by the Kenyan people at the Coast as part of their struggle against colonialism—first Portuguese and then British colonialism. She remains totally untouched by the centuries-old information collection and dissemination experience in Kiswahili at the Coast. The East African Coast has centuries-old history of literature, sciences and technologies, which had been preserved over centuries by local librarians and information workers. Kiswahili literature goes back over ten centuries. It is inconceivable that this wealth of the language could have been preserved without the work of librarians. Indeed book production at the Coast is among the first, not only in African context, but in world context as well. Yet Larby can find not a word about this proud achievement.

No movement against colonialism would have survived without organising its own information production and dissemination services. Larby is admittedly giving only a "largely personal backward look". But it is important to note that her account omits any analysis of the one topic that dominated every aspect of life not only in Kenya, but in Eastern Africa during the 50s—the Mau Mau struggle for independence. Librarianship in the British/U.S. tradition assumes that one remains apolitical, meaning that librarians are not even supposed to open their eyes to the social and political reality around them, let alone taking part in the on-going social struggle of which they are a part.

The Kenyan Context

The time of independence in Kenya was one of hope and also of betrayal—in political life as in the information field. While the working people who fought for independence had high hopes of changing the society to make it more just and equal, there were internal and external forces, which sought to subvert this process. Two groups of people played a crucial role in this exercise: foreign government and settler interests on the one hand and the local petty bourgeoisie, which had been nurtured by colonialism. It was the combined strength of these two elements that marginalised the progressive forces such as Mau Mau and all that it represented—the development of a new society based on principles of equality and social justice, in which the wealth of the country would be shared by all in the interest of all.

Just as in the wider social context, so also in the information field, these two groups played a crucial role by marginalising individuals, ideas and practices built up over generations and which had been developed further by Mau Mau information services. Thus the foreign expatriate interests played a significant role in ensuring that foreign ideas and practices prevailed in the information field. Their success was assured by local librarians promoted to important posts with the blessing of the British Council and the United States Information Services. Their power base and loyalty lay not among the people but with technocrats from foreign lands whose ideas of information services were far removed from the real needs of the majority of local people who had hoped for fundamental changes in society after independence in order that their interests would prevail. But this was not to be.

It is true that there were many meaningful changes taking place at the time of independence in 1963. By the late 1950s important changes were taking place in the library field, as in all aspects of social life. As Anthony Olden points out; "in 1958, the McMillan Library stopped operating on a racially exclusive basis. In 1962 the Nairobi City Council acceded to its request to take it over...the service within the city was extended during the 1960s through the opening of two branch libraries."[63] These were indeed important changes, which reversed decades of practice in library services as far as official libraries were concerned. As Diana Sidenberg says, "public libraries are a part of the ideological apparatus of the state."[64] As the colonial state ended, libraries ceased being its tool and became the tool of the new state, which represented the interests of the new African ruling class.

It is important to see the changes taking place in libraries in the overall context of the political and social changes taking place in these countries. It is only in this context that we can understand the weaknesses that emerged in the information field. We will look at the experience of Kenya in particular, but there are similar trends in other Eastern African countries as well.

The Political Scene

The 1950s were a decade of change in Kenya. Before this period it was assumed by colonial forces that Kenya would remain a colony forever, with settler interests being dominant. By the end of the decade it was clear that the African majority had achieved their right to power through a violent armed struggle, the Mau Mau. Before 1950, the social divisions were seen more in terms of colour — white, Black and Asian. By the 1960s another social phenomenon, which was always present but had not been visible on the surface, once again became clear for all to see: class contradictions and class struggle in Kenya.

What has become obvious now is that while the African interests may have prevailed and had brought about independence, it was the working people — white, Black and Asian — who lost out in the struggle for independence. Colonialism transformed itself into neo-colonialism by encouraging the growth of an in-between, buffer class — the comprador, known locally as the "Nyaparas" and the "Wabenzi"[65]. This development served the interests well of big business and the settlers. They were now happy to see the achievement of political independence as the power passed to an African petty-bourgeoisie which ensured their continued domination of the economy. Progressive working class heroes and heroines (Kimaathi, Muthoni) their Party (Mau Mau), and their ideology (struggle for land and freedom) were marginalised. Along came Kenyatta and Moi to represent the interests of a minority through manipulating the political process. All progressive thought and political activity were forced underground.

Ideological Struggle

The struggle on the ideological front has underlined every struggle in Kenya as it has in Africa as a whole. This is also true in the information and library field. The aim was to control the all-important economic resources. The prize to be won was the enormous natural and human wealth of Kenya. This struggle was waged at various levels but was well represented in the information field, which reflected the larger social struggles. One of its manifestations was the contradiction between "western" librarianship and national information systems. In an ideal situation there would have

---

[63] Olden, Anthony (1994): "Libraries in Africa; Pioneers, Policies, Problems". Scarecrow Press, Metuchen, New Jersey, USA
[64] Rosenberg, Diana, "The Colonial State and the Development of Public Libraries in Kenya prior to 1965", Fellowship thesis, British Library Association, 1984, ii. Quoted in Olden (1994)..
[65] "Wa Benzi" : those who own Mercedes Benz cars.

developed a new information system taking positive aspects from each system. But, the "advise" of expatriate information "experts" with their control over technology, finance and power structure ensured that only the Western ideas prevailed.

In broad terms, the ideological struggle was a reflection of the struggle on a global level between the forces of capitalism and those of socialism. In a local setting this struggle was evident in every field: in the political field, in education, in the cultural field, including theatre and language-use, etc.

As capitalism consolidated itself, the division among classes in Kenya sharpened, as did the struggle at the ideological level. While the state controlled important mass media, those opposed to the regime developed their own ways of communicating and distributing their information. The basic difference between the two contending forces remained the fundamental economic one: was the wealth of the country to be produced and distributed for the welfare of those who laboured to produce it, or should it end up with the comprador and their foreign backers. This contradiction was the basic dividing factor in the information field as well.

One key question was whether the libraries and information services should be organised for the working people or were they for the rich elite. Another issue was the matter of language usage. Undue emphasis was placed on English language material. The predominance of English as the medium of instruction in schools once again brought in foreign-imposed values, which were not suited to local social, cultural, or economic needs. As a result of this emphasis on English, the development of the national language — Kiswahili — and the various nationality languages was retarded. These issues remain fundamental even today.

The Information Scene

There is a strong parallel in the information field to what was happening at the political level. The balance of power was challenged in the 1950s. Before independence, the people of Kenya took the information field as their own preserve and took control of every form of social communication. As part of the struggle for *uhuru*[66], Mau Mau developed a strong oral communications policy and began to use songs, religious music and oral traditions to achieve its political goals. This was later extended through the use of the records industry to produce songs with strong political and social messages. At the same time, it published books of liberation and resistance songs, which become extremely popular.

...

The Situation at independence and after

Thus at the time of independence in Kenya in 1963, the information needs of the majority had already been assigned to a second-class status. All formal and official information and mass media reflected the economic and political interest of the new ruling class, which served the economic interests of imperialism.

Faced with this embargo on the information needs of the people, there developed underground forms of information systems that served the interests of the people. News of the corrupt activities of the ruling classes, for example, passed with great speed and efficiency throughout the country through the use of orature. In addition, progressive individuals in key information sectors ensured that people-orientated news kept flowing

---

[66] Uhuru — Kiswahili for "independence".

in the mass media. Small progressive publishers continued to publish whatever they could, given the strict censorship. Literature, drama and theatre once again took up the challenge to keep on propagating the message of the working class solidarity and mass action. Soon after independence, patriots such as Pio Gama Pinto were able to establish progressive printing houses such as Pan African Press to politicise and inform people about the current situation in the country as well as lessons of the working class struggle around the world. He also helped to establish the Lumumba Institute in order to train committed, well-informed party cadres. But in a few years all such progressive experiments had come to an end, brutally suppressed by the now-powerful ruling class. Pinto's brutal assassination signalled that the ruling class was ready to suppress the forces that had fought and succeeded in bringing independence to the country. The working people were once again faced with brutal oppression.

An important opportunity to develop and create a new society was thus lost. The chance to establish a new information and library service that were relevant to the needs of the majority of the people was also lost. The opportunity to fulfil Lenin's test of a public library service — "The pride and glory of a public library [is] not the number of rarities it contains...but the extent to which books are distributed among the people, the number of new readers enrolled, the speed with which the demand for any new book is met"[67] — was never taken up seriously. Encouraged by foreign "experts", the new generation of librarians unquestionably assumed that their task was merely to satisfy the information needs of the "educated" elite and ignored the needs of the millions who did not have formal education, and who had no proficiency in the English language.

The energy of the rank-and-file library workers which could have been used to develop new ways of satisfying the information needs of the people was wasted in fighting a library management which was far removed from the needs of the people, being interested in furthering their own careers only. These managers did nothing to challenge those in power who saw the free flow of information as a threat to their rule. In this battle, librarians trained by Western countries played an important role in suppressing any progressive ideas and experiments, which could have provided an appropriate answer to the country's information needs. It was the class that grabbed power at independence that did the most damage and allowed an important juncture in history to pass without making fundamental changes in the very structure on which the society was organised. This class grabbed power in every field and used this power to further their class interests at the expense of the masses of people.

Libraries and librarians were no exception to this general betrayal of people's hopes. It is indeed ironic that the new ruling class sought to complete the task begun by the colonial government. It was Kenyatta's government, which wanted to destroy a large part of the Mau Mau documentation collected over the years of the "Emergency". This included pictures and biographies of thousands of activists captured or sent to the gallows by the colonial government, extracts from high security colonial files obtained by Mau Mau activists from the Special Branch files among other valuable material. These were saved from Kenyatta's thugs by the quick action of activists who managed to ship them out of the country.

Neither the colonial government nor the Kanu government managed to suppress the information activities of those fighting for genuine independence. The progressive forces continued the tradition of underground publishing and established a new distribution network. Among the well-known underground publications are the ones issued by the

---

[67] Quoted in Public Library Journal. 9 (3) 1994, p.89 [Reviews].

December Twelve Movement (later emerging as Mwakenya): *Cheche Kenya, Pambana, Mzalendo Mwakenya, Mpango wa Demokrasia, Msimamo wa Mwakenya*, etc.

Conclusion

The struggle for a relevant information service is intimately linked with the political struggles of the people for organising a society that ensures that material, social, cultural and political interests of the people are met. The struggle on the information front cannot be separated from this larger social struggle. At the same time the triumphs in the information field strengthen the people's forces in the other fields as well. The final victory in one field is dependent on and in turn influences victory in other fields. It is thus important that information workers do not isolate themselves from the broader social struggles taking place in their societies. In order to be a good information worker, one must first be a good fighter on the side of the people in the class struggle.

The lessons to be learnt from the experience in the colonial and post-colonial struggles against imperialism are of practical interest not only to the present generation of library workers in Kenya and East Africa. It is of crucial importance in countries such as South Africa, which are embarking on the path of freedom after years of suppression. We would be doing a great disservice to the African societies if we keep quiet about the tragedies and the triumphs of the Eastern African countries in the 50s and 60s.

The opportunity for making fundamental changes, created as a direct result, of political victories in the early period of struggle for liberation was lost. The opportunity that history had brought to our doorsteps to provide a people-orientated information service was lost. Instead of challenging the very basis on which library services was built, we allowed ourselves to be manipulated into making merely quantitative changes in library services, but failed to make any qualitative changes. The *classes*, which were served by the colonial library service, continued to be served and the working people who had always remained outside the remit of such services remained unserved as before. Their experiences, their cultures, their very language remained outside the walls of impressive library buildings. Thus the advantage gained in the early period of the struggle for a society and an information system which served the needs of *all* its people was lost. The struggle for such an information service continues to date.

Information relevance, equality and material security — the Kenyan experience (1998)[68]

Information and class struggle

The wealth of a nation is produced by those active in the struggles waged by the people for survival. Workers, peasants, pastoralists and other working people struggle against nature to produce the basic material needs for survival — food, clothing, and shelter. They then engage in class struggle in order to protect the products of their labour.

---

[68] Library Review. Volume 47(1) pp. 20-25. October 1998. © MCB University Press- ISSN 0024-2535

Information and knowledge are also produced in the course of these struggles. Different societies find different ways of storing and disseminating this information depending on the technical level achieved by the society. The primary purpose of collecting, storing and disseminating information is to satisfy the material needs of the people.

In all class societies, libraries are institutions, which primarily serve the needs of the class in power. The contradictions in the information field arise because the information needs of different classes are different and libraries are supposed to serve all classes, all nationalities, all racial and ethnic groups and all interest groups. In practice, libraries end up serving primarily the needs of one class or race, while a myth is maintained that the needs of all are served. The question of which class will end up the winner in the information field will be decided in the final analysis on which class controls the means of production and hence power. The struggle of the working people for equality in the distribution of national wealth is the primary struggle in a class society.

The control mechanism which decides how resources are used, and which class has the deciding power is not very transparent and cannot be easily identified. The appearance is always that the information needs of all classes are provided for by a "national" information service. The reality is quite different.

The dynamic context

Libraries play a key role in collecting, storing and disseminating knowledge and information relevant to the lives of people. The term relevant is important because unless a library provides information that is of use to people, the library itself becomes irrelevant to the needs of those it is supposed to serve. Information can be examined from various angles to determine if it is relevant.

The global context

It is worth considering the social context of the global information world. A recent study in the U.S.A shows the reality of the world today, for example half the world's wealth is in the hands of only 6 percent of the world population—all U.S. citizens.[69]
...
It is true that the wealth of the West is dependent entirely on the labour and resources forcefully extracted from the majority of the world. It has now been recognised, for instance, that the commercial exploitation resulting from the Industrial Revolution in the West could not have taken place without the labour of slaves from Africa. Yet in the societies, which provided slaves, the descendants of slaves are daily dying from the lack of basic needs, with the rest barely surviving on the margins of life. There is more concern in the West for the wellbeing of animals than that of the working people.

It is obvious that all the developments in science and technology, including information technology, have not helped in satisfying the material, social and information needs of the majority of the people of the world. This is not accidental, as the wealth and power are concentrated in the hands of a tiny minority whose main aim is to satisfy its own greed and riot the needs of the majority world. The facts quoted above about poverty for the majority and concentration of resources in the hands of a few explain why the distribution of information is unequal. Inequality in

---

[69] Wesker, A. (1997): Welcome to the real world, art. The Guardian, 30 August, p.21.

the possession of wealth translates into inequality in the possession of information. Minority elite has thus become information-rich and the rest of the population is forced to live in information poverty. Nor does this majority have political power to bring about any meaningful change in social relations or in the possession of wealth and information. The final resolution of information poverty will come only when the question over the control of resources and power has been resolved.

It is difficult to understand the lack of action by the LIS[70] profession in the face of such monumental social injustice. It is a sad fact of life that questions of relevance and equality are considered of little or no importance in the LIS field, which has the power to play an important role in alleviating poverty by ensuring an equitable and effective distribution of relevant information. Perhaps it is only when we have a new breed of worker-peasant-based "barefoot" librarians that the profession will start to address the fundamental issues of inequality in the information field.

The users

One cannot discuss relevant information without first knowing the people and understanding their needs. There is no abstract, fixed group of people who need one constant, unchanging type of information. A library operates within a social context and reflects the ever-changing contradictions within society. Thus library users as well as the information they need are constantly changing, both historically from one time to another as well as geographically, from place to place in one country and from one country to another.

Thus the question of the relevance of information should be seen in this dynamic context. The information needs in a society are dependent on the division of labour within the society. The needs of a worker are different from those of the bourgeoisie. "Relevance" of information should be related to the lives and needs of the nationalities of Kenya and not to the needs of an abstract, foreign society. Information, as well as the institutions developed to organise the information (libraries) are class-based and librarians should be aware of their communities. The information profession often claims to be "class or colour blind", claiming to serve all classes, all races, and all nationalities. In practice, such "blindness" serves the needs of the ruling class who decide who will be served. The masses of working people have no means of influencing what resources are used to serve their needs. In their "neutrality", library and information workers ignore the needs of the working people.

The time has now come for a new class of LIS workers who will champion the needs of the working people openly and in practice. The question of the provision of relevant information is not merely an academic one: it relates to the very survival of people.

Classes and class struggle

It is generally the ruling classes who benefit most from "national" information systems. For example, a survey conducted in Tanzania found that the library services were geared to serving the following minorities:

> *Expatriates* – most of these people because of their acquaintance with public libraries at "home", wish to use the library service here. Their interests being different from the needs of this country, they thus exploit the service at the expense of the nation.

---

[70] LIS – Library and Information Services

The elite – the bourgeoisie in general whose literary interests are basically Western. Those quite probably read a lot of fiction, thrillers, "love" novels, detective stories, etc. The value of most of this kind of material can hardly be described as lasting or indeed relevant to the country.[71]

The situation in Kenya is no different. But what should be the priorities for Kenyan libraries: provide light foreign-oriented material that serves to increase the market for Western transnationals, or provide information that will make people self-sufficient and able to satisfy their basic material needs? C.A. Houlding says: "We are definitely not in the business to provide recreational reading for minorities, or to propagate the benefits of British, American or any other culture."[72] But those who control funding and policies of library services are intent on recreating a foreign-based model of library service that is totally removed from the needs of the people.

Houlding highlights two other important issues:

What we need to establish are sound collections of educational utilitarian literature, material that will enable people to acquire the skills and knowledge ... The literature of reality should everywhere have preference over the literature of the dream.[73]

The second issue is, that; the publishing field is dominated by foreign publishers; whose primary interest is profits and not satisfying the information needs of the majority of Kenyan people. Houlding says:

It is true that for the present we are largely dependent on the publishing industry of the West for our supply of books. The products of this industry are in the main aimed at populations with a reasonably high standard of literacy, plenty of time for recreation ... Books are spewed out, plugged unmercifully and unscrupulously, done up like attractive packages and sold like packets of washing powder. Brain-washing powder perhaps. A high percentage of its output is irrelevant to our needs.[74]

Although the situation is a little better today and more local publishers have emerged, the general situation remains the same. It is also obvious that the pricing of publications does not take into account the purchasing capabilities of the buying public. The industry has turned books into commodities available to those who have the means to buy them. They are not seen as a social and economic necessity.

A relevant library service in Kenya would then look at the needs of the workers and peasants, who form perhaps 90 percent of the population. A library service should undertake concrete investigations on what are the ongoing struggles of their potential users and what kind of information will best help the people succeed in these struggles.

Content and language of information

What the content of relevant social communication should be will depend on the class, which the library serves. But the medium (whether print or audio-visual such as sound broadcasts, films, videos, music cassettes or CDs, tapes, slides) as well as language (whether in any of the Kenyan nationality languages like Dholuo, Somali, Maasai; or in the all-Kenya national language, Kiswahili, in preference to a foreign

---

[71] Baregu, M.LM. (1969): A people's library service. East African Library Association. Bulletin, No.10, pp. 61-4.
[72] Houlding, CA. (1969): The importance of being relevant. East African Library Association. Bulletin, No.10, pp. 65-7.
[73] Ibid.
[74] Ibid.

language like English) is important areas of library investigations. Correct information, in terms of content, supplied in an inappropriate form or an inappropriate language does not satisfy the information needs of the people. If this happens, then the working people lose faith in the library service.

The question of what is relevant content of information and knowledge which libraries collect, store, disseminate and produce cannot be resolved without undertaking concrete investigations to find out what struggles workers and peasants are involved in. Over 85 percent of Kenyans live in rural lands, most as poor peasants or as underpaid farm and plantation workers. The question, which every Kenyan librarian should be asking is: Do we provide the people with the relevant information to enable them to win their struggles? The main problems facing the majority are linked to their poverty and how to alleviate it. But few librarians are aware of the real problems facing the people.

Lack of housing, food, clothing, droughts, food shortages and price rises, have become household topics in Kenyan working peoples' homes. The question then is: do librarians have any role in providing relevant information to help people in their struggle?

It is obvious that our scientists can provide us with accurate scientific information, for example, about future rainfall patterns. This information is available in libraries. But it is not made available by libraries, in a form and language acceptable to those who are engaged in the production of food; nor do the peasants have the means to act on the information to avoid food shortages, which follow droughts and floods. Libraries, in conjunction with other organisations, can play an important role to ensure that action is taken to abolish hunger.

Historical information

Supplying information of a technical nature alone, abstract and removed from its social context will not really satisfy the information needs of Kenyan people. Libraries will also have to provide information of a historical nature, explaining why African, Asian and South American countries with such rich resources are faced with the problems of starving workers and peasants. Some background to food scarcity for workers and peasants in East Africa, is given by Professor Kigoma Malima:

> The story of food security or insecurity in East Africa cannot be separated from the ravages of colonialism, with its devastating impact on agricultural production priorities. Indeed, as a result of the colonialists' emphasis on the so-called cash crop production, like cotton and coffee, the basic food requirements of the broad masses were without exceptions neglected. Thus, not only were peasant producers often forced to cultivate export crops for the metropolitan markets but government resources research and extension were also directed at cash crops with very little or none left for food production.[75]

The basic economic structural transformation that would have ensured economic independence along with the political independence has not yet been effected. The setting and policies have changed but little from those of the colonial days. Consequently, while most of the East African countries have more than adequate and suitable land for food not only of the protein variety but even grains as well.

---

[75] Malima, K. (1979): Food security in East Africa: some comments. Maji Maji (Dar es Salaam), No.37, pp.46-8.

A relevant library service should explain the historical and current facts of underdevelopment to the people; it should also plan its information services according to the concrete information needs of the people, taking into account their historical background and their ongoing social struggles.

Reorienting library services

A large amount of information, which would be of immediate benefit to workers and peasants, is available in libraries. This information is stored in libraries, and is classified and preserved very carefully. But why does this information fail to reach the people?

Has it failed to reach the people because most of the information is in print form and the majority of people cannot read? In that case we should provide the information in a more appropriate form, for example broadcast it over the radio service and provide free radio sets to the people.

Or does the information not reach Kenyan workers and peasants because it is supplied in a language they do not understand? That is, in a language that is foreign? If so, we should provide the information in Kiswahili and the various nationality languages.

Another reason why the information may not be reaching the workers and peasants could be because information workers do not know how to reach the people. Perhaps the education system has alienated the "educated" so much from the majority of Kenyans that they no longer know how to solve their information needs. In a society with sharp class divisions, the educated immediately join the ranks of the elite, further increasing the gap between them and the working people from whose ranks they came.

Librarianship training has also similarly disorientated graduates from their own societies. As a result, library services are modelled on a foreign, Western library system, which is not suited to solve local problems. Some people claim that information does not reach the people because of the lack of training of library workers. Jaffer says that this is not such a serious problem in itself, but is caused by our own mismanagement of our resources:

> We have so far been relying on technical assistance to train Tanzanians. A library assistant can be trained locally by the national organisation in the art of librarianship... they should be shown how to help people with their requests. After training, these people should be given bigger responsibilities, as we cannot afford to stick to the demarcation of professional and non-professional duties. Let us train them locally and give them more responsibilities.[76]

One concrete step that librarians can take to help the national population in its struggles is to provide more information from other "third world" countries and show how they solve some of their problems. The information that we can provide can be of a positive type showing success in the struggles of workers and peasants. An ILO Report found only one exception to the general poor performance (China), where "even the poorest families in the poorest region can provide their basic needs, receive communal services and still have 20 percent of their income to spend on other basic needs ... It is safe to say that the poorest 20 percent of China's population earn over 11 percent of the national income while the top 20 percent earn only 35 percent.

---

[76] Jaffer, M.H.A. (1969): What sort of system? East African Library Association. Bulletin, No.10, pp. 58-60.

No other Asian country can match that".[77] The reasons for the success of the Chinese experience, need to be disseminated widely.

The lesson for us in libraries to learn is how best to raise the technical and scientific knowledge of workers and peasants. With correct input of information, peasants can be mobilised to become innovators and scientists, to gain control over nature and thus avoid future famines.

The politics of information

There are serious barriers to the "right" information reaching working people in a form and language that is appropriate to their needs. The barriers are not caused by technological reasons nor are they limited to the information field. They are social and economic. The political reasons why information does not reach the people should be the chief concern of LIS workers if their concerns about information poverty are genuine. Until the profession takes this challenge seriously, no amount of breast beating will lead to the satisfaction of the information needs of people.

History has shown that people do not wait for "outsiders" to come and satisfy their needs. A time comes in all societies when people take it upon themselves to satisfy their own needs, as it is a matter of their survival. People cannot wait while LIS workers spend years discussing how and what information to provide. They have developed their own information systems and will continue to do so. The question is whether the LIS profession is with people or not and also whether the profession is ready to work with the people in deciding what service they will have.

Libraries have an educational role to play in society. They are not neutral collectors of information, but can play a positive, dynamic role by being proactive in satisfying the real information needs of the people. LIS workers will have to learn to work with other national, regional and international organisations as a special team to provide a meaningful service.

The question of the relevance of information is related to the question of equality in the distribution of information between different classes. There cannot be information equality unless there is equality in the ownership of economic resources and political power. Thus the information struggle for equality and relevance is directly related to the struggle for economic and political equality. The fact that the LIS profession, as a profession, in Kenya as well as in Britain, has chosen to turn its face away from these larger social struggles has led it to accept the present power relations in society. Thus the information poor are condemned by the profession to perpetual poverty.

But LIS workers can no longer claim to be neutral in the social struggles going on in their societies, but will have to stand up and be counted. It is easy to keep "tolling the bell" simply because it has always been tolled. The need now is to rock the boat and come up with new ways of providing service, in a democratic, "equal" and transparent way empowering the people on whose behalf libraries are run. The real challenge is to make all working people, librarians, and to make all librarians, workers, both in thought and in action. Only then will real power in the information field return where it belongs — to the people. Only then will questions of relevance and equality in the information field be resolved.

---

[77] ILO(1980): Profiles of rural poverty. Geneva. Reviewed by Nadkarni, H. V. (1980), "Political economy of rural poverty" Economic and Political Weekly. Vol. XV No. 34, pp. 1434-6.

Politics of information, information for politics

Setting the scene (2): A mere librarian doing research

September 1984. Nyayo House, Nairobi. The torture headquarters of the KANU-Moi regime. The Special Branch officials have found their next victim. There is no end to questions: Why are you writing about Pinto and Kimaathi, and not about Kenyatta? Even historians are not allowed to do research on the Mau Mau. Why are you, a mere librarian, doing this research? Do you not know that people at the highest level in the Government, are offended by your article on Pinto? Are you a communist? Why do you write about workers and peasants? What do you understand by workers—even Moi is a worker, why are you not writing about him?

It is important to ask questions so we understand the reality around us. But it is more important to listen to the answers, however unpalatable. The Special Branch officers were not really interested in listening to my answers or to understand them. Their minds were already made up—after all it was a job to question and torture people as instructed. Their performance was measured not in terms of understanding their victims, but in "outcomes" of how many were tortured, jailed, exiled or disappeared.

So why write about Mau Mau, Pio Gama Pinto and Kimaathi? Precisely because their histories, their contribution and their ideas had been suppressed and distorted initially by the colonial regime, and later by the independence government. Their vision of a society as explained in a Mau Mau document did not suit the new or old regimes:

> let us, in short, create a new society which allows to each the right to eat, the right to the products of their labour, the right to clothe, house, and educate their children, the right, in short, to live in dignity amongst equals. It is a socialist society we should be struggling to build, a system which, unlike capitalism, concerns itself with the welfare of the masses rather than with the profits and privileges of a few.[78]

It was in the interest of those who were in power to suppress such "dangerous" ideas. Hence the attacks on individuals, who held such ideas or who disseminated such ideas. And that included librarians and political activists. All democratic political organisations had to function underground. The first item in this section, "The politics of food" was written for an underground newspaper *Pambana* ("Struggle") published and distributed in 1984 by the December Twelve Movement.

Many other articles, some reproduced in this book, continue this process of documenting information about the political aspects of the struggle. This process is still not complete and more research needs to be undertaken to write a complete history of over 500 years of Kenyan people's resistance to colonialism and imperialism. There are no funds or other resources to carry out this task—neither

---

[78] Barnett, Donald L. (1972): "Kenya: two paths ahead". Introduction to Muchai, K.: "Hardcore: the story of Karigo Muchai" (1973). Richmond, B.C., Canada: LSM Information Centre.

from the Government, nor from international organisations, or from the otherwise ubiquitous aid agencies. Nor have Kenyan Universities taken up this challenge to research, document and teach about this important aspect of Kenyan history. It will be up to progressive individual researchers and political activists to take up this task.

The politics of food (1983)[79]

For many years now in newspapers and radio, we have been fed with government propaganda and that of the World Bank or other foreign "experts" that food shortages are a normal state of affairs in our country. They say there is not sufficient arable land in Kenya. They tell us that our population is too high and rapidly increasing and that not everyone can be fed. They tell us that we do not have enough Kenyan expertise. They tell us that capitalist agricultural production is the only type of agriculture possible.

These are brazen lies spread by imperialists and their agents so that they can continue exploiting our country. The production process and the distribution of wealth, is done in a way, which enables the imperialists to make high profits. For a capitalist maximizing, profit is the overriding concern. The aim is to invest as little as possible and with as little risk for the highest possible returns. A capitalist even makes profits from our misery. When the capitalist is a foreigner as is the case in our country, this means the continuous drainage of our wealth to foreign countries, thus making our country poorer and poorer as theirs become richer and richer.

We must therefore know and understand that there are other systems of agricultural production, which would enable us to produce more food, sufficient for everyone and even have a surplus. There is no doubt this is possible. It has happened in other countries, which have dared to throw out imperialists and have afterwards adopted a system of agricultural production that puts people's basic food requirements first. Let us have a look at some of these countries.

China

We can learn a lot from China. When China was dominated by imperialists from Britain and the U.S.A., famine was endemic. It is only after 1949, that is, after their victorious war against local and foreign domination, that Chinese people were able to make plans related to their own lives. In agriculture, for instance, the peasants were given land to grow food crops for their own consumption instead of cash crops for export. Science and technology were used to solve land problems like soil erosion, flooding or water shortages. Bridges and canals were built in addition to dams for storing water for irrigation during the dry season. Instead of importing expensive gadgets they developed appropriate machinery for the needs of their country and people. Thus within a few years of ousting imperialism China managed to do away with hunger. Today China is able to feed all its 1,000 million people.

In short, it is only when a country uses all the knowledge available to serve and meet the needs of its people that it is able to satisfy people's basic needs like food. But this is only possible when imperialist foreigners have been driven out of the country.

---

[79] Pambana; organ of the December Twelve Movement (Nairobi). No. 2 July 1983.

Cuba

Cuban history is similar to that of China. When Cuba was dominated by imperialism, starvation among people was chronic. Under Batista's puppet regime Cuba had became a paradise for millionaire playboys from the U.S.A. It was only after the overthrow of the Batista regime in 1959 and the overthrow of the imperialists, that Cuba was able to solve food problems for the working people. For the first time, it became possible for Cuba to use agricultural knowledge to satisfy people's needs instead of producing for the benefits of markets abroad. For example, very few Cubans were able to eat fish although Cuba is a fishing country with over 5,000 km of coastline. Fish was very expensive and only rich Cubans, tourists and other foreign visitors could afford it.

The anomalous situation changed after 1959. The lives of fishermen changed for the better. Better fishing methods were developed even as fishing increased. At the same time, fish prices came down and many people were able to afford it. Today, fish is a cheap but nutritious protein-rich food available in ordinary Cuban homes. It is no longer the preserve of the rich. As a result, hunger and food related diseases have been eliminated among ordinary people in that country.

Nicaragua

Before the people of Nicaragua, under the leadership of the Frente Sandinista de Liberacion National (FSLN), the Sandinistas, liberated themselves from neo-colonialism and U.S.-imperialism, over 40 percent of the land was owned by only two percent of the population plus a few rich foreign land owners. The peasants were squeezed on to only 3.5 percent of cultivable farmland, while the Somoza family and their close associates owned more than 2.5 million acres. Nicaragua was ruled by the U.S.-supported Somoza dynasty, one of the most corrupt and hated dictatorships in Central America. Most workers and peasants lived in hunger.

After 1979 when the Somoza puppet regime was overthrown through the Sandinista-led armed struggle, people's democracy was introduced and agricultural production was put on a new footing. Land was confiscated from the corrupt and rich land owners and their foreign associates without compensation and restored to the people or brought under state control. Food production rose and after only a short time, the Nicaraguans became self-sufficient in food; peasants were able to feed themselves properly, and the surplus was sold cheaply to other Nicaraguans and so food consumption rose by 40 percent. They were even able to export some of the surplus. A healthy well-fed population is the basis for development.

North Korea [DPRK]

Since North Koreans defeated imperialism and snatched back their independence, agricultural development progressed in leaps and bounds. Before 1959, total grain production was less than 2 million tons yearly. By 1979, it had reached over 9 million tons per annum with an expected increase to 15 million tons within the next few years. In the 70s, agricultural production grew by 30 percent every year. In 1974, one hectare produced about 6 tons of rice and 5 tons of maize. By 1980, this production had increased to 7.2 tons of rice and 6.3 tons of maize per hectare. This is only possible because in North Korea it is the people themselves who are responsible for their agricultural production led (unlike in the US-controlled South Korea, and where a few compradors and their US-backers control agricultural production). The food produced in North Korea is used to feed the people (unlike in South Korea where poverty and hunger reign amidst an overfed super-rich U.S.-backed oligarchy).

Lessons for Kenyans

These few examples of a system of agricultural production based on people's needs show clearly that food shortages are not caused by the lack of knowledge, or the size of the population or even indeed the size of arable land. It is caused by the system of land ownership and of capitalist export- and profit-orientated agricultural production pursued by the get-rich-quick comprador class and their foreign backers.

These examples teach us that in order to make agricultural production meet and satisfy the people's needs, we must first snatch back our economic and political independence from the imperialist foreigners.

Only after getting rid of imperialist-backed oppression, shall we be able to take new directions in food production:

1. Productive land must be in the hands of the masses;
2. The people must be responsible for the production and distribution of food;
3. Production of food crops and not cash crops must be given priority;
4. Food should feed Kenyan people first before it is exported. Feeding people is more important than earning foreign exchange for importing BMWs, Volvos, Mercedes Benzs and other luxury items.

China, Cuba, Nicaragua, North Korea and many other socialist countries have banished hunger and starvation by adopting a different path of development. But in Kenya, despite the fact that we have some of the best agricultural land in the world, many poor people still suffer from hunger, malnutrition and as in the case of northern Kenya, from mass starvation. The majority of our people go hungry in a country where the weight-reducing industry (massage-parlours, hormone-injections, weight-reducing clinics, saunas, etc.) for the overfed few is thriving.

In Kenya, imperialist foreigners and a few rich come first, but in Cuba, China, Nicaragua and North Korea, the peasants and working people come first. In these countries, the people had to wage an armed struggle to free themselves from the stranglehold of imperialist-backed oppression before they could be responsible for their own food production. A relentless struggle against the alliance of the comprador "mbwa-kali" ruling class and Euro-American imperialism is the only way we Kenyans can use the wealth of our country to satisfy our own needs and banish hunger. The defeat of imperialism in its neo-colonial stage is a necessary first-step for our development as a Kenyan people.

The other Kenya: underground and alternative literature (1997)[80]

Introduction

It is necessary to have access to the vast amount of underground and alternative literature about Kenya in order to understand the current political, social and economic state the country is in. This alternative literature can provide the real picture of the situation in the country today from the viewpoint of the majority. It provides a barometer of the state of the class struggle in Kenya.

While the ruling classes deny the very existence of classes and class struggle, the alternative material listed here provides an entirely different picture. So fearful have the current "leaders" become of the people's victory over oppression, they systematically distort records of Kenya's *past* and have even banned open discussion of Mau Mau. In view of this, it is becoming increasingly necessary to interpret and document the history of the struggle for independence from the working class point of view. The lessons of past victories are applicable to today's problems. This has been done by the underground movements and progressive activists and historians,— hence the attempt to silence their voice. Some of this "silenced" material is included in this survey.

The importance of underground movements and their publications is recorded by the underground itself:

> The most dramatic development...was the emergence of worker/peasant based underground groups. They began articulating an ideology that fully reflected the workers' struggle. The seventies saw the development of a vigorous underground press. Between 1974 and 1982, the underground groups and newspapers had become the real voice of the Kenyan people.[81]

This survey provides a broad picture of the alternative material—it does not aim to be a complete record of such material. But sufficient material is included to show the wide range of material that is available. It is not possible to list every document published underground as much of it is lost and no organisation in Kenya dare openly collect it.

It is not certain if any outside institution, with the possible exception of the CIA, has collected such material.

Nonetheless, much material has been collected by Mwakeny, both inside and outside the country. Copies of some of it are available from their overseas branches, including the ones in the U.S.A. and in Britain. Some such material is listed in Appendix 6.

Some Underground Publications

Kenyan organised underground resistance movement has had an "unbroken continuity – though not always along a straight path – from the 1970s, and in different guises and forms", as the article, "Roots of the Revolt" in *Africa Events* points out. This

---

[80] Collection Building (1997) Vol. 16(2) 80-87.
[81] Mwakenya (1987) Draft Minimum Programme. p. 13.

movement draws its inspiration from, and in a sense is a continuation of, the line taken by Mau Mau, especially in the years just before independence. In the early 1980s, it was the December Twelve Movement with the publications *Cheche Kenya* and *Pambana;* which carried on the tradition of resistance and of the underground press. The name "December Twelve Movement" was later changed to "Mwakenya", a Kiswahili acronym for Muungano wa Wazalendo wa Kuikomboa Kenya (Union of Patriots for the Liberation of Kenya).

...

Conclusion

This brief survey shows that much work needs to be done in documenting and making available relevant material on the real situation in countries such as Kenya. African countries are facing increasing marginalisation in all fields as a result of the new scramble for its resources in the 1990s. This is particularly evident in the field of information where the development of new technologies is used not to develop its resources, but to further impoverish its people.

Yet the situation is not hopeless. The present survey shows that there is a vibrant underground working class movement, which has the ideas and theories to solve their problems. Progressive people are risking their lives to ensure the free flow of information. In the long run, they will find their own solution to the information — and other — problems they face.

In this context, what role can progressive people around the world, especially in the information field, play? The first demand of the people in Africa is to be left alone by the Western countries to find their own solutions. Progressive people everywhere can demand this from their governments. In addition, support for the information activities of the underground and people's movements would obviously be helpful. Very little, if any, such support is forthcoming.

Documenting, collecting and making available alternative material would play an important role in supporting the information struggle of the African people. Collecting only the output from African government sources and from African-based multinational publishers will merely help to reinforce the message of the ruling classes. It is the alternative literature, which will redress the information imbalance, and in the long run help to reinterpret African history from the people's point of view. It is only from this that real progress and development can follow. The availability of such material in British and American Universities and public libraries can help to change people's attitudes.

It is hoped that by making alternative material widely available, libraries in Kenya as well as around the world will enable a better understanding of the struggle waged by the people of Kenya. The real proof of the freedom of information is whether libraries dare collect and disseminate this alternative material.

The lesson for library and information workers is that they need to make a conscious effort to collect and make available such alternative material. Without this effort, they are failing in their professional duty. It remains to be seen if the profession is ready for this challenge.

Information in Kenyan liberation struggle — facts and fiction (2000)[82]

Fact 1: Neo-colonial history books tell us that the route to India was "discovered" by Vasco da Gama. The reality is that there had been trade for hundreds of years between East Africa and India before Vasco da Gama was even born. In fact it was a Mombasa-based Gujarati pilot who guided Vasco da Gama's ships from Mombasa to India.

Fact 2: Kenyan children know that a large fort exits in Mombasa. Few know who built it and why. Fort Jesus was built by Portuguese colonialists in Mombasa to protect the Portuguese occupation army from the liberation forces of the Kenyan coastal people who waged an armed struggle to throw out the foreign invaders.

Fact 3: Neo-colonial history books show Mau Mau as a localised, primitive, "tribal" movement, which used violence against its own people in an orgy of senseless murders. Children in Kenya are still not taught that Mau Mau was a sophisticated armed movement with its military wing, Land and Freedom Army, with its own anti-imperialist ideology, was well organised among workers and peasants and had support in all parts of the country. In fact, the colonial forces had to declare a state of emergency in the country in 1952 in order to control the growing forces of the liberation forces. The whole British army was mobilised to fight the liberation forces — from Aden, Burma, and the U.K. Why was such a mighty army mobilised if Mau Mau was a local "tribal" "disturbance"?

Who is to document and interpret Kenyan history from a Kenyan, working-class point of view? The colonial government cannot obviously be expected to show history from the people's point of view. Nor can one expect the neo-colonial regime that was installed with colonial support after independence. It is a matter of fact that the most prominent Kenyan historian, Maina wa Kinyatti was imprisoned in solitary confinement for six years because of his research of the Mau Mau. His research involved interviewing Mau Mau activists, and collecting their liberation songs. Even after his imprisonment, Maina was not safe in Kenya and had to seek safety outside Kenya.

...

Thus the liberation forces of necessity had to set up their own underground liberation libraries. Perhaps the largest one was the one run by Nazmi Durrani, which provided a major reference point for the December Twelve movement, which published its own newspaper *Pambana* ("Struggle") in the early 1980s. The library contained material which was banned in Kenya and which could lead to indefinite detention if found out. This included works of Marx, Lenin, Stalin, Castro, as well as publications from the USSR and the Foreign Language Press in Beijing. This library also provided the source material for important document in the fight against the neo-colonial Moi regime such as Mwakenya's *Register of Resistance (1987)*, and Umoja-Kenya(1989).

The collection of books on Kenya, which are now being given to the Cuban Library Association contains material from this important library as well as material

---

[82] Notes accompanying donation of books to Cuba. February 2000

collected in London to support the struggle in Kenya. It is a matter of particular satisfaction to the Kenyan liberation movement, Mwakenya—which itself has published a large amount of material—that we are able to give this material to Cuba which has played a major role in the liberation struggle in Africa, in military, economic and political terms. The struggles of the Cuban people, their example in standing up to the imperialist forces led by the U.S.A. and their internationalist spirit have inspired many generations of African people. The underground liberation activists in Kenya absorbed the lessons of the Cuban struggle. Che and Castro inspired countless youth to stand up against imperialist forces.

We hope to continue this anti-imperialist cooperation in a stronger way in future.

Voices of resistance: underground publishing in Kenya, 1963-1998 (1990)[83]

Introduction

Most studies of publishing in Kenya have confined their scope to the above-ground legal publications allowed by the government machinery. And yet the KANU (Kenya African National Union) governments, first under Jomo Kenyatta and now under Daniel arap Moi have systematically suppressed press freedom. "In the past two years, "says *Africa Watch*, "the government of President Daniel arap Moi has become increasingly intolerant of freedom of expression in Kenya creating a general climate of fear."[84] The police in Kenya even go to the extent of checking library records in order to keep an eye on who reads 'subversive' material. It is a common knowledge that classrooms, lecture theatres, public transport, bars, and even funeral processions are regularly attended by government informers who report anyone found to be critical of government policies.

In such a climate of repression, people have resorted to underground publishing to express their opinions on the current situation. Kenya has one of the most flourishing underground publishing in Africa. As Umoja-KENYA has said, "The best literature about the Kenyan situation over the ten year period (1978-1988) has come from the underground press."[85] The existence of a large underground communication system is a reflection of the sharpening contradiction between the majority of working Kenyans and the ruling class, which gets much material and moral support from its Western backers. It also reflects the increasing militancy and resistance to the repression of the right to communicate.

In this study we shall examine the different means of underground communication in existence in Kenya, the various forms they take, look at their content in light of contemporary events, the distribution network in use, and the effects they have had on the political scene in the country. We begin with a brief look

---

[83] Internal document written for Ukenya (United Movement for Democracy in Kenya)
[84] Africa Watch 6 December 1989 (London): 1.
[85] Moi's Reign of Terror; a decade of Nyayo crimes against the people of Kenya. 1989. London. UmojaKenya: 40.

at the publishing scene before independence, during the Mau Mau struggle for independence as this experience has influenced the current publishing scene.[86]

...

Throughout the 1970s there continued to be issued various underground pamphlets. These included *Mwanguzi* and *Kenya Twendapi*,[87] which questioned the direction followed by Kenya after independence. Many former Mau Mau combatants began to recount their experiences and stated that they had not suffered to see a few getting all the benefits of independence. Many such views could not be published within Kenya and had to be published overseas. Among the best known are Kabiro's[88], Mathu's[89], and Muchai's[90] — all published in Canada.

The murder in 1975 of the popular politician, J. M. Kariuki brought out a national unanimity in anti-government feelings. It also saw the publication and distribution of a large number of underground leaflets in support of basic human and democratic rights.

The popularity of songs and plays performed by the Kamiriithu Community Culture Centre once again showed that the Kenyan people had rejected the culture encouraged by the government but were in support of progressive content in art and drama. Events were to show that such expression of free ideas could not be tolerated by the government. Ngugi wa Thiong'o, one of the authors of the play performed at Kamirithu was detained and the open-air theatre constructed by workers and peasants was razed to the ground by government bulldozers. This was the largest open-air theatre in Africa and had the added attraction that it was far from urban centres, in the middle of the peasant settlement in the countryside. It now became clear to all that no public expression of any ideas or opinion was possible in Kenya. Such expression had of necessity to be underground. This lesson bore fruit in the 80s when a popular underground press, could truly be said to have been established.

In general, the underground leaflets of the 1970s reflected the contradictions of the times. Many were written by University or school or college students, who played an important role in mobilising public opinion on important issues. The writers of these leaflets were also:

> conscious of the class dimensions of the post-colonial Kenya society and they often tried to show the connections between Kenya's problems — not in tribal or personality lines — but in terms of what they called 'the neo-colonial path' of development opted for by the government. The leaflets bearing Kiswahili names became part of a vigorous underground press that took a very different line on national and international affairs from that of the established press.[91]

"*Cheche-Kenya*" sets a new record

---

[86] This section is not included as it has been covered in the author's book "Never be silent; publishing and imperialism in Kenya, 1884-1963 (2006). London: Vita Books.
[87] Abdilatif Abdalla (1989). Personal communication, London. Kenya Twendapi? (Where are we heading in Kenya?) was a series of pamphlets (about 9 were issued) in 1989.
[88] Kabiro, Thiong'o (1973): The man in the middle: the story of Thiong'o Kabiro. Richmond, BC, Canada. LSM Information Centre.
[89] Mathu, Mohamed (1974): The urban guerrilla. Richmond, BC, Canada. LSM Information Centre.
[90] Muchai, Karigo (1973): Hard core. Richmond, BC, Canada. LSM Information Centre.
[91] Africa Events (London): Countdown to Freedom (Cover story). Vol. 6 (8-9) August-September, 1990.

There was a qualitative difference in forces opposed to the government by the end of 1970s. The on-going resistance of workers, peasants and students had been joined by professional people; such as lecturers, doctors, lawyers and teachers. This new unity resulted in a qualitative change in underground publications as well. Perhaps the most important publication of this period; was published by a group called *Cheche Kenya* (*Cheche* is a Kiswahili word meaning 'Spark'). The publication itself was called *InDependent Kenya*.

InDependent Kenya[92] was in fact a whole book in a cyclostyled form and numbered over a hundred pages. It was widely distributed throughout the country in 1981. The publication of the book marked a significant progress in the development of resistance forces as well as in the field of underground publication.

The first significant point to be noted is that *Cheche* brought together intellectuals and workers in an underground organisation. Gone were the days of individuals and small groups brought out a single page leaflet focusing on a single issue. The whole concept and approach of *InDependent Kenya* was different. The book was the study of Kenya's history and politics. It documented from the perspective of the Kenyan working people, the history of the struggle for independence, the struggle of militants and conservatives within KANU, the corruption that become a way of life within the regime, and the cultural dependency under the shadow of imperialism. *InDependent Kenya* represented an important ideological step in understanding the realities of neo-colonialism.

It was a major achievement on the part of the authors that they managed to distribute the book underground widely in Kenya under very difficult conditions. By the time the book came out in 1981, it was obvious that the change of Presidency from Kenyatta to Moi in 1979 had not heralded any change in bringing in a more tolerant government in spite of some initial indications. Repression had in fact increased. Resistance too had moved to a new, higher level. The publication of *InDependent Kenya* itself was an indication of this higher stage of resistance. But events showed that an even higher, *organised* stage of resistance had been achieved by 1982.

1982 – The Year of "Pambana"

"Pambana" (Kiswahili: "Kupambana" – "to struggle") became the national call for change in 1982. *Pambana* was the title of an underground newspaper that fired the imagination of a whole new generation. *Pambana* set new standards in politics as well as in publishing and communication.

...

What is more significant from the point of view of this study is the understanding that the Movement and *Pambana* showed about the importance of communication in society. It showed their awareness of the role of the press in any social conflict. The editorial in the first issue of *Pambana* is important as it deals mainly with the role of publishing in their struggle. Entitled *Cheche: A Spark can light a prairie fire,* it reads:

> This first issue of PAMBANA marks a major milestone, indeed even a turning point in our country's history. It is the first truly people's newspaper. It constitutes a step towards creating our people's own voice and our institutions. The government-

---

[92] InDependent Kenya (1982). Underground document circulating in Kenya in the early 1980s. Later published in London by Zed Press and sponsored by The Journal of African Marxists.

controlled, foreign-owned press, as well as the laughable *Voice of Kenya*; lie to us always. They misrepresent Kenya's reality and praise every crime and evil act the ruling class commits. They apologise for them and continually attack our people's struggles or at best ignore them. These newspapers sow confusion and disunity in their attempts to put "a lid on trouble" and stop the wheel of history. Our people want change, revolutionary change. The government and its mouthpieces want to keep Kenyans down. Just as these government-controlled, foreign-owned papers cannot be free; they cannot be neutral. In many real ways they support our enemies.

PAMBANA is similarly neither free nor neutral. It will accept no apologies for oppression or thievery and will forcefully represent the truth as seen from the majority poor, dispossessed Kenyans who have hitherto been so fully ignored. PAMBANA will therefore be militantly and proudly partisan. PAMBANA could not have come at a better time. The current regime, like the previous one, is fully exposed as unable to solve the political and economic problems facing us.[93]

...

In spite of the increased repression following the coup attempt in which reportedly over two thousand people were killed by government troops, the activities of the underground December Twelve Movement continued. The second issue of *Pambana* came out in July 1983 and was again widely distributed in the face of increased government surveillance. This issue summarised events since the coup and interpreted the role of the underground press in Kenya:

When the first issue of *Pambana* came out in May 1982, the people of Kenya received it with great joy. It filled Kenyans with hope, great expectations. It made them see that it was possible to change the prevailing oppressive conditions and to create a better life for all Kenyans. That is what they had always looked forward to—an organ which would unite the poor and the exploited against the Kenyan ruling class and their foreign masters. Such a unity is what *Pambana* stands for.

... *Pambana* will continue to voice the demands of all the protesting peasants, all the striking workers, all the defiant students, indeed of all the patriots who want to free Kenya. *Pambana* shall live.[94]

...

Resistance through orature

The use of an oral medium is yet another way in which the government's ban on expression has been broken. The use of progressive songs, plays, poems, and records is a well-established tradition. Poems of resistance have been in circulation underground from the group "Upande Mwingine" who have also done some pioneering underground work in documenting resistance in Kenya. The poems reflect the lives of working people and register people's rejection of oppression.

---

[93] Pambana. Underground publication of December Twelve Movement. Issue No. 1 (May, 1982) was reproduced in London by the Committee for the Release of Political Prisoners in Kenya in their publication, Law as a tool of political repression in Kenya. Copies of Nos. 1 and 2 are available in the archives of Mwakenya.
[94] Ibid.

Another method of resistance is through songs. Many have been issues and many singers, producers and even sellers of tapes have ended up in jails for this. *Africa Events* again reports on this:

> ...what is unique about the new songs was that their message had nothing to do with the pet theme of love; rather, they came laden with brazen, hard-core politics...the heavy hand of state security brought the songs' reign to a swift end...During the crackdown, music stores were ransacked by security officers, and about 100 shopkeepers and Matatu (mini bus) drivers (who took a special pleasure in playing the songs full blast to passengers) were arrested and charged with purveying or publishing seditious material. Some of them raised the KSh 2,000 fine the magistrate asked them to pay. Those who could not raise the money are in jail.

(One of the songs) was in Kikuyu language. Its subject matter can be loosely translated as "The trials and tribulations of the people of Muoroto" and the song strongly indicts the government for the forced eviction of the people and levelling of Muoroto, a Nairobi shanty, in May this year. A local cleric claimed that eight people died in the brutal operation, although the government has denied it.[95]

Upande Mwingine have also documented the Muoroto resistance in their poem simply entitled 'Muoroto'.

Distribution Network

No segment of Kenyan society is free from informers and the special branch of the police. They keep a watchful eye on who says and does what. Even the smallest facts are known to the government. Yet the underground organisations have managed to circulate their messages regularly and efficiently. In fact the distribution is so well coordinated that often the pamphlets appear overnight in different parts of the country so as not to alert government security machinery. Talking of Mwakenya's distribution work, *Africa Events* observed:

> But despite the severe crackdown, it seems the Kenya government was unable to get at the nerve centre of the organisation, which continues with its political work inside the country, with its publications sometimes finding their way into the pigeonholes of Members of Parliament, or in police stations and Army barracks. [96]

The impact of underground publications

There is no doubt that underground publications have had a major impact on the Kenyan society. In a society where no open debates, exchange of ideas, or discussion of alternative models is possible, people turn naturally to underground publications. Such publications are instrumental not only in passing on important information, but also carry important new ideas on how a more just society might be organised. Examples from around the world where such ideas have been turned into reality give the people hope that they too can benefit from a similar experience. Once such ideas have been disseminated, they become widely accepted and strengthened largely because they answer their needs for material necessities. Such ideas in fact originate among the people themselves. The positive work of the underground organisations involves collecting such ideas, organising them into an overall programme, and exploring methods of implementing them. Such programmes inspire confidence

---

[95] Africa Events (London): op.cit.
[96] Africa Events (London): op.cit.

because they are no longer individual hopes and aspirations but represent the collective will of the people.

Africa Events again looks at the question of the impact that the underground movement has had in Kenya:

> The organisation and its leadership (of Mwakenya) have largely been underground. But its above ground manifestations seem to have had direct and indirect effects on the intellectual, cultural and political life in Kenya.[97]

Underground publications in Kenya have become a major source of information and an important means of the communication of ideas, which then influence people's action. It is an aspect of mass communications that has been deliberately ignored or its impact minimised by the government, which has much to lose by accepting its true significance. But the reality of underground publications and the impact they are having on the politics of Kenya today can no longer be ignored. It is a reality that is forcing itself on the society as a whole, whether one agrees with the message it upholds or not. It is perhaps time that information workers took this reality seriously. The voices of resistance are loud and clear. They will not go away merely because some ears are closed.

Conclusion

This brief survey shows that much work needs to be done in documenting and making available relevant material on the real situation in countries such as Kenya. African countries are facing increasing marginalisation in all fields as a result of the new scramble for its resources in the 1990s. This is particularly evident in the field of information where the development of new technologies is used not to develop its resources, but to further impoverish its people.

Yet the situation is not hopeless. The present survey shows that there is a vibrant underground working class movement, which has the ideas and theories to solve their problems. Progressive people are risking their lives to ensure the free flow of information. In the long run, they will find their own solution to the information— and other—problems they face.

In this context, what role can progressive people around the world, especially in the information field, play? The first demand of the people in Africa is to be left alone by the Western countries to find their own solutions. Progressive people everywhere can demand this from their governments. In addition, support for the information activities of the underground and people's movements would obviously be helpful. Very little, if any, such support is forthcoming.

Documenting, collecting and making available alternative material would play an important role in supporting the information struggle of the African people. Collecting only the output from African government sources and from African-based multinational publishers will merely help to reinforce the message of the ruling classes. It is the alternative literature, which will redress the information balance, and in the long run help to reinterpret African history from the people's point of view. It is only from this that real progress and development can follow. The availability of such material in British and American Universities and public libraries can help to change people's attitudes.

---

[97] Africa Events (London): op.cit

It is hoped that by making alternative material widely available, libraries in Kenya as well as around the world will enable a better understanding of the struggle waged by the people of Kenya. The real proof of the freedom of information is whether libraries dare collect and disseminate this alternative material.

The lesson for library and information workers is that they need to make a conscious effort to collect and make available such alternative material. Without this effort, they are failing in their professional duty. It remains to be seen if the profession is ready for this challenge.

The Battle Continues
in a Colder Climate

The search for social justice

Setting the scene (3): No equality of conditions

Act 2, Scene 1. Date: 1986. Location: London. Change of scene, similar struggles.

There is no doubt that British public libraries are better resourced than most libraries in Africa. They have more resources and more staff; they have long-established library routines and procedures set to achieve high standards of service. But some of its very strengths are also the basis of their weaknesses. The society as a whole has become rather complacent. Long centuries of domination over resources of the Empire have created a culture of superiority. The library profession appears to have become fossilised, blinkered and puffed up with its own importance. New ideas from abroad or from new generations of librarians are not welcome. The status quo allows no alternatives. The end of the Empire, the rise of the U.S.A., USSR, and later Germany, Japan, China and India have all shifted the goalposts in every aspect of social, political and economic life throughout the world, yet policies and practices in libraries remain largely unchanged. The profession seems to be afraid of the challenge to change. Society refuses to accept the reality of classes and class struggles and libraries too reflect this blinkered approach to their social reality.

Following the end of the Second World War, what we see are major demographical changes in Britain. Labour and skills shortages after the war lead to a net import of labour from the former colonies whose economies have been ruined by centuries of plunder. While the labour and skills of the immigrants are welcome, they are not welcome as a people – nor are their cultures, their lifestyles and their world outlooks. This non-acceptance filters down to libraries as well. The work environment of black communities remains that of second-class citizens and refugees, to be tolerated but not accepted. Services to Black communities remain tokenistic. The prejudice reserved for working class people in general becomes the lot of the black people.

But the issue of racial inequality is closely entwined with an ingrained inequality in Britain and other "democratic" societies in the West. Ambedkar recognised this in the context of India, as Kumar notes:

> Ambedkar envisaged [the] establishment of equality – social, economic, and political – not just as a slogan but as a concrete policy. He made equality of opportunity a fundamental right. But he was conscious that in an unequal society, equality of opportunity could lead to further production of inequality because those groups which were already ahead in the social ladder would always have an advantage. Therefore, Ambedkar also enshrined "equality of condition" in the Indian Constitution. This condition was nothing but reservations for the Dalits.[98]

---

[98] Kumar, Vivek, (2004): Ambedkar, the nation-builder. The Pioneer. 28 April, 2004. Available at: http://www.countercurrents.org/dalit-vivekkumar280404.htm. [Accessed: 28 May 2007].

No such "equality of condition" exists in Britain. This is further compounded by a lack of democracy, which is the end result of capitalist globalisation. While this democracy deficit for the working class has been perpetuated in the countries of the South, it is equally prevalent in the industrialised North. The reasons for the lack of democracy are explained by Parenti:

> With international "free trade" agreements such as NAFTA, GATT, and FTAA, the giant transnationals have been elevated above the sovereign powers of nation states. These agreements endow anonymous international trade committees with the authority to prevent, overrule, or dilute any laws of any nation deemed to burden the investment and market perogatives of transnational corporations. These trade committees–of which the World Trade Organization (WTO) is a prime example—set up panels composed of "trade specialists" who act as judges over economic issues, placing themselves above the rule and popular control of any nation, thereby [en]suring the supremacy of international finance capital. This process, called globalization, is treated as an inevitable natural "growth" development beneficial to all. It is in fact a global coup d'état by the giant business interests of the world.[99]

This threat to democracy affects public libraries as well, as Parenti recognises:

> Under the free trade agreements any and all public services can be ruled out of existence because they cause "lost market opportunities" for private capital. So too public hospitals can be charged with taking away markets from private hospitals; and public water supply systems, public schools, public libraries, public housing and public transportation are guilty of depriving their private counterparts of market opportunities, likewise public health insurance, public mail delivery, and public auto insurance systems. Laws that try to protect the environment or labor standards or consumer health already have been overthrown for "creating barriers" to free trade.[100]

This section brings together articles on the theme of equality within an overall democratic framework—but this time within the British public library context. Crucial to the attainment of equality is the inclusion of the political framework missing from much of "professional" literature, especially in Britain.

---

[99] Parenti, Michael (2007): Globalization and democracy: some basics. 26 May, 2007. Available at: http://www.countercurrents.org/parenti260507.htm. [Accessed: 27 May 2007].
[100] Ibid.

Black communities and information workers in search of social justice (1999)[101]

The struggle for Black librarianship[102]

A matter of social justice in the LIS sector is crying out for a solution: institutional racism in information services. The unstated but implied question, which goes to the root of the matter is: does institutionalised racism exist in British society in general and in libraries in particular? Following the Stephen Lawrence Inquiry Report[103], almost every profession has begun to address the question of institutional racism within its ranks. Thus local authorities, lawyers, the police, trade unions, the National Health Service, housing associations, education, broadcasting, the press—all have begun dialogues to examine their own policies and practices in relation to racism. Among the few professions which has stood in silence is the Library Association ...

But the Library Association—"the most authoritative voice on library and information matters" by its own estimation[104]—finds nothing to say about racism in the profession. It is satisfied with its Equal Opportunities sub-committee taking whatever limited action it can take, given its limited powers.

This lack of official interest in the association means either that there is no institutional racism in LIS, or that it is so ingrained that it will not even admit to its very existence. The issues of the powerless of Black LIS workers and of their concentration in lower, non-decision making positions is linked to the lack of adequate service to Black communities.

Yet ample evidence exists to indicate that there is a deep-rooted institutional racism in the sector.

Some examples of racism in Britain in general and in the LIS field are given in the author's forthcoming working paper.[105] Other evidence of the existence of institutionalised racism in the public library field is now easily available. Olden, Tseng, and Mcharazo[106] and Roach and Morrison[107] have done useful work in

---

[101] New Library World, Vol. 100 (6) 1999 ISSN 0307-4803. pp. 265–279), Copyright © 1999 MCB. All rights reserved

[102] The term Black is used in its political sense to include all people from Africa, Asia, and the Caribbean and all those who consider themselves Black.

[103] The Stephen Lawrence Inquiry. Report of an inquiry by Sir William Macpherson of Cluny (1999). London: The Stationery Office 1999 . Cm 4262-I. Available at: http://www.archive.official-documents.co.uk/document/cm42/4262/4262.htm. [Accessed: 24 August 2007].

[104] Library Association. Annual Report. 1998.

[105] Durrani, Shiraz (2000): Struggle against racial exclusion in libraries; A fight for the rights of the people. Open to All? The Public library and social exclusion. (2000) Vol. 3: Working Paper 13, pp.254-349. London: Resource: The Council for Museums, Archives and Libraries. Available at: http://www.seapn.org.uk/opentoall.html [Accessed: 02 April 2007].

[106] Olden, A., Tseng, C.-P. and Mcharazo, A.A. (1996), A Review of the Published Literature on Black and Ethnic Minority/Multicultural Provision by Public Libraries in the United

exploring issues of racism in LIS. Pioneering work by Black and Ethnic Minority Workers Group (BWG), Hackney, with its report to DNH[108], numerous articles in *Hackney Libraries News*[109] and minutes of its meetings all provide perhaps the only written documentation of institutional racism in local authorities in Britain.

This is not to say that no attempts have been made to make the association address the issue of institutional racism in the profession.

...

Hackney's Black Workers Group also raises the question of whether racism exists in the library service:

> What is essential in this ongoing struggle is that we do not take an ostrich-like attitude and pretend that there is no racism in the library service. This attitude objectively serves those who advocate racism. It is better to admit that racism exists in library service — as it does in the society outside the library. There is no shame in admitting a truth. It is in fact wrong not to admit it. Once its existence is admitted ways can then be found to combat it.[110]

...

Such managers see institutionalised and individual acts of racism as results of "poor management" or "poor communication". Black staff who struggle against racism in various ways are often condemned as "emotional", "lazy", and accused of "using the race card". Victims of racism are condemned as liars because they cannot produce evidence of the existence of institutionalised racism, when by its very nature racism is hidden and operates at an underground level. The onus is always on the victims of racism to produce proof of racism, never on those perpetrating racism to produce proofs of their "non-racism". Asking victims of racism to prove the existence of racism is victimising the victim.

Allegations of racism are dealt with differently by different managers and in different workplaces. This results in having double standards in management practices, one for white staff and one for Black staff. This was raised, for example, at the Black Librarians' meeting organised by the Equal Opportunities Sub-Committee of the Library Association. Black workers who raise the question of workplace racism are subject to extreme pressures. This is mentioned in *Hackney Libraries News*:

> The existence of double standards in everyday work: mistakes by white staff are quickly forgiven, those by black ones result in severe punishment. Black staff need to be super efficient, white ones can get by with mediocrity. Black qualified staff remain on lower grades for ever or they resign in disgust. White ones find it easier to move

---

Kingdom, British Library Research & Development Department, Boston Spa, R & D Report 6204, 39 pp.

[107] Roach, P. and Morrison, M. (1998), Public Libraries, Ethnic Diversity and Citizenship, Centre for Research in Ethnic Relations, University of Warwick, Warwick.

[108] Black and Ethnic Minority Workers Group (BWG) Hackney (1994): Library Services for Black and Ethnic Minority nationalities in the UK: a report prepared for the Department of National Heritage (DNH) Review of Public Libraries. London: Hackney Library Services. See: Review of the Public Library Service in England and Wales. Aslib, 1995. ISBN 0 85142 353 1. Some information about the report available at: http://panizzi.shef.ac.uk/library-review/index.html [Accessed: 24 August 2007].

[109] Hackney Libraries News, Issues for 1993-94 carry a number of informative articles by Hackney Library's Black Workers Group on the existence of work practices that the Group indicates were inspired by racism.

[110] Hackney Libraries News (1993): Racism in Hackney Library Service. No. 11, pp. 14-16.

up, although there are a few "unfavoured" ones who have joined their black colleagues at the bottom of the heap. These "unfavoured" ones are often the articulate, the class conscious or strong union supporters — in other words "troublemakers".[111]

It is convenient and less stressful for (racist) managers to ignore the problems created by racism than to admit it exists and then be forced to take action against colleagues and friends in order to eliminate racism.

…

Once the existence of institutionalised racism is accepted, many possible ways of combating it can be explored. It is necessary to practice what can be called "Black librarianship" in order to eliminate racism. But this will immediately give rise to the question "Does Black librarianship exist?" The wide range of issues raised by Olden, Tseng, and Mcharazo[112] poses fundamental questions about the LIS profession as a whole. If the social and professional issues raised are ever to be addressed seriously and resolved, then the concept of Black librarianship itself needs to be recognised as a way of providing solutions. Reforming a basically Euro-centric library system by "bolting-on" some marginal policies to address race discrimination will not solve the basic problems. Nor will a token service to Black communities address their real information needs. A new concept and vision of service to Black communities is the only way of providing a relevant service to the dispossessed and excluded communities. Hackney Libraries took the appropriate step by producing *Vision Statement on Services to Black and Minority Ethnic Communities*,[113] perhaps the first such vision in Britain.

The lack of recognition of the need for special library practices to address problems of racism (broadly described as Black librarianship) is related to the lack of recognition of racism itself and an absence of the will to eliminate racism. The one is dependent on the other. By accepting the existence of Black librarianship, one implicitly accepts the existence of racism. Thus the first step in resolving the problems of lack of service to Black communities and the poor working environment for Black librarians is to accept the concept of Black librarianship, which can then become one of the tools of combating racism in libraries.

The two aspects of Black librarianship — service to Black communities and the work environment — are areas that require more attention from policy makers, library management and workers. Better community and outreach services address issues related to the economic, cultural and social needs of Black people. Improving the work environment for Black staff involves improving job and career prospects and ensuring fair work practices. Empowering Black staff and communities to be part of the real decision-making process in a structured, organised way, and generally creating more friendly working conditions for Black staff can result in improving services to Black communities.

Black communities and their information needs

It is necessary to examine the different Black communities and to understand their particular information needs. What, for example, prevents them from making

---

[111] Ibid.
[112] Olden, A., Tseng, C.-P. and Mcharazo, A.A. (1996): op. cit.
[113] London Borough of Hackney Library Services (1996): Vision statement on services to Black and Minority Ethnic communities. London: London Borough of Hackney Library Service.

full use of the traditional library which, in theory at least, has all the information that its local community needs?

...

One of the recommendations made by Hackney's Black Workers Group was:

> We need to go beyond the present "Equal Opportunities" policies and work on a new "national" vision and a strategic approach and framework. Standards of service for BEM communities must be set up, with procedures for monitoring their implementation.[114]

The majority of libraries see no need to change their traditional system as the new Black communities did not have sufficient economic and political clout to force a change in local services. An analysis of the first year of Annual Library Plans indicates that most authorities achieved poor results in issues surrounding "social exclusion" which incorporates exclusion based on race. Black librarians at the meeting organised by the Equal Opportunity Sub-committee lamented the lack of resources available for Black material. Even when the so-called "outreach" services such as housebound services existed, the chances were that they concentrated on services to non-Black communities.

...

It is then clear that a library service that claims to address the needs of all its actual and potential users needs to be proactive in seeking out their potential users. Developments to date do not provide evidence that this has happened in a systematic or organised way.

Change will only come when there are enough Black librarians in the position of power at local and national level. Those who wield power in the profession also control finances, research grants and make policies. It is a sad fact of the British society in the late 1990s that there are few, if any, Black librarians among this élite. A quick survey of the heads of public libraries—for example at the Association of London Chief Librarians—and of a meeting of the Library Association's Council will again show the lack of Black faces. Indeed many progressive white librarians feel equally concerned about this lack of fairness in the profession, yet are powerless to change the situation.

The unequal relations of power within the profession ensure that a so-called neutral position is taken on social, cultural and political issues, which are then dismissed as not being relevant to the needs of the "profession" which is supposed to be above such "unprofessional" matters. Far from ensuring neutrality, the view that the profession does not need to get involved in "politics" has in fact helped to serve the interest of one race and one class against the needs of others. Such views have made the profession seem irrelevant to those whose needs have largely been ignored.

Many members of Black communities and Black information workers feel that the library profession has failed to meet its own fundamental requirement: that libraries should first serve its users. Yes, they serve—but only insofar as the population is mainly white and petty bourgeois. When it comes to Black people, or working classes, this maxim seems not to be important. They are not considered a library's "natural users". Token service is considered good enough for them, especially if there are no organised protests from the community. Examples of how Black library workers see

---

[114] Black and Ethnic Minority Workers Group (BWG) Hackney (1994): op. cit.

the profession's failure to meet the needs of Black communities are found in *Hackney Libraries News*.[115]

Winston provides a similar view from the U.S.A.:

> Diversity as a value is quite a bit easier to articulate than it is to put into practice or make a priority in the minds of librarians and staff. What has become apparent to me is not everyone who voices support for diversity is equally committed to making the day-to-day decisions (and sacrifices) needed to institutionalize diversity and to create an environment conducive to the success of minority staff and patrons.[116]

Some White petty bourgeois groups can be extremely articulate in demanding — and getting — the lion's share of library resources at the expense of Black communities, and the working class as a whole. They are well connected to local or national political forces in power. They sometimes monopolise the use of valuable library exhibition space, meeting halls, or office space. It is very difficult to change the usage in order to allow, "excluded" communities the same facilities. This is confirmed by Roach and Morrison:

> The principles of "universality" as expressed in the Public Libraries and Museums Act of 1964, rather than enabling, actually defeats equality by imposing a standard based on the needs of the most powerful or influential groups whilst failing to recognise needs of less powerful or influential groups. In this way it has been possible for individual public library services to promote access for all whilst continuing to deliver, at best, colour blind (or, at worst, ethnically biased) service provision.[117]

Black communities and librarians have not yet established an equivalent power base.

Resistance to racism

It is not only the issues of Black library service that are ignored overall. The existence of the resistance to racism in the LIS field has also been similarly ignored by library educators and "mainstream" publications. It is true that in every workplace where there is racism, there is inevitably resistance to it — however open or underground it may be. For those seeking proof of this, I would recommend a visit to any workplace where there are Black information workers — but such resistance will become obvious only to those sympathetic to the cause.

...

Among the tools used to suppress the resistance of Black librarians is the extremely hostile work environment which has left the Black librarian isolated — culturally, socially, ideologically and often physically — in the workplace. Even when Black staff make up a majority of staff, they are usually at the lowest level. Thus the decision-making process is controlled by a well-knit white petty bourgeois leadership (male and female) which claims to be "colour blind" — in effect not wanting to understand racism, let alone trying to combat it. This élite controls the prevailing work policies and practices and buys out the loyalty of middle and lower levels of management (who are often racist themselves anyway) by means of small favours

---

[115] Hackney Libraries News (1993): op. cit.,
[116] Winston, M (1996) The minority librarian: why your role is different. in: Neely, T. and Abif, K. (1996) : In Our Own Voices; The Changing Face of Librarianship. Lanham, Md, USA, The Scarecrow Press, pp. 386-407.
[117] Roach, Patrick and Morrison, M (1998): Public libraries, ethnic diversity and citizenship. (British Library Research and Innovation Report 76). Coventry: CEDAR, University of Warwick.

and as a result of a perceived common interest. These facts are well documented, for instance in the minutes of Hackney's Black Workers Group, their articles in *Hackney Libraries News* as well as points raised by Black librarians at the meetings organised by the Equal Opportunities Sub-committee of the Library Association.

...

The full history of the struggle of the Black communities and of the Black librarians for a relevant library and information service has yet to be written. The Commission for Racial Equality (CRE)[118] and Roach and Morrison[119] have provided not only evidence of the problem but possible solutions.

Suffering from the glass ceiling

The situation in the U.S.A. is perhaps not so different in terms of the struggle that Black communities and librarians have to wage in Britain. A recent publication from the U.S.A. documents the struggle for equality waged by American librarians of colour. Abif explains the current situation; "Discussions have been taking place since the 1960s regarding the recruitment and retention of librarians of color. The past ten years has seen no real change".[120]

Yet in one sense at least, Black librarians in the U.S.A. have made more progress than those in Britain. They are better organised (e.g. they have formed a powerful Black Caucus within the American Library Association); more of them are getting higher level jobs, and they seem to have some control over the publishing field and manage to get into print their struggles "in their own voices". Black British librarians have not yet made any progress in controlling or being able to use the established professional journals, nor to publish their own books or have any control in the publishing field. If they are to articulate their struggles effectively, and indeed to form a unified front to combat racism, they will have to pay attention to the publishing field. In the final analysis, racism can only be defeated by uniting all anti-racist forces — black and white. This can be achieved only on the basis of regular and systematic exchange of views and practices to forge a common strategy. A dedicated press is essential for this. Any resistance movement, which ignores this fact does so at its peril. Developments in information and communications technology offer new opportunities, which need to be grabbed by those seeking a way out of "social exclusion".

Some things will never change…?

"Some things will never change", says Flowers. "It was obvious that racism played a key role in the office politics that surrounded me on a daily basis. … The bottom line—some things will never change".[121]

The situation is no different in British libraries. It does not take long for a group of Black librarians meeting for the first time to establish deep sympathy and understanding with each other on the basis of an exchange of common experiences of

---

[118] See: http://www.cre.gov.uk/ [Accessed: 24 August 2007].
[119] Roach, P. and Morrison, M. (1998): op.cit.
[120] Abif, K. (1996), "Epilogue", in Neely, T. and Abif, K., In Our Own Voices; The Changing Face of Librarianship, The Scarecrow Press, Lanham, MD, p. 408.
[121] Flowers, J. (1996), From paraprofessional to professional: the changing role of an African American librarian. In Neely, T. Y and Abif, K. K. In Our Own Voices; The Changing Face of Librarianship. Lanham, Md, USA, The Scarecrow Press, p.226.

racism at workplaces. But their discussions, experiences and solutions are not part of the "mainstream" issues of "professional" concern. Whenever such "ugly" topics of racism at workplaces arise at "polite" meetings, there are embarrassed silences all around and it is subtly made clear to the unfortunate victim of racism that their problems are not due to racism but are really a result of their own personal and professional shortcomings. In any case, it is made very clear, such issues should not be aired in public.

They who hold the stick ...

It is the lack of Black LIS workers in senior management and decision-making posts that has distorted library services to Black communities and provided a poor work environment for Black staff. The lack of Black staff at senior decision-making levels means that all policies and practices of relevance to Black communities have to be sanctioned by white managers.

What then are prospects for a non-racist library service? An indication of how the needs of Black people are considered officially is provided in the "largest piece of research into public libraries ever undertaken in the world"[122] Olden et al. point out, "Black and ethnic minority/multicultural provision is not treated at length" in the Review.[123]

Hackney Library's Black and Ethnic Minority (BME) Workers Group makes the following comment on the draft report:

> It is very disappointing and disheartening that the Draft DNH Report by ASLIB Consultancy has not included any evidence of special research/survey nor special recommendations for improving public library services to Black and Ethnic Minority (BEM) Nationalities. By this omission, the ASLIB Report assumes that the British society is homogeneous. It is therefore indirectly discriminatory to providing services to BEM nationalities.[124]

The Group provided a 20-page detailed report with recommendations on improving services to Black communities. It gave specific recommendations on staffing, funding, service delivery (including outreach, community links, promotion), education and training, and new technology.

...

But one important lesson to be learnt by Black librarians is that of "self-empowerment". As Prime says, "One of the things that I think is the biggest croak about empowerment is the idea that anybody can empower us; you have to be self-empowered".[125] Until this process of self-empowerment takes place among Black communities and Black library workers, there is little hope for any real, meaningful change.

At the same time, those struggling against racism need to learn a few lessons. It is important to relate the struggles within libraries to two important struggles outside the library: the anti-racist struggle in the society outside, and to the class struggle

---

[122] Review of the Public Library Service in England and Wales. Aslib, 1995. ISBN 0 85142 353 1. Some information about the report available at: http://panizzi.shef.ac.uk/library-review/index.html [Accessed: 24 August 2007].
[123] Olden, A., Tseng, C.-P. and Mcharazo, A.A. (1996): op. cit. (p. 29).
[124] Black and Ethnic Minority Workers Group (BWG) Hackney (1994): op. cit.
[125] Prime, E. (1998) High Profile: Eugenie Prime. SepiaNews; Libraries, Community & Technology (New York) Spring 1998. [<sepianews@juno.com>]. Accessed 3 July 1999.

within a capitalist society. Pateman[126] provides a well-researched discussion on the issue of classes in libraries. But these are taboo subjects in a "pure profession" such as librarianship. For those who take anti-racism, and struggle against exploitation and oppression seriously, there is only one way ahead: librarians need to be active participants in the social and class struggles in the society as a whole. Librarians are not an isolated group, vacuum-packed on library shelves. They are part of the larger struggles in the society.

A united front of all progressive people — Black and White — is the only force that can defeat racism. There are many progressive White people ready to join hands with Black people struggling for their rights. One of the main tasks is to identify all progressive people. Only by joint action will we ensure "equal" service for all. The struggle will be hard and long, but hopefully things will change. The Government's initiatives in addressing issues of "social exclusion" provide a new framework for the LIS workers to take a strategic approach to addressing the issues of racism in the information services. Without such a strategic approach, it will be very difficult, if not impossible, to eliminate racism.

In the final analysis, our goal is to make diversity "less of an issue", as Winston says:

> Our goal should not be to raise issues of diversity simply to hear ourselves talk or "keep our agenda on the table," but to create libraries with the staff, collections, policies, and services that embody diversity as a value so that it is far less of an issue.[127]

All LIS workers need to take up this challenge.

Combating racism in library and information services (2000)[128]

It is generally accepted today that the needs of Black communities are not being met by public libraries. This is shown, for example, by Roach & Morrison[129] who concluded that the "public library service has not yet managed to engage fully with ethnically diverse communities (and that) there is a lack of clear vision and leadership on ethnic diversity and racial equality matters within the public library service". A similar conclusion was reached by the Stephen Lawrence Inquiry[130] for local government services as a whole. More recently, this point of view was confirmed by

---

[126] Pateman, J (1999) Social exclusion and class. Working Paper No. 3. Open to All? The Public library and social exclusion. (2000) Vol. 3: Working Paper 3, London:Resource: The Council for Museums, Archives and Libraries. Vol. 3 available at:
http://www.seapn.org.uk/publication.html.
[127] Winston, M (1996): op.cit.
[128] Editorial. Information for Social Change. No. 11 (2000). Available at:
http://libr.org/isc/issues/isc11.pdf [Accessed: 27 August 2007].
[129] Roach, P. and Morrison, M. (1998): op.cit.
[130] Stephen Lawrence Inquiry: op.cit.

the Social Exclusion Unit,[131] which concluded that "people from minority ethnic communities are at disproportionate risk of social exclusion (and that) racial discrimination plays an important role in the disproportionate social exclusion experienced by people from minority ethnic communities".

Similarly, Black library and information workers are not allowed to play any significant role in deciding, implementing (except at the lowest level) and monitoring policies. The serious nature of the problem is reflected by the fact that out of over 25,000 personal members of the Library Association, only 1.2 percent—i.e. 286 individual members—are of African, Caribbean or Asian background. Even more worrying, only 3 Black members earned over £27,000 p.a.[132] What this means to individual Black members is reflected in one of the contributions in this issue of *Information for Social Change*—Case Studies and Comments. Going by some recent publications and some of the articles in this issue, the situation in the U.S.A., although marginally better, is not one to give hope that the concerns are seriously being addressed, by those in power in the LIS sector in U.S.A. either.

Yet there is no lack of ideas and actions for addressing this social injustice. The Comission for Racial Equality standards[133] provides an excellent tool to the struggle against racial discrimination, as shown by Susan White in her contribution in this issue. These Standards have been around for a long time, yet they have made no overall difference on the ground. At the same time, there are a number of other studies, reports, guidelines and recommended action that can help to change the situation, as shown in the "Combating racism checklist". Yet, as the reports on the last two years' Annual Library Plan indicate social exclusion has not been addressed adequately by most library authorities. A similar conclusion is reached by "Open to all?"[134]

To make matters worse, there is a lack of forum where racial discrimination in the public library service can be debated and possible solutions discussed. Few, if any, Black Library worker groups with significant power exist. Few, if any, authorities have the mechanism to consult, in a meaningful way, Black communities and Black LIS workers so that they can influence library policy, monitor implementation and ensure that the outcomes meet their needs. No journals or books exist to document the struggles of Black communities and workers for justice. The profession as a whole, dominated by white, male, middle class power-holders seem to have decided that if they do not acknowledge that there is injustice and discrimination in the service they provide, the problems will disappear.

It is for this reason that *Information for Social Change* is devoting this issue to combating racism in library and information services. What we need desperately today is an open debate about what the problems are and a discussion of new ideas

---

[131] Social Exclusion Unit (2000), Minority Ethnic Issues in Social Exclusion and Neighbourhood Renewal; a guide to the work of the SEU and the Policy Action Teams so far. Available at: http://archive.cabinetoffice.gov.uk/seu/publicationse340.html?did=114. [Accessed: 05 May 2007].
[132] Khan, Ayub (2000): Stamping out institutional racism. Library Association Record 102(1) pp. 38-39.
[133] Commission for Racial Equality (CRE, 1998): A standard for racial equality for local government; racial equality means quality; a standard for racial equality for local government in England and Wales. London: CRE.
[134] Open to All? Op.cit. Vol. 3: Working Paper 13. pp.254-349.Available at: http://www.seapn.org.uk/opentoall.html. Accessed 30 August 2007.

on how to address these problems. Many authorities and individuals are already doing much to address the issue, as shown by some articles in this issue. We hope this issue of *Information for Social Change* will help to carry this discussion to a higher level. The joint LINK-ISC Conference in November will provide another opportunity to come together and look at more creative and innovative ways of eliminating racism from society.

"Change, like death, is inevitable", Nduthu,[135] a Kenyan freedom fighter said. It remains to be seen if we, as a profession, change willingly and remain in control of the new agenda — otherwise forces of social change will surely drag us to a new, just and "equal" society.

Struggle against racial exclusion in public libraries (2000)[136]

Introduction: A library in every home

This year marks the 150th anniversary of the Public Libraries Act. Yet we are nowhere near having a system that provides "libraries for all" after this long period. Indeed we are still debating what this term means. We are not short of resources or ideas that can put a "library and information in every home." Why is it that Cuba can have such a vision which is rapidly being put into practice in spite of limited resources and a 40 year economic blockade, yet Britain "celebrates" 150 years of a public library system that has not reached at least 50 percent of the people whose needs are perhaps more urgent?

The fact that we still need to struggle against an exclusive library and information service at the beginning of the 21st century is indeed a sad one. Over the last 150 years, the world has seen major revolutions in every field. We have come to understand and control the forces of nature through enormous developments in science; human welfare is at a stage where there is a theoretical possibility for the material needs of every human being to be met; our understanding of the social forces ruling our lives has enabled major social and economic revolutions to take place. Developments in information and communications technologies have revolutionised the way we organise and use information.

Yet there are major contradictions in every aspect of life. With all the necessary natural and human resources readily available, a large proportion of the world goes hungry; while little or no resources are available to provide safe drinking water to every child in the world, vast fortunes are spent every day in military expenditure. With all the talk of democracy, most people of the world have no control over their lives. A few individuals control resources that total more than the combined wealth of

---

[135] Nduthu, Karimi: a life in the struggle (1998). London: Vita Books. ISBN 1-869886-12-7.
[136] Open to All? Op.cit. Vol. 3: Working Paper 13. pp.254-349.Available at: http://www.seapn.org.uk/opentoall.html. Accessed 30 August 2007.

billions of people. A few transnationals have cornered the wealth of the world in order to extract even more wealth for themselves.

The reason for this basic contradiction is seldom mentioned in the information field, yet it affects everything we do. This state of affairs is inevitable under capitalism, which is based on private ownership of the means of production. Its distribution system has nothing to do with equality: its main interest is in making profits for the few. It creates a divided society: a powerful few and powerless majority. Its relentless globalised march leads to imperialist plunders that replicates its divided society around the globe. It should then not surprise us that a system based on addressing the greed of a few creates millions of people who are "excluded" from even the basic means of survival. It would indeed be surprising if capitalism did produce an "equal, all-inclusive" society.

After hundreds of years of capitalist development, the people in the "West" have ended up with a divided society with millions who are excluded from the benefits that advanced technologies make possible. The ranks of the "excluded" include working people, Black communities, disabled people, lesbians, bisexuals, gay men and transgendered people as well as other communities whose needs are considered in other Working Papers of this Project.

It is in this context that we need to see the struggle of the Black communities in Britain today. They suffer from racist oppression as well as class exploitation. Thus their struggles are not restricted to library and information fields. What are the forces that stop us, as a society, from tackling racism in LIS services? Why have most white LIS "professionals" not accepted — in theory and practice — that the service they have created and wish to maintain today actively discriminates against Black communities and Black LIS workers? The very facts that Black people have to "prove" that their needs have not been met, that the voices of Black communities and LIS workers are nowhere to be heard, that their absence from the ranks of policy makers bothers few white policy makers, are proof enough that we have a racist library service. Perhaps it will need a white judge to pronounce the existence of racism before the LIS "establishment" accepts that the British library service is a racist one and starts taking action.

It is ironic that it was the resources from the majority world that enabled Britain to enjoy the wealth that enabled services like public libraries to be established. Yet people from the majority world in Britain today are among those "socially excluded" from the public library services.

Perhaps, all this will automatically be dismissed by some as of no relevance to the LIS community, as a matter of politics, which is supposedly miles away from libraries. But the basis of exclusion is the lack of power among Black communities and Black LIS workers. This inevitably takes us into the political field.

The changes needed to make libraries relevant to the needs of the working classes and Black people cannot come about unless libraries examine their role in the wider social context. It is the lack of direction and commitment at a national level that prevented developments in the past. With the new emphasis that the Government is placing on "social exclusion", there is a real possibility for change. A new set of tools is now available to ensure meaningful change.

Yet there are many barriers, both within the profession and within the wider society, which prevent the leap to a new service. If the difficulties are to be overcome, there needs to be a joint approach between Black communities, all positive workers in libraries and in Council departments (as well as other professions) to push for change.

There should also be a joint approach by all those excluded from libraries to create a service that looks after the needs of all those currently excluded.

There is an urgent need for a change in thinking on the part of those who hold power in libraries and local authorities. The first step is to admit that all is not well in the library world. As Sir Herman Ouseley said, "To tackle an illness, one must first accept one is ill."[137] A new vision of an all-inclusive, non-racist library service is urgently needed.

This paper looks at the library scene from a wide social and political point of view. It also takes a brief look at race issues outside the UK, as the experiences and ways of combating racism in other fields and other countries have valuable lessons for us. Too often issues in the library are seen in isolation from their social and political context. Too often libraries operate in an environment sealed from new creative ideas and developments in other fields and countries. This narrow outlook then prevents us from looking for broader solutions, which others are trying out. We thus lose the benefits of finding real solutions in a cooperative way. This paper deliberately places emphasis on looking at racism in the wider British society as well as looking at experiences in other countries. The debate in the LIS sector desperately needs to be informed by examples of combating racism in its wider national and international context. Its resolution in LIS will not be achieved in isolation, but will be informed by solutions tried out in the wider society, which are again influenced by successes or failures in other countries.

Concerns within the library field are taken up in the author's other papers mentioned in the Note and in the References. The Recommendations flow from issues raised in this paper and in its companion papers as well as from discussions at various conferences.

Part 1: Understanding race and class oppression

Six percent of the British population is Black, i.e. 2.2 million people of working age. This comparatively small proportion of population faces racism, which has become one of the greatest social and economic issues of our time. Racism is so much a part of life in Europe today that it is often seen as something inevitable, something based on "scientific fact". Yet modern science has shown that the biological category of "race" is meaningless when applied to the human species. "Biologically, the human species shares a common gene pool, and there is much more genetic variation within each so-called racial group than between them."[138]

It is at the economic, social and political level that racism has had profound effects on the lives of millions of people. Belonging to an oppressed race has often been used as justification for inequalities in the distribution of power, resources, advantages and benefits.

Hall captures the reality of racism in Britain today and sees the connection between racial oppression and economic exploitation; "The practices of racialised exclusion, racially compounded disadvantage, household poverty, unemployment and educational under-achievement persist, indeed, multiply".[139]

---

[137] Marks, K (1998): Trying to clarify the linguistic confusion. The Independent (London). October 16, 1998:8.

[138] TUC (1996): United against racism in Europe; tackling racism and xenophobia in Europe – a TUC handbook for shop stewards. London: Trade Union Congress.

[139] Hall, Stuart (2000): From Scarman to Lawrence. Connections. Spring 2000.

TUC[140] draws distinction between "personal racism" and "institutional racism." TUC[141] mentions "direct and indirect discrimination". All these aspects need to be addressed in libraries. John points to the ever-present existence of racism in our society:

> We live in a society with an overarching culture of racism that is all pervasive. Culture underpins and underlines racialisation of oppression, immigration, crime, and also of resistance to oppression itself. It is not possible to appreciate other oppressions (e.g. of women) without understanding this.[142]

John pinpointed a particular problem of racism that exists in LIS as well: "There is too little recognition of the fact that this society validates white people automatically while constantly expecting Black people to be proving ourselves".[143] The manifestation of such validations can be seen at every work place in LIS.

Moving the Centre

Thiong'o sees "moving the centre to correct the imbalances of the last four hundred years"[144] as a crucial step to win the struggle for liberation. It is worth examining Thiong'o's thoughts as they provide a dynamic analysis of the problems of oppression and their possible solutions. "I am concerned," says Thiong'o, "in moving the centre in two senses at least":

> One is the need to move the centre from its assumed location in the West to a multiplicity in all the cultures of the world. The assumed location of the centre of the universe in the West is what goes by the term Eurocentrism, an assumption, which developed with the domination of the world by a handful of Western nations... The Eurocentric basis of looking at the world is present in all areas (including) economic, political and... cultural studies.

A serious look at public library policy and practice reveals a Eurocentric approach, with the achievements and indeed the very existence of other cultures and practices merely given a nod in tokenistic projects. When the pressure to "move the centre" becomes too strong, cosmetic changes are made to release pressure for fundamental change. Such was the case, for example, when the name of a Library in Hackney was changed to C.L.R. James Library, but the essence of its work remained the same as before. The Eurocentric forces have gotten even stronger with the end of the USSR, which had provided a (less powerful, perhaps) second centre.

Thiong'o then looks at the second level at which the centre needs to move:

> Within nearly all nations today the centre is located in the dominant social stratum, a male bourgeois minority. But since many of the male bourgeois minorities in the

---

[140] op.cit.
[141] TUC (1998): Union Action for race equality; a negotiators' guide. London, Labour Research Department, Trade Union Congress.
[142] John, Gus (1995): Equality and Entitlement. Talk given by Gus John, Director, Directorate of Education and Leisure Services to Library Staff at Stamford Hill Library on Thursday February 23, 1995. (from notes made by the present author).
[143] John, Gus (1999): Talk given at the Conference The Significance Of The Stephen Lawrence Inquiry For Public Libraries. London and Home Counties Branch: The Library Association in association with the Association of London Chief Librarians (ALCL). Executive Briefing: 28 June.
[144] Thiong'o, Thiong'o wa (1993): Moving the centre; the struggle for cultural freedoms. London: James Currey.

world are still dominated by the West we are talking about the domination of the world, including the West, by a Eurocentric bourgeois, male and racial minority. Hence the need to move the centre from all minority class establishments within nations to the real creative centres among the working people in conditions of gender, racial and religious equality...Moving the centre in the two senses — between nations and within nations — will contribute to the freeing of world cultures from the restrictive walls of nationalism, class, race and gender.[145]

Thiong'o thus provides a basis for understanding issues of race, class and other forms of oppression, at international as well as at national levels. If the information field is to liberate itself, there is an urgent need to move the centre from the restrictive walls built by what Black[146] calls "the strength of the middle-class pressure exerted on the public library over 150 years". It is also interesting to note that Thiong'o has already moved the centre as far as the concept of majority/minority and language-use are concerned: the white "majority" of the West becomes "a Eurocentric bourgeois, male and racial minority" and the so-called Black "minorities" have become the majority in a truly world-wide perspective. It never fails to satisfy me, for example, to reflect that while I am a minority Gujarati speaker in Britain, Gujarati in India is spoken by more people than the entire population of Britain. Which "minority" do I belong to in a globalised world?

Five features of racism

Anybody really interested in understanding racism should read Thiong'o,[147] particularly Chapter 14, *The ideology of racism*. It is important to understand the "five interlinked features" which Thiong'o lists: obscurantism, divide and rule, political domination, exploitation, oppression.

Social and economic exclusion

Black people are "disproportionately deprived" in Britain. *Social Exclusion Unit*[148] finds that they are more likely than the rest of the population to live in poor areas, be unemployed, have low incomes, live in poor housing, have poor health and be victims of crime". It then looks at reasons why Black people are excluded.

Direct and indirect racial discrimination

An inadequate recognition and understanding of the complexities of ethnic minority groups, and hence services that fail to fit their circumstances and address their language, cultural and religious differences.

Social exclusion, of which racism is an important aspect, is an essential part of capitalism where social exclusion, social oppression and economic exploitation are the basis of organised life. The prevailing free market system ensures that economic activity satisfies the profit motives of the few, leaving the material, educational and

---

[145] op. cit.
[146] Black, Ian (2000): EU fights far right with laws on racism. The Guardian. May, 18. Available at:
http://www.guardianunlimited.co.uk/Archive/Article/0,4273,4019399,00.html. Accessed: May 21, 2000.
[147] Thiong'o: op.cit.
[148] Social Exclusion Unit Leaflet (2000). London: Cabinet Office. http://www.cabinet-office.gov.uk/seu/ Accessed: 24 April, 2000.

cultural needs of the majority of people unfulfilled. In this context, the issues of racial oppression and class exploitation are intertwined and cannot be considered in isolation. This also implies that racism is not a problem for Black people alone.

This essential connection between race and class should be kept in mind in any attempts to combat racism. This was emphasised in comments on the DCMS Guidance, *Libraries for All*:

> The social context in which English (and British) libraries exist is largely ignored in the Policy Guidance. The distribution of wealth and power in society as a whole influence the way public institutions such as libraries operate. The context of a society where private ownership of property and production for profit allow some to have excessive wealth, power and influence at the expense of the rest of the community needs to be taken into account. It is this reality, which leads to a large number of people being excluded from social wealth and power. Libraries cannot be seen in isolation from social forces all around them, nor can solutions be found if this reality is not understood.[149]

Kundnani refers to a "redefinition of equality" under New Labour:

> Equality as it used to be understood by Labour is now regarded as an outdated concept from before the Thatcher 'revolution'. It failed to recognise the importance of 'individual freedom' and 'economic pluralism'. What we have instead is equality of opportunity, with social mobility replacing redistribution. Instead of seeing the market as a system, which structurally produces and depends on inequality, the neoliberal view of the market as a rational and efficient system of rewards has been accepted wholesale...social exclusion no longer simply means a lack of access to material resources. It is now defined so that it refers to cultural attitudes as much as exclusion *per se*. Hence it can be combated by a change in perceptions... If Britain is a prejudiced country, it is not a matter of 'institutional' or 'structured' inequalities, it is a matter of cultural baggage tied to personal hang-ups.[150]

If the cause of inequality is incorrectly diagnosed in terms of its manifestations rather than its root causes, the solutions will obviously be similarly incorrect.

Language of exclusion...language of liberation

Liberation from any form of oppression implies a struggle at a cultural level. It requires those who struggle for liberation to first of all liberate their thinking from that imposed on them by the forces that seek to exclude them.

Thus the struggles that Black people need to engage in include the cultural front, at the level of language. The English language itself, as well as the meaning of English words commonly used and understood in the British society today often alienates Black people. For example, the term "asylum seeker", when applied to people from the majority world, has begun to have an automatic context of "bogus" added to it by actions of some media and politicians. White refugees from Zimbabwe are welcomed as citizens of Britain, while South Asian British citizens from East Africa become "economic and political migrants". It is not only the *form* of such communications (i.e. the language) that is racist; it is the *content* itself that is racist. Such distortion of

---

[149] Durrani, Shiraz (2009): Comments submitted to the Department for Media Culture, Media and Sport (DCMS): on Libraries for all – A tool for change? A review of Libraries for All: Social Inclusion in Public Libraries; Policy Guidance for Local Authorities in England. October 1999.

[150] Kundnani, Arun (2000): 'Stumbling on': race, class and England. Race and Class. 41(4) pp. 1-18.

language to serve a racist agenda is another indication of the existence of racism in Britain today.

It is for this reason that an essential aspect of resistance to racism is an assertion of the right of majority world languages to exist, as well as the creation of language and terms that serve the needs of Black communities struggling against racism. Thus the language of liberation is engaged in a fierce battle with the language of oppression. Young Black people have evolved their own language to oppose the imposed meanings of the "Queen's" English. Internationally, the "English" language of BBC is opposed by the "english" language of the people of majority world who have had to use the language of the former colonial power as a medium of communication.

The struggle at the level of language should be understood correctly as it reflects the struggle for liberation from racial exclusion. It is in this context that the terms and language we use should be understood. Such an understanding should then inform our policies and practices. In order to understand better the on-going debate about racism, it is important to be clear about the terms we use. Language can often play a divisive role if words and terms mean different things to different people. Use of terms and phrases should help us to understand social reality, not obscure facts and lead to confused thinking. We next examine a few terms in common use today to see their marginalising context, which helps to further exclude people of colour and the working classes.

Social and economic exclusion

"Social inclusion/exclusion" shows only a partial picture and is likely to lead the thinking of policy-makers and those excluded to a partial solution of the real problem. A better term would be *social and economic exclusion* as it takes on board not only the social *effects* of exclusion, but also the economic *causes* of exclusion. With this clarity of the problem and its effects, it will be easier to find appropriate resolutions to the problems. It also gives dignity to the excluded individuals and communities who are then seen not as being responsible for their exclusion, but as victims of economic and social forces in an increasingly globalised world created by transnationals as a means of increasing their profits.

...

However the effects of racism on the white community are perceived, there is no doubt that the effects of racism on Black working people has been devastating. While it is "less and less fashionable these days to consider too explicitly the kinds of costs that slavery and colonialism exacted",[151] the effects on the colonised and enslaved nations and Black people cannot be ignored. The Trade Union Congress looks for roots of racism in political and economic factors: "The background to racial discrimination lies in Britain's colonial past and willingness of governments and employers to see Black workers as a source of cheap labour".[152] The TUC publication points out an important fact about racism, which is often ignored — that racism is not merely a matter of a struggle between people of different colour. The crucial factor is power — "power to dominate, to exploit, and to abuse". It is the use of power by the white-controlled Western society against Black people that is the basis of racism. TUC

---

[151] Williams, Patricia J. (1997), The Genealogy of race. The 1997 Reith Lecture, No. 5. London: BBC. [Transcript, p.7].
[152] TUC (Reprinted 1989): Tackling racism; a TUC workbook. London: Trade Union Congress.

explains the process of how racism has become embedded and institutionalised in the British society:

> Western society is a white-controlled society, which has been built on the exploitation of the rest of the world. This exploitation at first was economic—extracting precious metals, slaves, commodities and foodstuffs from Africa, South America, and Asia. But it quickly led to ideas about the superiority of European people over others, as a way of justifying the behaviour of European traders and colonisers. These ideas appeared in literature, religion, and popular entertainment, and they became established in the way subjects like history and geography were taught in schools and colleges…So you don't have to be an "oppressor" or "exploiter" to be affected by racist ideas—they have become rooted in Western society.[153]

Thus the roots of British racism lie deep in the development of capitalism and imperialism. The issues of race and class are deeply inter-twined in this complex economic and social system. Economic development in the West depended on the exploitation of the working classes — in the colonies, the neo-colonies as well in Britain itself. This institutionalised system of exploitation depended on the labour of the Black working class, which had to prop up the whole system.

Britain has always imported labour to meet the needs of growing industrialisation, whether from Ireland, the Caribbean or Asia. This imported labour has always entered the class structure at the bottom, allowing the native English male working class a certain minimal mobility or 'privilege'.[154]

In the new "globalised" super-profit world of the last quarter of the 20th century, the role of the working class everywhere has changed, causing the white working class to lose some of the "privileges" it had clung on to at the expense of the working peoples from the majority world as well as from the Black British work force. Kundnani[155] explains how the race conflict, was fuelled by the changing economic forces:

> With the shift to a post-industrial economy, the large numbers of workers who used to be employed on factory floors, in the docks and in the mines are no longer needed and large tracts of the English working class have found themselves as unwanted as the Blacks who worked below them. All are now having to compete (still, however, on an uneven racial playing field) in the struggle to find work in the uncertain world of the service economy. Furthermore, those workers who still hold jobs in manufacturing industries find that they are in direct competition with workers in Asia… Meanwhile, the middle classes have found that the status and security which accrued to their 'jobs for life' has been run down. The earlier privileges that existed for all English classes, first under imperialism and, later, through racial discrimination in the domestic labour market, have been reduced, if not eliminated.

This shift in balance of economic power then creates an underground level of racism and gives rise to racist attacks on Black people from right-wing racist gangs. It is thus important to understand that racism is not inevitable or a "natural" way of organising a society. It is sustained to serve a particular economic and social agenda, and can be eliminated if there is a will to do so. But this will not be an easy task. As the British Prime Minister Tony Blair acknowledged, Britain "has a mountain to climb

---

[153] TUC. Ibid.
[154] Kundnani (2000): op. cit.
[155] Ibid.

before we have a decent modern, multicultural society we can all be proud of".[156] It remains doubtful if there is even an agreement on the need to climb the mountain.

The white race

Any mention of "race" is often automatically seen to imply that race means Black races and communities. This leads to a one-sided understanding of reality and to an inappropriate method of resolving the "race problem". As Williams says, "the notion of whiteness as a race is almost never implicated":

> One of the more difficult legacies of slavery and of colonialism is the degree to which racism's tenacious hold is manifested not merely in the divided demographics of neighbourhood or education or class but also in the process...called "exnomination" of whiteness as racial identity. Whiteness is unnamed, suppressed, beyond the realm of race.[157]

Race riots and the Scarman Report

Hall[158] traces the history of racism from the early race riots of Nottingham and Notting Hill in 1958, to various racially motivated murders and to police indifference to date. "Each of those events was followed by campaigns, inquiries, recriminations from authorities, and promises of reform. Yet very little seems to have changed", he concludes.

The Scarman inquiry was set up in 1981 following "some of the most serious riots in mainland Britain this century".[159] Lord Scarman's report into relations between Black communities and the police in the early 1980s was "one of the first official documents to address the issue head on. Though it acknowledged that racism may stem from inertia as well as assertion, his report denied that British society was institutionally racist or that 'the direction and policies' of the police service were racist."[160]

The 'temporary collapse of law and order' in Brixton, south London on April 10-12, 1981, caused widespread injury and the destruction of large numbers of vehicles and buildings.[161] The resistance of Black communities in other parts of Britain following the events in Brixton included demands that library services provide for the needs of Black communities. This was the case, for example, in Hackney:

> The history of C.L.R. James Library itself is interesting. In common with Black people's struggles nationally in early 1980s, the people of Hackney took to the streets for various grievances, including the need to provide a Library Service that reflected the needs of Black and Ethnic minorities of Hackney. In response to this demand, the Council decided in 1985 to change the name of one of its Libraries, Dalston Library, to C.L.R. James Library as a commitment that the Library service will in future respond to the needs of these communities. Cyril Lionel Robert James has come to symbolise the struggle of Black people throughout the world for their basic rights...But as is usual in such cases, the Library's name change remained a mere cosmetic change. It

---

[156] The Independent (London). March 1, 1999.
[157] Williams, P. J. (1997): op. cit.
[158] Hall, Stuart (2000): op. cit.
[159] Hall, Stuart (2000): op. cit.
[160] Naidoo, Seb (1999): Root and Branch. Red Pepper. February. www.redpepper.org.uk Accessed June 12, 1999.
[161] Bowling, Ben (2000): Facing the ugly facts. The Guardian. 17 February.

was considered sufficient for Black people that an empty shell be provided for them, without any meaningful content, for a dry bone to be thrown at them.[162]

Hall[163] sees the Scarman Report as distinctive for three reasons:

- It broke the prevailing law and order consensus by firmly locating the sources of unrest in 'insecure social and economic conditions and an impoverished physical environment'.
- Scarman put his trust in a much-expanded programme of police training on community and race issues as a way of trying to get to grips with the racialisation of routine police work.
- The statutory establishment of community consultative committees.

One reason why the Scarman Report did not have the desired effect was because "the wider social and economic reforms were seriously out of key with the political temper of the times and triggered no significant response". "In retrospect," Hall continues, "Scarman was to bewail the 'lack of implementation of the social and economic recommendations' and to acknowledge that he should have been 'more outspoken about the necessity of affirmative action to overcome racial disadvantage.'"[164]

The lessons of this failure have still not been learnt. The overall social and economic conditions are the same for the majority of Black communities—"still immured in poor inner-city housing with few amenities and severely-limited employment opportunities".[165] One possible solution—affirmative action—is not widely used in Britain although the Race Relations Act (1976) does allow for it. The opposition to it comes from those who have benefited from the lack of such action. Meanwhile the Stephen Lawrence Report (Macpherson Report) remains silent on any affirmative action. Whether it is ethical to let those with privileges to make policies on equality is not even a subject of debate in Britain today.

Combating racism in the USA

Racism is not unique to the UK situation. It exists in Europe as well as in Africa, Asia, and America. It is often used as a tool by the ruling classes to divide people and to take attention away from the facts of everyday poverty and exploitation of the working people. For example, it was used against South Asian communities in Uganda by Amin; South Asian Kenyans get attacked regularly by politicians seeking quick popularity.

If racism is common around the world, resistance to it is also found in all countries. While the oppressed communities have continued to struggle against it, many governments have also tried various methods to eliminate racism. In their search for "equality", many countries have tried different methods, including "constitutional guarantees, protective legislation, affirmative action and multicultural

---

[162] Durrani, Shiraz (1993): The facts behind the Three Continents Liberation Collection. Hackney Libraries News. No. 9, 7-9.
[163] Hall, Stuart (2000): op. cit.
[164] Ibid.
[165] Ibid.

programmes".[166] Yet, "glaring inequalities remain". Brown examines the experiences in the U.S.A., South Africa, India and Australia. Below we look only at the U.S.A.:

Brown says that the U.S.A. was "built on contradiction". He quotes President Bill Clinton who said in 1997:

> We were born with a Declaration of Independence which asserted that we are all created equal and a Constitution that enshrined slavery...We advanced across the continent in the name of freedom, yet in doing so we pushed Native Americans off their land, often crushing their livelihood.[167]

The U.S.A. has tried affirmative action legislation in the 1960s to compensate for the "racial disadvantages that were a legacy of slavery, segregation and discrimination". This allowed a minority applicant for a job or college place to be selected over an identically qualified white candidate. While affirmative action has often been criticised and recently outlawed in some states, it has brought about major improvements. Brown says that, "twenty-five years of affirmative action policies in public and private sectors have achieved levels of diversity in boardrooms, universities and political institutions that were unthinkable a generation ago".[168] Yet the playing field is still "far from level". The creation of a substantial Black middle class has been accompanied by the growth of massive poverty among Black communities. "Average Black incomes still lag behind those of whites; poverty and unemployment levels for African-American and Hispanic people are significantly higher than for whites".

In order to deal with continuing inequality and poverty among minorities, President Clinton, in 1997, launched a "national effort to deal openly and honestly with our racial differences and to address policies that will close the opportunity gaps that exist for minorities". In the following year, Clinton established a "race council—the first free-standing White House office with a remit to educate the public about race, identify policies to increase equal opportunities, and co-ordinate work on race between the White House and federal agencies". New Labour has borrowed many practices from the U.S.A. Perhaps the formation of a, "Race Council" should be its next priority.

At the same time, the young people of colour in the U.S.A. are changing the way in which race is perceived and allowed to influence every area of social life. They are thus creating a new world where people of colour are no longer at the periphery of society, but in the centre. Farai Chideya[169] "reveals how America's young people are deconstructing the white/Black definition of race and constructing a new pluralistic paradigm that encompasses the country's white, Black, Hispanic, Asian, and native peoples. Chideya shows us the trials and triumphs of several young adults who dare to brave the new multicultural world". Chideya says, "We do not obey the laws of race. We make them. Now is the time for us to choose wisely what we will preserve about our racial and cultural history, and what destructive divisions we need to leave behind".

---

[166] Brown, Matthew (2000): Seeking equality in a diverse world. Connections (London) Spring 2000.
[167] Ibid.
[168] Ibid.
[169] Chideya, Farai (1999): The Color of Our Future. HarperCollins Canada.

Libraries in the USA

Racism in society gets reflected in all its institutions, including libraries. Racism plays a big role in U.S. politics, as it does in U.S. libraries. The following section is based on some recent publications: Neely and Abif,[170] Tucker,[171] and Reese and Hawkins.[172]

"Racism is still alive in American libraries" says a contributor in Neely and Abif, which records 26 experiences of the "new generation of minority librarians". E. L. Josey sums up the experience in the Preface, "Racism is still alive and well in America and in American libraries" and highlights the fact that there has been little improvement over the years.

It is difficult for this young generation of librarians, hastening towards the twenty-first century to visualise the life of professionals who are well-educated, and having been well-endowed with the master's of library science (M.L.S.) degree and several are studying for a doctorate degree, to contemplate that they are experiencing some of the same problems and difficulties that minority professionals have confronted for the last fifty years.

...

Yet in many ways the situation is better in the U.S.A. than in Britain. For example, research carried out by the Local Government Management Board (LGMB)[173] points to various successful initiatives in the U.S.A. to attract and retain talented and productive people. These initiatives aim to:

- increase cohesiveness and effectiveness in the work force
- establish communication and rapport with minority groups in the marketplace
- promote creativity
- improved problem solving in relation to service needs
- reduce absenteeism, and turnover and recruitment costs

LGMB concludes: "Few British organisations follow this approach and so little has been done here to utilise the contribution of Black and other minority ethnic employees, or to break down barriers to progression for Black and other minority ethnic staff".

Nor do local authorities follow the example of the UK business-led Race for Opportunity, which aims to promote greater business involvement in racial equality as part of Britain's economic and community development. Reese and Hawkins[174] mention a whole range of policies and practices that are being adopted in the U.S.A.

In terms of professional organisation, the American Library Association is decades ahead of the British Library Association in supporting the needs of Black

---

[170] Neely, T and Abif, K (1996): In our own voices; the changing face of librarianship. Lanham, Md. Scarescrow.
[171] Tucker, John Mark (Editor) 1998: Untold Stories; Civil Rights, Libraries, and Black Librarianship. Graduate School of Library and Information Science, University of Illinois. Champaign, IL, USA.
[172] Reese, Gregory L and Hawkins, Ernestine L (1999) Stop Talking, Start Doing! Attracting people of color to the library profession. Chicago. American Library Association.
[173] Local Government Management Board (1998): Evening the Odds: research into management development for black and other minority ethnic managers LGMB: London.
[174] Reese and Hawkins: op.cit.

workers and communities. ALA uses its Office for Literacy and Outreach Services to "ensure that the ethnic caucuses of the ALA are supported in their effort to ensure that the issues and concerns of ethnic minority library professionals and ethnic minority populations are properly addressed".

...

Perhaps what is needed in Britain is a more open-minded approach towards the need to learn from other people and countries. The complacency that surrounds the LIS profession today can become a threat and marginalise the profession from the needs of ethnic minority people. Hendry[175] considers Britain's public library service to have once been the "jewel in the crown of our civilised society". Yet the jewel never worked for Black communities or for working classes.

Manifestation of racism in the UK

Racism is so all-pervading in our society that sometimes it is often difficult to see it as anything unusual. Gus John talks of recognising the importance of how people "define themselves and particularly the way they define themselves as groups with a common identity of group oppression". He continues:

> It is my view that if we are genuinely concerned about social inclusion, we have to understand the myriad of ways in which institutional racism acts as a structural barrier to any form of social inclusion. We must interrogate the practices that are sustained by a culture of institutional racism.[176]

The acceptance by the government that racism exists is an important step in the ultimate resolution of the problem. Tony Blair[177] has said:

> "...Not one Black high court judge; not one Black chief constable or permanent secretary; not one Black army officer above the rank of colonel. Not one Asian either. Not a record of pride for the British establishment. And not a record of pride for Parliament that there are so few Black and Asian MPs."

There are 9 Black MPs in the House of Commons out of 659. Jack Straw, the Home Secretary said in February 2000: "There are a large number of institutions, and some private ones, which are institutionally racist — and that includes the Home Office".[178]

The Stephen Lawrence Inquiry Report[179] asserts that institutional racism in the UK is the reason why the public sector has failed to provide an adequate and appropriate service to Black people. The evidence of the failure of local government to address racial discrimination, service provision and employment is also supported by the Audit Commission, whose 1997/98 report[180] on local authority performance indicators revealed that there are areas of local government employment practice and service provision which remain untouched by any equal opportunities programme. This apparent inaction is despite the fact that local authorities have a specific duty under the Race Relations Act of 1976 to have regard to the promotion of equality of

---

[175] Hendry, Joe (2000): Here comes the sun. Library Association Record. 102(5) pp.272-3.
[176] John, Gus (1999): op. cit.
[177] Blair, Tony (1997): Labour conference speech. Quoted in Travis, A and Rowan, David (1997) A beacon burning darkly. [Analysis: Ethnic equality] The Guardian October 2, 1997:17.
[178] Quoted in the Guardian, April 8, 2000,p.4).
[179] Stephen Lawrence Inquiry: Report of an inquiry by Sir William Macpherson of Cluny (1999). The Home Office. Cm 4252-1.
[180] Audit Commission (London): Annual Report 1997/98.

opportunity in carrying out their functions, and over £1830 million had been provided by the Home Office in the form of Section 11 funding to support this objective.

A brief look at how racism manifests itself in British society today will help to see the situation in LIS in its social context.

...

Racism and the law

Laws which oblige local authorities to consider equalities issues in the planning and delivery of their functions and services include the Local Government Act 1992 and the Race Relations Act 1976.

The Race Relations Act 1976 makes it unlawful to discriminate directly or indirectly on the grounds of colour, race, nationality (including citizenship), or ethnic or national origin, or to apply requirements or conditions which are disadvantageous to people of a particular racial group, and which cannot be justified on non-racial grounds. The Act covers all local government services as well as discriminatory treatment of employees and discriminatory recruitment and selection process.

Local Government Act 1966

Under the Local Government Act 1966, local authorities are required to make annual reports on citizen's charter performance indicators, a number of which cover equal opportunities in service delivery and employment. The Audit Commission's Equal Opportunities Performance Indicators aim to measure how successfully councils are implementing the Commission for Racial Equality's Code of Practice. Some external quality awards such as Investors in People and Chartermark also require equalities performance indicators.

Richard Howitt described the laws as "the biggest breakthrough in British race relations for a quarter of a century". Black describes the so-called race directive, which is strongly backed by CRE, as a "package of groundbreaking anti-discrimination legislation (which) will require amendments to the 1997 Race relations Act to incorporate harassment and the new definition of "indirect discrimination".[181] Black mentions some features of the directive:

> Under the new laws racial harassment and victimisation would be outlawed while sweeping protection against race discrimination in education, employment and in access to grants and scholarships, social protection and social security would be introduced.[182]

Part 2: Employment of Black workers

---

[181] Black, Ian (2000): EU fights far right with laws on racism. The Guardian. May, 18. Available at:
http://www.guardianunlimited.co.uk/Archive/Article/0,4273,4019399,00.html Accessed: May 21, 2000.
[182] Black, Ian (2000): EU fights far right with laws on racism. The Guardian. May, 18. Available at:
http://www.guardianunlimited.co.uk/Archive/Article/0,4273,4019399,00.html. Accessed: May 21, 2000. and Black, Ian (2000): Tories oppose EU anti-racism directive. The Guardian May 19. Available at:
http://www.guardianunlimited.co.uk/Archive/Article/0,4273,4019716,00.html Accessed: May 21, 2000.

As with other aspects of racism, employment of Black staff and managers in LIS should first be seen in the context of the employment situation in society as a whole. The situation in LIS can then be more meaningfully examined and an appropriate solution worked out.

A recent Government report[183] acknowledges the existence of racial discrimination in employment of Black people when it says, "People from ethnic minority backgrounds have higher unemployment rates regardless of their qualifications or where they live". It continues:

People from ethnic minority backgrounds face racial discrimination in the job market. Inequality is pervasive. People from ethnic minority backgrounds are not securing jobs in proportion to their total numbers in the population. People from ethnic minority backgrounds are rarely represented in proportion to their numbers in the workforce at senior levels of organisations in all sectors of the economy…the effect is an institutional bar to advancement based on race. This is unacceptable.

Labour Force Survey (LFS) for 1997 showed the level of discrimination against Black workers in terms of employment:[184]

Unemployment rate for Black workers is 15 percent, compared to 6.6 percent for white workers.

Unemployment of Black men is 18.5 percent and just over 15 percent for Black women, compared with 8.3 percent for white men and 6.1 percent for white women.

Unemployment rate for Black male workers under 25 years old was 32 percent, and 33 percent for Black women under 25 years. This compares with 13 percent (men) and 10 percent (women) for white people in the same age range.

The problem also goes further than service provision and employment. A recent study by the LGMB revealed that only 3 percent of local authority elected members are Black and other minority ethnic people, yet the Black and other minority ethnic population is estimated to be 6 percent in England and Wales.[185]

Cunningham[186] points out that:

in the case of the public authorities mentioned in the examples above [education, policing, urban policies such as Single Regeneration Budget, the Health Authority, local authorities] all have equal opportunity statements and policies, all have service standards, yet racial discrimination and disadvantage remain at unacceptably high levels.

She looks at the effects of this discrimination in the workplace:

Given this scenario it is perhaps not surprising that there is a fear of discrimination and of unequal treatment, which puts off ethnic minorities from entering the [LIS] profession. And I would suggest that it is also discrimination, direct or indirect, which leads to ethnic minorities being found at the lower grades.

---

[183] Department for Education and Employment (DfEE) (1999): Jobs for All. Nottingham: National Strategy for Neighbourhood Renewal (Report of the Policy Action Team 1).
[184] TUC (1998): op. cit. p.3.
[185] The Stephen Lawrence Inquiry: Home Secretary's Action Plan (1999). http://police.homeoffice.gov.uk/news-and-publications/publication/community-policing/slpages.pdf?view=Binary. [accessed: 29 August 2007].
[186] Cunningham, Marie (1996): Speech at the Open meeting for Black and Ethnic Minority Staff, Library Association, 17 April.

Research shows that Black workers face discrimination at work, which unfairly limits their ability to make the most of their skills and talents compared to white employees. TUC[187] reports on the situation:

> Data from the government's Labour Force Survey (LFS) shows that racism continues to be a major barrier at work for Black and Asian employees, unfairly limiting career progression and development once in employment. The LFS statistics also show that, proportionately, many more Black employees are trapped in part-time jobs against their will and that this further limits opportunities for career development. Furthermore, these trends have occurred against a backdrop of rising skill levels among Black workers, with the latest statistics showing that they are much more likely to hold higher level qualifications compared to their white counterparts.
>
> Meanwhile, even as the white unemployment rate is coming down, it is going up among Black communities. The level of joblessness among Black people is twice the white employment rate.[188]

Black and other minority ethnic people make up almost 6 percent of the British population. Yet "only 1.4 percent of chief executives, chief officers and deputy chief officers come from Black or other minority ethnic backgrounds." Overall local government in England and Wales employs over two million people. Of these approximately 700,000 are involved in white-collar administrative and professional functions. Local Government Management Board[189] found that, in a sample of 53 local authorities for whom ethnic monitoring data was available, there were 6000 BME employees in management positions at Senior Officer grades, i.e. SO1 and above.

The LGMB Survey substantiated the claims made by many BME local authority employees in terms of the obstacles they face in reaching high levels of management:

White staff generally occupy more senior positions in the hierarchy, whereas BME staff are much more evenly spread. A high proportion of BME staff remain at the bottom – with seven or more tiers of managers above them.

Considerable differences show up between BME and white managers in the length of time they have had management responsibilities. Only 9 percent of BME staff has managed for over 10 years against 43 percent of white. In general white officers manage greater numbers of staff.

The majority of the group participants agree that BME managers face unequal access for resources for development. This is supported in the survey findings.

There is only one Black member of staff at Senior Civil Service Grade 3. People of Colour are seen as "space invaders" in higher levels of civil service and in the academic world where there are only 2.3 percent of professors from Black and Ethnic Minority communities.[190] The few people of colour who reach this rarefied position find the environment extremely hostile.

It is important to examine what BME staff themselves see as barriers to their advancement in local authorities. Local authorities will need to investigate (in co-operation with BME staff) their own policies and practices to identify if such

---

[187] TUC (2000): Qualifying for racism; how racism is increasingly blighting career prospects. ESAD. London: Trade Union Congress.
[188] Travis, Alan (2000): Man with a mission [Gurbux Singh]. The Guardian (Society) March 22, 2000, pp. 2-3.
[189] Local Government Management Board. (1998) Equality control. LGMB: London
[190] BBC Radio 4: "Thinking Aloud" April 19, 2000.

perceived barriers are real and, if so, take steps to change the situation. If found to be not substantiated, reasons for such perceptions will need to be investigated.

...

The Library field

The situation of Black workers and managers in public libraries is no better than that in other fields. Khan quotes Bob McKee, the Chief Executive of the Library Association:

> He (Bob McKee) went on to say that our profession, particularly at senior levels, does not reflect the ethnic and cultural diversity of our communities. Figures show that 1.2 percent of LA members describe themselves as Asian, African or Caribbean—a total of 286 people [out of total membership of almost 24,000] of whom just three individuals declare a salary of more than £27,000 per year. [191]

It is only after the publication of the Stephen Lawrence Inquiry Report and the high level of publicity about the existence of racism in the country that the profession has begun to pay more than lip service to even admitting racism in libraries. The voice of Black librarians has been conspicuous by their absence in the debate on racism. When it is raised, it is either within the confines of meetings of Black workers or has to be issued anonymously, for example the comments about experiences of racism in libraries from nine Black librarians. These make eye-opening reading for those not aware of the situation of Black LIS workers. Those who preside over such work places need to be investigated.

...

Equality: a service development approach (2000 — SD, PJ)[192]

Durrani, Shiraz and Joyce, Paul

Is it time to challenge the assumptions we make about how to achieve equality in service delivery and the assumptions that are implicit in the strategies we use to bring about equal employment opportunities? Merton Library Services believes that challenging existing assumptions now could produce better value for the public and break some of the current sense of stagnation in the movement towards equality of employment opportunities. It is setting out to challenge these assumptions through its new pilot development project for the enhancing library services to better meet the "new needs" of the Black and Asian community. The key proposition of this project is that the project is itself critical as a vehicle for developing the new know-how that a new service requires for its design and delivery. (The new needs might be simply hitherto ineffective needs that were not addressed by current library services).

---

[191] Khan, Ayub (2000): Stamping out institutional racism. Library Association Record 102(1) pp. 38-39.
[192] Durrani, Shiraz and Joyce, Paul (2000) : Library Management. Research Note. 21(8).

Values for an equality development project

The values that are the starting point of a new approach to improving Merton's Library services to its Black and Asian communities are:

- The need for development projects to be guided by an assessment of the Black and Asian communities' current satisfaction and the scope for improving the services to them.
- The need for each service to tailor service improvements to exploit its distinctive resources as well as the public's requirements, rather than blind copying of other library services' initiatives.
- The need for the top managers of the service to provide the quality of leadership skills and commitment to make the success of the development project more likely.
- The need to expand the experience and managerial expertise of Black and Asian library employees through the activities of the development projects.
- The need for the top managers to win the support of all sections of library staff, and not just the managers and professionals who have an existing commitment and sympathy to greater equality in services and employment.
- The need for the learning and growth of capability developed during the development project to be recognised within the organisation and become the basis of increased responsibilities for Black and Asian managers and staff.

The design of the pilot

These six assumptions have been expressed in the design of a pilot development project agreed at Merton Library.

Stage 1: Feasibility Study

The feasibility study will involve interviewing members of the Black and Asian community, library professionals, and managers. The interviews with members of the black community are based on problem exploration (downplaying the search for solutions at this stage). The interviews will focus on the problems experienced in using the library service. In the case of users we want to know about problems experienced in using the service. From a non-user we are interested in identifying the nature of the problems that have prevented them from using library services. The interviews aim at identifying a number of problems and getting interviewees to rate the problems that have the highest priority from the user's perspective. The interview with the library professional takes the point of view that the professional is recognised in his or her service as an expert on the design of library services. The professional can recommend good ideas for developing the library service to solve the top priority of the problems identified. They can also identify resources that would be needed and what resources are already available for implementing the ideas. An interview with a senior manager can help with reviewing the problems and solutions and identifying what is acceptable or unacceptable or missing. They may veto any of the ideas for solutions and give in-principle support for any of the ideas. Top management would evaluate the results of the interviewing and select one of the ideas for a new service development. This stage of the pilot development project would also need to formulate local performance indicators and targets with the intention of mainstreaming new service developments by including them within the performance plan and the associated best value processes.

Stage 2: Development Project

This should not last more than six months. A part-time project team for the development of a new service will be established and led by a Black or Asian member of the staff with potential for development. The development team will develop the initial idea and make corrections to it on the basis of more thorough appraisal of the Black and Asian community's needs and meticulous planning of operational processes, resources, and implementation steps. The development team will also appraise and correct the local best value performance indicators and targets suggested by the feasibility study. Following on from this, the development team would need to confirm that the new service is the best value option by considering alternative ways of delivering the new services (procurement, partnership working) and by benchmarking the performance and cost parameters of the new service. This is essentially a cost-benefit exercise. The output of the development stage would be a comprehensive proposal for service development ready for submission through the relevant channels for authorisation.

Stage 3: Pilot new service

It is envisaged that a new service proposal might take at least two years to implement and would require changes to procedures, structures, and staffing in the library service. A manager for the new service would be required. The job description and person specification produced for such a role would define the essential know how or expertise required of the new manager.

The creation of managerial capability

The central proposition of the pilot project is that the meeting of unrecognised or under-recognised needs (new needs) requires new services, and new services require new skills and know-how (including new management know-how). The development of new services and new Black and Asian managers by Merton Library, and the evaluation research by the Management Research Centre of the University of North London, has been conceptualised in three stages.

The project team should be assembled with care. As well as Black and Asian library workers it needs to include experienced librarians and a senior member of library management. The team will need to be well resourced in terms of the part-time secondment of its members to work on the project. The team, including Black and Asian staff with development potential, will need to debate new ideas, solve issues, visit other library services, and test out ideas wherever possible.

We are testing out the proposition that development projects involving Black and Asian staff will be more effective in developing distinctive and valuable sets of know how and expertise. We are less concerned with standardised management competencies (managing people, budgets, information, and services) that are in any case more easily provided through conventional training. But the capabilities developed through the project are harder to acquire through traditional training formats and more valuable as a consequence. In summary, the pilot project is an expression of the idea of a 'learning council' and offers, we believe much more than off-the-job training courses in management ever could to Black and Asian staff. And of course this is all within a project offering to deliver better value to the public.

Mainstreaming equality, meeting needs (2003 – SD/ES)[193]

Mainstreaming equality, meeting needs; the Merton Library approach – Shiraz Durrani and Elizabeth Smallwood[194]

Introduction

The approach of Merton Library and Heritage Service (MLHS) to equalities has been a dynamic one. It has evolved and developed in keeping with the changing situation nationally as well as in Merton. Its policies and practices on equality are continually modified as a result of experiences. While there are many similarities between the experiences in Merton and those in other authorities, Merton is perhaps unique in accepting the need to change its policies on equality and in taking concrete action when the situation requires change. Innovation and calculated risk-taking have been at the forefront of the changes in Merton. This experience, then, has relevance far beyond the boundaries of Merton.

At the same time, Merton Library and Heritage Service have taken a proactive role in meeting the recommendations on social exclusion from DCMS[195] and Resource.[196] This has injected new ideas and creativity, which has helped the service to experiment with different forms of service delivery, arriving at a model that is suitable for the needs of Merton's communities.

This article aims to show the approach that Merton Library and Heritage Service has taken in order to address equalities in a meaningful way, rather than a superficial "gloss" for the sake of appearing to address equality. However, it does not cover the equalities aspect of the media fund and collection policy and practices. Much remains to be done in this field and the final resolution on this matter is still some way off. The article, then, covers some service delivery aspects and looks at the changing staffing structure to assess how the equality aspects have been managed. Unless there are appropriate structures and policies to address equality matters, no fundamental change, required for creating a service based on principles of social justice, can occur.

We look at the underlying vision and philosophy that guides the drive for greater equality in managing the library service. This is an on-going struggle and the various

---

[193] Durrani, Shiraz and Smallwood, Elizabeth (2003): Library Management. Vol. 24 Nos. 6-7. pp. 348 – 359. ISSN: 0143-5124.
[194] The views and interpretations expressed in this article are not of Merton Library Service or of Merton Council, but those of the two authors who are actively involved in the change process in Merton Library Service.
[195] Department for Culture, Media and Sport (DCMS,1999): Libraries for All: Social Inclusion in Public Libraries. London. Available at:
http://www.culture.gov.uk/NR/rdonlyres/42818901-0EA3-4AE5-B1C2-1689ABC069BD/0/Social_Inclusion_PLibraries.pdf [Accessed: 29 August 2007].
[196] Open to All?: op. cit.

contradictions inherent in the situation have by no means been resolved. What is significant in Merton is the total support for the drive for equality that has come from senior Departmental and Council officials as well as from Members.[197] Without such support, the progress made to date would not have been possible. At the same time, there are Library and Service Managers able, willing and committed to service improvement and principles of equality who take action to further equalities. There is perhaps a lesson here for other library services striving for developing a service based on the principles of equality, social justice and the requirements of human rights.

This article has been written not only for informing others outside Merton on our approach and experiences in equalities: it is equally an open and frank discussion of our successes and failures for internal (Merton) discussion and debate. The approach therefore is one of transparency and self-criticism — and self-congratulations, when appropriate.

Part 1: From Community Librarian to Equal Access Services

Early experience: 2000-2002

The period after 2000 has been the period of dynamic change in addressing the question of equalities in Merton Libraries. The period has seen major changes in the way the service is run and organised. This section takes a brief look at the changes that have been made in the period 2000 to 2002:

- Pre 2000: There was one post of Community Librarian who was expected to be the focus of equalities for the whole service. The post-holder was expected to be responsible not only for the acquisition and distribution of stock in all South Asian community languages, but also to take responsibility for service delivery to ethnic minority communities. The post was a follow-up from the former Sectional 11-funded post, which had been absorbed into the main staffing structure, but remained largely outside the work of the library service.
- In theory, the work of the post-holder was supplemented by staff at all libraries, but the reality was that she operated a generally isolated service on the margins of the "mainstream" library service. In addition, the focus of the work of this post was entirely on race basis and other equality aspects were not covered in the work of the post. In practice, the service became a rather narrow service for some South Asian communities and remained rather an operational one without any strategic approach.
- The year 2000 saw the conclusion of a 2-year Review of the Library Service. The Review report concluded that the one post of a community librarian was not adequate in providing a meaningful service to ethnic minority communities. The staffing structure, which became operational in June 2000 set up nine cost centres, one of which was the "BME/Outreach cost centre". This provided some form of equality to services to ethnic minority communities (which makes up almost 23 percent of Merton's population) by allocating similar managerial structure, power, staff and resources to services to ethnic minority services as it did to the rest of the service. Thus ethnic minority services moved slightly from the margins of library life towards the centre. The cost centre was also expected to take a lead in developing outreach services to all excluded communities, thus

---

[197] Elected Councillors running local authorities.

moving away from an essentially race-related service to ethnic minority communities.

- In 2001, a new manager (Elizabeth Smallwood) took up the post of Library and Service Manager at the BME/Outreach cost centre. She carried out an investigation of the working of the cost centre and the needs of the communities expected to be served. She studied the way the new cost centre was perceived by other managers and staff and concluded that the cost centre needed to change to a more strategic focus from an operational one. She noted a distinct lack of policy-focus without which "equal" services could not be delivered. She also identified the need to see services to ethic minority communities in the wider equality context if the service was not to remain in the margins of the library service. She wrote a number of reports and made a number of recommendations, which were considered by the Strategy, Commissioning and Scrutiny team (SCS)—the decision-making senior management—which agreed to many of these changes.
- As a result of the above process, the BME/Outreach cost centre changed to the new "Equal Access Services" (EAS) in 2001. This was expected to be the first stage of mainstreaming equality, as recommended by various Government reports. The new cost centre now had two strategic managers (Library & Service Mangers)—one to focus on services to ethnic minority communities (including the requirements under the Race Relations (Amendment) Act), the other to focus on other equality aspects covered by the Equality Standards as well as other aspects of social exclusion. The focus of the new cost centre changed from operational work to strategic work, especially in developing policies for the Library Service on issues of equality. Thus the operational post of "Site Manager" was deleted. The implementation of these policies was to be done by all cost centres (libraries and the Heritage Centre).
- As a further development of this process of mainstreaming equality, some other aspects of the work of EAS (including outreach and house visit service) were to be devolved to sites. The proposal was that the SCS would then monitor the performance of individual libraries to ensure that all equality aspects were delivered to the standards set by the EAS. A new post of Site Manager (based with SCS) was created to undertake performance management functions, which had hitherto not been fully addressed.

An evaluation

The changes recorded above resulted in a number of important successes. This was symbolised by the Merton Libraries winning the national "Libraries Change Lives" Award in 2001 for the pioneering services to refugees and asylum seekers provided by the BME/Outreach cost centre. This was to provide, in 2003, the blueprint for the "Welcome to your Library" project set up by the London Libraries Development Agency (LLDA) and funded by the Paul Hamlyn Foundation.

However, this success masked a number of weaknesses in the concept of an "equal" service to marginalized and excluded communities and people. The cost centre was becoming what Ngugi wa Thiong'o calls "a giant on mosquito legs". The perception of its achievement far outweighed the reality on the ground. The change from "BME/Outreach" to the EAS was a correct one to remedy some of the shortcomings identified in the BME/Outreach phase. Yet this did not go far enough to have a meaningful impact. At the same time, the new, second strategic post of Library and Service Manager (Ethnic Minority Services) that was created at the inception of EAS could not be filled due to recruitment problems, although it was advertised over five times. At the same time, the changes were not fully accepted by all the managers although many meetings were held and many reports were written in order to ensure the adequate flow of information and to provide opportunities for feedback on these changes.

Perhaps the most important reason that the BME/EAS experiment did not work as well as expected was that it was mainly a quantitative change in services to marginalized communities, not a qualitative one. The number of staff establishment and other resources were increased, but the cost centre still remained a marginalized one. The "mainstream" and prevailing culture of the service — consisting of the static libraries and a Heritage Centre — continued life as in the past, unaffected in the most part by the changes proposed by the EAS. The new performance-monitoring programme was not robust enough to challenge non-performance and to ensure compliance with new requirements, which were spelled out in the "SCS Manual". Thus there was no change in the culture of the organisation.

One positive aspect of the Merton experience is the readiness of those responsible for EAS services to admit that their policies had not brought about the fundamental changes that were required if libraries were to be at the heart of their communities. They operate in an environment that is not afraid to face facts and make changes to policies and practices if they need changing. It is this constantly challenging and critical attitude and willingness to take calculated risks that has driven the service forward in a search for an even better way of operating.

This approach has been incorporated into Merton Library and Heritage Service's new staffing structure.

Part 2: Creating conditions for strategic change

The shortcomings identified in the above section led the Service to start exploring more appropriate ways of addressing the equality question. At the same time, a challenge was issued to the Library Service by Merton's Assistant Chief Executive, Keith Davis, to provide a new model of library service in the context of the local authorities facing radical changes in the next five years.

This challenge was taken up by some of the managers and resulted in the creation of the concept of a "needs-based" service.

Needs-based service

A small group of managers[198] started looking at producing a new model of service, which could be piloted in three libraries in Merton. Smallwood[199] sums up the new approach adopted, under the title, "Communities Developing Communities". She explains:

> If libraries are to be at the heart of communities, they must be relevant to the local community. We feel that the best way to be relevant is to respond to the current and changing needs of the community. So, at the centre of all library activity in Merton, must be community needs. We have, therefore, put community needs at the centre of

---

[198] Besides the two authors of this article, others were Di Reynolds and Raihana Ahmad.
[199] Smallwood, E. (2002): "Communities Developing Communities". Diversity No. 3, pp. 22-33, 75. See particularly the needs-based chart on p.75. Available at: http://www.seapn.org.uk/docs/diversity_march01.pdf. [Accessed: 29 August 2007].

> our Community Development chart and not Community Development [one of the Service's strategic objectives] itself as we feel that the key role for libraries in providing opportunities for communities to develop themselves is in addressing the issue of community needs in a library and information context... Although particular needs may vary from community to community, we have identified several key needs that we think are common to all communities, particularly communities that need/could benefit from development. These are: information and knowledge; skills; empowerment and capacity building.

Smallwood goes on to explain the connection between equalities and a needs-based service:

> Equalities: this relates to balancing needs. We must take into account the needs of actual and potential users if we are to be truly relevant and this means considering equalities issues. It also encompasses issues of transparency and democracy. We need to be clear about the decisions we take and to impart this information to the community. Painful decisions may need to be taken but addressing any inequality in service provision is something we cannot, nor should not, shy away from.

The "Communities Developing Communities" approach was put into practice at three libraries: Mitcham, Pollards Hill and Donald Hope Libraries. This approach was not fully implemented as the tensions in the system between the "traditional" library service and the new approach to service delivery had not been resolved. The process was also interrupted by a new budgetary situation in 2002-03, which provided an opportunity to rethink radically the whole approach to equalities. This is covered later in this article.

New outreach programme

Outreach is meant to be an organised activity of reaching out to the large number of Merton people who were not connected to library services—as part of the mainstream activity, not a marginal activity carried out by a few dedicated members of staff. The approach to outreach during BME/Outreach phase (2000-01) was never clearly defined, and remained at an experimental stage. It was a daunting task, especially as there were only two dedicated "outreach" posts—one of which was vacant. Initial activities included visits to community groups where staff explained what the library service had to offer and attempted to make connections between the people who had previously not used libraries and their local libraries.

At the same time, all libraries were expected to take a proactive part in this outreach work. Workshops and training sessions were held in compiling community profiles so as to be able to compare actual usage against needs in the community. Some libraries were more proactive than others in seeing the need for outreach to their communities as part of their "normal" library service; others felt that their main responsibility was to provide a high quality of service to their existing communities. This tension has not been resolved, resulting in only a patchy outreach service. The situation was complicated by an increase in opening hours, and the outreach programme had to be modified.

It was then decided, as part of the "needs-based service" to create a post of a Site Librarian (SM) with specific responsibility for outreach. The SM was to coordinate the work of two other outreach staff who would be based at different libraries in the Needs Based Pilot project. This project showed the potential for this new approach. Important achievements included the establishment of new outreach activities from the Donald Hope Library and work with a youth group at Mitcham Library in a partnership project with Merton's Youth Service. Similarly, the Pollards Hill Library began a series of new activities as part of turning itself into a "community library". Such activities included close partnership with the Commonside Trust.

New Projects as engines of change

One difficulty encountered in bringing about changes needed to mainstream equality was the tension between the traditional building-based library service and the new, needs and outreach-based service. Lack of resources to develop new services was also an important constraint as it was not always possible to redirect resources from the "traditional" service to the new, innovative services being developed.

A way out of this "tension zone" was indicated when the Merton Library Service was selected as one of the five authorities nation-wide (the only one in London) for the DCMS-Home Office funded "Lending Time" Project managed by Community Service Volunteers (CSV). Merton's proposals were along the following lines:

> Merton's proposal for "Lending Time" is to put into practice lessons learnt as part of the review of the service. Their [volunteers'] contribution will add value to what we already do, but on the basis of empowering local communities through a network of volunteers who will have representation at policy making and implementation bodies of the library service. They will thus not be a group of people working "on the margins", but will be right at the centre of the Library Service, influencing policy and monitoring its implementation. They will be the eyes and ears of the community ensuring that the Library service meets the real needs of our communities.[200]

The equality aspect was expected to be at the heart of such project work. It was the expectation when the application for this Project was made that its example of mainstreaming equalities will provide an incentive and the necessary push to mainstream equality in the service as a whole. It is too early to say if the Lending Time Project provides the hoped-for push for change and for mainstreaming equality in the service.

It remains to be seen whether it is possible to use such Projects to mainstream equality and bring about the necessary cultural and structural changes to create a new model of library service.

Legislative and Standards requirements

During this period, a number of laws and library requirements were introduced that made the mainstreaming of equality a legal requirement. These included the enactment of the Race Relations (Amendment) Act (2000) as well as other equality legislations (for e.g. the DDA) and various EU equality requirements. In addition, the adoption by Merton Council of the Equality Standards for Local Authorities[201] added urgency to the need to mainstream equality.

Part 3: A new staffing structure, a new approach to equality (2003)

---

[200] London Borough of Merton: "Lending Time" Pilot Project: Expression of interest. 31 August 2001.

[201] Some legal and other requirements are covered in Durrani, S. (2001) "Social and Racial Exclusion Handbook for libraries, archives, museums, and galleries". 2nd edition, August 2001. Social Exclusion Action Planning Network. Nadderwater, Exeter.

Thus our approach to equalities is to mainstream equalities. As Smallwood notes, one cannot provide for marginalised groups through marginalised service provision and claim to be tackling social exclusion. The approach of Merton Library and Heritage Service, therefore, is to mainstream equalities i.e. make equalities the responsibility of all staff. In this way can its libraries be truly at the heart of its communities.

Such an approach requires that it is embedded at the heart of the Service. We have chosen to do this through our new staffing structure. Whilst retaining elements of the traditional service, we have found a balance, which helps us move in a new direction through the inclusion of a post focusing on innovation and development. Together with a post focusing on equalities and policy development, we can move towards change with a focus on meeting needs. The policy focus will help to ensure that we respond to equality legislation in library and information provision. This focus will also help us to mainstream equality—by providing the guidelines for all staff to follow. The post of Performance Manager will help to ensure that policies are implemented consistently across the borough.

A new staffing structure was thus adopted in April 2003. This aimed to meet the following needs:

- To address various tensions identified in the current structure. For example, current Library and Service Managers are required to manage both a library site, a borough-wide service area such as Young People's Services and jointly manage a strategic objective such as Community Development. Additionally, as Merton Library and Heritage Service is cost centred, budget responsibility for library sites and borough-wide service areas rests with Library and Service Managers. These demanding tasks have led to a number of tensions, massive amounts of paperwork and insufficient time for service development.
- To deliver required savings
- Attempt to meet some of the requirements of the Framework for the Future

Following extensive consultations with managers and all staff, the Human Resources section, Staffside, and the Finance Department, a new staffing structure was introduced in April 2003. The following section takes up some of the equality aspects of this structure:

Mainstreaming Equalities

The creation of the post of Equalities, Policy and Research Officer marks a sharp change in the way equalities is addressed. The changes implied in the creation of this post include:

- A shift from operational to strategic (not expected under BME/Outreach; not fully achieved under EAS);
- A strong emphasis on policies on equality without which achievement of equality cannot be guaranteed;
- Research on equality and on other aspects of library work is now included as an essential part of library work and should enable input from legislation, best practice and other creative ideas to inform library policies.
- A shift from focus on race (as under BME/Outreach) to looking at all aspects of equality (planned, but not achieved, under EAS). It is now possible to

address all aspects of the Equality Standard, EU legislation on equality as well as meeting the requirements of the Race Relations (Amendment) Act;
- The creation of a strong performance monitoring structure under the post of Operations and Performance Manager should ensure that implementation of policies on equality are better monitored, and corrective measures taken if there is non-compliance.

Meeting needs through targeted outreach and projects

The previous structures had attempted various methods of "scatter outreach" whereby all excluded communities and groups were expected to be reached by a few outreach officers. While this proved to be very popular, it became obvious that, at best, it could reach a very small proportion of people whose needs had not been fully met. The new structure takes a new approach to outreach—creation of specially targeted outreach posts created in partnership with other sections and Departments of the Council. The key ones are:

- Youth Library Development Officer: This is a joint post between Libraries and Youth Service. The post will be based in Libraries and will work closely with, and empower, the youth themselves. New services will be developed to meet their needs better. Already a Youth Magazine Group has been established.
- A new post of Older People's Services Officer is being created jointly between the Libraries, the Chief Executive's Department and Merton Association of Pensioners.

Change, Equality & Innovation

The above changes are part of a larger change underway, under a programme of "doing the change". A "Change, Equality and Innovation" initiative brings together a number of innovative initiatives and partnerships, which will change the whole way the Service operates. Already an "Innovation Centre" is being set up at Mitcham Library. The various project based at the Innovation Centre are shown in the Change, Equality and Innovation Chart, which forms part of the new staffing structure.

An important aspect of the projects' approach is that each element or project has the principle of equality at its very centre. Race, gender and disability issues form an integral part of the equalities agenda, especially as they are the three areas in the Council's priority equality work as part of meeting the Equality Standard for Local Authorities.

The Projects mentioned in the Chart are being developed as a way of introducing change and connecting with potential users. Some of the Projects are explained below:

- Merton's **'Communities Developing Communities'** approach. Merton Library and Heritage Services is committed to furthering community development by empowering communities to develop themselves. We feel that libraries cannot develop communities but can provide opportunities for communities to develop themselves. This approach has encouraged us to rethink our services and to begin a refocus of service based on the needs of users and potential users.

- Merton Library and Heritage Service has introduced its own award – **Merton Libraries Change Lives Award**. This award will be given annually to that

Merton library which develops the most innovative service to a marginalised group. In this way the legacy of innovation encouraged by the national Libraries Change Lives Award will remain with us. The Award is in two parts, one specifically for services to refugees and asylum seekers, the other for improvement in services to other excluded or other communities whose needs have not been fully met in the past.

- **The Lending Time Project.** Merton is one of only six authorities countrywide (the only one in London), which has been selected to participate in the DCMS/Home Office's Active Community Unit funded pilot project managed by Community Service Volunteers. It focuses on using volunteers to add value to library services. Volunteers can help us to develop our services to all excluded communities in a unique partnership. The Project will provide people with the opportunity for gaining skills and experiences, which can be taken forward into employment or indeed to enjoy a fuller life through activities such as reading, creative writing and drama.

- The London Library Development Agency **'Welcome to your Library'** Project, funded by the Paul Hamlyn Foundation. Merton will be working very closely with the LLDA and a number of other authorities in London to develop further services to refugees and asylum seekers. It is the intention of the project to develop a model of service which can be rolled out elsewhere, benefiting a wider range of refugees. The Project will pay particular attention to meeting the needs of disabled people and refugee and asylum seeker communities, many of which suffer physical and other forms of disability as a result of conditions, which create the need for exile.

- Merton has acquired funding for the national **Quality Leaders Project – Youth (QLP-Y)** from the National Youth Agency and the Paul Hamlyn Foundation and Resource. Merton not only manages the national Programme, but also has one of its staff participating in the Programme. Appendix F reproduces a press release giving details of this national Project managed by Merton Libraries. Some positive results of working with youth in Merton will be passed on to the national QLP-Y Project.[202]

Conclusion

Equality and diversity are much in the news these days. It is obvious that there is an urgent need for organisations to change in order to meet legal and moral requirements on equality. Many organisations have started taking active steps to ensure that the required change takes place. However there are no ready-made formulae or blueprints that can be used to bring about change. The obstacles to change are many and different in different organisations.

In this paper, we have attempted to give a brief record of the policies and practices in Merton Library and Heritage Service from the period 2000 to the present. We have gone through a number of phases of change. We do not believe that we have arrived at the "ideal" solution – if at all there is such a thing. What is obvious is that there is a constant need for change and development in order to keep up with

---

[202] Further information about QLP is available at: http://www.seapn.org.uk/qlp.html

changing circumstances and needs. Our experience points to the need for a number of key requirements that are essential for creating a service that is based on principles of equality. Some of these are:

- A total commitment to principles of equality;
- A clear vision of where the service wants to go;
- Member and senior management support;
- Willingness to experiment and take risks;
- Openness to new ideas and practices;
- Effective leadership at all levels;
- A creative partnership with other parts of the Council and community groups;
- A willingness to take action when required;
- Not be afraid to tackle resistance to change;
- Willingness to redirect resources in order to put your principles into practice and creative use of resources;
- Educating staff and others on the need and direction of change.
- Establishing appropriate staffing structures that enshrine principles of equality;
- Creating appropriate policies and willingness to be guided by them;
- The creation or strengthening of monitoring procedures to ensure that policies are converted into real practice;
- Willingness to learn from experiences of others and from your own weaknesses and strengths.

Achieving equality in practice needs the kind of resolute approach that can only be borne from a sense of passion. An impassioned approach to equalities is not, however, incompatible with a logical one. The only way forward is through strongly and logically argued debate. One may not immediately win hearts and minds through logical argument, but equalities issues cannot wait until everybody is on board with the issues. Logical argument lays the foundations for a closer focus on equalities issues. It is not always easy to stand up for equalities when it may mean being on the receiving end of approbation from less committed colleagues. Passion and commitment are necessary for such a resolute approach. The experiences of Merton Library and Heritage Service prove that this is the case.

Create a people-orientated public library service (2004)[203]

The Government's policy on public libraries needs to be informed by the following factors:

Globalisation and effects on libraries

The key issue is to decide what the social role of public libraries is. They should not take the social, economic and political situation they find themselves in as "given", but actively seek to understand why and how we arrived at this situation — and also ensure the public understands it too. It is their role to dig deeper into "facts" that are given to them by their social environment.

British libraries are in danger of using a commercial version of a "global library" much like McDonald's restaurant outlets, which serve the same product in every part of the world. While this approach may be a useful one in ensuring a standard level of service, and a useful model for maximising profits for the McDonald's chain, it is disastrous for libraries if they want to root themselves in their local communities. It is essential that a new model of needs-based library service is developed at the policy level and is implemented.

For this to happen there is an urgent need for setting up a "public library innovations & development" think tank with Government support. Further details of this proposal can be submitted to the Committee in oral evidence if considered appropriate.

Other important changes that need to be considered include the rules developed at the World Trade Organisation, especially in the context of TRIPS (trade-related aspects of intellectual property rights). IFLA has expressed its concerns over TRIPS in a number of areas such as "not for profit libraries", intellectual property and cultural diversity. Specific threats from these are mentioned by IFLA.[204]

These threats to public libraries need to be considered by the Committee, which needs to give a clear direction in ensuring that public libraries remain public in theory and practice and do not become a tool in the hands of a global corporate world for making profits.

Faced with a situation where libraries are blindly walking into extinction, it is important that public libraries stand up for a new role of libraries in society. In the world ruled by corporate globalisation, it is too easy to drift along with the tide of "neutral" librarianship and do nothing to make libraries play a central role in liberating people, their cultures, and their economies from the privatised future that globalisation has planned for them.

A new approach in terms of vision and practice of public librarianship is urgently needed. Real democracy and transparency needs to flourish if public libraries are to be at the heart of social life. The Committee needs to give leadership in bringing about these necessary changes.

---

[203] Submission to the UK Parliament. Select Committee on Culture, Media and Sport. Session 2003-04. 26 October 2004. New Inquiry: Public Libraries. Written Evidence. Available from:<http://www.publications.parliament.uk/pa/cm200405/cmselect/cmcumeds/81/81we19.htm>. Accessed 03 November, 2005.

[204] The IFLA Position on The World Trade Organization (2001). Available at: http://www.ifla.org/III/clm/p1/wto-ifla.htm#3.

Democracy deficit in libraries

The myth of a "neutral" public library service needs to be exploded. There is no way that libraries and librarians are or can be neutral in the social struggles of their societies. Every decision they make — how much to spend on books, which books to buy, what staff to appoint, how to manage the service — is a reflection of their class position and their world outlook, however much they deny this. The power they have been given in running their libraries is supposed to be used to meet the needs of ALL local people. But there is a basic lack of democracy in the world of libraries, which has created "dictator library managers".

What librarians do — and don't do — is not merely an academic question. It affects our understanding of our natural and social environment, which, taken in its totality, affects our world outlook, affects what we think and what we do. It influences the minds of the young generation and becomes the prevailing outlook of the adult world of tomorrow.

Manipulation of information, whether conscious or unconscious, is an important matter, not only in local life, but in international relations as well. Librarians can become tools in the hands of those seeking to manipulate whole populations to think along *their* lines — or stand firm to support the democratic rights of the people. There is no third way here.

Thus there is an urgent need to create a new type of people-oriented, democratic libraries and librarians who are directly answerable to the communities they serve.

Libraries and society in Britain

There is usually a time gap between the emergence of a new social reality and that reality being accepted in people's consciousness. In the case of Britain, changes after the Second World War resulted in the loss of the economic power of Britain, a fact reflected in the loss of the British Empire. However, at a larger social level, the British society has not fully absorbed this fundamental loss of economic and thus political power. Lessons and reality of history are shut out from social consciousness by denying the reality of a new world where Britain is no longer the superpower ruling the world, where China is flexing its muscles to become the most powerful nation in the world.

In a society that has sought to shut out the reality of a new globalised world, it is not surprising that its libraries have shut themselves in a dream world of presumed superiority and "professional" might. The fact that the library world has not come to grips with changes in British society is a reflection of the British society as a whole not coming to grips with its new reality.

The Committee needs to give urgent attention to having a reality check of what the current social role of public libraries is and what it ought to be. A greater awareness of the real international and national forces at play in modern society needs to inform public library policy and practice.

Creating a people-orientated library service

There is thus an urgent need to develop a library service that helps to create a new consciousness among people about their real role in society and also about the position of their country in the context of the wider world. Only on such wider awareness can a people-orientated library service be built.

If there is going to be a true people-orientated library service, it is necessary that there is a clear understanding of social forces within which a particular library service operates. Libraries and librarians face a number of challenges today. The first need is for all librarians to investigate their society and communities. Mao's recommendation at a political level—"no investigation, no right to speak"—is equally valid in the information field. It is important to understand working people's lives and struggles, be one of them, and then seek ways of creating a relevant library service.

In all societies with class divisions and class struggle, library services tend to be a service for elite by elite, providing a service to the dominating classes and their allies only. In situations like these, the process of liberating the library service for those previously excluded is the key role of library workers and professionals.

The challenge is to develop a service that is open to all irrespective of class, race, gender, ability, age, sexual orientation, political beliefs, etc. The service needs to be an inclusive one, which reaches out to all who are currently excluded. Yet this task is not easy and needs careful thought and planning.

As is the case in all social movements, there are no specific guide books on how to create a liberated, "open" library service. It is only the actual practice of learning from people that will provide a solution that is relevant to our particular social situation and will help us build libraries without walls.

But just learning from people is not enough. The next, and perhaps the more difficult, step is to turn our ideas into action. This is best done by empowering the excluded, so that it is *they* who decide how our library resources should be used and how our energies are spent. People themselves will then be the best judges of our success or failure. It is in putting these ideas into practice that a people-orientated, "open to all" service can be built.

Libraries can be at the centre of this vastly changing world. Effective leadership in the information field can make libraries places where different social, political and economic forces in conflict can deposit their various views, experiences, knowledge, and world outlooks and help create a society at peace with itself. By ensuring that these contradictory forces have an equal chance to be acquired, stored, heard and understood, librarians and libraries can create a new social role for themselves. They will then have played a meaningful social role in creating more just and "equal" societies.

Abdul Kalam, the President of India, has pinpointed the root cause of social and political conflicts in the world today:

> ... [the] world over, poverty, illiteracy and un-employment are driving forward the forces of anger and violence... But, societies,which includes you and me, have to address themselves to the root causes of such phenomena which are poverty, illiteracy and unemployment.[205]

Librarians everywhere have a role to play in eliminating the root causes of poverty, illiteracy, unemployment and inequality. It is no longer acceptable for libraries and librarians to refuse to take this social responsibility seriously. The choice is simple: if the information profession does not take its social responsibility seriously, it will no longer have a social role. People will then develop alternative models of information and knowledge communication, which do meet their needs. There will then be no libraries, as we know them today.

---

[205] Kalam, Abdul (2004): "Dynamics of terrorism and violence". Philosophy and social action. Vol. 30 (2) April-June, 2004.

> *The Committee has an important role in ensuring that public libraries emerge from the deep social sleep into which they have sunk – generally isolated from the people and communities they are expected to serve. There is a further danger of decision makers and managers living in a dream world where, regular assurances are given by interested parties, that all is well, and that libraries are at the centre of social life. The Committee needs to give a clear guidance about the future role of public libraries and help create a totally new mindset needed if we are to save the library for a new generation.*

Creating a new library, creating a new library manager (2005)[206]

PART 1: The need for change in public libraries

While the Government has recognised the need for change in public libraries, its methods of achieving change remain weak. The DCMS's *Framework for the Future*[207] does not provide a clear vision of what the public library should be in the 21st century to meet the information needs of all people. Some developments following the launch of this document have shown positive action, yet the overall vision remains patchy and unfocussed.

It is now accepted that public libraries are not open to all. *Open to all?*[208] found a "take it or leave it" approach which keeps a large proportion of the population out of the range of its services:

> The 150 year history of the public library reveals that UK libraries have adopted only weak, voluntary and "take it or leave it" approaches to social inclusion. The core rationale of the public library movement continues to be based on the idea of developing universal access to a service which essentially reflects mainstream middle class, white and English values. Attempts to break out of this mould, such as the "community librarianship" of the 1970s and 1980s, have been incorporated back into this mainstream. Attempts to target services towards excluded people remain patchy, uneven and are often time-limited.[209]

The research goes on to record some "key consequences of this approach to service provision":

- a continuing underutilisation of public libraries by working class people and other excluded social groups

---

[206] Paper presented at the 2005 efmd conference on public sector management development Management Development for Reform and Turnaround in the Public Sector Modernising Managers for Modern Services 3-4 March 2005. Nottingham Business School. The Nottingham Trent University. Nottingham, UK

[207] DCMS (2003): Framework for the future: libraries, learning and information in the next decade". London: Department of Culture, Media and Sport (DCMS). Available from <http://www.culture.gov.uk/libraries_and_communities/framework_for_the_future.htm> [Accessed 5 February, 2005].

[208] Open to All?: op. cit.

[209] Ibid.

- a lack of knowledge in the public library world about the needs and views of excluded "non users"
- the development in many public libraries of organisational, cultural, and environmental barriers which effectively exclude many disadvantaged people.[210]

The Government's aim is to ensure that public services do not reinforce the already existing social exclusion among this section of people. It also expects authorities to work actively towards eliminating exclusion and to create cohesive communities by supporting informal learning and meeting the information needs of all. Yet the role that libraries play in achieving this is actually declining. The Audit Commission concluded that the "traditional library services are in decline" giving the following facts:

> The proportion of the population who are 'active borrowers', people who have borrowed items in the last year, has also fallen significantly, from 37 percent in 1997/98 to 29 percent in 2000/01. At the same time, user surveys show a decrease in the proportion of users aged under 55 — with some library services having less than one-half of their users in this age band.[211]

...

> Since 1992/93 visits have fallen by 17 percent, and loans by almost one-quarter. Twenty-three percent fewer people are using libraries for borrowing than just three years ago.[212]

Leadbeater (2003) also found a similar picture. Observing that "Britain's public libraries are in serious trouble", he concludes:

> Unless decisive action is taken now, the decline of our public libraries could become terminal by the end of the decade. If that happened Britain would be writing off vital social and cultural assets.[213]

Public libraries used to be central to the life of many communities but they are increasingly marginalised. People now get books and information from other sources. Libraries need to respond by making themselves more attractive, while building on their traditional strengths.

They have to face up to the challenge and get to grips with it, starting by putting their own house in order. Only then will a once failing service start to attract additional resources, partners and support.

Recent figures show that the decline in the number of issues of public library material has continued:

---

[210] Ibid.
[211] Audit Commission. (2002): Building better library services: AC Knowledge Learning from Audit, Inspection and Research. London: Audit Commission. Available from: <http://www.audit-commission.gov.uk/reports/AC-REPORT.asp?CatID=&ProdID=9D0A0DD1-3BF9-4c52-9112-67D520E7C0AB> [Accessed 5 February, 2005].
[212] Ibid. Summary.
[213] Leadbeater, C. (2003): Overdue; how to create a modern public library service. London: Demos. Available from: <http://www.demos.co.uk/catalogue/default.aspx?id=262. [Accessed 5 February, 2005].

Year	Children's issues (million)	Adult issues (million)
1992-93	111.6	449.6
2002-03	89.2	270.8[214]

The Secretary of State, Tessa Jowell, has recognised the need for change in the sector and has posed a number of challenges to the profession:

> This is a critical time for the future of public library services. Although for over 150 years, libraries have given pleasure and provided opportunities to learn, it is now time to ensure that libraries are relevant and inviting to future generations... the challenge is to generate new users... it is important to learn lessons about why people do not use libraries — only one third do, so how do libraries attract the other two thirds?[215]

The Secretary of State made it clear that she wants change in public libraries. She explained what needs to happen so that libraries "become, once again, central points in local communities: But they can only take back this role if they consult local people, and put them in the driving seat. Not just once, but as a continuous dialogue".[216]

Yet the reality has not changed much. While a number of initiatives have been taken by Museums, Libraries and Archives Council (MLA), it appears that no fundamental questioning about the social and political role of public libraries in its global context has taken place. The general mould of the British public library has remained more or less the same for over 150 years, while society has seen major shifts on political, social, economic and cultural fronts. These changes have been accelerated in the last 20 years or so through changes associated with globalisation. Perhaps the main development that public libraries have seen is the availability of free access to computers and the Internet under the People's Network initiative. While this is a major development, it has merely been bolted onto the traditional mould of the public library and the rest of the system keeps operating the same as it always has. While technological aspects of library work are being responded to positively, the social aspects remain largely unaddressed. And yet the introduction of the People's Network computers has not halted the decline in the number of visits to libraries. Thus, visits to libraries declined from 355.9 million in 1997-98 to 323 million in 2002-03.[217] Presumably, the decline would have been even more serious without the People's Network.

While there have been some positive developments in finding a new, relevant model of public library service, these are not at a fundamental level to provide a viable new model of a new public service. A number of libraries have achieved Beacon status in some aspects of their work; the development of new library buildings (e.g. Peckham; proposed developments in Birmingham and Liverpool) have led to another approach of reinventing libraries, while Tower Hamlets had created a new

---

[214] LISU (2004): Library & Information Statistics Tables. Loughborough: Loughborough University.
[215] Jowell, Tessa. (2004, June 21). Department of Culture, Media and Sports public libraries seminar. Quotes taken from unpublished notes by Alison Bramley for Society of Chief Librarians (SCL) members.
[216] Lend it like Peckham! (2004, July-August). Library and Information Update. p.3.
[217] LISU (2004): op. cit.

brand, the "Ideas Store". Leicester City Library Service has started a process of reorganisation to make it more relevant to the needs of local people. Some initiatives at Merton Library Service, explained later in this article, point to yet another approach to redefining a role for the public library. Whether these experiences lead to long-term changes in the very fabric of public libraries remains to be seen.

The key question, then remains: what conditions need to be met in order to develop a new, vibrant model of public library service? IDeA identifies the key challenges to local authorities thus: "The challenge for local government is to change culturally, to seek new ways of working, and to reach beyond its organisational boundaries".[218] Whereas various sections of local authorities have responded to this need for change, few public libraries have aspired to meet the challenge set by IDeA in any meaningful way.

A key requirement for making meaningful change is leadership with vision, commitment and drive. Such leaders should be able to connect with the most progressive ideas and people within and outside the information sector. Yet these are the very competencies that are in short supply. There can be no innovation and development without creative leaders and ideas. Creativity and innovation need fertile ground to grow and build a strong foundation. It is in this area that the Government needs to turn if its desire for change in the information sector is ever going to be met. The formation of a "public library innovations & development" unit was suggested by the present author in 2004 in a submission to the Culture, Media and Sports Parliamentary Committee as a way of supporting innovation and change in public libraries.[219]

In order to make libraries relevant and meet new challenges, there needs to be development in two related areas:

- The need to develop new leaders with innovative ideas, clear vision and the ability to inspire and develop staff
- The need to develop new, relevant services to meet new or unmet needs in a creative environment that involves the end users of the service in planning and monitoring services, taking into account equality requirements.

The present author has worked, with others, on a number of projects which address the above needs. This paper will focus on two such initiatives: the Quality Leaders Project—Youth (QLP-Y), and the innovations approach in the Merton Library and Heritage Service.

...

The two projects covered by this article—QLP and Merton innovations projects—provide many useful lessons—negative and positive—in developing effective leaders and developing relevant service. The two aspects are related and cannot be seen in isolation from each other. Further insight into success and failure of different aspects of the QLP project will be available in due course from independent evaluators. Additional details about the project, as well as an assessment from those involved in the project, will be included in the forthcoming "QLP Manual".

---

[218] IDeA (n.d.): Local government improvement programme. Available from: <http://www.idea.gov.uk/lgip/> [acquired on 7 February, 2005].
[219] The submission is available at <http://lists.essential.org/pipermail/upd-discuss/2004q4/000857.html>. Acquired on 7 February, 2005.

The key issue

The key issue facing local authorities is to bring about changes in services which have remained more or less static in a rapidly changing world. The experience from both these projects indicates that change can come from a new kind of leadership with a vision and drive to create a new type of relevant, inclusive and "equal" service for all people. While such leadership is not widely available now, our experience shows that it is possible to develop it from the ranks of the middle management who currently remain largely powerless to make effective change, and whose effective leadership skills have not been fully developed.

It is thus clear that a key task is to develop new managers so that they emerge as future leaders with a new vision and commitment. They need to break away from the mindset created by many present "leaders" and from the prevailing ethos which has refused to change—except in words. Our experience shows that there is a layer of middle managers who are not only ready for change, but are actively supporting change. But in many cases, their attempts are thwarted by many of those who hold power in the system, who are often afraid of losing their positions of power and influence, and who cannot face the challenge posed by new ideas from a new generation. Yet they have no solutions to the many challenges facing libraries today. They are also active in stopping the empowerment of local communities to influence their local services. They have become the greatest obstacle to the normal development of a new generation of leadership as well as for developing relevant services which are open to all.

It is also important to realise that there is a powerful group of "traditional" managers who hold enormous power through having survived in the system over long periods. They rule by patronage and intimidation, installing fear, but no respect. They are extremely successful in scuppering any progressive ideas, having learnt bureaucratic tricks to thwart any change they do not agree with. "Middle class, white and English values", according to *Open to all?*,[220] is the prevailing mode in public libraries. Drastic surgery is needed if the very values running public libraries are to change.

...

At the same time, there are key lessons which the Government needs to take on board. While the approach of bringing about gradual change through persuasion may be an important way of ensuring that everybody is on board, this approach is not likely to lead to any meaningful change during the lifetimes this or next generation. Libraries, and local authorities as a whole, do not have that much time left—they are likely to be swallowed by forces unleashed by globalisation and rules from WTO, even as we argue about the best way of bringing about change.

What is perhaps needed is the declaration of a "state of emergency" to save local services in the interest of local communities. The Secretary of State was right when she identified the need for change in public libraries—and by implication in all public service. Her desire to see libraries "become, once again, central points in local communities"[221] will not be fulfilled unless a new leadership is born in the very struggle for change. Many information workers are daily involved in this struggle to bring about the change that the Government wants. Yet they are on their own in the battlefield, fighting an army of managers and power-holders who are armed to the

---

[220] Open to all?: op. cit.
[221] Lend it like Peckham! (2004) op. cit.

teeth with the weapons which have been supplied by the Government itself. It is about time that the Government "disarms" these power brokers and instead "arms" those who are active in creating a new information service. Change and innovation need to be legitimised in local authorities. Those in power need to be made accountable to their communities. It is necessary to ensure that creativity, equality and empowerment of communities and progressive staff happen in practice, not only on paper.

After 150 years of public library service, there is an urgent need to give a new legitimacy to an alternative information service. There is an urgent need for alternate effective leadership. New ideas, new vision and new structures are needed if local authorities are to meet the needs of a new world. It is only Government action that can kick start this process in a meaningful way. The conditions on the ground are ready. The experience with QLP is proof of that. The experience at Merton, however short-lived it may prove to be, shows the tremendous potential that is available in local communities and among progressive staff. But will the Government take up the baton?

Comments on "New direction in social policy" (2005)[222]

Some comments from Shiraz Durrani for the first meeting on 23 March, 2005.

The following concerns assume that what we are after is a new culture within the MLA domains. While the following comments focus on libraries, I believe the situation in the other domains is similar:

- It is clear that libraries need major changes and the social policy framework would be *the* place to start the process. This opportunity seems to have been lost.
- Public libraries existed for years without a proper planning regime, until the introduction of the Annual Library Plans and the Position Statements. While planning has now become part of life now, it can often become a routine process just to score marks on the paper exercise. A new policy approach needs to ensure that the planning is for a social purpose. There is no evidence in the material I have seen that this is being taken on board.
- Similarly, libraries have existed without an appropriate policy framework or culture. There needs to be an urgent need, to change the culture in a meaningful way. I would have assumed that the prime task of the "new direction in social policy" initiative would be to kick start this process as part of the new approach. This does not seem to have been proposed in the tender document, nor achieved in the draft report. There may well be other

---

[222] Museums, Libraries and Archives Council (MLA) Cultural Diversity Advisory Group. 22 March 2005.

initiatives to make this happen, about which I may be unaware.
- Connected with the need for a new policy approach is the need for committed people on the ground working with managers who themselves are committed. If anything comes out of this initiative, it should be an agreed and rigorous framework by which an authority's performance on cultural diversity is measured. Library authorities should focus on PROPER performance management systems with a clear equalities focus. While one hopes that the leadership initiative by MLA will start addressing this need, it should also be reflected in the policy initiative.
- The government is moving very clearly in the direction of community engagement (and councils are having to follow suit) but are libraries following their councils? For far too long libraries have existed in some kind of Dickensian time warp where the rules don't apply to them. The only way for Libraries to address any kind of cultural diversity agenda (rather than simply producing endless documents about them) is to wake up to the fact that they need a few simple things:
  - committed staff;
  - committed senior *and middle* management;
  - rigorous performance measures and willingness by senior management to introduce strict competency proceedings if performance measures are not met, or the losers will be the public — the very people we are trying to engage!
- This can only be addressed meaningfully if the policy brief addresses itself to this need. As it stands, it does not.
- Basically there needs to be policies from MLA/DCMS on performance requirements. It should indicate what is required from managers and staff:
  - This is what you have to do to indicate a culturally diverse service (itself requiring staff who are committed and who will produce meaningful policies and performance measures);
  - This is what will happen if you don't do it;
  - So get on with it and be ready to be disciplined if you don't do it.

There are currently no policies to make this happen.

- There is a danger of losing the plot when there is an assumption that the various domains, which administratively come under MLA, have similar needs and can be "treated" with the same medicine. The domains are quite distinct, and the addition of the health aspect complicates further what was already a confused picture. There needs to be an assessment of what the universal aspects of the different domains are (which can all be addressed with similar treatment); at the same time, one needs a clearer picture of the particularities within each of the domain which are particular to that aspect only and so need specific policy approach. In all this, the role of MLA (indeed of DCMS) needs to be clearly defined.
- A number of new reports have been published recently; some after the BOP Final report (2nd draft) was produced.[223] These need to be looked at before the

---

[223] BOP: Burns Owens Partnership, consultants who produced the report. Other reports include the following: Commons Culture, Media and Sport Committee report on public libraries Available from http://www.parliament.uk/parliamentary_committees/

final report is prepared and lessons on policies incorporated.
- There is a further danger in the approach taken in this consultancy tender document of being less than clear about what social role each domains plays, or is expected to play.
- At the same time, there seems to be a vacuum about various developments at the international level, e.g. what impact is globalisation having on public libraries around the world, and also in Britain; how are developments in ICT going to change the future public library service; what positive experiences from around the world can be used in Britain. Local authorities as a whole are changing, and libraries cannot expect to remain the same. Who is going to decide where they go? With a policy vacuum, they will be driven by private interests.
- Also what is needed is a willingness to focus on the qualitative rather than simply the quantitative. Mapping provision, evidence base and all the other things in the consultant's report seems very interesting but not remotely new. While it is good to put together results of various small bits of research, this is meaningless unless particular lessons for a *policy approach* are recommended. This is lacking.
- While the recommendation for setting up the "Social Policy Research Network" is a useful one, such a recommendation did not require external consultants to come up with. There is enough expertise within MLA to have worked this out. The final report needs to come out with more substantial recommendations.

Public library managers and staff need to be given a very strong framework to work under. This can only be provided by a robust policy framework. Change will not come without it — there are too many vested interests. Unless this comes out of the present exercise, it will all have been a major waste of time.

22 March, 2005

---

culture_media_and_sport/cms_050309.cfm [accessed 21 March, 2005].; Public Library Impact Measures. The Public Library Impact Measures have been launched. More details are available from DCMS website from: http://www.culture.gov.uk/libraries_and_communities/impct_ms.htm [accessed 21 March, 2005]. The Audit Commission has put forward proposals to give Public libraries stronger weighting in the Comprehensive Performance Assessment (CPA) of local authorities. Available from the CILIP website: http://www.cilip.org.uk/aboutcilip/newsandpressreleases/news050311.htm [assessed 21 March, 2005].

The challenge for libraries in a multicultural society (2007)[224]

Part 1 – Key challenges

Politics of information

Perhaps the most important challenge facing libraries and librarians is to accept the implications of the fact that they are part of the political situation of their societies. This means that their action – or inaction – in the political arena have important implications for their communities and their professional work. Libraries exist in particular political situations and librarians reflect their own particular class and social positions in the decisions they make in their professional life. In societies divided by classes, this means that the profession may often serve the interests of one class only – the ruling class whose world outlook the libraries may help to reinforce at the expense of the outlooks, visions and needs of the working class and poorer members of our communities.

The question about whether libraries meet the needs of marginalised communities is, in essence, a question of whether libraries meet the needs of their communities by providing relevant services. In order to do so, it is, first of all, essential that there is a clear vision of what type of society, and what type of library service, we want. Secondly, it is essential that the library service knows their local communities and understands their needs. There has to be a real partnership with local communities so that library services do not appear from the skies to "deliver" a service. The service and service providers have to be part of the community before the community will accept them as one of their own. Local communities, particularly those who have been excluded, should be empowered to be active players in making policies on services and resource allocation, on service delivery and monitoring its impact. Too often, it is the most articulate, the most politically connected and those with wealth and education who set local agenda. The need is for those excluded from this position of power to be empowered, to become active citizens and to influence policies and practices of public institutions.

Let us look at some other challenges library services face in developing innovative libraries for the future in a globalized, multicultural society that Europe is today.

Democracy deficit

I start by making some basic assumptions about our societies. The first is that we aspire to live in a democratic Europe – and a democratic world – where the rights and

---

[224] Presentation at a conference organized by the Danish Library Centre for Integration – konference den 23. Januar 2007. Eigtvedspakhusikøbenhavn. Integration og biblioteker. State and University library. Universitetsparken. Dk-8000 aarhus c • denmark. Www.statsbiblioteket.dk/sbci. Bibliotekscenter for integration (sbci).. Also available at: http://www.indvandrerbiblioteket.dk/data_editors/ibed//objects/Durrani.pdf [Accessed: 18 February 2007].

responsibilities of all are fully guaranteed and respected. But what does "democracy" mean? Here is one definition:

> Democracy is a system of political governance [where] decision-making power is subject to the controlling influence of citizens who are considered political equals. A democratic political system is inclusive, participatory, representative, accountable, transparent and responsive to citizens' aspirations and expectations.[225]

Some requirements for a functioning democracy are mentioned by Dahl:

- Effective participation: equal & effective opportunities to make views known before a policy is adopted
- Voting equality: all to have opportunity to vote in policy-making. All votes to be counted equally
- Enlightened understanding: opportunities for all to learn about policies & their consequences
- Control of the agenda: all to have the right to decide how and what matters are placed on the agenda
- Inclusion: All to have full rights[226]

There is a fundamental question here about democracy: what happens when the majority vote for particular policies that discriminate against minorities? Our constitutions and rules need to ensure that the rights of all are protected and this can only happen when a society is guided by principles of social justice and human rights, which protect the interest of all. Legitimate rights of minority groups should be protected by law.

The question then is whether there is real democracy in Europe. We all like to think that there is, but is there democracy for *all*? The reality is that many minority communities do not share the same democratic rights that should be theirs by right. There cannot be democracy without power, without adequate income or adequate wealth. There cannot be real democracy and equality in Europe when there is global inequality in wealth and income — often as a result of the profit motives of transnational companies and global financial interests. It is worth keeping in mind the facts about the distribution of global assets, as shown by Davis et al:

- The richest 1 percent of adults alone owned 40 percent of global assets in the year 2000
- The richest 10 percent of adults accounted for 85 percent of the world total
- The bottom half of the world adult population owned barely 1 percent of global wealth[227]

---

[225] International Institute for Democracy and Electoral Assistance. Available at: <http://www.idea.int/democracy/index.cfm>. [Accessed: 21 December 2006].
[226] Dahl, Robert (2001): The General Definition of Democracy, Research-Education-Advocacy-People (REAP). Available at: <http://www.reapinc.org/Defdem.html>. [Accessed: 06 December 2006].
[227] Davies, James et al. (2006): World Distribution of Household Wealth. New York: World Institute for Development Economics Research of the United Nations University. United Nations Secretariat, New York. Available at: <www.wider.unu.edu/>. [Accessed: 06 December 2006].

So the first challenge for establishing a fair and just library service is to address the question of democracy deficit in our world as a whole and in Europe also. The effects of inequality at a global level are then felt in Europe too as a result of the total freedom of capital to go all over the world in search of mega-profits, thereby disrupting the functioning of viable economies in other countries. At the same time, while capital moves freely, labour is restricted in its search for employment and livelihood, which they can no longer find in their own countries. We thus have a rich world and a poor world—a North-South divide—not only in different regions of the world, but within each country as well. It is this national and international inequality that is then reflected in our libraries.

It is inconceivable that the marginalised minority communities would remain marginalised for long if they had effective power and wealth. They would then have been in a position to demand—and receive—the services they need. Their marginalization is not self-inflected—they are victims of our economic and political systems whose very foundation requires a majority of people to be poor so that the minority can be super rich. Those caught in between the two extremes are engaged in a constant battle to rise up—or at least not to sink too low. It is also important to remember that people who are marginalised are engaged in active struggles against their marginalisation and inequality. The easiest way for us to connect with their world is to join them in their struggle for equality and social justice.

The question then arises about the role that librarians can or should play in order to ensure that there is real democracy in our societies, our world and in our libraries. This is not entirely a matter for individual choice. If we are serious as professionals in providing a service to all, then we also need to ensure that we play a part in removing the social, political and economic barriers that prevent us from delivering an "equal" service to all. At the very least, it is our duty to provide information to our active and potential users as to the real reasons for inequality in our world today. We should provide them with historical information about how this inequality came about and who benefited from it. We also need to show that those who suffer inequality do not suffer it in silence. Information about resistance to this inequality is often hidden and not generally available in our libraries. Thus the victims often begin to blame themselves for being victims. If we do not document this resistance, those resisting inequality find our libraries alien places that neither understand their world, nor provide them with information to help them get out of their social oppression and economic exploitation. Providing them with token information in the name of multiculturalism does not fool them into trusting a system and a society, which they see as remote and uninterested.

Those who are really concerned to reach out to minority communities should try to deliver an information service that reflects world reality from *their* point of view—and we will see an immediate take-up of such a service based on an alternative worldview missing from most of our libraries.

Policy challenges

The next challenge is to ensure that library services have appropriate written policies guided by national and international laws. It is important to ensure that policies meet requirements of human rights and social justice. Appropriate national information policies are an essential requirement and these should guide policies of individual institutions and libraries. Such information policies should cover the following areas:

- Diversity: bring people from "outside" into policy making teams
- Innovation: provide alternatives to the "usual" practices and procedures
- Risk Management: assess & manage risks
- Consult those responsible for implementation & those affected by policies
- Assess impact: monitor, evaluate & adjust

Thus the first test is to see if the library services are guided by appropriate policies. The second test is to see if the marginalized communities had any say in deciding on these policies and in monitoring their implementation. The CDF guidance on "community leadership" states, that "those at the receiving end of services and provision should begin to play a more active role in shaping the policies, programmes and services which affect their lives".[228] Unless this happens in practice, our services will not meet the needs of all, particularly those already marginalised by social and economic forces.

Ethical and professional considerations

The next challenge is to ensure that our services meet ethical requirements. The case for an "equal" library service has been made by international bodies such as UNESCO, as well as by IFLA, World Summit on the Information Society (WSIS), among others. UNESCO's Public Library Manifesto provides[229] guidelines on meeting needs of all.

Thus for example, IFLA/UNESCO Public Library Guidelines for Development state the need:

- to promote equal access to public library services for all;
- to raise the quality of services in public libraries by defining standards, developing guidelines and documenting best practices;
- to promote the importance of training and professional development in libraries;
- to defend the role of the public library in democratizing access to and the use of information technology.[230]

The World Summit on the Information Society sets a clear vision for library services "to build a people-centred, inclusive and development-oriented Information Society" where "everyone can create, access, utilize and share information and knowledge". It emphasises the need for "enabling individuals, communities and peoples to achieve their full potential in sustainable development and to improve the quality of life". In

---

[228] "Community Leadership" Guide Paper for the Community Development Foundation (CDF) Workshop. BVSC, Birmingham, 4 October 2005.
<http://www.cdf.org.uk/SITE/UPLOAD/DOCUMENT/Practice%20Links/leadershipguidepaperoct05.pdf>. [Accessed: 18 October 2006]
[229] Available at: http://www.unesco.org/webworld/libraries/manifestos/libraman.html [Accessed: 30 August 2007].
[230] IFLA Public Library Section:
<http://www.ifla.org/VII/s8/proj/s8_Guidelines_For_Development.pdf>. [Accessed: 18 Oct. 2006]

addition, in its Declaration of Principles, WSIS sets out a clear agenda for library and information services:

- To respect peace and uphold values of freedom, equality, solidarity, tolerance, shared responsibility, and respect for nature;
- Acknowledge the importance of ethics for the Information Society which should foster justice, dignity & worth of the human person;
- The use of ICTs & content creation should respect human rights and fundamental freedoms, including privacy, right to freedom of thought, conscience, religion in conformity with international laws;
- All to take actions, as determined by law, against abusive uses of ICTs, e.g. racism, racial discrimination, xenophobia, intolerance, hatred, violence, child abuse, and the exploitation of human beings.[231]

These are issues that we need to engage with actively.

Organisational and cultural change

Forces of globalisation have brought about major changes in societies in individual countries as well as globally. Developments in ICT provide new challenges and new possibilities that have changed the way we work and live. Major shifts in economic and political power can be seen in the rise of the BRIC countries (Brazil, Russia, India and China) and the relative decline in the power of the U.S.A. and Europe. Such major changes over a comparatively short period of time requires people and countries not only to understand this dynamic situation, but also prepare to meet new challenges by acquiring new skills and new world outlooks. Library services can play a key role in this process. At the same time, they need to make changes in the way they deliver service if they are to meet new or unmet needs of all people in their communities.

Change is needed at a number of levels: vision, organisation, management, culture, and in the way policies and decisions are made and implemented. Resistance to change by some managers, staff and even existing beneficiaries of the service has also to be addressed. Appropriate staffing structures need to be in place, and policies to mainstream equality have to be prepared and implemented. For all this to happen, an important area that needs to be addressed as a matter of urgency is the development of leadership within the workforce. At the same time, the need to provide appropriate developmental opportunities to staff in general, as well as all levels of management, should be addressed.

In general, staff needs to be seen as part of the process of change and not as mere bystanders who are expected to implement changes without real involvement in the decision-making process. At the same time, there needs to be a clear vision and leadership from the main decision makers.

The very vision of library services needs to be revised to ensure that a real people-oriented service is delivered. We do not have time here today to go into all these

---

[231] World Summit on the Information Society (WSIS): Declaration of Principles; Building the Information Society: a global challenge in the new Millennium. <http://www.itu.int/wsis/docs/geneva/official/dop.html>. [Accessed: 28 November 2005].

areas, but it should be realised that if there is a genuine desire for improving services to minority communities, all these areas will need to be addressed.

An equally important area of concern is whether libraries reflect their local communities in the proportion of staff they employ from minority communities. It is particularly important that this happens at all levels, particularly at senior and middle managerial levels where policies are made and implemented. This, in itself, does not guarantee that the service will be an "equal" one—after all there can be token minority representatives on management boards, others may side against their own communities to prove that they have "arrived", and many others—particularly women—may find the prevailing organisational culture, racism and xenophobia makes it impossible for them to be effective. Yet it is important to make a start by having minority representation in management boards. It is only when the minority communities see a fair representation in staffing that they begin to trust the service. It is instructive to see that India has an affirmative action policy for the Dalit community to ensure they have a fair representation in all fields of social and economic life. Perhaps there is a lesson here for us to learn.

...

The case studies in Part 2 gives some examples of how a progressive service can meet these challenges.

Conclusion: Innovate, dream, take risks and rely on people

The main task then is how to translate some of the ideas mentioned above into practice, to move from ideas to action. Perhaps the best advice one can give on this is that there are no ready-made solutions. Each of us needs to investigate our own local situation, understand our communities and work with them to find a relevant service, which meets their needs. We have to investigate and understand the power relations between different classes and communities in order to find the best solutions for our particular situation. We have to win the confidence of those seeking equality and social justice and they will become our best allies in bringing about change. As there are no textbook solutions, it is necessary that we take calculated risks and be creative in the way we manage library services.

We have an important leadership role in bringing about change so that the needs of all are met. The first requirement is to acknowledge the need for change and to have a commitment to making changes in the way we think, work and relate to people. We have the advantage that developments in information and communications technologies (ICT) provide us with new tools to address old problems of social division, inequality and disempowerment of some. These tools, if used correctly, can empower our communities to chart out a new future for them—with our help.

Further, it is important to understand the relation between race and class. People who suffer because of discrimination and exploitation face multiple disadvantages. Women, young people, and other cultural minorities then face an ever-heavier burden. Building trust with them is a priority.

While we try to bring communities together, the many divisive forces in our societies have been introducing artificial barriers and divisions. Religious differences, for example, need not divide people, but they do so in today's world. Differences between different communities can add value to the total sum of our culture and social lives—unless vested interests use these to increase divisions, hostility and conflict. It is our role as information workers to provide information, which can show the real factors that unite us and help develop a more equitable society where the right to information is a reality for all.

Let us affirm that change is possible, a new world is possible, and we can play a part in creating this new world. Let us:

- change through alternative vision and ideas;
- develop alternative leadership in action;
- innovate: turn ideas into action;
- legitimise alternative leaders, ideas, structures and services;
- build creative partnerships with those sharing our vision.

Finally, let's not stop dreaming of a society where there is real equality and social justice. Only then can it become a reality.

Politics of information and resistance

Capitalism and socialism — has the contradiction been resolved? (1992)[232]

Recent events in Eastern Europe and in the Soviet Union, have been hailed by bourgeois propagandists as victory for capitalism and the death of socialism. Many progressive people and indeed some activists have been confused by these events and their interpretation by the capitalist press. It is necessary for us to start a discussion on the events and also on their implications for us in Kenya.

First of all it is important to read what progressive people and parties have been saying about recent developments. It would be instructive, for example, to hear what Cuba and China are saying about recent events. The South African Communist Party has also begun a debate on this. Some articles on this are listed at the end of this section and should be read by all.

It is important to admit that changes in Eastern Europe and the Soviet Union have adversely affected the forces of socialism in the world. Their very existence had provided a rallying point for socialism and in many cases had provided not only moral but material support for liberation movements and to anti-imperialist forces everywhere. Their change of policy has left imperialist forces led by the U.S. a free hand to interfere in the affairs of any country without being challenged. The recent attack on Iraq testifies to this.

But this does not mean that capitalism has triumphed. The achievements of socialist experiences have been many and will live forever. But even socialism in these countries was of a particular type influenced by their own particularities. The conversion to capitalism will not in itself solve the problems facing the people. Already questions are being raised about production for profit, which disregards the satisfaction of people's basic needs. As time goes on more contradictions will arise.

More fundamentally, it is true that these changes, however important they may have been, have not resolved the basic contradiction between capitalism and socialism. Classes have not been abolished; class struggle has not ceased. Mois and KANUs still exist and are still in power. Their major backer, U.S.-led imperialism still exists, more powerful and more ruthless than ever before. Social oppression has not vanished: economic exploitation still deprives our people the fruits of their labour. Children still die in their thousands through malnutrition and their parents are even today massacred and shot by forces of oppression that is the hallmark of capitalism.

If capitalism is flourishing, if exploitation is still rampant, can socialism be dead? Ever since the formation of classes, class struggle has never ceased. And there can only be one resolution to class conflict — socialism. Historically, the struggle against imperialism has been waged throughout the world, but different countries and different nationalities within a country have taken the lead at different times. It was the Paris Commune in France that led the struggle in one historical period, the

---

[232] Mpatanishi Vol. 2 No.1 Sept. 1992, pp.11-12. Originally published in Matukio Duniani (Ukenya, London).

Bolshevik Revolution at another, and the Chinese revolution in yet another period. At other times, the lead has been taken by people of Cuba and Vietnam. At another level, the anti-colonial struggles in Algeria, Kenya, and Ghana have played their part in nibbling at the feet of the imperialist giant-dwarf. The struggle of the South African people even today plays its part in the overall struggle against imperialism in its local manifestation. Similarly our own struggle testifies to the on-going struggle against neo-colonialism.

Do these struggles imply that imperialism has won, that socialism has been defeated, that the people's search for a democratic solution to their problems has been abandoned? On the contrary, they imply a further sharpening of the basic contradictions.

The only certainty for the future is that the anti-imperialist struggle will continue. They may be more difficult, having been deprived of the material and moral support that came from Eastern Europe and the Soviet Union. More self-reliant forms of struggle will have to be evolved. More cooperation among struggling people will have to be resorted to. This may delay final victory, but a stronger foundation for long-term success will have been laid in the process. In the short term, some people may be disillusioned. This merely implies that more ideological work among the people and even among cadres is needed. On our part it calls for more study to understand the current forces for and against progress.

The experience from Europe and in Africa has placed the people's power back where it belongs — with the people. No amount of propaganda can alter this basic fact that people's power belongs to the people and they are not about to hand it over to imperialism to continue their exploitation.

So let us sing even louder our songs for total liberation and stand firm against everything that imperialism represents. Tomorrow truly belongs to the people — and to us if we march with them.

Suggested Reading

Slovo, Joe: "Has Socialism Failed?" Umsebenzi Discussion Pamphlet. South African Communist Party pamphlet. 1990. pp. 28 [Also published in *The African Communist*, No.121, pp. 25-52 (1990).

Castro, Fidel: They gave their lives for the most treasured values of the revolution. Dec. 7, 1989. Reproduced In *The African Communist*, No. 121, pp. 52-63 (1990).

Marrero, Juan: Nicaragua — Big setback that leads to new stage of Struggle. *Granma*. March 11, 1990. Reproduced in *The African Communist*, No. 122, pp. 93-96 (1990).

Returning a stare; people's struggles for political and social inclusion (2000)[233]

PART 1: INTRODUCTION – Capitalism and Social Exclusion

...

Public libraries have an important role to play in these worldwide struggles of the people of all nationalities and all countries. Yet as international finance consolidates its stranglehold over lives of people and countries following the end of the so-called Cold War, national governments and local authorities are being forced to follow the social and economic policies laid down by international finance and its agencies, the International Monetary Fund and the World Bank. The resources available to governments to support education, information and knowledge through public libraries are consistently shrinking. The relentless drive towards "privatisation" results in an ever-reducing role of local authorities by decreasing the funds available to them to run social and educational services such as public libraries. While the international finance capital can tolerate Mobotus, Mois and Marcoses who drain away huge proportions of national wealth, it cannot tolerate a relevant information and education system that can liberate people from their bondage to international finance.

This does not imply that people have given up their struggle for a relevant information system. While their main struggle is at the economic level, the provision of relevant information and education is considered essential for success in people's struggles everywhere. There is a general recognition that no liberation can be won without getting control of the means of mass communications.

...

PART 2 – EXCLUSION AND GLOBALISATION

The process of exclusion is evident in all capitalist countries. This is not accidental, as the division of society into classes implies that some people are "over-included" while others are excluded from social, political and economic life. The process of exclusion has been accelerated in the last part of this century with the collapse of the USSR. Capitalism is now free to extend and intensify its ideology of "profits before all else". The process of globalisation of this period has created its own record of social exclusion.

Globalisation and exclusion have had a profound impact on the information field. We need to see what these terms mean and exactly what effects they have had on the information field.

---

[233] Open to All? The Public library and social exclusion. (2000) Vol. 3: Working Paper 6. Public Library Policy and Social Exclusion. London: Resource: The Council for Museums, Archives and Libraries. Available at: http://www.seapn.org.uk/opentoall.html [Accessed: 02 April 2007]. Also published in *Progressive Librarian* No. 17, Summer, 2000 pp.3-34.

Social exclusion

Social exclusion is a concept proposed by the social policy think tanks of the European Union's Commission, and adopted by the United Nation's International Labour Office. Castells describes social exclusion as:

> the process by which certain individuals and groups are systematically barred from access to positions that would enable them to an autonomous livelihood within the social standards framed by institutions and values in a given context. Social exclusion is, in fact, the process that disenfranchises a person as labour in the context of capitalism.[234]

The British Government's Social Exclusion Unit uses Duffy's definition of Social Exclusion: "an inability of individuals to participate effectively in economic, social, political, and cultural life, alienation and distance from the mainstream society".[235] King discusses the differences between the terms "poverty" and "social exclusion". He defines poverty as a "lack of material resources" and social exclusion as a "highly dynamic and complex notion which explains not just how many poor people there are, but what poverty actually *is*, and how it fits into the larger social, economic and political makeup of a given locality". [His emphasis].

For the purpose of this paper, the terms "poverty" and "social exclusion" will be used to indicate both aspects mentioned by King. The term "social exclusion" may be comparatively new, but the phenomenon it describes has been with us for a long time. Poverty in the South as well as in the North has existed for hundreds of years. Whatever name it has been given, the majority of the population of the world has always lived an excluded life.

It is thus important to understand the conditions that give rise to a person or a group being "socially excluded". As used in literature currently, the term needs to be understood as a particular manifestation at a particular historical stage in the development of capitalism. The globalisation context of capitalism at the end of this millennium will be examined in the next section. The process of exclusion is a dynamic one, changing over time and space affecting different groups of people in different ways. Castells explains this aspect thus: "social exclusion is a process, not a condition. Thus its boundaries shift, and who is excluded and included may vary over time, depending on education, demographic characteristics, social prejudices, business practices, and public policies."[236]

It is worth remembering that it is not only individuals and individual communities that are excluded from enjoying economic benefits that a society is capable of generating. Entire countries and regions are often excluded, for example Sub-Saharan Africa with its 500 million people. The reason for this exclusion can be explained in the context of the development and expansion of capitalism worldwide. Castells says that these regions are excluded because they are:

> non-valuable from the perspective of informational capitalism and they do not have significant political interest for the powers that be and so are bypassed by flows of wealth and information, deprived of the basic flows of wealth and information, and ultimately deprived of the basic technological infrastructure that allows us to communicate, innovate, produce, consume, and even live, in today's world. This

---

[234] Castells, Manuel (1998): The power of identity. Oxford, Blackwell. p.73.
[235] King, Ewan (1999): Social Exclusion; reflections on the definition and measurement of social exclusion. London, Office for Public Management.
[236] Castells (1998): op. cit.

process induces an extremely uneven geography of social/territorial exclusion and inclusion, which disables large segments of people while linking up trans-territorially, through information technology, whatever and whoever may offer value in the global networks accumulating wealth, information, and power.[237]

It is thus clear that exclusion is not an isolated phenomenon, an unexplainable side effect of global development. It is in fact an essential outcome of capitalist development and is allowed to continue as a basis for the development of capitalism. A sobering fact that forms the background to our discussion is worth mentioning here: the world population is 5.9 billion. Out of this, 800 million people are hungry today—excluded from the very basic means of staying alive.[238] The world already produces enough food to provide everyone with a nutritious and adequate diet—on average, about 350kg of cereal per person. A clue to understanding causes of world hunger is in these facts: The poorest 60 percent of the world's population share just 4.5 percent of the world's income, and 20 percent of the richest share 83 percent.[239]

Capitalism does not distinguish between the North and South in inflicting exclusion on people. It is not only in the poorer, industrially undeveloped world that exclusion exists. In the U.S.A., for instance, " the human rights situation is such that that the social vice whereby the rich get ever richer and the poor get ever poorer has reached its extreme; tens of millions of vagabonds, beggars, destitute, and unemployed wander on the edge of their basic right to live."[240] Yet the U.S.A. boasts the most advanced industrial and electronic base in the world, creating unbelievable wealth for a small proportion of its population. It is not beyond the realm of possibility to eliminate exclusion if economic and political will existed. It is the financial/industrial capital, which, in the U.S.A. as well as internationally, opposes such elimination.

Globalisation

By its very definition, capitalism divides people along class lines. Working class people as a whole are historically excluded from enjoying the social wealth created by their labour. Hence the system creates a class that is automatically excluded from wealth, power, education and information. But this process of exclusion has been intensified in recent years. There has been a qualitative change in the process of social exclusion in the last quarter of this century on a global level. Castells explains these changes as a:

> technological revolution, centered around information (which) has transformed the way we think, we produce, we consume, we trade, we manage, we communicate, we live, we die, we make war, and we make love: a dynamic global economy has been constituted around the planet, linking up valuable people and activities from all over the world, while switching off from the networks of the power and wealth, people and territories are dubbed as irrelevant from the perspectives of dominant interests.[241]

---

[237] Castells (1998): op. cit. p.74.
[238] Pretty, Jules (1999): Southern comfort. The Guardian. February 24, p. 5.
[239] Brittain, Victoria (1999): High pressure. The Guardian. February 3, p. 4.
[240] Democratic People's Republic of Korea (1999): Statement by the Foreign Ministry. Broadcast on Central Broadcasting Station, Pyongyang, March 6, 2100 GMT. Picked up and translated by BBC Worldwide Monitoring. The Editor (the Guardian supplement), March 13, 1999:18.
[241] Castells (1998): op. cit. p. 1.

Capitalism began a new phase with the end of the international communist movement in the 1970s and 1980s and used the networking logic of the Information Age. Capital, no longer having to contend with opposition from socialism was now free to roam the world, wherever excessive profits were to be made. While this aggressive phase of capitalism resulted in increasing economic growth in some countries and regions, its own logic ensures that millions of people and large parts of the world remain excluded from growth. Many areas have thus experienced a decline in gross national product as capital moves out of less profitable countries and regions. The social and economic consequences of this global search for profit inevitably leads to marginalising and excluding millions of people around the world.

An important qualitative change brought about by globalisation is the change in the balance of power between labour and capital. Thus globalisation serves the interests of the minority rich elite, which control the wealth and resources of the "global world". As Lazarus says, "globalisation directly serves the interests of some people and that there is an intricate structural connection between the obscenely burgeoning prosperity of this minority and the steady immiseration of the vast majority of the world's population".[242]

The social, political and economic control over the majority world by forces of global capital has resulted in massive poverty—total "social exclusion"—for a majority of people.

Globalisation destroys workers' rights, suppresses civil liberties and negates democracy. It dismantles the public sector; privatises the infrastructure and determines social need. It free-floats the currency and turns money itself into a commodity subject to speculation, so influencing fiscal policy. It controls inflation at the cost of employment. It creates immense prosperity at the cost of untold poverty. It violates the earth, contaminates the air and turns even water to profit.[243]

In effect globalisation has created deeply divided societies (both in the Capitalist developed countries as well as in the majority world)—what Sivanandan[244] calls "that third of society that Information Capitalism and the market have consigned to the underclass as surplus to need" and which Hutton[245] calls "the absolutely disadvantaged" 30 percent of the "thirty, thirty, forty society". These developments have resulted in an increased social exclusion for an increasing number of people. Kundnani explores the dynamics of social exclusion; "The relationship between the wealthy and the poor is changing from one of exploitation to indifference".[246]

Gray records the social effects of globalization:

> over a hundred million peasants becoming migrant labourers in China; the exclusion from work and participation in society of tens of millions in the advanced societies; a condition of near-anarchy and rule by organised crime in parts of the post-communist world; further devastation of the environment.[247]

---

[242] Lazarus, Neil (1999): Charting globalisation. Race & Class 40(2/3) pp. 91-109.
[243] Sivanandan, S. (1999): Globalism and the Left. Race & Class 40(2/3) pp. 5-19.
[244] Sivanandan (1999): op. cit.
[245] Hutton, W. (1995): The State we're in. London: Cape.
[246] Kundnani, Arun (1999): Where do you want to go today? The rise of information capital. Race & Class 40(2/3) pp. 49-71.
[247] Gray, John (1998): False Dawn; the delusion of global capitalism. London: Granta Books.

Castells[248] dates the forces of globalisation and informationalisation from the end of Soviet communism and the "hurried adaptation" of Chinese communism to global capitalism. Previously, the 1917 Russian Revolution and the international communist movement had been the dominant political and ideological phenomena of the twentieth century. Castells sees the end of the Soviet Union as resulting from its inability to "manage the transition to the Information Age".

...

Elliott looks at the contradictions crated by globalisation and technological developments at the end of the second millennium:

> This is the age of the Internet, yet 80 percent of the world's population has never made a phone call. This is the age of democracy, yet the world's richest three men have assets that exceed the combined GDP of the 48 poorest nations.[249]

Muddiman sums up the relation between capitalism and social exclusion:

> The key thing is that the "Information Revolution" has actually *made things worse*. The "Information Society" is not just neutral or "up for grabs", but actually bound up with the forces that perpetuate exclusion and intensify it.[250]

This intensification of exploitation of the majority world has created a corresponding intensification of contradiction within countries and globally. People throughout the world are struggling against increasing exploitation and against capitalism as a whole. Thus as globalisation creates the global capitalist, so it also creates conditions on a global scale for resistance to it. It is this resistance to capitalist super-exploitation, to the total social exclusion, that we now turn to.

PART 3 – RESISTANCE TO EXCLUSION

Resistance to the new global disorder

Globalisation is unleashing contradictory forces that provide the dynamics of life at the end of the second millennium. The tremendous possibilities for improvements for a better life for all are reduced to the reality of marginalisation and exclusion for the majority.

On the one side, the levels and capacity of production are increasing at a tremendous pace with the immense capacity to satisfy the material needs of all people. There is greater scope to communicate on a global level in an increasingly efficient way. New creative and cultural activities are possible at a scale not even thought of 20 years ago. Increased productivity has the potential to transform the lifestyles of people by increasing leisure time

On the other side, is the fact that such possibilities are available to only a minority of countries, societies and individuals. As the world is dramatically divided in ever sharper class divisions, the majority of working people are excluded from all the wealth and possibilities made possible by the increased capacity to produce wealth.

---

[248] Castells (1998): op. cit.
[249] Elliott, Larry (1999): Economics. The Guardian. Weekend section. March 13:70.
[250] Muddiman, D. (2000). Theories of social exclusion and the public library. In Open to all? op. cit. Working Paper 1, pp. 1-15. Available at: Available at:
http://www.seapn.org.uk/opentoall.html [Accessed: 02 April 2007].

Castells concludes, "globalisation and informationalisation are disenfranchising societies". With the exception of a small elite, "people all over the world are losing control over their lives, over their environment, over their jobs, over their economies, over their governments, over their countries, and over the fate of the earth".[251]

The resistance by those who have lost control over their lives is resolving this basic contradiction. Thus "resistance confronts domination, empowerment reacts against powerlessness, and alternative projects challenge the logic embedded in the new global order, increasingly sensed as disorder by people around the planet". [252]

It is however an aspect of globalisation that information about resistance itself has also been marginalised and banished from the mass media controlled by the same global controllers. Thus begins people's resistance at the level of information and communication. The struggle then is not only to end poverty and exclusion but also to end the embargo on progressive information about the struggle of people around the world to end their exclusion.

It is obvious from the previous section that social exclusion is not an accidental outcome of some misguided policy. It is a natural outcome of capitalist development in the period of globalization, which has entered a new phase in the last quarter of this century. It affects the "developed" capitalist countries as well as the non-developing majority world. The struggle of the people around the world to be included in the distribution of products, which sustain life, is also global. It is global in two senses: One, in every country the marginalised and excluded people are struggling to be included in the economic, political and social life of their country. Secondly, the struggle is global in the sense that there is an increasing cooperation by people in different countries to work together on joint campaigns as their struggles and the causes of their exclusion are also linked.

Before the collapse of the Soviet Union, people's struggle everywhere, were primarily defined by the presence of the two super powers. People's struggles were clearly a struggle for liberation from capitalist marginalisation with a hope of creating a new society based on social justice and for socialism. With the material, ideological and symbolic support of Soviet Union and Eastern Europe gone, and with China increasingly adopting capitalism, the struggles of people have undergone a qualitative change.

These struggles take place in the "developed" as well as the majority world. Sivanandan examines both these struggles:

> In the developed countries, political power is diffused and mediated, and dissidence centres around specific issues. Resistance, therefore, takes on the form of protests and demonstrations and direct action politics.[253]

Resistance on a global level to forces that create social, political and economic exclusion is intensifying as we come to the end of the second millennium. The combatants are peasants, workers, intellectuals, academics and many others. The important qualitative difference in their resistance is that they are united, articulate, organised and are able to use the latest technologies in support of their resistance. Their target is no longer just the local tyrants, dictators and financiers. They have targeted the worldwide network of transnational companies, official bodies, unfair

---

[251] Castells, 1998: op. cit. p.69.
[252] Ibid.
[253] Sivanandan, S. (1999): op. cit.

treaties and speculators who use the neutral image of the UN to hide their real motive of mega-profits.

In the following section, we look at some examples of resistance to social, political and economic exclusion by people around the world.

The Battle of Chile

The control over mass media by a few transnationals has resulted in people's history either hidden from view altogether, or distorted to such an extent that events become non-events, heroes become villains, and atrocities against people never see the light of day. But once again the courage of individuals and organisations fighting oppression and exclusion has used appropriate technologies to give people's history its rightful place — centre stage.

Patricio Guzman's documentary film, *The Battle of Chile: the fight of an unarmed people* is an "epic of reportage on the events that extinguished democracy in Chile in 1973".[254] It was shown at the Human Rights International Film Festival in London in February 1999. The film is in two parts: Part One is entitled *The Insurrection of the Bourgeoisie (1975)* and Part two, *The Coup d'Etat*. Guzman and five colleagues who made the film were detained and tortured in Chile during filming.[255] Guzman made a sequel, *Chile, Obstinate Memory*, which reveals that after the film was smuggled abroad, the cameraman, Jorge Muller was arrested, and taken to a torture camp, where he "disappeared" until his grave was found years later.

The film records the events in Chile from 1972 onwards — on the streets, with the student unions, and in the factories, "to document the melodramatic reality of revolution. Guzman and his crew were there to record every significant event, every tiny speech, every road block, in the last year of Allende's rule".

...

Lessons for Public Libraries

It is obvious that no public library will be able to document openly state oppression against its own people. Yet it is important that library workers do not use this as an excuse for not recording, preserving and making available, at a later stage, records of events taking place around them. The film crew managed to do this and there are obvious risks they faced. But if library workers are part of the people they seek to serve, they face similar risks anyway. If they cannot become activist-librarians, the least they could do is to join hands with activists to ensure that the library's functions are kept in the forefront of the struggle. Perhaps library and information workers need to study the examples of journalists who often risk their lives in the course of their professional work. The concept of risk and danger in professional work needs to be incorporated in the core values of the LIS profession if it is to be socially relevant.

The video activist

The use of cameras and videos in support of struggles has a long history. Photo-documentation of events as they happen gives an instant authenticity to events. They are also more accessible to communities, which may have been kept away from

---

[254] Pilger, John (1999): Armed only with a camera. The Guardian. February 12: p.2.
[255] Hattenstone, Simon (1999): "I didn't take time enough to cry". The Guardian. February 12. p. 3.

literacy skills. For the first time, activists themselves take control of the medium and present news from their own point of view. As *Undercurrents* says:

> The video magazine is an alternative news distribution outlet that sets out to challenge mainstream definition of news. *Undercurrents* relies on volunteer video activists using domestic camcorders. Ignored but important local issues now can have an international audience.[256]

The visual images, the commentary and the voice of Leyla bring to life a situation that Western business interests and the mass media, which supports it, would rather suppress. As Tony Benn says, "I think *Undercurrents* is doing a marvellous job because you're providing [news that you do not see] in the media and with that little box of tricks you can beat Rupert Murdoch and John Birt and CNN and NBC and you've got to do it."[257] It is an alternative voice and image that needs to be heard and seen.

Lessons for Public Libraries

Libraries need to pay more attention to forms other than printed book: sound recordings, photographs, video filming, recording and preserving oral histories should become important forms that they actively collect and promote.

The Alternative Davos

The Alternative Davos was set up by Ahmed Ben Bella, the former President of Algeria and is supported by some of the best organised mass movements in the majority world — such as the landless of Brazil (MST), led by Mario Luis Lill; the organisations of the Indian farmers; the National Federation of Peasant Organisations (Fenop) in Burkina Faso, as well as the substantial social movements in Europe, especially in France.

The Alternative Davos got together to challenge the meeting of the global financial elite as they met in Davos. "It was the first time that the world's economic and political powers had had to confront the intellectual challenge to their fundamental premises on their own doorstep".[258]

...

The Alternative Davos attacked the power of the transnational companies, the Bretton Woods institutions, and the speculators. It called for the imposition of a tax on capital movements, the cancellation of all majority world debts, the replacement of the International Monetary Fund and the World Bank with a democratic UN body. No longer are the financial controllers of the world able to sit in isolated splendour planning world plunder. Resistance has reached their doorstep.

Protest and campaign movements

Various protest and campaign groups have now started using both, the overground and underground, alternative press to mobilise their supporters and disseminate their information. The availability of relatively cheap and easy means of communication that the Web and e-communications allows has revolutionised the way protest and social justice movements can be active. This has given new power to united and organised forces of those struggling against transnational companies and

---

[256] Undercurrents (1998) No. 9: Video Magazine. Oxford. www.undercurrents.org
[257] Undercurrents (1998) No. 8 Video Magazine. Oxford. www.undercurrents.org
[258] Brittain, Victoria (1999): op. cit.

their Western financial supporters. Vidal gives some examples of how the protest and campaign movements use the electronic media:

- Twelve environmental justice protesters and a video activist walked into Shell UK's London HQ and occupied three offices on January 11, 1999.
- The campaign to stop the Multilateral Agreement on Investment (MAI) depended on the Web and spread like wildfire. The MAI was being debated in secret by OECD countries and would have been nodded by Western parliaments, giving massive legal and economic advantage to transnational corporations around the world.[259]

Thus the Web technology, which is being used by speculators to acquire massive profits by "whizzing trillions of dollars around the world every day" has now become the most potent weapon in the toolbox of resistance to globalisation and the rampant free market. It has given instant information to activists around the world. "Small" events in one part of the world get immediate worldwide exposure, which leads to massive global campaigns within days or even minutes. The days when information was controlled by a few who disseminated only those aspects considered "safe" are over.

Lessons for Public Libraries

Public Libraries need to pay attention to underground and alternative material, which are becoming the main communication media for people struggling for change. The possibilities of cheap and easy means of communication that the Web and e-communications allow need to be harnessed by libraries to acquire, store and disseminate information that the struggling people consider relevant. Those who are active in the struggle have already adopted these technologies as tools for their struggles. If libraries are to be considered partners in the people's struggles, they will need to accept the new media, not to satisfy the business and other needs of the "already rich", but for the needs of the socially excluded.

The Adivasis and Social Exclusion

It is instructive to see social exclusion from the point of view of the Adivasi of the Nilgiri Mountains in Tamil Nadu. They struggle against transnational companies such as Unilever, which evicts them from land they have lived and worked on for generations. Marcel-Thekaekara compares the Adivasi experience with the struggle against social exclusion in a number of other countries:

- The experience of those struggling against social exclusion among the housing estates in the inner cities of England and Scotland. In Easterhouse housing estate in Glasgow, considered "Europe's worst slum", the reality of poverty included the fact that "most of the men in Easterhouse hadn't had a job in 20 years; they were dispirited, depressed, often alcoholic. Emotionally and mentally they were far worse off than where we worked in India; [we saw] underdeveloped Scottish children — a whole generation were growing up a head shorter, smaller than their parents and grandparents. Malnutrition in Britain"!
- The struggle of the Aboriginal Australians: "Our people in Tamil Nadu were

---

[259] Vidal, John (1999): Modem warfare. The Guardian. January 13. p. 4.

shocked beyond words by the Australians' stories of children wrenched from their families, of the treatment meted out to them by the white Australians. For months afterwards the Adivasis talked about the Aboriginal Australians' visit: "Poor people, how they've suffered", they said. "Our problems are nothing compared to what they've been through". The Adivasis visited the "super-developed Germany" but they were not impressed. They did not hanker after German consumer goods, and were speechless when they saw an old people's home, saying, "We must ensure that such things never happen in our society". They were shocked at the spectre of unemployment that haunted the society. Yet they admired the fact that everyone treated them with respect and dignity, as equals.[260]

For those struggling against social exclusion, satisfying basic material needs is obviously an important concern. But for many, the notions of wealth do not equal the possession of money. Wealth to the Adivasis is "our community, our children, our unity, our culture, the forest". Marcel-Thekaekara comments, "We realised that the Adivasis didn't see themselves as poor. They saw themselves as people without money".[261]

Their contacts with other struggles around the world provided a new source of strength, which is a result — an unplanned one, no doubt — of globalisation: solidarity of people struggling against exclusion, exploitation and oppression in different parts of the world. Marcel-Thekaekara quotes Bomman's speech in the village square after his overseas visit:

> Unilever is very powerful. But the days when Adivasis were totally powerless are over. We now have friends in Germany and the UK. If we tell them what Unilever is doing here they will start a campaign to inform all the people of Europe to stop buying Unilever tea. They will fight on our side. We are not alone".[262]

As Marcel-Thekaekara[263] says, "The global links between people usually considered poor, and therefore powerless, had made a difference". Thus globalization, which brought poverty and powerlessness to every doorstep in the world, also brought the means of overcoming the very poverty and powerlessness on which capitalism thrives. New battle lines are drawn. Combatants of a new generation take on the new struggles.

Lessons for Public Libraries

Public Libraries in Britain and other "developed" countries need to examine their work practices, outlook, mission statements with a view to making them less Euro/U.S.A.-centric. There is an assumption in the profession that the "Western" model of public libraries is the best. This model has failed to stop the exclusion of perhaps a third or more of our populations from the informational world. It is time we asked for some technical expertise from those Majority World countries which have had more success than ourselves in providing a relevant educational and information service.

---

[260] Marcel-Thekaekara, Mari (1999): Poor relations. The Guardian. Saturday Review. February 27, p. 3.
[261] Ibid.
[262] Ibid.
[263] Ibid.

We need to question and challenge the static role that public libraries have acquired in Britain. The class bias in public libraries is analysed by Pateman who says, "There is plenty of evidence to suggest that, while public libraries are used by all social classes, they are a predominantly middle class institutions...; the service is managed and operated by middle class people who share their middle class values with middle class library users."[264]

LIS is a sanitised profession that wants to keep away from getting involved in people's struggles, that wants to remain "neutral" while those with power and wealth gobble up an ever-increasing proportion of library budgets. Again a comparison with another profession may help to understand our real situation: NHS doctors insist on the best medicine for their patients irrespective of their financial or social standing. What matters are the needs of the patients. The library profession needs to come up with a similar "needs-led" approach to satisfying the information needs of people.

The Kimaathi tradition

Kimaathi led the Kenyan forces in the political as well as military fronts. He was elected to lead the Kenya Parliament founded as an alternative state in the liberated areas; he also led the Kenya Land and Freedom Army on the battlefield. Because of these roles he had of necessity to be involved in the communication strategy of Mau Mau. He helped to plan an elaborate underground library network in the liberated forest areas; he ensured that Mau Mau reports and documents were well looked after and preserved (it was the British forces which destroyed or hid, even to this day, much of this valuable resource); he supported the work of underground and overground press controlled by Mau Mau; he actively distributed Mau Mau newspapers, carrying them in baskets and travelled around the country in buses and *Matatus*. Kimaathi is a good role model of a library/information worker in tune with his people's needs and struggles.

Lessons for Public Libraries

Public Libraries need to see themselves as part of the society as a whole. People's struggles for social justice and economic liberation are waged at various levels: political, economic, social, cultural and educational. Communications can be at the heart of these struggles, linking all the different struggles and providing a basic support mechanism. Any search for relevance will need to explore this dynamic role of libraries.

Library workers will need to become activists in the various struggles of the people, in the Kimaathi tradition. Only thus will they become relevant to the people they serve and avoid the one-dimensional approach that is the rule today. There needs to be a new debate about what being a "professional" means.

No public library collects underground and alternative material from the people's struggles. Many important documents may already have been lost already as no organisation in Kenya dare openly collect it. It is not certain if any outside institution, with the possible exception of the CIA, has collected such material.[265] In order to avoid

---

[264] Pateman, John (1999): Open to all?. op. cit. Public Libraries and Social Class. Working Paper No. 3. Available at: http://www.seapn.org.uk/opentoall.html [Accessed: 02 April 2007]

[265] Durrani, Shiraz (1997): The Other Kenya: underground and alternative literature. Collection Building. 16(2) 80-87.

losing the experiences of people's struggle, public libraries need to have an active collection policy, possibly in conjunction with international bodies such as UNESCO.

Kurdish resistance

"No friends but mountains" goes a Kurdish song. That indeed seems to be borne out by the plight of the Kurds people this century. Together with the Palestinians, the Kurds, as a nationality, are among the most excluded people in the world today. Both suffered at the hands of the post-First World War carve-up of their territories by Britain and France.

The Kurdish people number between 25-40 million, according to different sources. They are divided over 5 main countries: Turkey (13 million); Iran (4.8 million); Iraq (4.3 million); Syria (1 million); Germany (0.5 million); Russian Federation (0.3 million); Armenia (0.1 million). They are also spread in Lebanon and Syria as well as in most European countries in varying numbers. Yet they have no state they can call their own. Kemal Attaturk "tore up the 1820 Treaty of Sevres which had envisaged an independent area for the Kurds in Eastern Turkey and cancelled their right to be seen as a people separate from the rest of the Turkish nation".[266] He also "swept aside their freedom of language and culture that had been written into the Treaty of Lausanne".[267] As Butt[268] says, "The Kurds were doubly cheated after the First World War. Not only did they fail to get a state of their own, but they found their mountainous territory chopped up by the new borders of Iraq, Iran, Syria and Turkey".

... Wherever they live, they tend to be highly politicised and organised. Just as the Zapatistas *(see next section)*, they make extensive use of orature, so that news spreads fast between isolated community members within each country as well as between different countries.

However, the Kurdish community also uses modern means of communications to carry news about their struggles, their culture and their language. Publishing is an important aspect of their struggle for survival. Publications in the Kurdish language are important, as it has been suppressed over the years. New publishing houses in Kurdish language material have sprung up in France as well as other European countries. These serve the needs of the Kurdish people throughout Europe.

In addition, the community runs the Med TV, a satellite television station based in London. Med TV has become the "Kurdish voice, not only in Turkey, but throughout Europe", as Estella Schmid, the coordinator of the Kurdistan Solidarity Committee says.[269] Med TV played a crucial role in keeping the Kurdish communities throughout Europe informed about developments surrounding the arrest earlier this year of Abdullah Ocalan, the leader of the Kurdish Workers Party. Its communications work was perhaps responsible for ensuring that there was widespread protest in more than 20 cities in Europe when Ocalan was arrested.

Pinter highlights a sad fact about the flow of information about the Kurdish struggle in Britain, with all the freedom of press it boasts. The Today programme on

---

[266] Butt, Gerald (1999): Plight of a divided and forgotten people. Evening Standard. February 17, p.8.
[267] Black, Ian (1999): Kurdish anger as TV station closed down for incitement. The Guardian March 23: p. 5.
[268] Butt, Gerald (1999): op. cit.
[269] Black, Ian (1999): op. cit.

Radio 4 interviews Professor Norman Stone who describes Ocalan as a "thug". Pinter continues:

> The appalling repression of the Kurdish people in Turkey is generally unreported in the British media and virtually ignored at Government level...the issue is not simply of what is happening to the Kurds but also what is happening to freedom of expression and independent thought. Something has been occurring beneath our very noses in Turkey for years: many thousands of people confront substantial and persistent persecution and yet we read little about it in the press and our government is silent while trade with Turkey flourishes—Turkey provides rich business opportunities for all Western 'democracies'.[270]

Meanwhile the struggle of the Kurdish communities continues...

Lessons for Public Libraries

Public Libraries need to become friends to all those who have *No friends but mountains*. This can happen only when they establish active relationships and communications links with people's struggles. The real solution would be to recruit people from these struggles as librarians and information workers. Perhaps then we can start making links at the national and international level with struggles of different people. Perhaps then we can start breaking down the "what's it got to do with me" mentality among a large number of middle class library professionals.

The Zapatistas and the electronic struggle

The Zapatistas came to the attention of the world on January 1, 1994, when about 3,000 armed men and women took control of several municipalities in Chiapas in Southern Mexico. They were the Ejercito Zapatista de Liberacion Nacional. They are Mexican patriots "up in arms against new forms of foreign domination by American imperialism".[271] The Zapatistas staged an armed uprising on behalf of Indian rights and fought the Mexican army for 10 days before a cease-fire was declared and negotiations began.

They thus launched what has come to be known as the first "cyber" or "Net" war. "Even as the government mobilised its army to occupy the state of Chiapas and tried to deny the revolutionaries access to the mass media", says Vidal, "they and their supporters were mobilising words and images to disseminate ideas electronically".[272]

...

Lessons for Public Libraries

The Zapatista's ability to grasp with enthusiasm new communications technologies and use them actively for their struggles holds a lesson for libraries.

PART 4 – LESSONS OF PEOPLE'S STRUGGLES

Social exclusion is an essential part of capitalism and so long as capitalism survives, social exclusion, social oppression and economic exploitation will also remain. Nor can such exclusion be totally eradicated as long as the prevailing free

---

[270] Pinter, Harold (1999): The Kurds have lifted the veil. *The Guardian: Saturday Review* February 20, p. 3.
[271] Castells, Manuel (1998): op. cit. p. 78.
[272] Vidal, John (1999a): Global conflict @ internet. *The Guardian* January 13, p.4.

market system ensures that economic activity satisfies the profit greed of a few rather than the satisfaction of material, educational and cultural needs of the majority of people.

Social exclusion can be eliminated on the basis of people's determination to be included in the processes that control their own lives. Experiences from around the world indicate that excluded people everywhere struggle to include themselves in deciding their future as individuals, nationalities, communities and countries. The level of exploitation and exclusion they face decides the strength of their determination to struggle against their exclusion. They thus create the conditions for their own inclusion. They do not need to depend on outside agents to "include" them in the share of power, which belongs to them by right. Their success in the process of self-inclusion is determined by a number of factors: their class consciousness; their understanding of the causes of their exclusion and knowledge about the struggle waged by other people (hence the importance of relevant education, information and knowledge); the organisations they create as part of their struggle; their control over appropriate technologies; the availability of a correct ideology which can guide them and, perhaps the most important factor, what actions they take in ending their exclusion.

In this paper we have seen the forces that have changed the playing field on which libraries are set; we also examined some struggles waged by people from different societies to participate fully in moulding their own lives and to take control over their destinies. The lesson from this is that the struggle for social inclusion is in essence the struggle for *economic, political and social* inclusion. And that is where the difficulty arises, as they come into direct conflict with the forces of international finance capital. The economic interests of finance capital are in direct conflict with the interests of the people struggling for inclusion.

History records that finance capital will go to any length in order to ensure that it continues to maintain its hold over labour and resources. It even uses the state power of powerful nations such as the U.S.A. to ensure its control over the lives and resources of entire countries. Examples of Chile, Congo and Cuba immediately come to mind. The extent to which the U.S.A. has gone to suppress people's actions to eliminate exclusion is revealed in recently published documents and in President Clinton's apology to the people of Guatemala:

> The findings of the independent Historical Clarification Commission concluded that the US was responsible for most of the human rights abuses committed during the 36-year war in which 200,000 people died.[273]

Thus people's struggles for inclusion are not waged in a vacuum. They are waged against powerful economic and political interests, which seek to appropriate the wealth of the whole world — no less. In this struggle, public libraries need to decide whether they support the interests of finance capital or those of the people struggling against exclusion. One reason why libraries have failed in the past to play an active part in people's struggles against exclusion is perhaps because they have avoided this decision and have thus quietly provided support to those opposed to people's struggles. Muddiman gives what is probably the real reason for their failure when he says that, "libraries have usually existed as part of the apparatus of a capitalist state

---

[273] Kettle, Martin and Lennard, Jeremy (1999): Clinton apology to Guatemala; leader is first president to admit US role in slaughter of thousands of civilians in 36-year civil war. The Guardian. March 12, p.16.

and hence, by and large, embodied the values of that state—i.e. acquisitive individualism".[274]

Given this, what role can there be for public libraries? Some lessons for public libraries are suggested in the above section. In general, the examples of the struggles examined in this paper, show that if libraries are to be relevant to the needs of the people, they need to make a conscious decision to side with the people in the on-going struggle. The challenge to information workers is to raise their heads and be counted among people's forces seeking to end exclusion. A new breed of activist librarians can possibly save the profession from becoming totally irrelevant to those who have been "socially excluded".

Liberation movements everywhere have had to create new information services to serve their own needs. People's struggles against exclusion will continue — with or without public library services. Official public libraries can fulfil a new role as information providers to people's forces in their search for inclusion, provided there is a conscious decision on the part of information workers and decision-makers in local and central governments to support people's liberation struggles. A cultural revolution is needed for this to happen. How to become involved on the side of the people's struggle is the real challenge to information workers and local and central governments throughout the world.

The professional is political: redefining the social role of public libraries (SD-ES) 2006[275]

Shiraz Durrani and Elizabeth Smallwood

Part 1: Librarians and their societies

The first question to consider is "what are libraries and information all about?" Let us take an experience from Kenya to answer this question. A library attendant lived in an area that produces coffee. When he went home for holidays one year, he was asked by a number of peasants a simple question: "You work in a University library; you have information from the whole world around you. We want you to answer a simple question for us: we work from dawn to dusk growing coffee, right from tending little shoots, to weeding, to harvesting, to drying coffee beans, day after day, month after month, year after year. We hear that our coffee sells for thousands of pounds in London, yet we do not earn enough from our labour to buy our own coffee in local shops let alone feed and clothe our families. You tell us why not, you who have all the information at your finger tips, you tell us what happens to our coffee money?"

---

[274] Muddiman, Dave (1999): op. cit.
[275] Progressive Librarian. No. 27 (p. 3-22) Summer 2006. http://www.libr.org/PL/.

It was not as if the University library did not have information about coffee. It had one of the best agricultural libraries in Eastern Africa. The library's collection on coffee and other cash crops was rated world class. Yet the library was not equipped to answer these simple economic-political questions from local peasants.

Now the questions asked by the peasants are fundamental to the work of librarians. The local library did have adequate resources to meet the needs of its users. It is just that its services were not aimed at peasants and workers. More important, the information that was available was depoliticised. It took the agricultural world around it as a reality that could not be challenged. It failed to see the difference between the natural world in which the coffee was grown and the social world, which had created social relations, and which decided on who owned the land, how labour was remunerated and where the profits went. Nor was it considered necessary to understand and explain that reality, to examine its history and, perhaps to see the need to change that reality — as the Kenyan peasants were demanding.

Globalisation and effects on libraries

The key issue then is to decide what the social role of librarians is. Should they take the social, economic and political situation they find themselves in as "given" without understanding why and how we arrived at this situation? Is it their role to dig deeper into "facts" that are given to them by their social environment? Is it appropriate to see the role of librarians in the same light in which Marx saw the role of philosophers: "The philosophers have interpreted the world in many ways. What matters is changing it".[276]

But before we consider the question of librarians trying to change the world, we need to question whether they even interpret their worlds. A large number of professional libraries remain unconnected to the social and political reality around them. Their model of a "global library" is much like McDonald's restaurant outlets, which serve the same product in every part of the world. While this approach may be a useful one in ensuring a standard level of service, and a useful model for maximising profits for the McDonald's chain, it is disastrous for libraries if they want to root themselves in their local communities.

Librarians trained to run such global libraries take professional pride in being "neutral" in the social divide all around them. They thus become increasingly isolated from the majority of people in their local communities. Forces of corporate globalisation then push them even further from their communities by offering to save staff time and mental effort by supplying pre-packaged "best sellers", guaranteed to meet the wants of the 30 percent[277] of the population — and to boost the profit margins of transnational publishers and booksellers. The success of their libraries is then judged by the number of such best sellers they manage to loan out. No critical questions are asked or answered here: What is a library all about? What is its social

---

[276] Marx, Karl (1969): Theses on Feuerbach. Marx/Engels Selected Works, Volume One, p. 13 – 15; Moscow: Progress Publishers, Moscow, USSR. Translated: W. Lough from the German. Available at: Marx/Engels Internet Archive http://www.marxists.org/archive/marx/works/1845/theses/theses.pdf). [Accessed: 23 August 2007]..

[277] "Almost 30 per cent of the population use libraries for borrowing books or other items". Audit Commission. (2002). Building better libraries: Learning from audit, inspection and research. London: the Commission. Available from: http://www.audit-commission.gov.uk/reports/AC-REPORT.asp?CatID=&ProdID=9D0A0DD1-3BF9-4c52-9112-67D520E7C0AB.

role? Who has the power to make key decisions, and on whose behalf are decisions made?

The "global library", then, is a standard library service that can be located in any geographical, social or political situation, in any historical period, and still be expected to function normally as a "library". The global librarians who run these global libraries take pride in their non-political stand, in their "neutrality" in the social struggles going on all around them. They claim to be outside social struggles taking place in their societies, somehow uplifted to a loftier position by their "professional" training. Their class position in their societies isolates them from the struggles of working people whose basic need for information is ignored by their libraries.

Corporate globalisation can be described as the "process enabling financial and investment markets to operate internationally, largely as a result of deregulation and improved communications".[278] We do not intend here to go into details of what globalisation is and how it affects libraries, as this has been dealt with adequately in a number of sources.[279] However, a key point that needs to be made is that not only are new technologies making it possible to rationalise tasks and work practices, but it makes it necessary to change at a faster rate as technological progress is changing the world around them. At the same time, many traditional library tasks are increasingly being handed over to private companies, rather than being done in-house. As the whole local authority sector is redefined to become facilitators of service rather than direct providers, significant changes are on the way. Other areas of local authority work are also changing. For example, household waste collection is no longer being done by local staff, and schools and education are being removed from local authority control. It is inconceivable that libraries will continue existing as they now are for very long.

We are not arguing that all changes associated with globalisation are necessarily bad. But we would like to see more librarians in Britain adopting the 10-point plan, proposed by Mark Rosenzweig, supporting "democratic globalism" as opposed to corporate globalisation:

> We shall oppose corporate globalization which, despite its claims, reinforces existing social, economic, cultural inequalities, and insist on a democratic globalism..., which acknowledges the obligations of society to the individual and communities, and which prioritizes human values and needs over profits.[280]

Iverson explains how the politics of globalisation affects libraries and their local communities. The inherently political role of librarians is clear:

---

[278] Collins online dictionary. http://dictionary.reverso.net/english-definitions/globalization) [Accessed: 23 August 2007].
[279] The politics of globalisation is covered admirably by A. Sivanandan in his article "Globalism's imperial war" (12 March 2003), available from <http://www.irr.org.uk/2003/march/ak000008.html>. The library aspects are covered by IFLA at: <http://www.ifla.org/III/clm/p1/wto-ifla.htm#3>; see also Durrani (2000), especially pp.89-94.
[280] Ten point programme presented to the groups which met at the Vienna Conference of progressive librarians sponsored by KRIBIBIE (2000) Available from <http://www.libr.org/PLG/docs.html>.

> As our global society becomes increasingly based on the commodity of information, power becomes increasingly focused and managed by those with access to information. Those without such access remain marginalized.[281]

However, Iverson notes, librarians often reject any stated political stance, seeing themselves as "neutral service providers" a position encouraged by their training:

> While librarians are trained to maintain an objective or neutral stance they are also expected to make decisions regarding "good" and "bad" materials. Unfortunately, they do not often recognize the inherent bias at work in making these decisions... and generally regard the selection of materials as apolitical.[282]

Few librarians have taken Muddiman's warning seriously:

> Exclusion thus challenges public agencies like the library service to produce policy and practice which will challenge social division and create a harmonious, diverse and more equal civil society where access to knowledge is a fundamental right of social citizenship. If the public library can rise to this challenge it might begin to successfully reinvigorate and reinvent itself. If it fails, then the public library too, like the poor and excluded communities it exists to serve, might find itself consigned to the margins of the "information" society in the twenty first century.[283]

Faced with a situation where libraries are blindly walking into extinction, it is important that those with conviction and commitment stand up for a new role of libraries in society—and actively practice this new role. In the world ruled by corporate globalisation, it is too easy to drift along with the tide of "neutral" librarianship and do nothing to make libraries play a central role in liberating people, their cultures, and their economies from the privatised future that globalisation has planned for them. This is not merely something that may happen in the future. It is already happening, as Rosenzweig points out:

> Trade ministers and negotiators alike are under increasing pressure to expose more services, like education, healthcare, culture, ... to the market powers of transnational corporations.[284]

A new approach, in which real democracy, equality and transparency flourish, is essential.

The myth of neutrality

Thus the myth of the "neutral" librarian needs to be exploded. There is no way that librarians are or can be neutral in the social struggles of their societies. Every decision they make—how much to spend on books, which books to buy, what staff to appoint, how to manage the service—is a reflection of their class position and their world outlook.

What librarians do—and don't do—is not merely an academic question. It affects our understanding of our natural and social environment, which, taken in its totality, affects our world outlook, affects what we think and what we do. It influences the

---

[281] Iverson, S. (1998/99): Librarianship and resistance. Progressive Librarian. No.15, 14-20.
[282] Ibid.
[283] Muddiman (2000): op. cit.
[284] Rosenzweig, M. (2005, February 19). Tell WTO trade negotiators: "Hands off services." Message posted on PLGNet-L listserv. 19 Feb 2005 to: alacoun@ala.org, srrtac-l@ala.org, plgnet-l@listproc.sjsu.edu. Available at: http://lists.essential.org/pipermail/upd-discuss/2005q1/000987.html [Accessed: 23 August 2007].

minds of the young generation and becomes the prevailing outlook of the adult world of tomorrow.

Manipulation of information, whether conscious or unconscious, is an important matter, not only in local life, but in international relations as well. Recent events have shown how misinformation can be used to generate popular support for wars of somewhat questionable legality, for example when the U.S.A. and Britain invaded Iraq, killing thousands of people in the quest for non-existent "weapons of mass destruction".

If librarians are involved in the world of information, then surely they have social responsibility to ensure that people get correct information. It is a matter of ethics that they challenge misinformation, particularly when, this is used by a small, powerful clique to wage wars and kill people on false pretexts. But our average "professional" librarians are too "neutral" — or too scared — to challenge the hand that feeds them. At the very least, they need to make alternate views and opinions as freely available as they do the views of the ruling classes. But this is not what the "globalised librarian" is trained to do. However, many progressive librarians in the U.S.A. are taking a stand for theirs and communities' information rights against the Patriot Act, which seeks to take these rights away from people. Their example needs to be followed globally.

Two aspects of the job of a librarian can be seen to be to *collect* and then to *disseminate* information, in a relevant form and language, to all those who need the information. This gives librarians tremendous power as it is they who decide what material to acquire and how and when to disseminate it. However, the easy availability of information on the Internet is fast changing their monopolistic role as it democratises the flow of information.

Libraries and society in Britain

There is often a time gap between the emergence of a new social reality and that reality being accepted in people's consciousness. Jacques refers to the gap between the perception and the reality:

> We still like to consider ourselves a global player, but in reality we are not: our pretensions are now more like pastiche, substance has been replaced by vacuity... Post-imperial Britain has become deeply parochial—yet we remain almost utterly oblivious of the fact (the liberal elite included).[285]

Thus, lessons and reality of history are shut out from social consciousness by denying the reality of a new world where Britain is no longer the superpower ruling the world, where China is flexing its muscles to become the most powerful nation in the world. Yet most public libraries have very little relevant material in English from or about China — a fact reflected in the lack of awareness among people as a whole about that part of the world.

In a society that has sought to shut out the reality of a new globalised world, it is not surprising that its libraries have shut themselves in a dream world of presumed superiority and "professional" might. The fact that the library world has not come to grips with changes in British society is a reflection of British society as a whole not coming to grips with its new reality.

---

[285] Jacques, M. (2004). Our problem with abroad: Britain has become a deeply parochial place in the era of globalisation. The Guardian. 21 August. Available from: http://www.guardian.co.uk/comment/story/0,,1287822,00.html

Creating a people-orientated library service

There is an urgent need to develop a library service that helps to create a new consciousness among people about their society and also about the position of their country in the context of the wider world. Only on such wider awareness can a people-orientated library service be built. Libraries cannot tell people what their "real role" is. They can only provide information to help people decide for themselves.

If there is going to be a true people-orientated library service, it is necessary that there is a clear understanding of social forces within which a particular library service operates. Librarians face a number of challenges today. Let us look at some of them:

The first need is for all librarians to investigate our society and our communities. Mao's recommendation, at a political level, is equally valid in the information field: "no investigation, no right to speak". It is important to understand working people's lives and struggles, be one of them, and then seek ways of creating a relevant library service.

In all societies with class divisions and class struggles, library services tend to be a service for elite by elite, providing a service to the dominating classes and their allies only. In situations like these, the process of liberating the library service for those previously excluded is the key role of library workers and professionals. The challenge is to develop a service that is open to all irrespective of class, race, gender, ability, age, sexual orientation, political beliefs, etc. The service needs to be an inclusive one, which reaches out to all who are currently excluded. Yet this task is not easy. The very language of this struggle has been removed from the "mainstream" by Government action. Thus class differences are not mentioned in Government reports and policies; racism is hidden under the bland term "social exclusion" thereby not only removing the reality of racism from public mention, but resistance to it is also disguised as criminal acts or as "terrorism". No society can be serious about addressing social oppression and economic exploitation when it chooses not to admit the very existence of such.

If librarians are to build truly people-orientated libraries, they will need to stop operating in isolation from the progressive forces that are already struggling for liberation. It is thus important that we develop creative partnerships with progressive forces, such as trade unions, workers' and peasants' social, economic and political organisations, youth groups, etc. Alliances also need to be made with all those struggling against all forms of social oppression.

But before librarians reach that stage, they need to liberate their minds from the norms of a class-divided society, its social, cultural and political norms. Its information systems and education provides us with a one-sided view of life. We will need to see the whole picture and not just the aspects we are shown. In the library context, we will need to free ourselves from the commandments taught at traditional library schools. We will need to learn not to be "neutral" but, instead, take sides on behalf of those previously excluded in everything we do in order to build an "equal" library service.

As is the case in all social revolutions, there are no specific guide books on how to create a liberated, "open" library service. It is only the actual practice of learning from people that will provide a solution that is relevant to our particular social situation and will help us build libraries without walls.

But just learning from people is not enough. The next, and perhaps the most difficult, step is to turn our ideas into action. This is best done, by empowering the excluded, so that it is *they* who decide how our resources are to be used and how our energies are spent. People themselves will then be the best judges of our success or failure. It is in putting these ideas into practice that a people-orientated, "open to all" service can be built.

PART 2: Public libraries in England

Speaking to the Society of Chief Librarians in June 2004, the Secretary of State for culture, media and sport, Tessa Jowell, posed a number of challenges to the profession:

> This is a critical time for the future of public library services. Although for over 150 years, libraries have given pleasure and provided opportunities to learn, it is now time to ensure that libraries are relevant and inviting to future generations... the challenge is to generate new users... it is important to learn lessons about why people do not use libraries—only one third do, so how do libraries attract the other two thirds?[286]

The Secretary of State made it clear that she wants change in public libraries. She explained what needs to happen so that libraries "become, once again, central points in local communities":

> But they can only take back this role if they consult local people, and put them in the driving seat. Not just once, but as a continuous dialogue.[287]

This challenge, however, is not reflected in the initiatives that the Department of Culture, Media and Sport has taken, primarily through the *The Framework for Future*,[288] (F4F) programme. The key development since the publication of F4F has been a programme to put the key points of the *Framework* into practice, led by the Museum, Libraries and Archives Council (MLA). MLA explains what the *Framework* is all about:

> Framework for the Future, published by the Department for Culture, Media and Sport (DCMS) in February 2003, is the Government's ten-year vision for public libraries—how libraries can best serve their communities in the 21st century. It aims to promote public libraries, give them improved visibility, and to set out why libraries matter.

The Framework aims to do this by focusing on three key areas for libraries to develop: books, reading and learning; digital citizenship; community and civic values.

Recent developments led by the Museum, Libraries and Archives Council (MLA)[289] are positive moves in the right direction and go some way to make up for what some feel to be immense failures of the *Framework*.[290] This includes the "Fulfilling their potential" programme, which provides a useful guide to developing services for young people. Other developments include the redrafting of the Public Library Standards focus on "impact measurement". It remains to be seen how far,

---

[286] Jowell, Tessa. (2004, June 21). Department of Culture, Media and Sports public libraries seminar. Quotes taken from unpublished notes by Alison Bramley for Society of Chief Librarians (SCL) members.
[287] Lend it like Peckham! (2004, July-August). Library and Information Update. p.3.
[288] Department of Culture, Media and Sport. (2003). Framework for the future: Libraries, learning and information in the next decade. London: DCMS. Available from: http://www.culture.gov.uk/Reference_library/Publications/archive_2003/framework_future.htm.
[289] See MLA website for further details: <http://www.mla.gov.uk/index.asp>.
[290] See for example: Durrani, S. (2003): Review of the Framework of the Future. Library and Information Update. March 2003.

taken as a whole, they will challenge and change the foundations of the public library structure in Britain to ensure they meet the needs of all current and potential users of library service.

At the same time, unless issues mentioned in Part 1 around commodification and globalisation of information, "neutrality" and politics of information services are addressed on a national level, any changes that come about are likely to be partial and not able to address real problems.

Iverson, commenting on the important role that libraries have to play, raises concerns about their role:

> I would argue that their role should not be to act in "collusion with the forces which perpetuate disadvantage" but to redefine their role to assist in the establishment of a truly equitable society.[291]

British librarians have generally ignored the fundamental issues about the role of public libraries that Iverson raises. The Department of Culture, Media and Sport, through its enthusiastic endorsement of what is perceived by some to be the visionless F4F, has failed to give leadership to a field desperate for change.

PART 3: The Merton Library approach

It is in the context of the Secretary of State's challenge that developments in Merton Library & Heritage Service (MLHS) between 2000 and 2004 need to be seen. Change and development for a relevant service can only be made if a foundation for change has been created.

The following section considers how a changed environment made it possible for a project involving young people to become self-sustaining and, in doing, create a new model of public library service that sought to place the needs of a particular community at its heart.

Creating conditions for change — staffing structure & equalities

MLHS's staffing structure, introduced in 2003, aimed to address some weaknesses identified in the 2000 structure within an overall perspective of developing a relevant, needs-based service. It was partially driven by the need to make savings in the service in keeping with savings being made in the Council as a whole. The structure was split into two distinct "wings": Operations and Performance Management (O&PM) and Innovations and Development (I&D) in such a way that an equalities approach could be mainstreamed. This approach allowed the targeting of services to key sections of communities whose needs have not been fully met. The two-wings approach was expected to ensure that innovative services were initiated and developed in the I&D wing. The O&PM wing was expected to ensure that the day-to-day existing work of libraries was carried on within a strong performance management culture, guided by policies developed in the I&D wing. Its role was also to ensure that new projects developed in the I&D wing would be nurtured and embedded as part of a mainstreamed service. The majority of the staff and resources were in the O&PM wing.

This approach was meant to resolve some of the contradictions identified in the service during the service review beginning in 1998. These included the contradictions between the needs of current users and potential users; between developing new

---

[291] Iverson, S. (1998/99): Librarianship and resistance. Progressive Librarian, No.15, 14-20.

services and maintaining current ones; between resource allocation for new services and allocations to established services. Implicit in these contradictions was the key contradictions between new ideas and "traditional" ones; between staff and managers who support the "traditional" mode of service and those keen to develop a new model of service to meet new and unmet needs of current and potential users.

Two key requirements were considered essential for the success of the new approach. The first was the support and commitment from senior management in the library service, within the Department, the authority as a whole, and crucially, from Members.

The second requirement was the need to address, in a clear and appropriate manner, clear resistance to change from some senior and middle managers who did not support the change programme and were unhappy about meeting the targets set out in the new programme. Addressing such resistance is considered a key factor in ensuring that planned change takes place.

The existence of this resistance was identified as a key risk factor by the team from the Management Research Centre of the London Metropolitan University, which had guided the service through the early period of change as part of an ESF-funded change management and management development programme.

Another area where the Service placed a great deal of emphasis was the need to have a policy approach in all its work. MLHS had a deficit of written policies, resulting in uneven practices between library sites. The aim of the policy approach was to address this deficit through the provision of policies that would, through effective performance management, ensure that there was uniformity in service delivery and resource use. At the same time the mainstreaming of equalities, with responsibility for equalities being transferred from the Equal Access Services cost centre to individual libraries was also to be governed by the policy and performance management approach, with the overall strategy being decided by the Libraries Senior Management Team.

The staffing structure recognised the fact that public libraries are at crossroads. The Audit Commission report, "Building Better Library Services"[292] notes that while libraries have a place in people's hearts, they "are losing their place in people's lives". Libraries thus need to change if they are to be relevant to the communities they serve. MLHS believed that, for public libraries to be relevant, they needed to respond to needs within local communities and that they needed to be well placed to respond quickly to changing needs. This, it was realised, would necessarily involve moving away from the traditional "books-based" approach to embrace a closer focus on informal learning through a wide variety of activities, providing information through a variety of means that would help people in many different aspects of their lives. Additionally, it would mean the recruitment of people with the types of skills not traditionally found in libraries e.g. skills in working with youth.

Innovations Project approach

In order to develop the needs-based approach, MLHS developed a number of strategic partnerships, enabling it to acquire new skills and enabling it to focus on what were key needs in Merton. The development of an innovations projects approach was thus a response to the need for change on several levels. It was recognised that the new staffing structure had to do the following:

---

[292] Audit Commission. (2002): op. cit.

- Respond to community needs
- Mainstream equalities
- Develop new skills within the Service

The aim of the innovations projects approach, therefore, was to take a targeted approach to outreach, develop library services based on need, which could then be embedded into mainstream service delivery. Such an approach was a key part of the new staffing structure, which had policy and performance management very much at its core.

The Innovations and Development wing was thus set up with key aims in mind:

- To mainstream equalities through a policy approach (the implementation of which would be performance managed by the Operations and Performance Management wing)
- To develop new services and reach out to marginalised groups of people via a programme of "Innovations projects" targeted at specific groups
- To develop policies to support the mainstreaming of new services
- To ensure that managers and staff at all levels and sites take ownership and responsibility for services to all groups and communities in the catchment area of their site.

It was recognised that library services needed to develop and reach out to a wide range of people. At the same time, budget restrictions did not allow the service to increase the staffing establishment. MLHS's response was to develop a number of partnerships both within, and without, the Council, allowing it to target key groups of people, using dedicated staff, in developing new services to these groups. Staff were either wholly or partly paid for by the partners.

There was a shift in the service focus as part of the new staffing structure. The previous approach was to devote staff and resources towards Black and Minority Ethnic (BME) communities. However, this did not allow MLHS to develop services where the needs were greatest, and targeting services to BME communities, irrespective of needs, began to create unnecessary tensions among staff and communities.

The new focus was on age, as age was seen as the one equality issue that cuts across all groups. With a mainstreaming equalities approach the aim was to ensure that, within each age group, all equality aspects are addressed e.g. race, disability, gender, etc. By adopting this approach, the Service contributed to community cohesion and reduced the tensions that could exist when one community feels that resources are being directed away from its services to services for other communities in a narrow area. MLHS was therefore taking a needs-based approach to ensure that the limited resources were targeted to meet the needs of current and potential users.

Why the Innovations projects approach?

It was decided to use a project approach to bring about change and development in the service. This approach has a number of positive aspects, for example:

- Allowed risk taking
- Could be stopped if they did not meet requirements

- Could be operationalised if successful, thus becoming part of the "mainstream"
- Could develop new partnerships
- Could generate new resources
- Could help connect libraries to sections of the community not using the service before
- Could develop new skills in staff

Space does not permit consideration of all Innovation Projects, so there follows a focus on one project only, Merton Sense, and an examination of its development.

Merton innovations project

This section focuses on one of the Innovations Projects, Merton Sense, as an example of how libraries can be community, rather than management, driven resulting in relevant, sustainable services responsive to community needs, as dictated by the community itself.

Recent reports on public libraries reveal declining usage of libraries by young people. New and creative ways of reaching them need to be found to attract them to use the service. Discussion with Merton's Youth Service revealed that young people in a less advantaged part of the borough were interested in exploring creative avenues not available in the local area. MLHS consulted with a group of young people, which revealed that they were interested in setting up and running their own project — a magazine by and for young people. MLHS, seeing this as an opportunity to connect with young people, worked with Merton Youth Service to provide the space, ICT facilities and staff support needed to bring the magazine into being.

Merton Sense leads the way

The magazine was called *Merton Sense*, a title chosen by the young people themselves. Its aim was to connect young people, many of whom, were from socially excluded groups, with their library service by actively engaging young people in designing the new service. The magazine was then produced by them, with the financial and management support from the library service.

The first need was to find a home for the magazine. Thus was created the "Youth Space" in the newly established Innovations Unit based at Mitcham Library. The Youth Service provided computers, which set the group going. The young people themselves decided how they wanted the Space decorated and what furniture they wanted.

The youth group consisted initially of about 12 young people, and grew to over 45 within the first year. This number has now grown to over 50 young people aged between 14 and 24 years old. The staff time that went into the support of young people producing the magazine was very important to the project. Often, library staff spent additional time in the week working with group members on article writing and graphic design to make their pieces presentable for the magazine. *Merton Sense* works with some writers for whom English is a second language and believes that all young people have something to add, irrespective of their varying abilities. However, such young people benefited enormously from the input of staff, who were able to advise them on writing in English. The qualitative nature of staff input enabled young people eventually to write without any assistance and, as such, was highly empowering. The success of *Merton Sense* would thus not have been possible without the commitment and input of MLHS staff.

The group produced the first issue of the quarterly *Merton Sense* in June 2003 with a print run of 1,000 copies.[293] A network of writers has been set up with different young people from around the world. Writers from Australia, Spain and the U.S.A. have already printed articles and plans are in place to encourage writers from Kenya, Pakistan and Brazil to contribute articles. *Merton Sense* has empowered the young people of Merton to take action and put their views and ideas into a creative and enjoyable experience. The group has learned about writing styles, how to compile a magazine, cohesive teamwork and working to reach deadlines.

Many of the young people involved with *Merton Sense* had never used the library service; some had never even been inside a library! As a result of MLHS initiating this project and introducing young, hitherto, non-users, to the libraries, they are all now members of the library service and much more aware of the diverse resources available to them. Libraries have also been an invaluable resource for the group in terms of background information for writing and composing articles electronically and in book form.

A retired journalist who had worked for the BBC was a volunteer through the Lending Time Project.[294] He offered support and advice for a while, from a professional prospective, on how to compile a magazine and provided invaluable experience on writing styles and skills and on how to compose articles. His involvement was one example of how MLHS encouraged inter-generational work. The magazine has developed in many areas the skills of the young people involved. These include ICT, writing styles and desktop publishing, thus improving their employability and further education options. The Welcome To Your Library Project, through its connections with Asylum Welcome, provided the group with young people who were new to the country and were from an asylum seeker or refugee background. The magazine gave them the opportunity to interact with other young people who may, or may not have been from a similar background. For those not from a similar background, this experience helped to gain a greater understanding of refugee and asylum seeker issues.

Some outcomes

The magazine connected many young people, some of who had never used the library service before, to the libraries but perhaps *Merton Sense's* greatest achievement is that it has empowered the local young community and brought a tremendous sense of community amongst the team and its readers. Among achievements of the magazine, the following can be listed:

- Involves communities: Wide range of youth from different groups, are able to speak not only to youth but to the wider community of Merton through the pages of *Merton Sense*. The young people are now openly tackling difficult subjects maturely, that are of interest to a wide group of people.
- Encourages reading: The use of the Internet and library resources to research

---

[293] This was covered in Library & Information Update 2(8) August 2003, p. 17.
[294] This was a British Home Office and Department of Culture, Media and Sport-funded project whereby library services worked with Community Service Volunteers to encourage local people to volunteer their services to local libraries in the aim of service development.

articles is now commonplace among the young people involved in the Project. *Merton Sense* itself is a literary product.
- Encourages learning: Participants have developed a wide range of new skills in a friendly, informal manner—these had not been provided by the formal educational sector. Besides the "job specific" learning of publishing skills such as ICT, layout, design, desktop publishing, writing styles, artwork, editorial work, etc., the young people have also developed a wide range of social and leadership skills, such as teamwork, people skills, and dealing with difficult issues in a mature manner.
- Shares information: *Merton Sense* speaks not only to young people, but to the whole community and keeps all informed of a wide range of issues from a youth perspective.
- Has the potential to be developed and adapted elsewhere: The model developed in Merton can work anywhere, with appropriate management support, resources and quality staff input and a trust in young people. In fact, the approach can also be adapted for other projects.

One of the key achievements for all team members, however, is the engagement in a learning process entirely driven by individual wishes to develop in particular areas. Examples include creative writing; journalism; language and communication skills; marketing and fundraising skills. Although informal learning is a key aspect of public libraries, without such a project it would have been extremely difficult for MLHS to offer such a range of relevant, community-driven learning opportunities. The opportunities afforded by this project have led to a number of achievements including:

- Two of *Merton Sense's* writers were picked up by national magazines to write articles in a freelance capacity.
- Three of the young people involved are now studying towards a career in the media, with *Merton Sense* forming an important part of their portfolios and increasing their employability options.
- *Merton Sense's* resident poet, Amie Russell, won a local poetry competition in which this project encouraged her to participate and her work will now be published by Xpress in a new poetry anthology book.
- A number of young people have been awarded the Millennium Volunteer Award.

The Editor of *Merton Sense*, Duane Melius, recalls what working on the magazine has meant for him:

> For the first time since I left school there was a valuable opportunity for me... From here *Merton Sense* began. It has been a joy to watch the birth of an idea and witness its refinement. Being part of Merton Sense gives me a sense of identity. It is heartening to realise there are agents in the community willing to give people like me a chance.[295]

---

[295] Melius, D. (2003, August 13). Best thing I ever did. Young People Now. Available from: http://www.ypnmagazine.com/news/index.cfm?fuseaction=full_news&ID=1684. [Accessed: 30 August 2007].

The magazine has gone from strength to strength and the initial print run has grown from 1,000 to 15,000. A *Sense* website has now been developed.[296]

Merton Sense — strategic issues and lessons

There is no doubt that *Merton Sense* has played a key role in reconnecting the library service to a large number of young people in Merton. These include not only the ones directly involved in all aspects of producing and writing the magazine, but also hundreds on the mailing list or who get copies through libraries, youth clubs, schools and in other ways. In the process, the library service was learning a new way of connecting with its potential users. The success of the project was recognised by the Youth Ofsted inspection in 2004:

> At the *Merton Sense* magazine group, young people took responsibility for project development, set challenging targets, evaluated their own progress and gained formal accreditation.[297]

One of the areas recognised as requiring attention in local and public service is the need for innovation. The *Merton Sense* project can be seen as an example of an innovative service development, which at the same time helped to develop new skills in managers and staff.

Another issue that should be understood in the context of making organisational change is the need for effective leadership with a clear vision, commitment and a strategy for ensuring success. In the case of Merton, this was certainly available during the period under review. *Merton Sense* also provides a very clear example of how service users can take total ownership of a new service if they are able to influence the direction of the service and are allowed to have control over it. The key point is that an idea and a service should grip their imagination. The young people at *Merton Sense* are keen to keep the magazine going and are developing financial and political skills to meet the needs of this complex project. There are enough lessons here for local government managers to digest.

Conclusion

As societies develop, as new technologies create even more possibilities for growth, the communications and information sectors needs constantly to develop in keeping with major changes in society. There is thus huge potential for developing services that meet the new needs of all people and it is quite possible for libraries to be at the centre of this vastly changing world. Engaging with the traditional library commodity of information in a "non traditional" way that responds to local contexts, via the involvement of local people in service design and development, will enable libraries to help bridge the gap between the information rich and the information poor. Libraries can thus play a part in better-enabling local people to make informed decisions.

However, realising this potential requires creativity, innovation, commitment and vision on the part of service leaders. Effective leadership in the information field,

---

[296] See: <http://www.sense.ik.com/>. The magazine has now been renamed "Sense".
[297] Office for Standards in Education (Ofsted) Youth Service inspection in 2004: http://www.ofsted.gov.uk/. Reproduced as Appendix 2 – Report following the inspection of Merton Youth Service by OFSTED in:
http://www.merton.gov.uk/democratic_services/ds-agendas/ds-archived_reports/_000-5363/3177.pdf [appendix 2 not currently available].

therefore, is the key to making libraries places where different social, political and economic forces in conflict can deposit their various views, experiences, knowledge and world outlooks. By ensuring that this contradictory information and knowledge has an equal chance to be acquired, stored, heard and understood, librarians and libraries can, perhaps, find a new social role for themselves. They will then have played a meaningful social role in creating more just and "equal" societies.

As custodians of information, librarians everywhere have a role to play in eliminating the root causes of poverty, illiteracy, unemployment and inequality. It is no longer acceptable for libraries and librarians to refuse to acknowledge this social responsibility. The choice is simple: if the information profession does not acknowledge its social responsibility and act upon it, it will no longer have a social role. People will then develop alternative models of information and knowledge communication, which do meet their needs. There will then be no libraries as we know them today. The choice is ours to make — today.

The role of the Library Association[298] [299]

The British Library Association's Annual Report for 1998 — celebrating the "Royal Charter Centenary" — fails to mention the Association's and the profession's relevance or otherwise to the Black communities. This was in a year when the Government challenged library authorities to address the question of social exclusion in the British society, when the first ever Annual Library Plan scored a very poor mark in social exclusion.

The Association has an Equal Opportunities Sub-Committee, which has the responsibility of overseeing race issues. It has published a number of guidelines on equal opportunities (Library Association). It also organises the annual "Black Contribution to Librarianship" conferences which to date have not led to any action to combat racism. The Association also has an "in liaison" relationship with two Black associations: African Caribbean Library Association (ACLA) and Asian Librarians and Arts Officers Group (ALAG) — which themselves have not only not been active in combating racism in libraries, but have actively opposed the formation of a Black Workers Group within the LA. Nor do they have any credible membership in the communities they supposedly represent. It seems convenient for the Library Association to be seen to be "in liaison" with inactive, unrepresentative organisations so that it can claim to be "in contact" with Black LIS workers and thus avoid any accusation of institutional racism within the organisation.

While there are useful initiatives from individuals and some Library Association groups, the organisation has, until very recently, remained rather aloof from taking an

---

[298] Selection from *Open to All?:* op. cit. Vol. 3: Working Paper 13. pp.254-349. Struggle against racial exclusion in public libraries; A fight for the rights of the people. Available at: http://www.seapn.org.uk/opentoall.html. [Accessed 30 August 2007].
[299] The Library Association is now known as the Chartered Institute of Library and Information Professionals (CILIP)

active part in addressing institutionalised racism and in addressing the lack of action by public libraries to respond actively to the needs of Black populations. To a large extent, the LA remains a "white" organisation concerned more with its royal charter and procedures and formalities than trying to address the real needs of a changing population. While almost a hundred Black LIS workers attend its annual "Diversity: Black contribution to British librarianship" conferences, very few choose to become members.

For the Library Association, it seems enough to spend a little time every year on such a conference, clear its conscience, and go back to its "normal" lifestyle for another year. No fundamental issues about Black librarianship are considered, no debates about giving power to Black LIS workers to put some of their ideas into action. A few nice speeches from worthy personalities and an opportunity for Black LIS workers to be present at the citadel of library power is all that emerges from these conferences. As Khan[300] asks, "But we are still talking about the issue of multicultural library services—just how far have we come?"

An attempt was made by some librarians to make the Association take some action to address the question of race in the profession. ...

The essence of the motion was lost through some technical amendments. The annual Black conferences are being held, but no progress has been made on the formation of the Black Workers Group. The Association was happy to hide behind technicalities of wanting 100 signatures before such a group could be formed. This creates a Catch-22 situation: the Association does not attract Black librarians and few white members are interested in signing-up for a Black Workers Group. The Association's conscience is clear—it has not opposed the formation of a Black group. Yet its technicalities prevent such a formation. Meanwhile Black LIS workers and communities remain unserved and under-represented.

Yet there is reason to be optimistic for the future. A promising development in 1999 is the endorsement of the findings of Roach and Morrison[301] by the Association of London Chief Librarians (ALCL). As the President of the ALCL says, "This study suggested that there is a need for a radical rethink of the role of the public library within a multi-ethnic, multicultural society. These findings were of special concern to chief librarians in London".[302] The Association has adopted a strategy for implementing the recommendations of the Warwick (Roach and Morrison) study and has included this in its Action Plan. "This will enable London's public libraries to enter the next millennium in a strong position to meet the needs of its ethnic minority communities". This is indeed a welcome development. As part of its reorganisation, the ALCL has also set up a Social Exclusion Group, which has been extremely active in the few months it has been in existence. It has also co-sponsored the Quality Leaders Project for Black LIS workers.

As far as the Library Association is concerned, the new Chief Executive has now given assurance on the action he expects to take:

- The LA will listen to the experiences and views of Black library and information workers and will seek to learn from them;

---

[300] Khan, Ayub (1999): How far have we come, in this multicultural society? Library Association Record. 101(2): 111.
[301] Roach and Morrison (1998): op. cit.
[302] Timms, M. (1999) Black and Asian services worthy of the millennium. Library Association Record. 101(2): 85.

- These views will help to shape the future policy of the LA...the LA Council has resolved to hold a full debate on the Black contribution at its June 2000 meeting;
- LA support will continue.[303]

The new commitment from the Chief Executive is a welcome initiative. Already there is more coverage of Black issues in the pages of the *Library Association Record* — although not regular columns as recommended by the resolution at the LA AGM in 1996 — "a regular column in the *Library Association Record* or quarterly supplement to the LAR".[304]

One hopes that Black library workers and community members will be able to participate in the "full debate" at the Council and that it will result in the empowerment of Black workers and communities and the formation of a Black Library Workers Group and that there will be more Black people on the decision-making bodies of the Association.

In April 2000, Bob McKee, the Chief Executive of the LA presented a draft "LA Corporate Plan (2000)" to progress his vision for "an integrated, inclusive and influential professional body".[305] The Plan's "framework of strategic objectives and key actions" includes "Working towards integration and inclusion". In order to achieve a "clear profile and strong role for the L/I (Library and Information) sector", McKee proposes that the Association will "seek to reflect within the Association the ethnic and cultural diversity of UK society... in order to address the issue of institutional racism and promote the Black contribution to the library and information sector". This is a welcome development and one hopes that action to implement this will include meaningful ways to address the poor record in service to Black communities and the lack of a Black presence in decision making levels, not only in the profession as a whole, but within LA as well.

"Working with bodies such as ACLA and ALAG" as the Plan proposes will not result in any meaningful change as experience of "working with such bodies" over the last three or four years shows. There is no point in hanging on to failed methods of bringing about change just because it may be too difficult to take a strategic approach. Past failures need to inform action for the future. More imaginative and bold vision and means of achievement are needed if the Association hopes to make itself relevant to Black communities. In particular, new tools such as Best Value show the importance of empowering Black communities and L/I workers and a new approach along these lines can provide grounds for meaningful change.

While libraries in the U.S.A. are not at the cutting edge of race policies, they certainly make more effort than the profession does in Britain. Some of their practices need to be studied for implementation in the UK. The existence of a large number of Black Universities in the U.S.A. over many years has, no doubt, contributed to strengthening the profession there.

Culture of change; change of culture

---

[303] Khan, Ayub (2000): Stamping out institutional racism. Library Association Record 102(1) pp. 38-39.
[304] Library Association Record: 8(9) September 1996.
[305] McKee, Bob (2000): Letter to LA membership, April 2000.

While the need for "change of culture" is gradually becoming accepted in the LIS world, its role in combating racism has not been sufficiently explored. There seems to be a general reluctance to talk openly about the need to address racism in the workplace. From casual conversation with library workers, it would appear that there is a lot of management bullying on the library workplaces, made more difficult for Black workers by racist attitudes mixed with such bullying. There is a feeling in some workplaces that any attempt to address racism automatically implies a criticism of the management and staff's commitment to an "equal" service. The attitude often is: "we are already providing a 'good' service to Black communities, so there is no need for change". In essence, this is a refusal to change, a refusal to look at service provision from the point of view of Black communities, a refusal to accept results of research such as Roach and Morrison, a refusal to accept the conclusions and recommendations from the Stephen Lawrence Inquiry.

> "Race equality must be a key part of our political and managerial agenda for change," says Local Government Association.[306]

...

John quotes the example of Hackney — which reflects experiences in many other London Boroughs — and provides useful insights on how change in culture can prove a useful tool against racism:

> How do you enable staff to participate fully in the running of the organisation? Policy and practice are two important ways in which these problems will be addressed [in Hackney]. The Action for Change will guide the Directorate of Education and Leisure Services to resolve the problems that exist in Libraries. Issues to be addressed will include stock, staffing, and access to library service. Policy and Resource implications of the necessary changes will be addressed. Change of culture is necessary to address the issues of rights, entitlement, quality with equality, service delivery, and management issues.[307]

Not much progress, however, seems to have been made as was confirmed by an inquiry in 1999:

> Hackney has embarked on an ambitious programme to eliminate racial discrimination from its workforce. The council ordered an independent inquiry into race discrimination in 1997. This inquiry found that although the council was very good at recruiting Black, Asian and ethnic minority staff, it discriminated against them once they were in post. Following this inquiry, the council has committed itself to a cultural change programme to eradicate institutional racism. One priority is to ensure that unacceptable action and practices are not only challenged but also prevented from occurring in the first place.[308]

---

[306] Local Government Association (1999) The Stephen Lawrence Inquiry and Home Secretary's Action Plan; initial guidance for local authorities. Produced by the Local Government Association, the Employers' Organisation and the Improvement and Development Agency.
[307] John, Gus (1995) Equality and Entitlement. Talk given by Gus John, Director, Directorate of Education and Leisure Services to Library Staff at Stamford Hill Library on Thursday February 23, 1995. (from notes made by the present author).
[308] Local Government Association, 1999: op. cit. p.18.

The experience in Haringey is similar. Travis says that 48 percent of the workforce is drawn from Black and minority communities.[309] However, Gurbux Singh, the new Chair of CRE who was the Chief Executive at Haringey says:

> But the vast majority are located at the bottom of the system. At the top…there is this glass ceiling. Minority ethnic communities have not broken through at assistant director or director level. We want to address that. We did it by setting targets and not quotas. Once you have any sort of target system it helps to focus minds.[310]

PART 3: THE BLACK COMMUNITY PERSPECTIVE

Many sections of the Black communities seem to be caught in a vicious circle of greater unemployment, poorer education, worse housing than white people. These make it difficult for them to demand their fair share of national services, including library services. Their disadvantage is compounded by the lack of interest among some libraries to make genuine efforts to reach out to them.

…

Community librarianship

A number of studies have looked at the development of community librarianship—for example, Vincent,[311] Black and Muddiman,[312] Muddiman,[313] Black.[314] Community librarianship "advocated a more flexible and diversified form of public library provision which would enable resources to be targeted at the disadvantaged", says Muddiman[315], who sees it as a "significant (if ultimately unsuccessful) attempt by some public library authorities to address disadvantage and social exclusion in library terms".

Black traces the history and scope of "community librarianship":

> Drawing on this example [in the U.S.A.] as well as their own tradition of social realism, many British librarians similarly embarked on a new course of action, one which discriminated in favour of the socially and economically deprived. This mode of service came to be known as 'community librarianship' which embodied 'a recognition that public library services are for all, not only for the better educated, more affluent "middle class" minority from whom the service has tended to draw its clientele, but also for the less literate, the disadvantaged, those who are perhaps less book-oriented but whose need for information and for life-enrichment may be greater'.[316]

---

[309] Travis, Alan (2000) Man with a mission [Gurbux Singh]. The Guardian (Society) March 22, 2000, pp. 2-3.
[310] Singh, Gurbux (2000), Quoted in "CRE harangues inflammatory language". Morning Star. 15 April. p.4.
[311] Vincent, John (1986): An introduction to community librarianship. London: Association of Assistant Librarians.
[312] Black, Alistair and Muddiman, Dave (1997): Understanding community librarianship: the public library in post-modern Britain. Aldershot: Avebury.
[313] Muddiman, Dave (1999): Open to all?: op. cit. Working paper No. 2: Public libraries and social exclusion: the historical legacy. Available at:
http://www.seapn.org.uk/opentoall.html [Accessed: 02 April 2007].
[314] Black, Alistair (2000): Skeleton in the cupboard: social class and the public library in Britain through 150 years. [Written for Library History, May 2000].
[315] Muddiman, 1999: op. cit.
[316] Black, Alistair (2000): op. cit.

An integral part of community librarianship was service to Black communities. As early as 1986, Vincent identified racism as a "major concern [which] is overlooked or ignored in much of the writing about provision of services". Years before Macpherson brought "institutional racism" to prominence, Vincent recognised its existence in the society and in the library:

The problem of poor service for Black communities which community librarianship sought to overcome was recognised long ago. Black[317] quotes some cases:

> Librarians began to express guilt over the exclusion of lower socio-economic groups from the public library. These groups included the unsuccessful ethnic minorities. In 1972, for example, in considering services to immigrant groups, Westminster City Libraries admitted that the 'public libraries are continuing to serve their communities as they existed 10-15 years ago, oblivious to the changes that have taken place in the intervening period' (R. Brown). Six years later, the chair of the Commission for Racial Equality wrote that an inadequate provision of books in public libraries *about* the ethnic minorities, as well as *for* them in their vernacular languages, represented 'a hole in the multi-cultural fabric of our contemporary society'.[318]

In order to succeed, community librarianship needed to undertake "wholesale 'deinstitutionalisation' of the public library service" instead it remained "an uneven and limited phenomenon—extensive activity running throughout the whole library service was exceptional".[319] Eventually, from the mid-1980s, community librarianship "lost momentum and support. Against the backdrop of political hostility and cuts in public services, [some?] librarians began to believe that its expense could not be justified".[320]

Indeed, the positive aspects of community librarianship were never accepted by the profession as a whole. Nor were any alternatives suggested. Black again examines professional hostility to the practices of community librarianship:

> Community librarianship required a reorientation of the librarian towards community work, a trend which some viewed as a threat to professional status: 'There is no doubt that some of the activities engaged in by librarians in the course of community librarianship were not entirely appropriate', remarked one of the pioneers of services to the disadvantaged in the early 1990s (P. Coleman).[321]

Further, the targeting of the disadvantaged in preference to other user groups appeared to counter the welfarist creed of universalism to which many public librarians deeply attached.

Black again highlights a fundamental tenet of community librarianship, which perhaps made it a target of attacks from the traditional, "non-community" librarian:

> Whereas equality of opportunity has been an unassailable tenet of public library philosophy, community librarianship's pursuit of *equality of outcome*, where intervention is based on positive discrimination in an attempt to raise the

---

[317] Ibid.
[318] Quoting D. Lane in Foreword to Clough, E. and Quarmby, J. (1978): A public library service for ethnic minorities in Great Britain. London: Library Association.
[319] Muddiman, Dave (1999): op. cit.
[320] Black, A. (2000): op. cit.
[321] Black, A. (2000): Ibid.

disadvantage to a level and quality of use commensurate with that experienced by users in the middle of the social scale, was difficult for many to swallow.[322]

The roots of the failure of community librarianship can be traced to what Black calls "strength of middle-class pressure".[323] This then led to the community librarianship becoming "de-radicalised from the mid-1980s onwards, its meaning being devalued into a slogan describing little more than a combination of community information, customer care and traditional outreach and extension services". This de-radicalisation can even today be seen in many traditional housebound and mobile services being grandly called "community service" when they do not even reach any Black communities. In contradiction to such pseudo-community services, many community groups set up and run their own library and information services, quite unconnected to the public library service. Although starved of resources, they serve the needs of their communities much better than the public library service, which then happily concentrates on serving its white, middle-class users.

Those seeking to improve service to Black communities need to understand this basic contradiction in British public library service — between the white, middle-class control on the one hand and the Black and working-class (potential) usage of the service. The problem of bringing about any meaningful change is so enormous that in most cases only minor, unsustainable projects are possible. This will remain the case until a revolutionary change takes place in the library world.

Hendry[324] looks at the "malign neglect by successive Conservative governments" from 1979 to 1997, which saw "public services reduced, externalised, starved of resources, put out to 'competitive' tender...The ethos of community service was dismissed".

The positive lessons from community librarianship were thus never learnt. It was a loss to the society as a whole, but particularly to all those who were disadvantaged, including Black communities. But the lessons are being learnt today through policies and practices currently associated with "social exclusion". "Libraries for all" would have been much closer if community librarianship had been allowed to evolve with the changing needs and times and to evolve its own theories and practices. The pioneers of community librarianship would have been considered heroes and heroines today instead of being condemned to closed chapters of history.

Empowering local communities

Excluded communities know what they want, in what form, when and how. The role of library and information workers and Council services is to enable change to be put into practice so that the communities receive services they need. They hold a key responsibility because they are the holders of the resources and control the power to decide how these resources are used. Thus if the service is to change, library workers must be prepared to change themselves. And that requires a bold decision that there is a need for change, that past practices have left many communities excluded.

Empowering communities can too easily become an empty gesture, a mechanical *form*, which avoids the *content* of giving the power to the community. As Halpin says, "A number of elements are required to deliver full and inclusive representation.

---

[322] Black, A. (2000): Ibid.
[323] Black, A. (2000): Ibid.
[324] Hendry, Joe (2000): Here comes the sun. Library Association Record. 102(5) pp.272-3.

[Communities] have to be *part of the debate, part of policy making and part of implementation and development of policy*".[325] [Emphasis added]. Hilary Armstrong says:

> In reality, many, if not most, public service organisations fail the Macpherson test because they do not have the basic systems in place, research into community needs, consultation with community organisations, ethnic monitoring of service use, policy analysis of the results to enable them to know whether or not services are free of discrimination and sensitive to the different needs of minority ethnic communities.[326]

A recent Institute for Public Policy Research (IPPR) survey provides a useful checklist of methods that can be used to consult Black communities. The report emphasises the "need for a more comprehensive approach if Black and ethnic minority people are to be genuinely engaged in the decision making process". The recommendations of the report need to be taken seriously by libraries:

> The Government's legislative drive towards public involvement to ensure better service delivery and responsiveness to need is clearly an important development and a major opportunity. The challenge is how to ensure that this is fairly applied to all groups including Black and ethnic minority people.[327]

...

The BME Sub-Group of voluntary sector representatives under the Working Group on Government Relations secretariat has produced a draft "Compact Code of Good Practice on Government Relations with the Black and Minority Ethnic Voluntary Sector".[328] It aims to set a new framework for the relationship between the BME voluntary sector and the government at all levels. The Code aims to achieve a new partnership between Government and the BME Sector and to achieve a positive difference in the relationship between government and the BME sector in improving outcomes for BME communities.

Capacity building, developing infrastructure and sustainability

The library and information sector needs to work closely with voluntary organisations and sign up to the Code as a way of ensuring appropriate community consultations. Thus even in places where there may be few Black communities or where there may be difficulties in working with local community organisations, such national bodies can represent the interests of local Black communities.

Many Black communities perceive current library services as inappropriate and "unequal." The collective failure of public libraries is indicated by the fact that three major reports and action plans have not been accepted in the planning process, and not systematically implemented.

---

[325] Halpin, Anita (2000): The new fight for union democracy. Morning Star. 10 March.
[326] Armstrong, Hilary(1999): Speech given at the Federation of Black Housing Organisation Conference. London. October 29, 1999.
[327] Ali, Rushanara (2000): Involving Black and ethnic minorities in decision making. Seminar hosted by the London Borough of Camden at the British Library on 19th January 2000. London: Institute for Public Policy Research.
[328] The National Council for Voluntary Organisations (2000): Compact BME!

Roach and Morrison

Roach and Morrison's[329] research provides a useful picture of the current situation nationally. Some key findings of their research "to examine how public library services have engaged in response to the issue of ethnic diversity".

Stephen Lawrence Inquiry

"Racism does not only affect Black, Asian and ethnic minority people; it impacts all communities" says the Guidance for Local Authorities.[330] The Guidance recommends the preparation of an overall equalities strategy, which encompass Black, Asian and ethnic minority community groups, asylum seekers and refugees. It sets out the benefits in eliminating racism – something needed in a society steeped in racism:

> The full impact of the Macpherson Inquiry's conclusions was attacked by the right wing press and their backers. Its programme was "the familiar English elite technique of integrating protest into a long-drawn-out process of reform which eventually results in the barest minimum of concessions".[331]

The response to the Macpherson report by the Government is summed up by Kundnani:

> The Macpherson report was meant to open up the issue of racism but, fearing a right-wing rebellion, the government brought in a reduced set of reforms, while tightening up a racist asylum policy.[332]

PART 4: SOME PROBLEMS, SOME SOLUTIONS

Equal opportunities, diversity or anti-racism?

Many local authorities have abandoned the practice of having race equality units and have replaced them with equality units which address not only race inequality but inequalities faced by lesbians, gay men, bisexuals and transgendered people, other equality matters such as lesbigay, women, and disabled people as well. While aiming to "equalise" anti-discrimination policies and practices, the effect in many cases has been to dilute action against race equality.

Cunningham says, "many employers have adopted the term "Managing diversity" in place of equal opportunities when discussing programmes designed to promote fair treatment in employment".[333]

John follows the history of "diversity":

> We started off with multi-culturalism, then we went into anti-racism, then that was thought to be not so impressive so you get rid of the race equality units and

---

[329] Roach and Morrison's (1998): op.cit.
[330] Local Government Association (1999): The Stephen Lawrence Inquiry and Home Secretary's Action Plan; initial guidance for local authorities. Produced by the Local Government Association, the Employers' Organisation and the Improvement and Development Agency.
[331] Kundnani, Arun (2000): Stumbling on': race, class and England. Race and Class. 41 (4) pp. 1-18.
[332] op.cit.
[333] Cunningham, Marie (1996) Speech at the Open meeting for Black and Ethnic Minority Staff, Library Association, 17 April.

committees and you have something generic called Equal Opportunities. But that wasn't really quite sharp enough and it made it sound as through the race thing had gone off the agenda altogether, which it did and has and consequently we must adopt the Valuing Diversity that is the new ball game. We are all committed these days to valuing diversity, workplace diversity, libraries diversity, bookshop diversity, all sorts of diversity; we value everything. The question is where was the agenda of valuing diversity long before any Black person landed on these shores.[334]

While there is no overall picture of a service relevant to Black communities emerging, it is true that a large number of initiatives are taking place throughout the country. *What's New*[335] regularly records such initiatives.

Managers, commitments and structures

Perhaps the greatest resistance to eliminating racism comes from managers. Their position of power makes them "mini Hitlers". They control policies and practices in the workplace. However much Councillors and senior executives want equality, however many "Equal Opportunity" policies there may be, without the active participation of middle and senior managers, there will not be any meaningful change. It is no longer enough merely to be "non racist" — managers should prove that they are actively anti-racists before they are allowed to continue having power over policies, staff and other resources and service delivery.

There is a growing awareness that business, civil service, as well as local authorities need to reflect the cultural diversity of the community they serve. While this has been put into practice in many local authorities, Black staff has tended to remain at the lowest levels. Urgent action is needed now to ensure that such diversity is reflected in the higher, decision and policy-making levels of local authorities.

There can be no progress in providing an "equal" service for people of colour without having senior managers from these communities. They need to be involved in decision- and policy-making positions so that the concerns of their communities are represented and given adequate representation at the highest levels, not only in the Library Service itself, but in the local authority as a whole. No meaningful change in policy and practices can result if there are an inadequate proportion of Black managers.

The Local Government Management Board (LGMB) says, "Black and other minority ethnic managers can make a unique and valuable contribution to improving performance and service delivery to the diverse communities local councils serve".[336]

While serious action is necessary to redress this imbalance, it is not enough to aim merely at increasing the number of Black managers at senior level. Two other issues

---

[334] John, Gus (1999): Talk given at the Conference The Significance Of The Stephen Lawrence Inquiry For Public Libraries. London and Home Counties Branch: The Library Association in association with the Association of London Chief Librarians (ALCL). Executive Briefing: 28 June 1999.

[335] What's New; LARRIE's Quarterly Update. No. 16 (p.2); No 17 (2000). Details about Local Authorities Race Relations Information Exchange can be found at www.lg-employers.gov.uk/equal-info.html from where racial equality action plans and special reports can be downloaded.

[336] Local Government Management Board (LGMB,1996): Evening the odds; research into management development for Black and other minority ethnic managers. Executive Summary. Details about LGMB are available at:
http://www.laria.gov.uk/content/newsletr/59/news13.htm.

are important. Essential criteria for all managers should include commitment to change and to improving the service to all marginalised communities, not merely in improving the personal professional development of managers. Ways also need to be found to enable minority communities to be actively involved in deciding how library resources are used and what services are provided.

Secondly, there should be organisational policies, structures and support mechanisms to enable Black managers to implement change. LGMB recommends that any schemes to support Black managers must be part of the mainstream and must not be seen as separate or marginal. In addition, LGMB says:

Merely increasing the number of Black and other minority ethnic managers in senior positions will not, by itself, improve organisational practices or services to the communities they serve. In development terms, Black and other minority ethnic managers need to emphasise their capacity to transform their organisations. However, this must be matched by an organisational development framework which links service enhancement with employees' development. It must be clearly supported by senior management.

An essential ingredient for success of a programme to ensure that there are more Black managers in local authorities was highlighted by LGMB.

Without the leadership and commitment from the very top of their organisations Black and other minority ethnic managers fear that measures taken to develop them will not create a fast track for development and career progression in local government.[337]

Such commitment from top leadership has had success in other management development programmes run by LGMB, such as the Top Managers Programme and the Women's Leadership Programme. Similar Black Managers Programmes need to be initiated as a matter of urgency. The Quality Leaders Project takes this approach.

All authorities serious about redressing the imbalance in BME managers in senior positions need to study and implement the key findings from the research conducted by LGMB. The Survey's Recommendations[338] should be essential reading for all working in or interested in local authorities. They are grouped under three sections: recommendations for The LGMB, for local authorities, and for Black Individuals.[339]

Barriers to change — race & class connections

Changing hearts and minds

Change can come about only when structural barriers to change are removed. These include having an appropriate legislative framework, an appropriate staffing structure, management commitment to change, an adequate level of Black leadership within the organisation, and an appropriate mechanism for Black communities to influence policy and procedures of the service. Perhaps one of the most difficult changes to achieve is the work environment.

Contradiction between "democracy" and equality

---

[337] Ibid.
[338] Ibid. And: Local Government Management Board (LGMB, 1998): No quality without equality — best value and equalities. By: Baldwin, Pam and Foot, Jane.
[339] Ibid.

The Government's drive towards greater devolution and democracy is commendable in empowering communities. But there is a danger in the process of local empowerment coming into conflict with the Government's other drive towards equality. As Richard Thomas says, "Labour could soon be faced with the choice between a fairer, more equal society and a more open and democratic one".[340] On the one hand is the need to direct greater resources to eliminate poverty and unemployment in some parts of the country and among some sections of the community, including the Black community. On the other, if the decision to transfer these resources is given to the affluent parts of the country or to the well-off people, then there is obviously a conflict, which may well see equality sacrificed. The Government will have to resolve this conflict. "Let us hope, for the sake of the poor", says Thomas, "that he [Tony Blair] is not too democratic".[341]

The problem at the local authority level is equally acute, especially in situations where the Party in power is not able or interested enough to support equality at the expense of "democracy". The danger for the public libraries in this political set-up is real. In many cases it is politically expedient to give in to some white petty bourgeois groups which are extremely articulate in demanding—and getting—the lion's share of library resources at the expense of Black communities, and the working class as a whole. They are well connected to local or national political forces in power. Black communities and librarians have not yet established an equivalent power base. Leaders at every level need to put equality in the forefront of their agenda.

Black (2000) looks behind the public library's "sound, democratic façade" only to find "illiberal motives and the exclusion of the poor".[342] He urges the public library movement to first acknowledge the "conservative foundations on which it has grown" and to "appreciate the strength of the middle-class pressure exerted on the public library over 150 years". It is this conservatism and middle-class pressure that defeated community librarianship and, at the same time, marginalised services to Black communities. Any struggle for improvement in service to Black communities will need to work closely with those struggling for the information rights of the working people. Thus issues of race and class are very closely related, as recognised by the publishers of *Race and Class*.

Information revolution for a few?

Technological innovations have generally prompted the kind of economic and social leaps that have left the Black community struggling. "Blacks have participated as equals in the technological world only as consumers", wrote Anthony Walton in the American magazine *Atlantic Monthly* earlier this month. "Otherwise [they exist] on the margins of the ethos that defines the nation, underrepresented as designers, innovators, and implementers of our systems and machines. As a group, they have suffered from something that can loosely be called technological illiteracy".[343]

Yet new technologies can also provide a powerful tool to eliminate racism for people of colour. Like any other tool, it needs to be used as a positive method of

---

[340] Thomas, R (1998): The big trade off. Prospect, Guardian Taster. p. 6.
[341] Ibid.
[342] Black, Ian (2000): EU fights far right with laws on racism. The Guardian. May, 18. Available at:
http://www.guardianunlimited.co.uk/Archive/Article/0,4273,4019399,00.html
[Accessed: May 21, 2000].
[343] Quoted in Younge, Gary (2000): Paying up. The Guardian. Jan. 8, p. 20.

liberation. This needs a new quality of positive leadership on the part of LIS managers who will need to work with Black communities to open out the ICT potential to Black communities and workers. As the National Black Caucus in the U.S.A. says:

> The inventions of humankind are not the property of any one race to be used to gain artificial superiority. Technology can be as much an instrument of liberation as it is of domination. Liberators must gain control of these new technologies and employ them for the proper advancement of all humanity.[344]

Department of Trade and Industry's "Closing the digital divide"[345] is thus a welcome initiative with its concern for the needs of Black communities. If appropriately implemented, this can be a powerful tool to "include" Black communities in the information revolution.

The need to fight institutionalised racism

It is necessary to realise that people of colour are not passive recipients of racism. Wherever there is oppression and exploitation, there is resistance too. Resistance to oppression is a normal reaction among the oppressed.

It is not only the issues of the Black library service that are ignored overall. The existence of *resistance to racism* in the LIS field has also been similarly ignored by library educators and "mainstream" publications. It is true that in every work place where there is racism, there is inevitably resistance to it—however open or underground it may be. For those seeking proof of this, I would recommend a visit to any workplace where there are Black information workers—but such resistance will become obvious only to those sympathetic to the cause.

Again, it is in the interest of those in power to ignore or play down the existence of such resistance. It is very seldom that one hears of resistance to racism in LIS. The resistance of Black communities and librarians to institutionalised racism is hardly recognised, let alone being used as an example of how to combat racism. It is ironic that a profession devoted to the free flow of information itself practices censorship of information and does it so efficiently.[346]

Gus John explains how this resistance is then racialised:

> Our fundamental instinct is towards justice. Although the slaves knew that they would lose a limb if caught resisting, they continued to resist. Wherever there is oppression, there the oppressed will unite to resist. When Black people resist, this resistance is racialised and seen as another reason to stereotype and marginalise Black people.[347]

Moodley highlights an important factor in eliminating racism: "This is the issue of changing attitudes, especially where the operation and organisation of the institutions

---

[344] Quoted in Black Information Link (BLINK). Available at: http://www.blink.org.uk/. [Accessed: 24 April, 2000].
[345] Department of Trade and Industry (2000): Closing the digital divide: information and communication technologies in deprived areas. (Report of the Policy Action Team 15). The Department is now called Department for Business, Enterprise and Regulatory Reform (see: http://www.dti.gov.uk/index.html. Accessed on 09 September 2007].
[346] Durrani, Shiraz (1999): Black communities and information workers in search of social justice. New Library World. Vol. 100 (1151). pp. 265-278.
[347] John, Gus (1995): Equality and Entitlement. Talk given by Gus John, Director, Directorate of Education and Leisure Services to Library Staff at Stamford Hill Library on Thursday February 23, 1995. (from notes made by the present author).

are concerned. The need to achieve this is now urgent".[348] This places the culture of resistance at the centre of tools needed to eliminate racism.

Gus John warns about the danger of side-stepping the issue of racism:

> There will always be problems when we side-step issues either to maintain consensus or to disenfranchise people. We ignore this [truth] at our peril. It is necessary to examine our attitude towards staff: how is staff valued, how seriously we deal with issues of marginalisation.[349]

The struggle against racism is then the responsibility not only of people of colour but of everybody. In the LIS sector, it is particularly the responsibility of management to ensure that they not only create conditions for the elimination of racism, but take an active part in its elimination.

Using anti-racism to defeat racism

There is a real danger that those opposed to fundamental change may use the term "institutional racism" to merely mouth formulas without doing anything about racism. The Campaign Against Racism and Fascism warns of two dangers:

First, institutionalised racism has become a new buzzword. Wherever the term discrimination or racism would previously have been used, people now say "institutional racism." It is as though they think of it as some new politically correct term that has now to be utilised, rather than a specific aspect of racism.

Second, those agencies, which assert that they are concerned about tackling institutional racism are not examining racism in new ways to find radical cures but merely resorting to old-style palliatives (reminiscent of 20 years of equal opportunities programmes).[350]

PART 5: TOOLS FOR CHANGE

Perspectives on combating racism

Ngugi provides a fundamental lesson on combating racism:

> Those fighting racism must never forget that racism, no matter how all-pervasive, is nevertheless an ideology founded on an economic system of exploitation and social oppression and today this is imperialist capitalism.[351]

The economic, political, cultural and psychological empowerment of the social victims of racism as part of the overall struggle against the roots of racism is the only way of defeating it.

In the information field, much has been written about how to combat racism. What is missing is the practice of combating racism. Until the Government took on the matter of social exclusion, until Annual Library Plans became compulsory, until social

---

[348] Moodley, Ronnie (1999): BME associations need to fight institutionalised racism. Black Housing. No. 108 (October-November) p. 4.
[349] John, Gus (1999): op. cit.
[350] Campaign Against Racism and Fascism (2000): Wasting the Macpherson opportunity. (CARF Features 53, December 1999/January 2000). Available at http://www.carf.demon.co.uk/feat33.html Accessed: 24 April, 2000.
[351] Thiong'o, Ngugi wa (1993): Moving the centre; the struggle for cultural freedoms. London: James Currey.

exclusion came to be highlighted as having a poor record in the Plans, libraries were happy to do whatever little they could get away with.

In order to combat racism, one needs to see the problems from a number of perspectives:

- Historical imbalance
- Black community point of view
- Organisation and the power of Black staff in the LIS sector
- Responsibility of library management

Solutions can be found only when there is an acceptance, especially among those who hold power, that there is a problem. Black communities know that they are excluded from "mainstream" life, that there is racism in Britain today, and that nothing will change unless they actively struggle for change. But it needed the death of Stephen Lawrence, the communities'[352] struggles and the pronouncements from a white judge to get a wider acceptance among the non-Black community that we suffer from "institutional racism".

Gurbux Singh makes clear what is required if we are to eliminate racism: "We need to have a clear national framework on how government intends to tackle institutional racism and it needs to set out clearly where ministerial accountability lies."

Never be silent — launch, Nairobi (2006)[353]

Shiraz Durrani: *Never be silent; publishing and imperialism in Kenya, 1884-1963*
London, Nairobi: Vita Books. ISBN: 978-1-869885-05-9

I would like to start by reading a news item from yesterday's *Daily Nation*:

> Algiers: Algerian President Abdelaziz Bouteflika said France's 130-year rule of the North African country was one of the "most barbaric forms of colonization in history". Bouteflika made the comment less than two months after renewing a call for France to officially apologise for the massacres of Algerians during the colonial era.[354]

The situation in Kenya was similar to that in Algeria. Yet there is a deafening silence today on many aspects of Kenya's history. Two generations have grown up since independence, yet they are not fully aware of the history of those who fought and sacrificed for us to have the freedom today to meet here without harassment. The stories of those who were active in these struggles have yet to be fully documented.

---

[352] Singh, Gurbux (2000): Quoted in "CRE harangues inflammatory language". Morning Star. 15 April. p.4.
[353] Book launch: Goethe Institute, Nairobi. 5 July, 2006. Information for Social Change. Available at: http://libr.org/isc/occassional_papers/Shiraz.htm [Accessed: 04 April 2007].
[354] "Algeria hits at France rule". Daily Nation (Nairobi). 4 July 2006, p. 15.

Many sacrificed their lives, their shambas, and their chance for education so that we can be a free nation. Their sacrifices have not yet been documented fully.

But we have not always been silent. Throughout the 500 years of struggle against Portuguese and British colonialism, our people have fought, have sung freedom songs, have written about their opposition to colonial massacres, domination of our land, and exploitation of resources and the enslavement of people. Yet we were forced into silence after independence — the very time when we expected to have the freedom to research, document and teach our children all about our heroic struggles.

It is only in the last few years that more is being heard about our history. The launch of this book today is a testimony that we are gradually liberating ourselves from the imposed silence. There is ample evidence all around this room of this new age of freedom. Witness the posters of Bildad Kaggia and Karimi Nduthu produced by the MwaKenya- December Twelve Movement; look at the posters of Pio Gama Pinto and Makhan Singh and publications from *Awaaz* which is setting new standards in documenting the history of South Asian Kenyans; examine the publications from Vita Books on display here. All this was not openly possible some years back.

It is also to the credit of the National Book Development Council that they co-sponsored this launch with Vita Books. They have an important role to play in the delivery of the millennium development goals. Without the free flow of ideas, creative works and appropriate learning material in all forms and languages, there can never be development.

Yet the struggle for new ideas and information is a long and hard one. The world is moving fast and we need to keep up with the best. There have been major changes globally. We need to learn from the rapid economic and hence political rise of the BRIC countries (Brazil, Russia, India and China). South and East Asia are fast becoming the growth engine of the world. China has already overtaken Britain as the fourth largest economy in the world. Africa needs to develop at an even faster rate so as not to fall further behind. We need to learn lessons from the new models of development practiced in Cuba, Venezuela, Bolivia, Nepal, among other places.

Free and easy availability of relevant information is crucial in order to learn from these examples. Moreover, developments in information and communications technologies (ICT) provide us with new tools to stop years of stagnation and catch up with the world. But this will not happen automatically. African governments need to give priority to education, to learning and to skills development. National policies in Africa need to reflect the central role that information plays in national economic development. As a first step, we need to eradicate illiteracy, inculcate lifelong learning skills and the love of reading, even as we introduce computer skills for all. Appropriate reading and learning material, backed by relevant research, is urgently required for our prisons, schools, colleges and Universities as well as for adult learning programmes. We need to emphasize the transfer of the latest scientific and technological information from around the world to budding Kenyan scientists, researchers. It is only then that we can broaden horizons and expand the awareness of all Kenyans. The process of real development starts in earnest after that. The need for new ideas and experiences from around the world is an essential ingredient for any social change.

In this context, I would like to commend the National Book Development Council for their campaign to develop a national book and information policy — without which our hopes for meaningful development will remain just that — hopes and dreams. There is also an urgent need for having library standards based on the

UNESCO Library Charter to ensure our services meet the learning needs of all. The Ministry of Education, Science and Technology can play a leading role in this.

Not starting from zero

But we are not starting from zero. The struggle for relevant information is being taken up actively by many. The latest is the newly-registered Kenya Centre of the Progressive African Library and Information Activists Group (PALIAct) where librarians are taking the innovative approach of linking up not only with other professionals, but, perhaps more importantly, with communities whose information needs have not been met in the past. They are also linking up with progressive activists in other African countries, as well as in the U.S.A., Scandinavia, Latin America and other parts of the world. I would like to commend Esther Obachi, the Chair of PALIAct-Kenya (who is among us today) and her colleagues who are taking leadership in developing this new approach to development.

And that is not all: PALIAct has taken the initiative with the support of the Finnish Government to run a workshop for over 30 librarians from Kenya, Uganda and Tanzania to ensure that information about and from the Word Social Forum (WSF) which takes place in Nairobi in January 2007 is made available to those who need it most—workers and peasants of East Africa through their public library services. They are also ensuring that information about Kenyan people's struggles is also made available to the WSF as a whole. PALIAct points the way of a more policy and practice for Africa as a whole. In this, the re-energized Kenya Library Association (KLA) under new leadership is playing an important role too.

The right to relevant information, to communicate freely, to acquire and disseminate ideas, information and knowledge is enshrined in Kenya's constitution and in several UN conventions signed by Kenya. They are also a part of basic human rights based on social and economic justice. But such paper rights will not automatically ensure free information for all. People need to be actively involved in the practice of achieving these rights. They can be active through free expression of ideas in newspapers and books, by undertaking research and disseminate results of such research, by developing appropriate policies, by publishing books and encouraging reading and learning.

20/20 vision

The presence here today of Hon. Dr. Kilemi Mwiria, Assistant Minister in the Ministry of Education Science and Technology is a clear indication of the commitment of the Government of Kenya to the basic rights mentioned above. But in a democracy, Governments need the active participation of citizens in all aspects of public policy formulation and implementation. We need to work together to develop a new vision for our society, focusing on the right to information and knowledge. It is for all of us here (and also those not here) to grasp the opportunities available to us to become active partners with the Government to decide our future to achieve a new vision of a free, democratic Kenya where rights to the free flow of information is not only a paper right but also a lifestyle. The process of liberating our minds starts here. Perhaps the first step is to formulate a vision of a knowledge-based Information Society in Kenya by 2020.

Research on the Kenyan struggle for liberation

Vita Books has taken a small step in making such rights a reality by publishing various books on display here. It is facing all the difficulties that an independent publishing venture faces. It has taken advantage of positive changes in the political situation in Kenya in recent years and has begun the process of coming back home from exile. I hope that the publication of *Never be Silent* will encourage further research and documentation of the real history of Kenya — something not possible in the past. Perhaps it is time to revisit the points I made in my submissions to the Task Force on Truth, Justice and Reconciliation Commission in 10 August, 2003, where I suggested the following:

- Erect national monuments in all major towns in Kenya to honour the memory of Pinto and other freedom fighters, who have sacrificed their lives for Kenya's struggle for liberation.
- Set up of a National Liberation Research, Museum and Archives Centre where the histories, publications and material culture of all national heroes can be collected and used as part of Kenya's heritage. This needs to happen urgently... Many such prominent people have died over the years.
- Set up a Pio Gama Pinto International Award to honour those who make an outstanding contribution to the political, economic and social liberation of Africa.
- Set up a Pio Gama Pinto Chair of History at the University of Nairobi to encourage research on the Kenyan struggle for liberation.

Urgent action is needed today — so that future generations do not suffer as previous ones have. The cry for never being silent is as urgent today as it was during the Mau Mau War of liberation.

The extent of the silence that surrounds the real history of colonialism in Kenya is illustrated by the lack of knowledge today among people in Kenya as well as in Britain about actual happenings during the colonial period in Kenya. Few people know about atrocities such as the following, referred to in *Never be silent*:

Mobile gallows

Taking the Mau Mau oath was made a capital offence. Between 1953 and 1956 more than 1,000 Africans were hanged for alleged Mau Mau crimes. Public hangings, which were outlawed in Britain for over a century, were carried out in Kenya during the emergency.

Professor Lonsdale explains, "A mobile gallows was transported around the country dispensing 'justice' to Mau Mau suspects...Dead Mau Mau, especially commanders, were displayed at cross-roads, at market places and at administrative centres.[355]

Five shillings a head

---

[355] Slaughter, Barbara (1999): "How Britain crushed the 'Mau Mau rebellion' – Channel Four TV's Secret History – Mau Mau". A report on the programme is available from: <http://www.hartford-hwp.com/archives/36/026.html> [Accessed: 2 April 2005].

Other reports told of officers who paid their men five shillings a head "for every Mau Mau they killed". One soldier testified in court that his officer had said he could shoot anybody he liked as long as they were black, because he wanted to increase his company's score of kills to 50.[356]

With a history of such terrorism against the people of Kenya, how dare we remain silent about the real history of Kenya?

Nairobi, 4 July, 2006

Communications for liberation: launch of *Never be silent*, London (2006)[357]

I have been asked by our legal people to read out this health warning: Putting into practice what the title of the book says may render you liable to ordinary or even extraordinary rendition. The University or the publishers will not accept liability for any consequences for you, your family or your country if you decide, "never to be silent".

In all countries, the ruling classes have used their control over information to influence people's world outlook and social awareness. Developments in information and communication technologies in recent years have given them even more power to control the destinies of peoples, countries and the world as a whole. Those who control information and systems of communications also decide what interpretation to give to our history and culture. They decide which ideologies, individuals and political and social movements "live" and which will die. This is no crude mind control. This is a silent and hidden hand going into our collective minds to organize our collective information and knowledge. Aspects of information that are unpalatable to the ruling classes are deleted and those that legitimize their rule are magnified. This newly recreated world is then projected through all means of social communication: mass media, the education system, arts and culture, as well as through libraries and archives.

Perhaps the most important example in recent years of the (mis)use of information for political and economic use is the propaganda mounted by the Bush and Blair administrations about the "existence" of weapons of mass destruction in Iraq. It did not matter that there was no real evidence for this, it did not matter that "evidence" had to be created to suit the political aims of those keen on waging wars—wars that have led to the death of over 700,000 people in Iraq. It did not matter that other countries are allowed, as a "natural right", to develop and use weapons of even more deadly mass destruction. No, what mattered was that people had to be

---

[356] Slaughter (1999): ibid.
[357] Celebrate the publication of Shiraz Durrani: *Never be silent; publishing and imperialism in Kenya, 1884-1963*. 22 November 2006. Graduate Centre (GC108). Tower Building. London Metropolitan University.

convinced by incorrect information about the existence of such weapons in Iraq and to designate Sadam Hussain, once an ally of the same powers, as a monster who had to be destroyed—together with the country and citizens as "collateral damage".

The fact that those who invaded Iraq controlled, directly or indirectly, mass media to silence the oppositions to the wars was a crucial factor that allowed the invasion to be given a superficial gloss of "agreement" in national and international terms. Millions of people around the world marched and shouted their opposition to the wars, but this had no effects on the so-called democratically elected "leaders" who used the most advanced weapons of mass destruction to rain death on people of an independent country. The same mass media were used to hide crucial facts—that the real interest in destroying Iraq as a viable country was to meet their geo-political interest in West Asia, to control oil in a major oil producing country, which was threatening to stop using U.S. dollars for oil transactions. The same media are used to misinterpret resistance as sectional wars. Those opposed to the invasion of their country are not seen as part of resistance, and their resistance is interpreted as religious wars in the well-used imperialist tactic of "divide-and-rule".

A world created by imperialism

Does all this appear to be too removed from the topic of this evening's discussion? Not really. Such brutality and destruction—as well as the control over information about them—have been used in the history of the world as created by imperialism for over 500 years. One needs to look at just a few books published recently to see this as very much part of the British Empire. Those who may not have time to read all the new material can perhaps look at just two books:

- Caroline Elkins (2005): *Britain's Gulag: The Brutal End of Empire in Kenya*. London: Pimlico.
- John Newsinge (2006): *The Blood Never Dried: A People's History of the British Empire*. Bookmarks.

These books provide details about historical brutality and terrorism employed by imperialism for centuries in Kenya, Ireland, China, India, Egypt, Palestine, and Malaya. No part of the world has escaped this brutal onslaught in which whole nations and communities have been wiped out. Yet such facts are not common knowledge as our media, information and educational institutes do not make us aware of them, preferring instead to focus on a few "benefits" bestowed on people around the world in the name of Empire.

I was surprised to read in January 2005 that Gordon Brown wants Britain to stop apologising for its colonial past.[358] I seem to have missed the apologies that Britain is supposed to have made. Instead, the Chancellor called for the "great British values"— freedom, tolerance, civic duty—to be admired as some of our most successful exports. Well, I would like the Chancellor to read the two books I have quoted—and also *Never be silent*—and talk again about "our successful exports"—which in Kenya have included mobile gallows to "pacify" the rebellious natives.

---

[358] Brogan, Benedict (2005): It's time to celebrate the Empire, says Brown. Last updated at 08:49am on 15th January 2005. Available at:
http://www.dailymail.co.uk/pages/live/articles/news/news.html?in_article_id=334208&in_page_id=1770. [accessed: 21 November 2006].

The native is looking back

But the same technology that enables "difficult" parts of history to be deleted from our consciousness also provides people with tools to retrieve that same history from the recycle bin and put it in the forefront of life. As Derek Walcott says, *"The native, the exotic, the victim, the noble savage, is looking back, returning a stare"*.[359] The process of returning a stare is made easier today as people everywhere claim back their histories and break embargos placed on their information. Everywhere, they are breaking controls on the means of the production of books, news and information. The people's war of liberation in the information field has started in earnest.

In fact, the process of resistance has never stopped — whether reported or not. Greatest theories and philosophies are created as part of liberation struggles. People make creative use of whatever means they have at their disposal to communicate, to organize and to create their own ideologies and organizations that help their liberation. Songs, orature, music and culture are used when other methods are not possible. It is not an accidental fact that music and songs from areas of intense wars of liberation are at their best and most intense. Witness the literature and songs of resistance and liberation from Vietnam, revolutionary China, USSR, South Africa under apartheid, from Palestine today, and from many African countries during wars of liberation.

500 years of resistance

Never be silent documents such a process of communication for liberation in Kenya during the last half of the last century. It documents not only the information struggle against the colonial regime and their allies, but also a struggle among Kenyans themselves for liberation. The enemy is not only out "there". As Mao taught, the enemy hides among the people and it is as essential to struggle against them, as it is to struggle against the foreign invaders and looters.

The liberation struggle against colonialism in Kenya started over 500 years ago with the entry of Portuguese colonialism in Eastern Africa. This struggle intensified when British colonialism took over in Kenya and Uganda. The people of Tanganyika took up their own struggles against an equally brutal German colonialism.

An aspect of African history that has not been fully documented is the resistance of people against colonialism and imperialism. This is where the brushing out of history takes place in its most brutal form. The wars of liberation are shown as primitive activities of a backward people. Africa is not allowed the dignity of their resistance being seen as conscious actions of a people against their exploitation. Slaves are usually seen as victims only. Victim they no doubt were, but they also organised resistance to their enslavement, never accepting their slave status. Documenting the resistance of slaves would expose the injustice of the whole system that sunk to the lowest level of civilization by enslaving people. Similarly, accepting resistance of the oppressed would expose the process of exploitation, and expose the beneficiaries of such exploitation. Those who benefit from slavery and today's exploitation thus seek to hide and misrepresent all such resistance.

---

[359] Derek Walcott (1998): What the Twilight Says. London : Faber and Faber.

Turning heroes into villains

The resistance of the Kenyan people needs to be documented and explained as an expression of resistance of the people against foreign invaders out to loot and steal. Every Kenyan nationality resisted the initial British intrusion until they were "pacified" by massacres, mass punishments, and confiscation of cattle. This was an open betrayal of the Kenyan people's trust in allowing the foreigners a foothold in their country as a gesture of friendship. This resistance reached a peak in Mau Mau, which was a coming together of a strong trade union movement with progressive nationalist forces now united under a new liberation ideology and organisation. Their aim was to recapture their land and freedom and provide basic worker and human rights to all. The movement of armed resistance changed the history not only of Kenya, but that of colonialism in Africa and the whole venture of the British Empire — which Lala Hardayal, the founder of the Ghadar movement, called the "British Vampire" in 1913.[360]

Surely such a major resistance movement deserves a more serious analysis and documentation, not the silence and distortion that it has faced. Many people are still left with the impression, created by colonialism and reinforced by imperialism, that Mau Mau was a backward, primitive movement of only one "tribe" to revert to its "tribal" ways thus defying facts and historical evidence. Fighting for one's land has been turned into a "primitive" activity. Personal and community sacrifices of a people, made as part of their fight to regain their land and freedom has been shown as backward and "uncivilized" behaviour. Heroes have indeed been turned into villains.

Social justice under attack

But these are issues not only for historians. The relevance of this is to be found everywhere in our world today. The right to question politicians and the right of the free flow of information are all under attack in Britain and the U.S.A. today in the so-called "war on terrorism". A new terror is being unleashed in the name of "fighting terrorism" — a real *1984* scenario.

In an environment that seeks to impose an ever reducing right to information, when the very freedom to express political opinion is under attack, surely the only option open to people is never to be silent. That is the lesson taught by the courageous people of Kenya half a century ago — taught with their blood and sweat. The very language used to describe the movement and its people exposes the attempt to denounce the movement: thus "guerrillas" become "terrorists"; "nationalities" become "tribes"; "wars of liberation" become "tribal and primitive wars". At the same time, the ideology and organisations of the movement become non-existent in an attempt to deny any legitimacy to the movement as an anti-colonial, anti-imperialist movement.

Never be silent documents the tremendous support that the people of Kenya received from progressive people in the UK in 1950s and 60s. This is part of a growing global movement of solidarity with those struggling for liberation. Such solidarity has given increasing strength as progressive people in all countries are brought together in a global agenda by using the new opportunities opened up by new technologies. It is thus appropriate that the 2007 World Social Forum takes place in Nairobi in January.

---

[360] Quoted in Durrani, Shiraz (2006): Never be silent; publishing and imperialism in Kenya, 1884-1963. London: Vita Books. p.44.

Progressive forces in Britain—as in other parts of the world—need to support the people of Kenya once again today as they demand that historical injustices be acknowledged—and be compensated for—by the British Government for its reign of terror maintained in Kenya during the entire colonial period. The same spirit of solidarity needs to prevail on a global level as we mark 200 years of the "Abolition of the Slave Trade in the British Empire". It is not aid that Africa needs. Africa demands justice—political justice, economic justice and social justice.

I conclude by quoting Digby Warren of the London Metropolitan University. He says, "the need for critical public debate remains so crucial in our post 9/11 era". I hope the publication of *Never be silent* encourages such a debate.

Trade union movement in Kenya & their communications system (2006)[361]

The working class in Kenya has brought about fundamental change in the political and economic fields. While every progressive social class has been struggling for change, it was the working class that ensured major qualitative changes and influenced other classes in the process.

Kenyan workers began struggling for their economic and political rights as soon as foreign capital came to Kenya for its resources and labour. The first mass campaigns against colonialism were organised by peasants and were nationality-based. Although they scored valuable victories, they were defeated by a better armed colonial force. The lessons of these struggles were not lost on the growing working class who soon took leadership in the anti-colonial movements.

The working class began to set up their own organisations—trade unions—and used the strike weapon to achieve their goals. The first strike was organised in the year 1900. The colonial administration tried to divide the working class by preventing the formation of non-racial trade unions. Early trade unions included the Indian Trade Union (Mombasa and Nairobi, 1914), Workers Federation of British East Africa (for European workers, 1919) and the Indian Employees Association (1919).

The first African workers' movements had to take the form of Associations, for example the Kenya African Civil Servants Association, the Railway African Staff Association, and the various local government staff associations—all formed after the First World War. Workers in Mombasa organised the Trade Union Committee of Mombasa in 1931 at a mass meeting of artisans, masons, and workers, while in Nairobi. The railway artisans formed the Kenya Indian Labour Trade Union in 1934. But by April 1935, it was decided to make the Union non-racial and to change the name to the Labour Trade Union of Kenya. This was a significant development for the working class in Kenya as it brought together workers of all races. It was also to prove an important development for publishing in Kenya.

In the early period of worker organisations, their newspapers and publishing as a whole helped to give publicity to worker meetings and news about strikes. They informed workers throughout the country about worker actions in one town or in one

---

[361] Extract from Durrani, Shiraz (2006): *Never be silent; publishing and imperialism in Kenya, 1884-1963*. London: Vita Books. pp.74-84.

industry. The formation of workers' organisations was an event of great significance. But this could not have been achieved without an effective communications strategy, which ensured that all workers were informed and involved in the work of such an organisation. It was necessary to publicise their activities and to gain more support from other workers. This was initially done by the use of established friendly newspapers. An example of this was the use of newspapers to report the aims of the Trade Union Committee of Mombasa. These reports were carried by *Fairplay*, which was edited by Dr. A.C.L. de Souza. *Fairplay* reported the speech of R. M. Shah, the President of the Trade Union Committee, giving particular emphasis to his reference to "the position of the artisan and labour class in this country and their various grievances arising out of the social injustices being done to them".[362]

> *Fairplay* also carried reports from another meeting, which was attended by about a thousand people. It asked the Government to ensure that "in fixing the common electorate and the qualification of the voters it should include the people of the artisan, labour, workman and mason class".[363]

One of the first acts of the Union was to purchase a typewriter and a rotary cyclostyle machine. Thus began a new phase in Kenyan publishing. Previously, publishing was beyond the reach of most nationals, particularly the working class, as a consequence of the exorbitant charges for printing. The costs were high not only because the machinery had to be imported from Britain, but, the charges were kept high to discourage Kenyan publishing. Most presses were owned by colonial interests, while the few that were controlled by Kenyans, could not meet the needs of all.

Thus the decision of the Union to use cheap cyclostyling was significant as it brought relevant technology within its reach. In addition, the Union developed the use of handbills, which could be produced cheaply and distributed easily without colonial censorship, formal or informal. These handbills contained information of relevance to workers about their rights, and also about union matters and activities. In addition, they carried news items of interest to workers, since not many newspapers catered for the needs of workers. The Union produced its handbills in the main worker languages such as Kiswahili, Gikuyu, Gujarati, Hindi, and Punjabi, as well as English. These handbills then provided relevant content to activists who used the well-established oral channels of communication to pass on the messages to people throughout the country. The easy availability of relevant news, in a form and language that made it easily accessible, played an important part in raising class consciousness of Kenyan workers and helped to strengthen their organisations.

One of the early activities of the Union was to struggle for an eight-hour working day. This was the decision of the Second Annual General Meeting of the Labour Trade Union of Kenya, held from 6-13 September, 1936. Makhan Singh explains some of the ways in which mass publicity was given to this important decision and examines the contents of one of the Kiswahili handbills:

> The decision [to campaign for an eight-hour working day] was further popularised through handbills, meetings in residential areas, work discussion, and public announcements (preceded by ringing of a large bell) in the main thoroughfares of

---

[362] Fairplay February 14, 1931, quoted in Singh, Makhan (1969), pp. 41-42.
[363] Colonial Times April 27, 1935, quoted in Singh, Makhan (1969), p. 42.

Nairobi. After about ten days of this campaign, daily mass meetings began to be held. The campaign created a new spirit among workers.[364]

Such handbills became a regular way for the Union to announce its meetings, to organise workers for strikes, and to educate workers on their rights...For example, the handbill calling workers to a meeting on 29 November, 1936 combined encouragement to workers, and asked them to be steadfast in fulfilling their historic mission with news about a strike in progress:

> **Struggle between capitalists and workers has started in earnest**
> Our worker comrades! Come forward! March ahead! If you do not march ahead today, then remember that you will be crushed under the heels of capitalists tomorrow. Workers should have a united stand and should stand up strongly against the capitalists so that they should not ever have the courage to attempt to exploit workers again, nor to take away workers' rights from them.
>
> - LABOUR TRADE UNION OF KENYA. 29 November, 1936[365]

A strike for an eight-hour day and wage increases finally came to a successful end after 62 days and ended on 3 June, 1937. The Union brought out another handbill informing workers about the success of the strike. All Nairobi employers agreed to an eight-hour day, and gave between 15-22 percent increases in wages and recognised the workers' right to be represented by their Unions. All workers dismissed during the strike were reinstated. The Union announced a demonstration to celebrate the Nairobi workers victory.

The Union was successful in the strike because of good organisation and solidarity, which could only be achieved with a good communication system. The "mainstream" newspapers could not have given the Union total control over its communications during the course of the strike. Using a relatively cheap and simple technology and controlling the distribution network, the Union ensured that its communication lines were not disrupted by employers or by colonial authorities.

Besides producing handbills, the Union also started a monthly newspaper called the *Kenya Worker* with Makhan Singh as the editor. Makhan Singh was the main person behind the consolidation of the trade unions at that time and he brought with him working class experience from India, which he creatively applied to the Kenyan situation. Not only was he a good organiser and trade unionist, he was also an excellent communicator and understood well the needs of ensuring effective communications between trade unions and workers. It was largely his influence that shaped the successful strikes and publishing policies of the trade union movement in Kenya.

The Annual Return made under the Newspaper Registration Ordinance indicated that *East African Kirti* was published weekly and that the average circulation was 1,000 copies per week.

Throughout the colonial history of Kenya, there has been a very close link between trade unionists and those involved in national politics. Many trade union activists saw that the only way to achieve their aims was to be active in direct political activities. In addition, trade union and political activists were involved in the

---

[364] Singh, Makhan (1969), p. 55.
[365] Makhan Singh Archives (translated from Gujarati by the author).

publishing field as well. Earlier, we saw Makhan Singh's involvement in trade union work, which inevitably involved him in publishing. Similarly, Chege Kibachia carried out his trade union and political work through the publishing field as well. In 1947 he was an assistant editor of *Sauti ya Mwafrika*.

Politics of information & knowledge in Africa (2007)[366]

Politics of information & knowledge in Africa; the struggle for an information inclusive society in a globalised world

Abstract

The article looks at contradictions facing libraries in Africa where the information and developmental needs of workers and peasants remain largely unmet, while libraries tend to meet the needs of a minority.

It maintains that the model of public libraries remains the same as the one introduced by the colonial powers and the opportunity at independence for bringing about a change to a people-orientated service was lost. The profession remains aloof from the political and social struggles of communities, thus alienating itself from the very people it seeks to serve. The article sees opportunities now for change in some positive aspects of globalisation and in developments in information and communications technology. The rise of China can create new possibilities for change.

It calls for information professionals to be activists in information as well as in social and political struggles of people. They need to work with communities in partnership with other service providers. It makes the point that the profession is not neutral if it supports the status quo by remaining silent on social and political issues.

The article calls for action to put ideas and a new vision into practice and gives some details about the Progressive African Library and Information Activists' Group (PALIAct) proposal which aims to create an alternative vision, strategy and practice of a people-orientated service in active partnership with communities and service providers.

The article calls upon countries, which benefited from the African slave trade to support initiatives, such as PALIAct, as a small way of acknowledging their debt to Africa. It ends by providing elements for an "African activist information programme", including suggestions for leadership development, collection building and "liberating the mind" collections.

Information in Africa—"Silence in the library"

Perhaps the best way to understand the contradictions facing libraries in Africa today is through a story. It is only when social contradictions are accepted and understood that attempts can be made to resolve them. And resolve them we must, if

---

[366] Mcharazo, Alli and Koopman, Sjoerd (2007): Librarianship as a bridge to an information and knowledge society in Africa. Munchen: K.G. Saur. (IFLA Publications 124).

libraries and information are to play their part in creating a new Africa where there is justice, democracy and development for all. The story is "silence in the library":

> Nyanjiru wakes up at 4 a.m.; a water debe on her head, she walks for an hour and a half to the nearest stream. Then she climbs back from the river to her home, picking dry wood on the way for fire; she arrives home three hours later to start the day's other work: crying children to be calmed with bits of left over food, chicken to be fed and watered; then to start digging her half acre shamba in the hot, burning sun. This is the daily routine for a peasant.
>
> And then there is Kamau. Kamau pats his dogs fondly as they surround his new Volvo. This is his daily ritual. He realises that the gates are not open yet and hoots loudly. Where is Mutua? Does he not know that today is the library board meeting and he has to report early? They are to discuss library regulations. He has prepared a long list of "don'ts". As Mutua opens the gates, Kamau speeds out, the silent sound of the Volvo soothing his mind. He starts thinking about library rules. Yes, users must be controlled. Only last week he found a fellow eating mandazi in the library. How can that be allowed? Kamau had him thrown out. The first rule is going to be about eating in the library. And then of course "Silence: silence in the library".
>
> Kamau feels happy as he enters the library parking. "Silence Please, Silence in the Library"; "No eating in the library" ... In such an atmosphere of threats; works the modern librarian. Inside the stone walls of the library, in total peace and calm among the well preserved volumes, he is oblivious to the ruin and chaos of hunger, starvation and mass exploitation outside.
>
> The contrasting lives of Nyanjiru and Kamau can be found anywhere in Africa. Their activities are taking place within miles of each other and on the same day. Yet the two are so removed from each other that they may easily be on different planets or in different historical ages.
>
> The library is a concrete structure inaccessible to Nyanjiru, and Nyanjiru as a library user is unacceptable to the librarians. For Nyanjiru there is no time to waste, no compromises to be made. All her labour and thoughts are to satisfy her family's basic needs: food, clothing and shelter. Anything that helps her in this work, she accepts with open arms and mind. Anything that prevents her from acquiring what she needs, she will fight. Her information needs are clear—she wants information, which will help her to support and protect her family.
>
> On the other hand is the library service—set up during colonial days, with a colonial vision, through 'assistance' from a colonial, neo-colonial 'mother' country. A mother whose very touch brings death. "Silence please; please, silence in the library".
>
> Silence, in spite of Nyanjiru's dying children; silence, in spite of Nyanjiru's twenty hour working day; silence, even though Nyanjiru's hard labour fails to fill her family's stomachs.
>
> Nyanjiru knows no library. No library wants to know Nyanjiru.

The story of Nyanjiru and Kamau highlights the key need in Africa today: development—development of people, resources, industries, agriculture, art, culture... But "development" does not take place in a vacuum. In order to develop, people and societies need relevant information and knowledge in a number of fields such as science, history, geography, history and technology. Yet, under capitalism, information and knowledge and the very process of learning and education have become commodities to be bought and sold on the "open" market. Those without resources to purchase information end up having no access to it. The irony is that even those who produce information often have no access to that information which is taken from them, copyrighted, patented, repackaged, and sold at prices, which the original producers cannot afford.

Thus peoples, countries and societies have been forced into "un-development" and inequality by the economic policies and practices of international finance and transnational corporations using the mechanisms of international financial and political control, such as the IMF, WTO and the UN.

But are these issues that should concern the library profession? Some say it is not our "business" to get involved in "politics" as we are professional people, not politicians. But if we accept that Africa needs a second war of liberation — economic liberation this time — then we need to accept that no liberation can be successful without appropriate information vision, strategy and tactics, as well as trained information activists. This is the lesson from the major revolutions in the world. This is also the lesson from Africa's long history of wars against colonialism and imperialism. And this is where we find a relevant social role for African librarians and information professionals and activists today.

The first requirement for liberation from an inequality imposed on Africa is access to information about the real reasons for poverty. Yet the information and communication systems created by the departing colonial powers were not expected or equipped to put this information before people. They were merely tools for a small, rich elite to impose its world outlook and culture on the poor and exploited majority of people. Post-independence systems and policies have made no fundamental change in this colonial-inspired information framework. We urgently need to seek a role for the information profession that is relevant to the needs of Africa in the 21st century.

An important task for Africa is to document fully the achievements, successes and failures of the anti-colonial struggles in Africa. Information about these can arm us for current and future struggles. This has not been fully documented. But if the history of the African struggle for political and economic liberation is poorly documented, the struggle for African information liberation is even less well documented and understood. It is not a matter of general knowledge, for example, that during the Mau Mau war of liberation in Kenya, the combatants controlled over 50 newspapers and many printing presses; they set up libraries in liberated territories, in forests, in cities, ran an efficient information collection system, and created their own distribution network using "traditional" and modern methods available to them. This complex communications system was created and managed by activist librarians and information workers who were active not only in the information field, but in the larger political and social fields as well. Their experience, if fully documented, can help us find a relevant role for the information professional in Africa today.

And yet today, we tend to follow blindly the "Western" model of public library services, which actively seeks to remove politics from information theories and practices. This model has not been successful in the "West" itself to provide information to all, particularly to those politely referred to as "socially excluded". Yet we in Africa have not fully challenged this situation. It is only by subjecting our current policies and practices to a vigorous challenge that new and relevant theories, policies and practices can emerge.

Opportunities for information liberation

Just as in the political field, so in the information field, there are major developments when social contradictions are at their sharpest. It is at such key points in history that opportunities arise for making revolutionary changes in the way information and politics are organised. Colonial Africa has had a number of opportunities to change its societies for the better and serve the needs of the majority of people. One such opportunity was in late 1950s and early 60s, which saw achievement of political independence in many countries. It was a time when foundations of the old colonial world were being destroyed and those of new free societies were being laid. Many activists had the vision of a society where all would have free access to information and knowledge created by the work of all. It was a time of immense change and high hopes for a just, equitable future after decades of colonial oppression and exploitation. This was the time when people did influence events in a major way, underscoring what was said at the World Summit for Information Society: it is "people who primarily form and shape societies, and information and communication societies are no exception".[367]

But the opportunity at independence to challenge the very basis of social organisations such as libraries was lost. Library services continued to function on the same basis as under colonialism, targeting their services to the elite, although now this included some more people and became "multiracial". Class divisions, which formed the real divisions in the society, were deliberately played down, and racial, "tribal" and other "divisions" were brought into prominence. An information service operating in the real interest of people would have ensured that this "information blind-spot" was removed and the question of who the library actually serves would have been resolved in favour of the majority of working people. Thus an information service using resources from all, but serving a few, was developed. This situation has more or less continued until today.

Today, however, there is another possibility for change. Changes at a global level in the last 25 years now present Africa with another opportunity to make a fundamental shift in the way societies are organised—and in the way information services are organised. If managed correctly, we can make the transition to a people-orientated library service that did not take place at independence. Let us look at two major changes: globalisation and the rise of China.

Globalisation

An intensified corporate globalisation is the current phase of capitalism and imperialism. This has been made possible by rapid changes in information technologies. The collapse of the U.S.S.R. has left only one imperialist world power (U.S.A.) with global imperialist ambitions and resources to impose its will on the world. This has major political, as well as economic, implications for countries around the world, as evidenced by the invasion of Iraq by the U.S.A. in pursuit of oil and strategic advantage for profit-driven transnationals.

By its very definition, capitalism divides people along class lines. Working class people as a whole are historically excluded from enjoying wealth created by their labour. Hence capitalism creates a class that is automatically excluded from wealth,

---

[367] World Summit on Information Society, Civil Society (2003): "Shaping Information Societies for Human Needs; Civil Society Declaration to the World Summit on the Information Society". World Summit on the Information Society (WSIS) Plenary. Geneva, 8 December. [Accessed 21 December, 2005 at http://wsis.ecommons.ca/book/print/218].

power, education and information. There has been a qualitative change in the process of social exclusion in the last quarter of this century on a global level. Castells explains these changes as a:

> technological revolution, centred around information (which) has transformed the way we think, we produce, we consume, we trade, we manage, we communicate, we live, we die, we make war, and we make love: a dynamic global economy has been constituted around the planet, linking up valuable people and activities from all over the world, while switching off from the networks of the power and wealth, people and territories dubbed as irrelevant from the perspectives of dominant interests.[368]

While this aggressive phase of capitalism resulted in increasing economic growth in some countries and regions, its own logic ensures that millions of people and large parts of the world remain excluded from growth. Many areas have thus experienced a decline in national product as capital moves out of less profitable countries and regions. The social and economic consequences of this global search for profit inevitably leads to marginalising and excluding millions of people around the world. Africa is a prime example of such exclusion.

Castells explains the essence of corporate globalisation:

> ...this is a brand of capitalism that is at the same time very old and fundamentally new. It is old because it appeals to relentless competition in the pursuit of profit, and because individual satisfaction (deferred or immediate) is its driving engine. But it is fundamentally new because it is tooled by new information and communication technologies that are at the root of new productivity sources, new organizational forms, and the construction of a global economy.[369]

Thus, while developments in technologies and science make it possible for rapid changes to be made, Africa lags behind. Yet possibilities exist in the world today, and within Africa, to bring about major changes in the way our societies—and information services—are organised. Possibilities exist in Africa today to put information at the service of people so that they help them meet their real needs, and not for an (mostly foreign) elite to enrich itself on African labour and resources.

There are other aspects of globalisation and development of information technologies, which affect the development of Africa.

Information society and knowledge economy in Africa

The term "Information Society" can be used to describe a society in which the "creation, distribution, and manipulation of information has become the most significant economic and cultural activity":

> An Information Society may be contrasted with societies in which the economic underpinning is primarily industrial or agricultural. The tools of the Information Society are computers and telecommunications. Progress in information technologies and communication is changing the way people lead their lives, how they work and

---

[368] Castells, Manuel (1998): The power of identity. Oxford, Blackwell.
[369] Castells, Manuel (1999): Information Technology, Globalization and Social Development. UNRISD Discussion Paper No. 114, September 1999. The United Nations Research Institute for Social Development (UNRISD). Available at:
http://www.unrisd.org/80256B3C005BCCF9/(httpPublications)/F270E0C066F3DE7780256 B67005B728C?OpenDocument&panel=seriespapers. [Accessed: 26 October, 2005].

do business, how they educate their children, study, carry out research, train themselves and how they are entertained.[370]

Africa needs to make the shift from reliance on agricultural and industrial activities to a society based on knowledge. The term "Knowledge Economy" refers to using the generation and exploitation of knowledge as a predominant player in the creation of wealth. KoïchiroMatsuura gives a background of the emergence of the knowledge economy and looks at the process of turning information into knowledge:

> The scientific upheavals of the 20th century have brought about a third industrial revolution. This revolution, which has been accompanied by Globalization, has laid down the bases of a knowledge economy. Yet information is not knowledge; and the world information society will only fulfil its potential if it facilitates the emergence of pluralistic knowledge societies that include rather than exclude.
>
> There is a clear awareness today that the development of societies predicated on the sharing of knowledge is the best way of waging effective war on poverty and forestalling major health risks such as pandemics, of reducing the terrible loss of life caused by tsunamis and tropical storms, and of promoting sustainable human development. For new modes of development are today within our grasp: these are no longer based, as in the past, on "blood, sweat and tears", but rather on intelligence, the scientific and technological capacity to address problems, intellectual added value, and the expansion of services in all sectors of the economy.[371]

These "new modes of development" appear to be far away from African shores. Yet it is possible to turn the new potential into reality by using existing visions and commitments as well experiences from other countries. The Vision of the Information Society, as summed up in World Summit on Information Society is the one that best serves African interests:

> We... declare our common desire and commitment to build a people-centred, inclusive and development-oriented Information Society, where everyone can create, access, utilize and share information and knowledge, enabling individuals, communities and peoples to achieve their full potential in promoting their sustainable development and improving their quality of life, premised on the purposes and principles of the Charter of the United Nations and respecting fully and upholding the Universal Declaration of Human Rights.
>
> We are aware that ICTs should be regarded as tools and not as an end in themselves. Under favourable conditions, these technologies can be a powerful instrument, increasing productivity, generating economic growth, job creation and employability and improving the quality of life of all. They can also promote dialogue among people, nations and civilizations.
>
> We are also fully aware that the benefits of the information technology revolution are today unevenly distributed between the developed and developing countries and

---

[370] The Net Result: Social Inclusion in the Information Society. Report of the National Working Party on Social Inclusion in the Information Society (1997). London: Community Programmes Manager, Corporate Affairs, IBM United Kingdom Limited. Available at: http://www.eric.ed.gov/ERICWebPortal/custom/portlets/recordDetails/detailmini.jsp?_nfpb=true&_&ERICExtSearch_SearchValue_0=ED433009&ERICExtSearch_SearchType_0=eric_accno&accno=ED433009. [Accessed: 09 September 2007].

[371] Matsuura, Koïchiro (2005): "Towards knowledge societies". Available at: http://www.kantipuronline.com/kolnews.php?&nid=56661. [Accessed: 13 November, 2005].

within societies. We are fully committed to turning this digital divide into a digital opportunity for all, particularly for those who risk being left behind and being further marginalized.[372]

The above declaration surely provides a powerful weapon at an ideological level. Other developments at a political level can also support Africa's demand for an equal share in the new information and knowledge world. The political, economic and ethical developments in the "non-Western" world provide a more relevant experience and example for Africa. On the one hand is the rapid rise of the BRIC countries (Brazil, Russia, India and China). On the other hand is the experience from the principled stand taken in Cuba, Venezuela and Bolivia, which provides a real chance for improvement in the lives of working people. Both these are relevant models that Africa can use for real development. Changes in the information level cannot take place in a vacuum. It is changes at the economic and political level in these examples that provides the possibilities for change in the information field.

The rise of China

The rise of China as a major international economic and political power is rapidly changing our world today. Already it has become the sixth largest economy in the world and is likely soon to become the fourth. It has enormous potential for the future. The significance of the rise of China is not only at the economic and political level; it has the potential for developing an entirely different moral framework for development, international relations and world outlook. Unlike previous superpowers which resorted to the occupation of land and subjugating people in order to satisfy their need for resources, China sets about developing mutually beneficial relations with countries such as Brazil, India and other "developing" countries so that there is mutual benefit. It seeks no colonies nor to enslave or colonise people. As Martin Jacques explains:

> The past two or three years have marked a new moment in the global perception of China. There is suddenly a new awareness that encompasses both a recognition of China's economic transformation and an understanding that, because of its huge size and cohesive character, it will have a profound impact on the rest of the world, albeit in ways still only dimly understood ... China has arrived and will increasingly shape our future, not just its own.[373]

Africa has much to gain from developing relations with China in a way, which benefits people of both continents. It will set a new standard of moral, economic and political relations between peoples and countries.

The rise of the BRIC countries (Brazil, Russia, India and China) as a whole, provide a totally new global scene, which can have tremendous impact on Africa. At an economic level, it challenges the monopoly of Western transnational companies to decide the terms of trade, which have historically worked against Africa. Thus the objective condition for positive change has been set. It remains for Africa to take advantage of this positive development. But we do not have to look far for examples of how these global changes can be used in the interest of their people—there is an alternative way which increases social spending and turns away from free-market

---

[372] World Summit on Information Society, Civil Society (2003): op. cit.
[373] Jacques, Martin (2005): "China is well on its way to being the other superpower". The Guardian, December 8. Available at:
http://www.guardian.co.uk/china/story/0,,1661736,00.html. [Accessed: 02 January 2006].

policies which have been imposed on Africa, causing increased poverty and stifling development.

There is an alternative

This alternative way of developing societies has been shown to work in Cuba, which, in spite of a U.S.A.-instigated blockade of over 40 years, is developing today at a highly enviable rate. Its GDP growth in 2005 was 11.8 percent—among the highest in the world.[374] As an example in just one field, Cuba has become a major bio-medical power. Gary Marx sums up Cuba's achievements:

> Cuban scientists have produced a hepatitis B vaccine sold in more than 30 countries and streptokinase, a potent enzyme that dissolves blood clots and improves the survival rate of heart attack victims. The country also makes recombinant interferon that strengthens the immune system of cancer patients and a meningitis B vaccine.
>
> In the pipeline are products ranging from an injection that closes ulcers and improves circulation in diabetics to vaccines against cholera and hepatitis C, according to Cuban officials.[375]

Similar changes are taking place in Venezuela which is also following an alternative economic and political path to development of its people, using oil revenues to set up Universities, literacy and health care programmes for working people, and other social projects. Similarly, in Bolivia, major changes are expected once the new President Evo Morales takes office in January 2006. What is perhaps more significant is that not only are these three countries taking the alternative path, but they are also developing an alternative support and cooperation structure among themselves and with other progressive countries. As Derrick O'Keefe says, "there is an alternative". He sums up the new situation:

> Today, global capitalism is being challenged most directly in Venezuela. Hugo Chavez's own discourse has sharpened dramatically against international capital in recent months and years. The Bolivarian leader has made repeated calls for the building of 'socialism for the 21st century'.
>
> The Bolivarian Revolution is carrying out a transformation of both the reality of Venezuela and of the global alignment of political forces. The gains of *el proceso* are preciously concrete, as seen in rising rates of literacy and education, mass expansion of health care services, land reform, new housing for the poor, and an explosion in cooperative worker co-managed enterprises. These reforms are part of a revolutionary process with a continental and global dynamic.[376]

Such positive news about development can provide important examples to people of Africa, but our information services rarely provide such information to

---

[374] Jacques, Martin (2005): "China is well on its way to being the other superpower". The Guardian, December 8. Available at:
http://www.guardian.co.uk/china/story/0,,1661736,00.html. [Accessed: 02 January 2006].
[375] Marx, Gary (2006): "Cuba cits [sic] 'world class' trail in biotech research". The Chicago Tribune. Available at thesouthern.com.
www.thesouthern.com/articles/2006/01/01/business/doc43b6e887be9f4564996873.txt. [Accessed: 02 January, 2006].
[376] O'Keefe, Derrick (2005): "There is an alternative: Bolivia, Venezuela, and the struggle against neo-liberalism". December 27, 2005. Available at Seven Oaks
http://sevenoaksmag.com/commentary/91_comm3.html. [Accessed: 29 December, 2005].

working people who need it the most. Such examples of development activities are highly relevant to Africa and perhaps the model of the "Community of South American Nations" may be a good one for Africa to follow.

A key requirement for the development of Africa is a redrawing of the "information map" to reassess our information work. We need to assess the relevance of the sources of information we provide to the people and to review whose point of view such information reflects. We need to look afresh at the form and content of information in our libraries and look at what languages they cover. We need to see if the information is targeted correctly and review how outcomes are monitored. Our information needs to reflect Africa in a new perspective and reinterpret its history from the point of view of African working people. The world-view that people are daily presented by the Western media needs to be challenged for African people to see themselves as equal partners in a global context. An alternative vision and view of the world needs to be made available to *every* African. No people can develop under a situation of daily images of their own powerlessness and inadequacy, where facts about their exploitation are hidden and their suffering is shown as resulting from their own fault. In order to build our self-confidence we need to see the world from our own perspective in which the "other" is just that—the other.

Technological developments mentioned earlier already provide a basis for making this alternative position for Africa a reality. An example, of this new way of thinking and doing, is provided by the pioneering Pambazuka *News, Weekly Forum for Social Justice for Africa.*[377] This is "a tool for progressive social change in Africa" and is produced by Fahamu,[378] "an organisation that uses information and communication technologies to serve the needs of organisations and social movements that aspire to progressive social change".

It is in initiatives such as this that African librarians need to get involved. We need to form new alliances with global movements such as the World Social Forum. Another area in which librarians need to be active is initiatives such as the pan-Latin American TV channel, Telesur, which, as Iain Bruce reports, aims to "counter cultural imperialism, which the Channel's president, Andres Izaara said had gone unchallenged in the region for 50 years".[379]

But a key requirement for ensuring a meaningful information change is to re-assess the social role of librarians and information workers. Too often we are satisfied with a very limited social role and have shied away from any active involvement in the political reality around us. But our so-called "neutrality" is not real neutral; it is, in effect, siding with the status quo, which we reinforce if we do not challenge inequality and injustice.

Social and political role of librarians

"The people's hour has arrived", said Bolivian President-elect Evo Morales while reiterating promises to recover Bolivia's natural resources, including natural gas, for all Bolivians.[380] Such a programme for Africa is well overdue and needs active

---

[377] Pambazuka News is available at: http://www.pambazuka.org/en/. "Pambazuka" means "arise" or "awaken" in Kiswahili).
[378] Details about Fahamu are available at: http://www.fahamu.org/.
[379] Bruce, Iain (2005): "First broadcast for Latin channel". BBC News. 24 July. Available at: http://news.bbc.co.uk/1/hi/world/americas/4713361.stm. [Accessed: 04 January, 2005].
[380] Bolivia's Morales, Chavez Pledge to Strengthen Ties (2005, update2). Available at: Bloomberg.com.

participation of information and community activists. Again, we need to work closely with progressive Pan African movements and activists, as the problems facing Africa can best be resolved on a continental-basis, and in partnership with others whose aims match ours.

Henry Blake examined the role of librarians in very clear terms:

> There are those who, clinging to the idea that the library profession should be politically neutral, would contend that contributing to social projects is not an appropriate activity for librarians. However, without a clear and vital set of philosophical and political ideals acting as a guiding beacon, the library profession will not remain neutral, but will drift aimlessly with the currents of power and privilege.
>
> Librarians must forcefully articulate their commitment to serving the information needs of all segments of society. They must rededicate themselves to assuring the widest and most equitable access to information by opposing fees for services and the commercialization of knowledge. Furthermore, librarians must be willing to enter the political arena and advocate for these principles.[381]

This call for involvement in the political arena is even more urgent in Africa today in view of the changes taking place in the context of corporate globalisation and marketisatiion of services.

The rest of this paper looks at one attempt in the African information field to make a positive change in the way information services are managed and delivered.

Progressive African Library and Information Activists' Group (PALIAct)

It is perhaps time for information professionals to move away from lamenting the situation to turning their ideas into action. The Progressive African Library and Information Activists' Group (PALIAct) initiative is one such attempt. It was set up as a way of taking on board some of the issues raised above. It is being supported by the Department of Applied Social Sciences of the London Metropolitan University. It also has the potential to bring together the African Diaspora with progressive people in the "West" to create a powerful partnership with the information professionals in Africa to develop innovative information services, which can help develop people and communities.

PALIAct seeks to develop people-oriented information services decided upon by workers, peasants, pastoralists, fisher people and other marginalised individuals and groups whose needs have not been met. It involves working in partnership with other professionals and service providers. PALIAct operates on principles of equality, democracy and social justice and encourages a Pan African world outlook among information and community activists.

PALIACT recognises the right to relevant information as a basic human right.

The struggle for a relevant information service is intimately linked with the political struggles of the people to meet their material, social, cultural and political needs. PALIAct believes that the opportunity for creating a people-orientated information

---

http://www.bloomberg.com/apps/news?pid=10000086&sid=amUh3706gyHU&refer=latin_america. [Accessed: 04 January, 2005].

[381] Blake, Henry (1989): Librarianship and political values: neutrality or commitment. Library Journal, pp. 39-42.

service at the time of political independence was lost. Instead of challenging the very basis on which library and information services were built, we allowed ourselves to be manipulated into making merely quantitative changes in library services, but failed to make any qualitative changes. The *classes* who were served by the colonial library service continued to be served, and the needs of the working people who had always remained outside the remit of such services remained unmet. Their experiences, their cultures, their very language remained outside the walls of impressive library buildings. Thus the advantage gained in the early period of struggle for a society and an information system, which served the needs of *all* its people was lost. The struggle for such an information service continues to date.

The PALIAct programme is therefore an activist agenda to ensure that the information rights of African people are recognised in theory as well as in practice. PALIAct will set up pilot projects in a number of countries to develop ideas and practices to develop people-orientated information services.

PALIAct aims to relate directly to meeting the Millennium goals for development. One of the challenges identified at the World Summit on the Information Society is to "harness the potential of information and communication technology to promote the development goals of the Millennium Declaration".[382] PALIAct provides one very practical answer to this challenge.

PALIAct principles[383]

In its commitment to developing a people-orientated information service, PALIAct is committed to:

- The principles of social justice, equality, equity, human welfare, and the development of cultural and social democracy; thus we shall actively address historical inequalities in the information field in Africa;
- Achieving equality of access to and inclusiveness of information services, especially extending such services to the workers, peasants and the poor, the marginalized and those who have been discriminated against;
- The provision of a relevant service to those active in the struggles for social justice and who are working towards the creation of a liberated Africa;
- Supporting the collection, organization, preservation and dissemination of the documents of people's struggles in all forms and languages;
- Making available alternative materials representing a wide range of progressive viewpoints from within Africa and overseas, which are often excluded by traditional libraries, mass media and educational and information systems;
- Encouraging the exploration of alternative models of services; promoting and disseminating critical analysis of information technology's impact on libraries and societies; and to support the fundamental democratization of existing institutions of education, culture, communications;

---

[382] World Summit on Information Society (2003): Declaration of principles; building the Information Society, a global challenge in the new Millennium. Document WSIS-03/GENEVA/DOC/4-E. Available at:
http://www.itu.int/wsis/docs/geneva/official/dop.html. [Accessed: 17 November 2005].
[383] Based on the Ten program developed by Mark Rosenzweig for the groups which met at the Vienna Conference of progressive librarians sponsored by KRIBIBIE in 2000. Copyright Progressive Librarians Guild, 2000. http://www.libr.org/PLG/ .

- Undertaking joint, interdisciplinary research into fundamental library issues (e.g. into the political economy of information in the age of neo-liberalism and corporate globalization) in order to lay the basis for effective action in our spheres of work;
- Investigating and organizing efforts to make the library-as-workplace more democratic and encourage resistance to the managerialism of the present library culture;
- Promoting international solidarity among librarians and cooperation between libraries across borders on the basis of our commitment to the Universal Declaration of Human Rights and related covenants which create a democratic framework for constructive cooperative endeavours;
- Organizing in partnership with other activists in the cultural and educational fields, to help put issues of social responsibility on the agendas of international bodies such as IFLA and UNESCO;
- Opposing corporate globalization which, despite its claims, reinforces existing social, economic, cultural inequalities, and working towards the creation of a democratic globalism and internationalism which respects and cultivates cultural plurality, which recognizes the sovereignty of peoples, which acknowledges the obligations of society to the individual and communities, and which prioritizes human values and needs over profits.

PALIAct is discussing the possibilities of setting up pilot country centres in a number of countries. The experience gained in these pilots will help to develop further centres in other countries or regions of Africa. Such pilots require a committed group of local information professionals willing and able to work with local communities. Discussions are taking place for setting up the first pilots in Ghana and Kenya.

The Kenya chapter of PALIAct has now been registered and has already started making a mark on the information scene in Kenya. Further details about PALIAct and the work of the Kenya chapter are available in PALIAct's newsletter, *Information Equality, Africa*.[384]

The success of the PALIAct initiative will, in the end, be decided upon by how actively the information professionals in Africa support it. The ideas are ready to be implemented, but whether they will be taken up remains to be seen. They offer a possibility of reconciling the lives of Nyanjiru and Kamau in the story we heard earlier. I hope there will no longer be silence in the library.

An African activist information programme

It is not within the scope of this presentation to discuss in detail what an activist information programme for Africa would or should look like. Such a programme will emerge when local information activists engage in the struggles of the people for their material and cultural rights. However, some possible direction for such a programme can be mentioned here:

---

[384] Details about PALIAct are available at http://www.seapn.org.uk/PALIAct-new.html. Information Equality, Africa, PALIAct's newsletter (formerly entitled PALIAct Ideas & Action) is also available there.

Leadership development

No country, organisation or profession can expect to achieve its vision without developing its members in areas such as appropriate ideological awareness and orientation, an understanding of historical and current contradictions facing the country or organisation, a clarity about who and what their allies are in terms of achieving their goals, an understanding of organisational change brought about by innovation and creativity. The development of leadership requires that these theories are then, reinforced by opportunities for practical work as a way of gaining experience which can give increased confidence to individuals as well as to organisations. It is only through such life-long learning programmes that there can be any hope of ensuring the sustainability required for long-term development.

These points were well understood in Kenya in the early 1960s when Pio Gama Pinto, Bildad Kaggia, Oginga Odinga and others set up the Lumumba Institute for developing political cadres. Those who killed the Institute (and Pinto) did a great disservice to the cause of African liberation. Today we can learn from this history and develop a thousand Lumumba Institutes as a way of developing our people to lead the war for African's second liberation, which starts with liberating our minds.

The need for effective leadership in the profession is now well recognised. What the African information sector needs are leaders who are not only good managers but provide a new vision, develop staff, create a new culture and appropriate organisational structures and remove habits that deaden, as Beckett's character Didi says in *Waiting for Godot*.[385] We need to pay attention to the warning sounded by Mao and stop working "half-heartedly without a definite plan or direction... work perfunctorily and muddle along". He goes on to warn of the danger of unthinking work: "So long as one remains a monk, one goes on tolling the bell".[386] We need to ensure that teaching institutes are delivering a learning programme to actively nurture and develop leadership, including all the attributes mentioned by various authors below:

- A leader needs to provide direction; it's the vision thing. To get a collective definition of success, leaders must engage, motivate and animate people in their organisations. It isn't enough just to have the vision; they really have to engage with their people.[387]
- Leadership is a balancing act. It requires communicating a compelling vision, convincing others to buy into that vision, and marshalling resources and talent to make it happen.[388]

---

[385] In Samuel Beckett's Waiting for Godot, Didi, one of the two tramps, says to Gogo, the other tramp: "Habit is a great deadener".
[386] Mao Tse Tung: Correcting mistaken ideas. Available at: http://www.marxists.org/reference/archive/mao/works/red-book/ch24.htm. [Accessed 05 September, 2006].
[387] Bennis, Warren: Leading from the Top—An interview with Warren Bennis. EFMD. Available from:
<http://www.efmd.org/html/Knowledge/cont_detail.asp?id=050209igbk&aid=050510mkfp&tid=1. Accessed 18 October, 2005.
[388] Becoming an effective leader; the results-driven manager series (publicity). Harvard Business online. Available from <Harvard_Business_Online@hbsp.ed10.net> Accessed 31 August, 2005.

- Your ability to lead is only as good as your ability to motivate. [389]
- You earn leadership from those that you lead. You earn leadership from earning the respect of the people.[390]

A number of programmes being delivered or developed at the London Metropolitan University's Department of Applied Social Sciences are suitable for such a leadership programme. All of these are capable of being delivered in partnership with African Universities if there is interest. These include:

- the Quality Leaders Project (QLP), "management development through service development", with its "combating racism, managing equality", and other project management modules
- various information management modules and short courses, including "leadership for innovation, equality and change", "society, information and policy", and "information and social exclusion". The new module "information for development" would be of particular relevance in Africa.

Collection building

An important area that needs to be addressed urgently is the collection policy and practice of African libraries. Again, this is not the forum to go into this in detail, but the following needs to be addressed:

- Material from the African liberation struggle. The enormous amount of oral and written material generated during the long history of the African struggle against colonialism needs to be collected, documented and made available. Developments in information and communications technologies make this task easier than it was some years back. Part of this process is the need to get back from colonial countries, the vast amount of African documents, material culture, and archives stored in London, Paris and other colonial capitals.
- Documents of the Pan African movement need to be included in the above, as do material on slavery whose effects Africa has not recovered from even today.
- Documentation on the policies and activities of organisations and leaders active in the anti-colonial, anti-imperialist movements (before and after independence) need to be made available through every public and University library in Africa. These should include organisations and leaders in every African country. For example, films on Lumumba and other anti-imperialist activists need to be collected or commissioned.
- African libraries seem to be flooded by material from a Western, imperialist point of view. There is a need to actively collect material from an alternative, people's point of view. This should include material on the World Social Forum (WSF) as well as on the people's anti-globalisation movements. The

---

[389] The right kind of leadership: how to motivate people to achieve their full potential (publicity). Harvard Business online. Available from:
<Harvard_Business_Online@hbsp.ed10.net> Accessed 31 August, 2005.
[390] Mintzberg, Henry: Engaging Leadership; An interview with corporate strategist Henry Mintzberg. European Foundation for Management Development. Available from: http://www.efmd.org/html/Knowledge/cont_detail.asp?TID=1&AID=050209czte&ID=050209igbk>. Accessed 18 October, 2005.

WSF has already included library events as part of its programme for its meetings in Bamako in 2006 and in Nairobi in 2007. Two representatives of the PALIAct Kenya Centre have been sponsored by the Finnish Foreign Ministry to attend the Bamako event. It is important for African library professionals to be actively involved in this important initiative. A large number of East, Central, and Southern African librarians need to attend the Nairobi meeting in January 2007.

- Material from a Pan-African and internationalist perspective. African libraries need to collect material from other African countries, organise a translation service to make material available to all, and promote major regional African languages throughout the continent (e.g. Kiswahili, Arabic, and Yoruba).
- Collections on social and economic development. Experiences on development in other parts of the world needs to be made available to African planners, teachers, lecturers, extension workers and others as a way of disseminating it to people. Thus experiences from China, Cuba, Venezuela and India should be actively collected.

The "liberating the mind" /"kuvunja minyororo"[391] collections

As a practical way of putting some of these ideas into action, I would like to suggest that a new information partnership be set up in interested countries, under the name "Liberating the mind" /"kuvunja minyororo" partnership.

Key partners would include the local PALIAct country centre, a local University and the public library service. Other organisations such as museums, archives, and relevant government ministries would also be able to join the partnership. International organizations, such as the International Federation of Library Associations (IFLA), the African Union, UNESCO, etc., could be invited as partners. The national partnerships would have representation in a continent-wide partnership.

The "liberating the mind" service would collect and disseminate the material mentioned above. It should include an "audience development"[392] approach taken by the Quality Leaders project and develop activities in areas such as film, radio, music, drama, all of which can be developed in partnership with other professionals. As a start, each country should have at least one library designated as a "liberating the mind" centre. A start can be made, for example, by making available material recommended by the World Social Forum as relevant for Africa. It would be in a language appropriate to the country and be in paper, as well as electronic format.

This Conference can set up a working party to take these ideas forward, if there is sufficient interest. This proposed partnership can set the African librarian free from the colonial/imperialism shackle and can finally re-emerge with a new, socially responsible role. The future is ours to make.

---

[391] "Kuvunja minyororo" – Kiswahili for "to break the chains".
[392] The QLP approach identifies two aspects under the term "audience development": The first aspect is to increase the reach of libraries and youth services to meet the needs of all young people, particularly refugees and asylum seekers and those who have not been reached before. The second aspect expands on what has come to be known as "reader development".

A new beginning?

The year 2007 marks the bicentenary of the British Parliamentary abolition of the slave trade in the former British Empire. We hope to formally launch PALIAct at the IFLA Conference in South Africa in 2007. At the same time, it would be appropriate for the library profession in Africa to make it a year of change to rededicate and reorient information services to meet the needs of the majority of its people. It would be appropriate for countries, which have benefited from African slave trade, to support initiatives such as PALIAct as a small way of acknowledging their debt to Africa.

But the prospects for a real new beginning for information services in Africa depend on whether African information professionals, activists and workers take up the challenge of development as part of their profession and work in active partnership with the people they are supposed to serve. There is much interest among a younger generation of information professionals and activists to change the information scene. But they operate in an inappropriate environment that kills all initiatives and creativity, offering no chance for advancement to those proposing ideas and visions not liked by the "information establishment". What is required to ensure a meaningful change, is a real desire for democracy in the workplace as well in the society as a whole, an environment that encourages risk taking and innovation, and a willingness to challenge status quo in the interest of developing services for people.

Perhaps the greatest challenge for information professionals is to develop a new model of an "activist" librarian. Information in Africa needs to be seen in its true political perspective and information professionals need to address their information role within the political context. Denying that information work has any connection with politics means denying development to people. As Durrani and Smallwood say:

> it is important that those with conviction and commitment stand up for a new role of libraries in society – and actively practice this new role. In the world ruled by corporate globalisation, it is too easy to drift along with the tide of "neutral" librarianship and do nothing to make libraries play a central role in liberating people, their cultures, and their economies from the privatised future that globalisation has planned for them.[393]

A new beginning for African librarians is possible only if the profession can take up this challenge.

In every home, there will be a library that was once the privilege of the rich. These books will be at the disposition of the poorest classes who, before, had no books or libraries, because we are now going to struggle for the culture of the people.
- Fidel Castro (2000)

---

[393] Durrani, Shiraz and Smallwood, Elizabeth (2006): The professional is political: redefining the social role of public libraries. Progressive Librarian. No. 27 (pp. 3-22) Summer.

Taking a Stand

Setting the scene [4]: Need for active involvement

A common thread running through the articles reproduced in this book is the need to understand the social and political context of the public library services. Libraries reflect the social, political and cultural reality of their societies and it is this reality that needs to be understood before one can analyse that society or its libraries. However, understanding libraries and their social background is only one aspect that these articles deal with. The other is the need for an active involvement in bringing about change not only in the library field but also in addressing the social conditions, which prevent the development of relevant libraries. It is in this context that these articles differ from the "mainstream" approach to librarianship.

Two related themes here are information and political activism on the one hand, and the development of staff and relevant services on the other. Another important aspect relates to a key role of the information profession: documentation of information, learning and knowledge. The acquisition, documentation and dissemination of information are essential requirements if that information is to lead to the development of knowledge. It is also essential for social development, particularly in the context of alternative information and experiences, which the transnational-controlled mass media do not collect, document or disseminate. An event or an experience that is not recorded is an event and an experience which soon dies and does not help to enrich human experience for social or economic development.

Similarly, people's heroes and activists cannot exist for a younger generation if their lives and experiences are not documented. This aspect of information documentation provides an important social role for the information profession. In this context, the action of East African librarians to document the World Social Forum in Nairobi in 2007 indicates the willingness of librarians to accept their social responsibility role. The Progressive Librarians Guild in the U.S.A. is now set to continue the process at the U.S. Social Forum.

Alternative information and political views do not often get an opportunity to be heard and are often not seen as significant in the academic, professional or political fields. Even when reported or documented, they are seen as isolated perspectives, and their overall framework is not recognised.

It is within this framework that this section, "Taking a stand" addresses the lack of material by providing some thoughts and ideas on alternative approaches to information work. The first part explains some aspects of what the alternative approach means in specific situations. The second part, "information activism" records some aspects of taking action to address information inequality.

As mentioned earlier, an important aspect of information activism is to develop the thinking of information workers and professionals in order to expand their horizons and widen their perspectives. It is the responsibility of our schools of information studies in Universities to develop this wider awareness among librarians. Unless students of librarianship are equipped with an all-around education, which should include an awareness of alternative approaches, we are in danger of allowing the status quo to continue. The section "Study and Teaching", records some changes brought about in the curricula and in teaching practices at the London Metropolitan University.

The final section, "Ideas into action", takes up the challenges of implementing various ideas on alternative methods. It is not enough just to state what alternative methods are. For students, professionals and activists to take these ideas seriously, they need proof that ideas work in practice. This calls for taking some calculated risks to allow for possible failures. One way of doing this is to develop pilot projects, which can be expanded if successful, modified or abandoned in response to the actual performance. It is important to test out ideas in practice so that lessons can be learnt and ideas modified in an active struggle for survival and change on the ground.

Explaining the stand

Three questions from *bis* (2001)[394]

In information sent to Sweden, you describe the formation of the Diversity Council as a historical event. Why?

There are a number of levels at which the formation of the Diversity Council is an historical event. Black and Minority Ethnic workers have struggled for a long time to get their managers, the profession, employers, and local and central governments to take serious action and address discrimination within the information field. Part of the reason for the lack of progress was the fact that a number of different groups were working on their own, or with minimal cooperation and so failed to make a national impact. With the coming together of the four main groups[395] as the Diversity Council, new possibilities have been opened up under a united strategy, action plan and aims.

At another level, the Diversity Council opens out the possibilities of other oppressed groups joining in, in an even larger movement. Such areas include oppression on the grounds of class, gender, sexuality, disability, etc. Much work has been done recently in the field of "social exclusion" and the Diversity Council can help to focus action along all these fronts.

At the same time, for the first time, the Library Association has been very supportive of this initiative and it is hoped that the Diversity Council will be recognised as a Library Association Group, thus "mainstreaming" an area of exclusion, which has previously struggled outside the professional organisation. Meaningful contacts have also been made with the Black Caucus of the American Library Association, which is providing valuable experience in organising and solidarity work.

---

[394] Three questions from *bis*, the journal of the Swedish organisation, Bibliotek i Samh. Answers by Shiraz Durrani . 8 April 2001. bis No. 1, 2001.
[395] The organisations that form the Diversity Council are the African Caribbean Library Association (ACLA), the Asian Librarians and Advisers Group (ALAG), and Race and Class Group (RCG), SPICE (Specialist Provision in Community Languages and English). Also expected to join is the Chinese Library Support Group.

What is, briefly, the situation for librarians in the UK with a third world background?

Their marginalisation, powerlessness and discrimination is reflected in the fact that out of 25,000 members of the (British) Library Association, only 286 are from African, Caribbean or Asian backgrounds and only 3 of them earn more than £27,000 p.m. At a recent meeting on Annual Library Plans, the lack of Black librarians was glaring; this is true also among senior LIS management generally, among ranks of the Library Association Councillors, at ALCL (Association of Chief London Librarians) and at the Society of Chief Librarians (SCL). All of this indicates a lack of input from Black librarians in the planning process itself. They remain outside the power structures that decide on policies, resource allocation and service delivery.

At the same time, workplace discrimination places additional pressures on the majority of world librarians who, in most cases, have to survive extremely oppressive work environments where they do not receive the same support, information, and training or experience that non-majority world library workers receive. In many cases, work places are run by dictatorial white managers whose main interests seems to be in maintaining the power *status quo*.

Following the publication of the Stephen Lawrence Inquiry report, it has now been recognised that institutional racism exists widely in Britain. Libraries are no exceptions. While new legislation makes it a requirement for all public authorities to address institutional racism, it remains to be seen how much meaningful change will be made in LIS.

Which is, in your opinion, the biggest challenge to LIS in the UK?

A number of major social, economic, and technologic forces are changing the world of information in Britain today. The forces of corporate globalisation are breaking old relationships and creating new ground rules that favour corporate profit. New moves from the WTO to "corporatise" services, including information and education, create yet more challenges. The exploitative forces that have affected information in the majority world for decades are now doing similar damage in Britain and other industrialised countries. New technologies provide new possibilities to solve many social and economic problems, but, in the wrong hands, they also carry the danger of further marginalizing the majority of working people who have traditionally remained outside the remit of "public" information services.

While people all around the world and in Britain too, are organising to face these challenges with a powerful international movement of people's globalisation, it remains to be seen if the British LIS profession joins the progressive forces or not. Change is always brought about by a minority, and signs of these in LIS are activities of organizations such as Information for Social Change, LINK, and the Diversity Council, among others. Many senior managers controlling the direction of British libraries as well as the Library Association have yet to indicate their stand in harnessing the positive aspects of the new technological and social forces in the interest of serving the needs of the excluded working people. Thus, the biggest challenge to LIS is to make itself relevant to the majority of British people and to move out of the 150-year old tradition of "the middle class running information services for the middle class". Success will be measured on the basis of a real shift of power from a minority white, usually male, middle class to a representative and diversified majority of working people.

Interview with Shiraz Durrani 11th May 2004 (Anna Goulding)[396]

AG: We'll start off with staffing and leadership then because I know you are very involved in the Quality Leaders Project so if we can start by talking about the key issues of ethnic diversity in the workforce, what do you think are the key problems and issues?

SD: I think one thing to keep in mind is that the issues in the library are a reflection of what's happening in society so it's not an isolated box that we live in. The library profession exists in its social context. I think it's obvious that there's a lack of commitment to equality on the basis of diversity in the country and within libraries. Whichever way we define it—not only in the staffing issues, but in the service as well. The issue is around organisational culture and connected with that there is a lot of lip service to diversity. All that lip service is not making much of a difference on the ground.

In the past, people used to go for equality training and many came back better equipped to avoid being caught in providing an "unequal" service. There is a danger of the same thing happening now. With reference to issues around the Steven Lawrence Inquiry or even the Equality Standard, we need to see from the point of view of what's happening on the ground, talking to people. If we are honest, we have to admit that it's again another of those exercises where you tick boxes and go away and do your own thing.

There is a lack of leadership or direction or guidance in the profession and definitely a lack of commitment to equality and that goes right across—it's at middle management level and also at a more senior level.

The danger point also is that some of the things that have been coming from CRE itself in terms of ethnic diversity may be giving the wrong message. Some of their statements seem to imply that political correctness is a thing of the past and not a matter of human rights. Political correctness to me means sticking to equality principles.

In the library field the Library and Information Commission commissioned the diversity report by Roach and Morrison. I don't think anybody's ever seriously bothered with looking at it or implementing it. It's nice to have those kinds of reports, but what use are they if they are not taken on board at all.

...

---

[396] Contemporary Discourses of Public Libraries. Arts & Humanities Research Board Research. Leave Scheme. AHRB research on discourses of contemporary public libraries. The research was subsequently published in Goulding, Anne (2006): Public libraries in the 21st Century: defining services and debating the future. Aldershot, Hampshire: Ashgate.

I don't think CILIP is giving leadership on this either, again they have their own ways of appearing to be doing something, but I don't think in real terms it makes a difference. I think the whole problem in the profession as a whole is that there doesn't seem to be a vision for libraries, someone looking ahead five years from now from the point of view of the majority of British people. There are no new ideas coming in, there is stagnation and people in positions of power are there to maintain their position. The whole issue around what libraries are for is kept out of public discussion.

AG: So things like Framework for the Future then you would say, well it has been said, not aspirational enough, not visionary enough.

SD: No. Well it does go some way, but it's not very much... I read in the paper yesterday about this new Equalities and Human Rights Commission. They say the Government will take a softly, softly approach and not pose any real challenge to ensure social justice. Similarly, the whole issues around Framework for the Future is that it takes a softly, softly approach... they don't want to challenge, they don't want to say this is what you have to do. Then there is the whole question surrounding the public library standards, which are again taking a very traditional approach, and not helping to bring about necessary change.

...

The crucial point about diversity and equality is that unless you involve the people directly, empower them, nothing is going to change. ...

Now unless you involve people like that, unless you involve the community, unless they're empowered, you will not bring about any change. It will then be the same old characters sitting in offices making decisions without understanding their communities. I don't think that's the way to run a public service.

Another thing we set up was the Diversity Council. As with every oppressed group, there was a lot of in-fighting, but we did overcome that to a certain extent and formed the Diversity Council which brought together a number of organisations which were active at different levels. It has now become the Diversity Group of CILIP. It now makes all the right points and all the rest of it, but I don't think it's going to make much of a difference.

AG: OK shall we move on and talk about social exclusion, you mentioned the public library standards and there are none covering social exclusion, do you think that's disappointing or that it's not appropriate?

SD: It's disappointing but I'm not surprised, put it that way. When I was in Hackney we ran a Black Workers Group which submitted ideas on developing services to BME communities to the then Department of National Heritage who were doing a survey of libraries. Later on, I wrote to the Social Exclusion Unit when they started discussing services to BME communities; I wrote to the Parliamentary Culture, Media & Sport Committee. So "they" are not unaware about what needs to happen or that something needs to happen.

...

There is no doubt that in the last seven years or so, there has been a lot of progress. There is a new momentum and a lot of positive things have happened under this government, but I think they're too scared to take a bold stand and say, "this is where we want to go and this is how we want you to…" and I think the other danger is that ICT can take a higher profile. I think it's absolutely essential; it's brilliant that every library has computers, so that is breaking down those barriers in a very basic way. I think it's an essential first basic step, but it has stopped there unless something new comes and this year's position statement guidance maintains that position, they don't want to shake the boat. It's almost as if they're scared of the heads of libraries, like the whole thing's around Framework for Future, "oh, we're taking on board what the heads of libraries think", but who are these heads of libraries, what class do they represent, whose interests do they represent?

...

Within the library world there is a danger of us not understanding the forces of globalisation. It's changing lots of things, not only technology but where things happen and not happen and all the rest of it, and we are simply sitting with closed eyes and minds and there are storms all around us and we think they'll go away. And the profession doesn't do much to challenge or to break people's thinking.

AG: So you think there needs to be more imaginative thinking?

SD: One of the things I've been talking about with the Paul Hamlyn Foundation was… I think one of the two key things that need to happen in the profession, is possibly developing an innovations unit in a big way which would collect innovations, ideas and support other people to put it into practice and document it.

AG: So there you're saying it's very fragmented and yes, there are pockets of good practice, but that needs to be brought together?

SD: We need to mainstream those activities. I've no problem in a sense with what Framework for the Future is trying to do. I think it's brought important things on to the agenda. The same thing with the report that came out last week, I think there are some very positive thoughts in it, which challenge us in a number of ways, and I think we need to be able to respond to those. We've been running libraries for 150 years, where have we taken them? We've taken them down a big hole I think. There are people who are challenging us and we need to start responding to that and then bringing it back to life.

...

AG: You did talk a bit about the People's Network, saying it's not enough just to shove these machines in libraries and think that it is going to overcome exclusion.

SD: OK, I think it's a positive development; it's something that is fantastic that has changed the thinking. We had librarians or library workers sometime saying we don't want to get rid of books from libraries, why do you want space for the computers, but they've now just come to be accepted. But the danger is that technology is not going to automatically address the needs of everybody, with the book and reading and the rest of it. I think it's a [specific class] of people who use the book service for instance, and there's the same danger there, that unless we change and challenge the way we do things, it's the same class of people, same group of people who know how to take advantage of things, who will make use of it, so that again it's going to be a marginalized service.

...

So it's the same kind of thing; computers are there but what are they being used for and I think the whole issue around learning is marginalizing people like this so if computers are a tool, a tool for what? For whom? Those basic questions have not been even asked, let alone answered and putting computers without those kinds of things... OK, put more money in books, but you keep buying Mills and Boon and mindless fiction, OK it's good to read, but is it always good for people to read more of what they always read while the rest of the population gets nothing.

...

So computers have their role in terms of preventing social isolation and for learning new skills, etc. Some of the greatest users of computers and email are older people because they're establishing a new community. Now what are we in libraries doing? We have the Lending Time project where we take some volunteers to teach people to use computers, but that's at the margins of real possibilities which the technology provides to us, and technologies are out there, we don't know what to do with them.

...

AG: Let's move on to this last section then, you've said that you can see the public library service going down and down into a hole, I think you said unless it gets its act together.

SD: Very much so. Kevin Harris from the Community Development Foundation asks: "does it really matter who provides information service to the community, as long as somebody does that?" We don't have a right from some high authority saying that librarians are the only ones who can provide information. The world is moving on; new technology is cheaper than ever. One of the things I said in the Kenyan context is that peasants need information, public libraries don't give them that information so they're not going to wait and starve until public libraries get their act together, they develop their own systems and the information they need whether it's about rain or fertilisers or whatever, people are developing their own ways, we need to connect with them.

If libraries don't provide that information and somebody else does, it could be a college, it could be a bookshop or whatever, I think it's something as librarians we should be pleased, these people are getting information, and we shouldn't be protective, we should not say "only I can give it", it's very macho thinking that we seem to be some kind of elite with particular skills and only we know how to stamp a book or whatever we do. So whether we like it or not, information in the learning world is changing and if we are proactive we will guide and give some sort of sense of direction because we do have certain skills which are essential, I'm not running those down either, but if you don't do it, people are finding their own ways and we won't be part of that changed situation. Maybe libraries won't be there but something else will take its place and there's no guaranteed right of existence as far as libraries are concerned.

AG: OK, ideas around the role and purpose of public libraries, well, I think you said that they don't really know what they're for or we don't know what they're for, there's no vision.

SD: I don't think there is one.

The Government itself has put a lot of money around the Learning and Skills Councils and all sorts of places, and whereas libraries... if you read *Update* there are lots of positive things going on and I don't want to run those things down either but it's little bits here and there. Where is the leadership going to come from? Again, I don't know that many universities teaching departments but the little that I know indicate that there is a gap there as well. At the same time, training in management skills has also not made that much of a difference. So where is the leadership going to come from, somebody needs to provide leadership, but part of the problem is political. Britain lost its empire, it was overtaken by the U.S.A. and possibly, as a country, it has not recovered from that shock. When it had an empire it was much easier to do things, there was ready money coming up. And the loss of the empire was a terrible cultural shock, and the U.S.A. taking over and Blair running behind Bush; there's no national political leadership either to give us confidence as a nation. Nor has Britain found an alternative identity in Europe as the centre of progress and development moves to the South, South East and East Asia. There is thus a cultural and political vacuum nationally and its effects are felt in libraries as well. So there is no answer to the question "where are we going?" The "mainstream" goes on about refugees flooding this country, which is in a state of panic; we don't know where we're going. So it's the broader social-political situation in which libraries exist that we need to look at.

AG: OK, so what's your vision then? If you have to give a vision, what would your vision be of the public library service?

SD: The vision would be a library service, which redefines the term "library" in a much broader way. The vision would accept the fact that this is a society divided by classes and that certain classes, because of the resources they control, have their own means of satisfying their needs. The service needs to reassess the role and purpose of the library in a class-divided, diversified society. We need to accept the fact that public library service is not open to all, and develop a needs-based service, which meets the needs of people who cannot afford information and other library services, such as informal learning. The new role of libraries should ensure that the resources are used to meet the needs of people who do not have other ways of satisfying their needs. We are going through major technological change and need to look at how new technologies can help us develop new services.

It would be a library service that is possibly located in the community in a different and challenging kind of a way. Buildings are important, but buildings in themselves are not libraries, so we need to move out of the buildings, spiritually at least, and meet the needs where people are, become the people, be where their needs are. Such a library service is "libraries without walls".

AG: But people need community space as well, don't they?

SD: Yes, but redefine what library is, there are community spaces, community halls, but this is not what libraries are all about and I think that one of the things we're looking at here is to connect to people's social and community life; there are other cultural needs where we don't expect libraries to take all those roles but work with the people and make it... like *Merton Sense*,[397] empowering young people, enabling them or giving them power to do their own thing, and then our next move is to have a music group.

But we have to wage a cultural war to change people's thinking about the role of libraries, both within libraries, and also in the society, if libraries are to play a greater social role. Some youth workers have asked us: "why are libraries involved in this kind of thing (youth magazine production), it's nothing to do with you, it's our job, working with young people".

Part of that vision is to change the thinking of people we provide a service to. People need to know what libraries can be, and can do; otherwise they cannot make a meaningful choice as to what they want libraries to do. I think we have to develop new ideas and broaden the thinking of staff and the people in the communities. We have an important role to play in that. I think libraries should be working with arts workers, with cultural workers, with educationalists, I think redefining the term "librarian" and the term "library" is a part of the process that needs to start urgently. Those terms have created barriers for our audience in terms of physical space, and also in our thinking and in what and how we do things. Breaking those barriers should be the start of the process of starting to see a new vision for libraries.

Dr Anne Goulding
Reader in Information Services Management
Department of Information Science
Loughborough University
Loughborough LE11 3TU
A.Goulding@lboro.ac.uk

Contemporary Discourses of Public Libraries
Arts & Humanities Research Board Research Leave Scheme
AHRB research on discourses of contemporary public libraries.

---

[397] See: http://www.sense.ik.com/.

Breaking the culture of silence (2006)[398]

The idea of writing this book was born when a group of progressive librarians at the University of Nairobi were searching for relevance in the information field in Kenya by organising a workshop at the Kabete Campus of the University of Nairobi in 1979. I decided to look at the history of mass communication and publishing to see what lessons could be learnt from those experiences. I presented a short version of my paper at the workshop. The fuller version was too big for inclusion in the proceedings of the workshop, which carried another paper I wrote.[399]

But the subject matter of the paper on publishing became an obsession with me the more I read. The fascinating struggles in the information field that unfolded with each new angle explored began to reflect the totality of anti-imperialist struggles in Kenya. I needed to devote more time to the research into publishing. I planned to take sabbatical leave in 1985 to research at the Kenya Archives, as well as the Colonial Office files. But the research seemed to take a life of its own and in a curious turn of events became "political" and led to my exile to Britain in 1984.

In the early 1980s, the underground opposition to the KANU-Moi regime penetrated every field of activity. It was led by the December Twelve Movement, which published its own underground newspaper—*Pambana*, which circulated widely throughout the country. The students at the University of Nairobi joined hands with the underground resistance. They lost no opportunity to attack the regime in every possible way. One of the ways was to publish progressive material on the history of resistance and the progressive anti-imperialist stand of the Kenyan people of all nationalities. A new generation was growing up, they argued, without the awareness of the real history of the struggle that created the current society. They approached me in early 1994 for help in some aspects of their publication, *The University Platform*. They also wanted me to write articles on the history of Kenya from a working class point of view. I provided three articles, two from my research on the history of publishing: one on Pio Gama Pinto and the other on Kimaathi.[400] The third was an article I had written as part of the publicity of the progressive play *Kinjikitile – Maji Maji*, which was directed by Naila Durrani and staged to full houses at the Education Theatre by the Takhto Arts of Nairobi in conjunction with the University Library's Sehemu ya Utungaji ("creative wing"), which I had set up with a group of progressive library workers.

All three articles proved popular and I decided to give them wider circulation. 1984 was in many ways a crucial year: following the 1982 coup, the KANU regime savagely attacked the forces of democracy. The subsequent killing, arrests and exile of thousands of people, whose only "crime" was opposition to the Moi dictatorship, meant that 1984 saw the nation recovering from the ravages of much government-led savagery. The publication of the articles in the national press, I decided, would give a message to those active in the struggle that, in spite of the jailing and exiling of many

---

[398] Durrani, Shiraz (2006): Never be silent; publishing and imperialism in Kenya, 1884-1963. London: vita Books. pp. vii-ix.
[399] "Agri-Vet information: production, organisation, storage and retrieval". University of Nairobi Library Magazine (Nairobi). 2 (23-37) 1979.
[400] This is the spelling used throughout the book.

activists, progressive forces were still active in Kenya. It was necessary for the dispersed groups to come together once again and continue their struggle. The underground opposition forces were regrouping and finding their feet once again and different groups were using different methods to re-establish connections with each other.

It was in this national context that my article on Pio Gama Pinto was published in *The Standard* of 17-18 September, 1984. The following week, *The Standard* was scheduled to publish a three-part follow-up article by me on Kimaathi, to be followed in the future by a series of articles on Makhan Singh. But it was at the publication of the first set of articles on Pinto that the regime struck and unleashed a series of events that forced me to seek political asylum in Britain. However, in the brief space of time between the publication of the articles and the Special Branch starting to take "special interest" in me, a large number of activists, including many from Mau Mau days, started sending messages of support. Their main message was that they wished to continue and consolidate the process of recording the true history of Kenya and to apply the lessons of history to the current struggle.

The questions that the Special Branch fired at me during interviews at the Nyayo House give an indication of how hurt the regime was at my research into the history of publishing and the anti-imperialist struggle in Kenya: Why are you writing about Pinto and Kimaathi, and not about Kenyatta? Even historians are not allowed to do research into Mau Mau. Why are you, a mere librarian, doing this research? Do you not know that people at the highest level in the Government are offended by your article on Pinto? Are you a communist? Why do you write about workers and peasants? What do you understand by workers — even Moi is a worker, why are you not writing about him? Do you think that you will escape the wrath of the Government machinery just because you are "an Indian"? And on and on.

It is a matter of utmost satisfaction to me that in the years that I have been in exile in Britain, I have continued work on the struggles in the information field in the context of the national struggle for liberation. This has included a number of articles published in various journals on the politics of information. Among other publications is *Kimaathi, Mau Mau's First Prime Minister of Kenya*.[401]

It also gives me personal satisfaction that the very reason for my exile from Kenya has enabled me to complete the documentation of an important aspect of Kenya's history — something that the KANU-Moi regime found so unpalatable. It is also a matter of pride to me that I completed the project while still remaining a "mere librarian".

The work of the underground movement contributed in no small measure to the events that led to the overthrow of KANU-Moi in December 2002. The new social climate in early 2003 has enabled a new debate about the whole colonial and post-colonial history of anti-imperialism not only in Kenya, but in Britain as well. This book, I hope, will throw light on some aspects of the history, which had been suppressed by successive KANU regimes.

---

[401] Durrani, S (1986).

Three questions from *bis* (2006)[402]

1. Why did you write the book? Your book has the title: *Never be silent*. Why?

The book started as a paper for a workshop entitled, "Libraries and rural development in Kenya". It was an exploration of the role that information workers should play in ensuring that the information needs of people were met. This was a way of understanding and redefining the social role of librarians in Kenya. That was the first reason for writing the book.

The second reason was to re-interpret the history of Kenya from the people's point of view. A large amount of history has been written and interpreted by those who sought to justify colonialism and imperialism. Facts were often distorted, hidden or misinterpreted. Those who sought to see history from a people's point of view were not free to carry out research, or to publish their findings. I used secondary sources to give the events a new interpretation. Thus the book seeks to provide an alternative and, from my point of view, an authentic, version of colonialism and resistance to it in Kenya. The history of publishing in Kenya, as an important aspect of social communications, provides a prism for seeing and understanding the reality of social and political struggles in Kenya.

The third reason for writing the book was an act of political activism at a time when there were few democratic avenues for political activists. All progressive political activities in Kenya from around 1965 had to be carried out underground. A new generation of cadres needed to be nurtured in theories of liberation and tested in active struggles. They had to be given a new, Pan African and anti-imperialist world outlook, based on principles of socialism.

A missing element in this process was a lack of appropriate study material. The underground opposition needed progressive material from overseas (e.g. writings of Marx, Lenin, Stalin, Mao, Castro, Lumumba, Nkrumah, Cabral, etc.) and organised their supply through underground networks – note that this was before the Internet made such material easily accessible. But it also needed material that reflected local history, struggles and achievements. Such material had to be written locally. Thus activists of the underground December Twelve Movement wrote and published *InDependent Kenya*,[403] as well as issued its own newspaper, *Pambana*.[404] My publications, including *Never be silent*, aimed to supply such material for political use. My other publications included a short introduction to Mau Mau.[405]

---

[402] "Three questions from bis (Bibliotek i Samhälle – "Libraries in Society") to Shiraz Durrani regarding his newly released book Never be silent; publishing and imperialism in Kenya. 1884-1963 (2006, London: Vita Books)". http://www.foreningenbis.org/index.html/
[403] London: Zed Books (1983).
[404] Further information about these, and other underground publications is available from: Durrani, Shiraz (1997): The other Kenya: underground and alternative literature. Collection Building. Vol. 16(2) 80-87.
[405] Durrani, Shiraz (1986): Kimaathi, Mau Mau's first Prime Minister of Kenya. Middlesex: Vita Books.

The title, "Never be silent" is taken from a liberation song sung by the Mau Mau activists as a way of recording their history, and to organise and mobilise their supporters. The song was called "We will never be silent".

2. In a popular movement, what is the role of the professional librarian or information worker?

It is important to see professional librarians in their social context. They are part of a social setup, which under capitalism, is divided into various classes. The information sector, in common with other aspects of life, is in effect a tool of a particular class, which uses it to further its class interests. At the same time, classes with less political or economic power are engaged in a constant resistance to assert *their* class interests. The professionals in this context are not neutral. Whether they admit it or not, they are involved in this struggle on one side or another.

A popular movement in such a situation seeks political power to meet the needs of those it represents. A key requirement for their struggle to succeed is control over social information. The information needs of the popular movement are, of course, related to the needs of their struggles. In essence, they need to know everything their enemies know, but in addition, they also need to know and understand the reality of the situation from their own point of view, both national and international, so that they draw correct lessons for their struggles. They need scientific and technological information, which can further their social struggles as well as provide means of satisfying their material needs. For this to be done, they need to control tools of social communication — printing presses, books, radio stations, ICT, videos, photo documentation, libraries and all the other tools made possible by developments in ICT.

Thus a popular movement needs its activists to have skills to ensure that it can control and use all these technologies — just as they need the skills of lawyers, doctors, peasants and workers.

Professional librarians can contribute to the success of a popular movement by being active in the struggle and contributing their skills to provide informational support for the popular struggle. All the traditional skills of the information professional — acquiring material relevant to advance their struggle, storing, dissemination, cataloguing and classifying information, etc. — are needed in the struggle. Librarians are the collective information banks of the struggle upon which the organisation can draw.

No popular liberation movement can succeed in achieving its vision without ensuring that its information needs are met. Thus the Mau Mau had a comprehensive information strategy to meet its information and communications needs, as documented in *Never be silent*. They controlled newspapers, printing presses, teaching programmes; they organised field hospitals and gun factories, they established libraries in secret locations — all of which needed appropriate skills and information. They developed methods of information dissemination and used orature and freedom songs to reach people who could not read or write. They also collected and used intelligence to monitor enemy movement and battle strength. In all this, the trade union movement played a key role.

The Mau Mau did not have professional librarians, as we know them today, to do this work. But the need for the librarian's skills was there. In fact it was the activists themselves who became librarians and documented events, wrote and collected information, organised secret libraries in the forests and ensured that correct information reached those who needed it in an appropriate form and at the right time. Today's "professional" librarians can learn much from their example of how to be activist librarians.

Given the stranglehold over mass media globally by a small number of media conglomerates, it is important that alternative information is made available to people in a form and language appropriate to local needs.

At the same time, a popular movement needs to work with other popular movements to strengthen itself. Imperialist forces work globally, forming "coalitions of the willing" to maintain their stranglehold over people, countries and resources. In the same way, popular forces need to work in unity in a global alliance with those struggling against imperialism. Information activists need to take a leadership role in this process of global cooperation of popular forces and facilitate information transfer to bring people and organisations together on the basis of awareness about each other's programmes, visions, experiences, successes and failures.

The vision of a global popular movement, such as the World Social Movement, can emerge only if there is this active information exchange. It is the role of the professional librarian to create networks for such exchanges.

3. "What is the role of ICT in the information provision to popular movements?"

This is tied with the previous question. Popular movements need all the tools they can get hold of in order to achieve their vision. Such tools vary according to the particular stage of the struggle in particular countries. But at every stage there is a need for relevant information to be assessed, collected and disseminated. Given the rapid growth in the amount of information available today, it is no longer possible or practicable to rely on tools used in previous struggles.

Developments in ICT have created new tools and technologies that can help in collecting and disseminating material from various liberation struggles. The enormous amount of oral and written material generated during the long history of struggles against colonialism in Africa, Asia, Latin America, as well as in Europe and the U.S.A., can now be collected, documented and made available more easily with ICT. Similarly documentation on the policies and activities of organisations and leaders active in the anti-colonial, anti-imperialist movements (before and after independence) need to be made available. With the possibilities opened up by ICT, this can be a manageable task, especially if there is greater cooperation between various popular movements.

One does not expect any organisation to use manual typewriters today to draft their manifestos. Nor can all activists be reached by the traditional postal mail. The enemies that the popular movements are fighting against use technologies that can take people to the moon and Mars. There can be no hope for victory if the movements themselves do not upgrade their tools and technologies to match those of their enemies. One cannot fight modern warfare using catapults. Similarly, one cannot hope to win people's wars by using pen and paper. ICT as a tool for communication is crucial for victory in people's movements. Not only can it provide an efficient and effective means of communication, it can also help to organise its supporters as well as train an army of advanced cadres for new battles.

It is easy today to reach millions of people by the use of emails and text messages within seconds. "Video guerrillas" take pictures of enemy atrocities and broadcast them to the world. Satellite television stations, using people's culture and languages, can help to break the imperialist embargo on people's communications. Radio stations can still be a powerful means of reaching people right in their houses, factories and fields. While the corporate companies seek to use these channels for diverting people's attention away from the reality of their exploitation and its causes, the popular movements can use them to open people's minds to the reasons for their suffering. They can provide a world outlook that imperialism seeks to block out. In essence, ICT has changed the whole balance in the struggle against corporate globalisation and created a new generation of activists who will help liberate the people of the world.

> *Injustice anywhere is a threat to justice everywhere.*
> - Martin Luther King, Jr. (1963) — letter from prison, "The Negro is your brother".
>
> *It is not enough to deal with racism at the individual level. Combating racism must entail a redistribution of social, economic and political power from the powerful to the powerless.*
> - World Council of Churches (1969) Quoted in *Goan Overseas Digest* 7(4)1999

Information activism

Library Association Motions on race and class (1996)[406]

The Library Association's Annual General Meeting held on Wednesday 23 October 1996.

Motion 8

Due notice having been given in accordance with bylaw 61, the following motion will be presented: 'Issues of race and class are as relevant and important to the library community as they are to society at large. A well-attended meeting of Black library workers held at the LA in April revealed that the Association needs to be proactive in its recruitment of these workers and that those who are already members should be encouraged to be more involved in LA activities. We therefore call upon this AGM to recommend to the Council: (1) that the LA establishes a formal Black Library Workers Group, which will have the same status (capitation, Council members, etc.,) as other LA groups; (2) that the LA organises an annual conference for Black Library Workers; (3) that the Black Library Workers Group is allocated a regular column in the Library Association Record or quarterly supplement to the LAR.' The contents of this column/supplement will be edited by the Equal Opportunities Sub-Committee.

Proposed: Mr Shiraz Durrani (Mbr No.0039636)
Seconded: Mr John Pateman (Mbr No.0032146)

Motion 9

Due notice having been given in accordance with bylaw 61, the following motion will be presented: 'Public library research indicates that there is a link between social class, deprivation and library usage. We therefore call upon this AGM to recommend to the Council: (1) that social class is included in the LA's Equal Opportunity Statement and supporting literature; (2) that the LA issue a guidance note on social class, similar to those on sexual orientation, older people, etc.; (3) that the LA commission further research into the usage and non-usage of libraries by social class.'

Proposed: Mr John Pateman (Mbr No.0032146)
Seconded: Mr Shiraz Durrani (Mbr No.0039636)

---

[406] Library Association Record. 98(9) September 1996.

Comprehensive and Efficient: Standards for modern public libraries, a response (2000)[407]

The initiative by DCMS in issuing the Consultation paper on standards is indeed a welcome one. However, in order to make the Standards relevant to the needs of people, it is necessary to examine the context of social and economic conditions in Britain today. The standards do not operate in a vacuum, but in specific conditions at a particular historical time. Perhaps the greatest weakness of the proposed standards is that they ignore the particular needs at the beginning of a new millennium. They similarly ignore initiatives taken by other Departments, and indeed seem to be unaware of the conclusions from research done by the Government and other research bodies. There is thus a lack of the "joined-up" thinking and action on the part of DCMS in devising the Standards.

General

The need to provide relevant and "equal" services for all social class is urgent. A recent research report concludes:

> What is clear is that, despite their origins as working class institutions, public libraries were never heavily used by the majority of working class people. They were taken over, in effect, by the middle class, and are now, it can be argued, characterised by a form of "institutionalised classism". As we shall see in Section 3.4, public libraries are used to a disproportionate extent by the middle class (in terms of their percentage of the total population), while working class use is relatively low. In this sense public libraries are not socially inclusive.[408]

The Standards approach this imbalance in a roundabout way. While the standards are set for "active library borrowers" there is no reason to believe that this extension will be targeted to include all social classes. Unless stronger standards are set to change the pattern set over 150 years, the situation in addressing the needs of working classes is not likely to change.

The Government's agenda on social exclusion shows the need for urgent action to address the needs of excluded communities. Unless action is required by the proposed standards, little action will be taken.

The Public Library Policy and Social Exclusion Project concludes; that if libraries are to "more convincingly respond to the needs of socially excluded people in Britain, most (libraries) will need to adopt comprehensive and sometimes radical change". The Standards similarly need to aim for radical change. Unfortunately, the draft Standards do not give evidence of such an approach.

---

[407] Response to "Comprehensive and Efficient – Standards for modern public libraries: A consultation paper". 2000. London: DCMS.
[408] Open to All? (2000): op. cit.

Research by the Social Exclusion Unit[409] highlights the discrimination faced by Black communities:

> People from minority ethnic communities are at disproportionate risk of social exclusion; they experience a double disadvantage. They are disproportionately concentrated in deprived areas...they also suffer the consequences of racial discrimination; services that fail to reach them or meet their needs; language and cultural barriers in gaining access to information and services. They are more likely to be poor and to be unemployed, regardless of their age, sex, qualifications and place of residence. As a group, they are as well qualified as white people, but some black and Asian groups do not do as well at school as others.

Yet the proposed standards do not address this discrimination in a meaningful way. The recommendations from the Hackney Library Black Workers Group pointed to the need for strict standards on services to Black communities. Their recommendations included:

> We need to go beyond the present "Equal Opportunities" policies and work on a new "national" vision and a strategic approach and framework. Standards of service for BME communities must be set up, with procedures for monitoring their implementation.[410]

These do not seem to have been considered by those drawing up the draft standards.

There is thus a need to develop standards that reflect the needs and usage of specific communities, especially those currently excluded. In the case of Black communities, for example, an overall minimum figure of 6.5 percent of all services and resources should be targeted to minority ethnic communities to reflect their proportion in the country. However, where the proportion of ethnic minority communities exceed this figure—as they do in London Boroughs—the library authority will need to target their activities to these higher figures. This was tried out in Hackney, for example.[411] Similar practices need to be extended to other excluded people, for example women, disabled people, lesbian, gay men and transgendered people, travellers, refugees, etc. Such targeting then needs to be monitored by the standards.

The needs of many excluded communities will not be met by static building-based services. Merton, for example, has set up strategic goals around outreach activities as well as around non-traditional activities in libraries. Services will then be measured against these local performance indicators. The national standards also need to include such performance indicators.

The research done by the LIC-funded QLP highlighted the need to develop performance measures to address the needs of Black communities. Their recommendations point to the need to develop appropriate standards and performance measures:

---

[409] SEU (2000), Minority ethnic issues in social exclusion and neighbourhood renewal; a guide to the work of the Social Exclusion Unit and the Policy Action teams so far.
[410] Black & Ethnic Minority Workers Group. Hackney (1994), Library Services for Black and Ethnic Minority Nationalities in the U.K. — A Report Prepared for the DNH Review of Public Libraries.
[411] See Durrani, S., Pateman, J. and Durrani, N. (1999) The Black and Minority Ethnic Stock Group (BSG) in Hackney Libraries. Library Review 48(1)1999.

Local authority best value performance plans and appropriate local performance indicators might be used to position services to Black, Asian, and other ethnic minority communities in the mainstream of efforts to modernise services.

Local performance targets for the percentage of members of Black, Asian, and other ethnic minority communities using key library services should be set and should reflect an ambition to make the services more relevant and accessible to these communities.[412]

Specific Standards

PLS 18 – Professional staff. The need to have staff with community development skills should be emphasised here. The traditional library and information-trained staff do not necessarily have skills and competencies to serve the needs of communities

PLS 22 and 23: The definition of the quality of book stock needs to include material from the majority world, as a large proportion of material in libraries is very Eurocentric. If libraries are going to be inclusive, they need to acquire a fixed proportion of alternative and majority-world-oriented material in different languages. Otherwise, we will reinforce the current practices of white, European centred material and outlook in libraries.

---

[412] A Quality Leaders Project for Black Library & Information Workers. Final Report of Research Findings, Feasibility Study, and Proposals (2000), Report Commissioned by the Library and Heritage Services of the London Borough of Merton for a Project Supported by the L.I.C. Management Research Centre, University of North London.

Progressive librarians & activists campaign to save CRE library (2004)[413]

Open letter to the Chair of the Commission for Racial Equality on his decision to close the "leading specialist race relations resource centre" to members of the public.[414]

We understand that CRE is proposing to close the library at the Commission for Racial Equality to members of the public.[415] This will also involve job losses for its library staff.

This is a short-sighted decision at a time when there is an even greater need to disseminate facts and figures on issues of race and other aspects of equality. In the absence of a nationally coordinated information campaign to give correct information to people, it is the racist media and parties whose views will be dominant. Far from closing access to the CRE library, it is essential that it should be given more resources to become an active player in disseminating the true picture of racism and xenophobia in the context of corporate globalization, which has led to increasing racial tension in the world.

This is the time when concerns about institutional and personal racism in Britain and Europe, as a whole, are increasing. Race relations in Britain have been damaged greatly by all political parties increasingly using misinformation around refugees and asylum seekers as an election issue. Britain's involvement in invading Iraq, and the subsequent anti-Muslim climate created by the U.S.A.-U.K. policies; need to be counter-balanced by the corrective force of real information – a role that CRE should be playing through its library.

It is ironic that at a time when the Government is talking about finding a new relevance for the public library service through its programme of "Framework for the Future",[416] an important resource that should help public libraries meet their equality targets is being restricted in its use. A model CRE library should be able to provide guidance to public libraries on how to achieve, in practice, an "equal" library service, but all we get from CRE is a further reduction to the already restricted service on offer now. We doubt that the Government's aim of achieving greater "social cohesion" can ever be met when the "leading specialist race relations resource centre" is being cut

---

[413] Select Committee on Culture, Media and Sport Written Evidence. Memorandum submitted by Shiraz Durrani . Available from:
<http://www.publications.parliament.uk/pa/cm200405/cmselect/cmcumeds/81/81we18.htm#note21#note21> [Accessed: 04 April 2007].
[414] The CRE library, as described by the CRE itself.
http://www.cre.gov.uk/about/library.html accessed: 16 August, 2004.
[415] Jenny Bourne (2004): "Plans to close CRE library". 4 August 2004..
http://www.irr.org.uk/2004/august/ha000002.html
[416] "Framework for the Future" is available at the DCMS website:
http://www.culture.gov.uk/Reference_library/Publications/archive_2003/framework_future.htm. [Accessed: 04 April 2007].

down. A society where only one-sided sources of information prevail can never be a coherent one.

This action by the CRE also indicates a lack of commitment to the spirit of the Stephen Lawrence Inquiry, which challenged institutional racism in the British society. The Race Relations (Amendment) Act gives public authorities a new statutory duty to promote race equality. Does this proposed action by CRE itself meet this requirement?

We would like the CRE to inform the public if its decision to close down an important public service meets the following requirements of the Race Equality Scheme, which is one of the specific duties under the Act. A body, which advises the rest of us on how to meet the legal duty to "promote race equality", surely needs to set an exemplary example itself. Does the CRE decision on its library meet the following requirements of the Race Equality Scheme?

- Assess whether their functions and policies are relevant to race equality;
- Monitor their policies to see how they affect race equality;
- Assess and consult on policies they are proposing to introduce;
- Publish the results of their consultations, monitoring and assessments;
- Make sure that the public have access to the information and services they provide;
- Train their staff on the new duties.

If CRE cannot meet these basic equality requirements, then it gives us further cause for concern about its ability and commitment to achieving racial equality in Britain.

We would like to receive assurance from you that the CRE library will remain a public access service. We would like you to re-prioritise the CRE budget and ensure that the essential information role of CRE is, in fact, enhanced. Further, we would like to receive assurance that there will not be any job losses for the CRE library staff.

We are also keen to hear what vision the CRE has to ensure that the information rights of the British people are met.

Study, teaching and learning

The educational role of public libraries in combating racism and xenophobia (1999)[417]

Abstract

The paper looks at the role of public libraries in combating racism and xenophobia, a subject often ignored in the library profession in Britain. It is based on a number of related publications by the author.

It looks at the existence of institutionalised racism in the British society and at the legacy of imperialism and its role in encouraging racism. Historically, the non-racist policies and practices of people of the South were destroyed by the onslaught of imperialism. Some examples from Kenya are provided.

It examines the record of public libraries in Britain in providing an "equal" service and the lack of leadership in combating racism from the professional body, the Library Association. A number of recent research projects have highlighted the problems. Olden et al.[418] provides a useful review of published literature on the provision of library service to black communities; Neely and Abif[419] provide a picture of racism in libraries in the U.S.A. Perhaps the most important research on the subject is Roach and Morrison,[420] which should form the basis for any work on services to Black communities. Their findings make grim reading, e.g. (1) The public library service has not yet managed to engage with ethnically diverse communities; (2) social distance exists between the public library and ethnic minority communities; (3) lack of clear vision and leadership on ethnic minority and racial equality matters; (4) lack of coherence in strategies to identify the needs of ethnic minority communities.

The article examines the action Black library workers and communities have taken to combat racism. The success achieved so far is limited, achieved in small, isolated cases rather than an embedded, national non-racist service. The author provides some reasons for this lack of progress. Some examples of "good practice" are also given: the Black Workers Group (BWG) at Hackney Libraries produced important policy documents, such as the Report to the Department of National

---

[417] A paper presented at the Second European Conference: Equality in Education Towards the next millennium. Collaborating to combat racism and xenophobia across Europe. Verona, Italy. 17-19 May 1999.
[418] Olden, Anthony, Tseng, C-P., Mcharazo, A. A. S. (1996) : Service for All? A Review of the published literature on black and ethnic minority/multicultural provision by public libraries in the United Kingdom (1996) Boston Spa, Wetherby, West Yorkshire: British Library Research & Development Department, 39pp. R & D. Report 6204.
[419] Neely, Teresa Y and Abif, Khafre K. (1996) In our own voices; the changing face of librarianship. Lanham, Md., The Scarecrow Press.
[420] Roach, Patrick and Morrison, M. (1998): Public libraries, ethnic diversity and citizenship. University of Warwick. British Library Research and Innovation Report 76.

Heritage[421] and documented workplace racism for the *Hackney Libraries News*. The BWG also helped set up pioneering practices such as stock work recorded by Durrani, Pateman, and Durrani,[422] the Three Continents Liberation Collection, the Nationality Languages Project, etc.

Initiatives from the British government and from the Commission for Racial Equality and the Stephen Lawrence Inquiry Report are also examined insofar as they can be applied to the library situation and can provide a framework to achieve equality.

The next section looks at the role that public libraries *can* play in providing a non-racist service. The article goes beyond this and examines the proactive role that public libraries should be playing in educating the public about the need and possibilities of eliminating racism.

On the whole, the author holds, racism can be eliminated only when victims of racism are empowered or self-empowered to combat racism. In the final analysis, racism survives on the basis of the powerlessness of its victims. In the information field, power, is held by members of the entrenched white middle class most of which are not committed to equality. They do not personally, or as a class, suffer from the effects of racism, and thus do not play an active part in combating it. Thus the question of racism is closely related to the question of class. The resolution of racism is dependent on the elimination of exploitation and oppression generally from the society.

In the meantime, until Black communities possess power to eliminate racism, legal and structural framework is essential in order to combat racism. The article makes several suggestions about a possible framework to eliminate racism.

Evidence of racism

The Stephen Lawrence Inquiry Report defines institutional racism as:

> The collective failure of an organisation to provide an appropriate and professional service to people because of their colour, culture or ethnic origin. It can be seen or detected in processes, attitudes and behaviour which amount to discrimination through unwitting prejudice, ignorance, thoughtlessness and racist stereotyping which disadvantage minority ethnic people.[423]

The Inquiry report asserts that institutional racism in the UK is the reason why the public sector has failed to provide an adequate professional and appropriate service to black and other minority ethnic people. The evidence of the failure of the local government to address racial discrimination and harass service provision and employment is also supported by the Audit Commission, whose 1997/98 report on local authority performance indicators revealed that there are areas of local government employment practice and service provision which remain untouched by any equal opportunities programme. This apparent inaction is despite local authorities having a specific duty under the Race Relations Act of 1976 to have regard

---

[421] Black & Ethnic Minority Workers Group (Hackney) (1994) Library Services for Black and Ethnic Minority Nationalities in the U.K. — A Report Prepared for the DNH Review of Public Libraries.
[422] Durrani, Shiraz, Pateman, John, Durrani, Naila (1999): The Black and Minority Ethnic Stock Group (BSG) in Hackney Libraries. Library Review. 48 (1) pp. 18 -- 25.
[423] Stephen Lawrence Inquiry: Report of an inquiry by Sir William Macpherson of Cluny (1999). The Home Office. Cm 4252-1.

to the promotion of equality of opportunity in carrying out their functions, and over £1830 million from the Home Office in the form of Section 11 funding to support this objective.

The problem also goes further than service provision and employment. A recent study by the LGMB revealed that only 3 percent of local authority elected members are black and other minority ethnic people, yet the black and other minority ethnic population is estimated to be 6 percent in England and Wales.[424]

Roots of racism

Social exclusion, of which racism is an important aspect, is an essential part of capitalism and so long as capitalism survives, social exclusion, social oppression and economic exploitation will also remain. Nor can such exclusion be totally eradicated as long as the prevailing free market system ensures that economic activity satisfies the profit greed of a few rather than the satisfaction of material, educational and cultural needs of the majority of people. The issues of racial oppression and class exploitation are intertwined and one cannot be eliminated without eliminating the other. This also implies that racism is not a problem only for Black people.

The position of the trade union movement is made clear by TUC which emphasises that racism and its solution are issues not only for Black people:

> Racism affects all workers, and we must all oppose it. Black workers suffer in several ways — from unfair treatment at work to verbal abuse, and physical attacks... It is still possible to hear comments that "Racism isn't our problem ... there are no blacks around here..." At best, this ignores the deep roots that prejudice has laid in British culture. Often it is an excuse for turning away from real problems of discrimination.[425]

This position is reinforced by the Stephen Lawrence Inquiry and the Government's response to it. The Home Secretary's Action Plan explains:

> The "colour blind" approach, favoured by local authorities whose populations are mainly white, is no longer acceptable as it ignores racism and will not deliver an anti-racist society in which racial and cultural diversity is embraced.[426]

TUC looks for the roots of racism in political and economic factors: "The background to racial discrimination lies in Britain's colonial past and willingness of governments and employers to see black workers as a source of cheap labour".[427] This valuable TUC publication points out an important fact about racism which is often ignored — that racism is not merely a matter of a struggle between people of different colour. The crucial factor is power — "power to dominate, to exploit, and to abuse". It is the use of power by the white-controlled Western society against Black people that is the basis of racism. TUC explains the process of how racism has become embedded and institutionalised in the British society:

> Western society is a white-controlled society, which has been built on the exploitation of the rest of the world. This exploitation at first was economic — extracting precious metals, slaves, commodities and foodstuffs from Africa, South America, and Asia. But

---

[424] Local Government Association (1999) The Stephen Lawrence Inquiry and Home Secretary's Action Plan: op. cit.
[425] Trade Union Congress (TUC): Tackling Racism; a TUC workbook (Reprinted 1989). London: TUC.
[426] Local Government Association (1999) The Stephen Lawrence Inquiry and Home Secretary's Action Plan: op. cit.
[427] Trade Union Congress (TUC): Tackling Racism: op. cit.

it quickly led to ideas about the superiority of European people over others, as a way of justifying the behaviour of European traders and colonisers. These ideas appeared in literature, religion, and popular entertainment, and they became established in the way subjects like history and geography were taught in schools and colleges...So you don't have to be an "oppressor" or "exploiter" to be affected by racist ideas — they have become rooted in Western society.[428]

It is thus important to understand that racism is nor inevitable or a "natural" way of organising a society. It has been created to serve a particular economic and social agenda, and can be eliminated if there is a will to do so. But this will not be an easy task. As the British Prime Minister Tony Blair acknowledged in *The Independent*, Britain "has a mountain to climb before we have a decent modern, multicultural society we can all be proud of".[429]

The reality of racism

In order to set the ground for a fuller exposure of racism in library service it is important that its manifestations are exposed. It is the shadow that reveals the shape of the hidden substance of racism, the slow poison in our society that will kill the patient if not stopped in time. The reality of racism in public libraries in Britain was shown in the findings of research by Roach and Morrison.[430] Their findings included national as well as local issues, such as:

The National Agenda

1. Developments in race equality and ethnic diversity within public library services have been largely ad hoc and progress has been limited. There is no effective champion for race equality within the public library movement and future developments and progress are uncertain.

2. Public library services are one of a number of providers of information at the local level. Our study indicated that for many ethnic minority communities, the local network of ethnic minority community sector organisations is often more relevant and appropriate as an access point to information. Yet the work of many of these local community based providers is not sufficiently recognised and there is often a failure to ally the work of these agencies to the work undertaken by public libraries in order to ensure coherence and effectiveness of the provision. Many of these community based provisions are also seriously under-resourced.

3. Few library services have established measurable objectives and service standards linked to racial equality and ethnic diversity. Where initiatives have been taken to develop performance indicators and measurement systems these have largely failed to consider ethnic diversity implications.

4. Ethnic minorities are under-represented amongst staff within the public library service and there are few opportunities for ethnic minority citizens to influence service provision. The current uncertainties about, and the potential

---

[428] Ibid.
[429] The Independent (London): 1 March 1999.
[430] Roach and Morrison (1998): op. cit.

demise of, special funding regimes such as the Home Office *Section* 11 programme could further weaken the link between public libraries and ethnic minorities.

5. Few library authorities have devised explicit programmes of research to investigate the service needs of ethnic minority communities. Whilst many library authorities routinely collect ethnic origin data in respect of service users, few undertake any detailed monitoring and review of such data as a means of assessing changing patterns of library need.

6. Library managers and staff are often unclear about the most effective ways in which they can develop more inclusive service provisions. In many library services the experience of policy development, strategic planning, research, monitoring, performance review, public consultation, marketing and networking does not include a focus on ethnicity implications.

7. Professional attitudes and skills may present barriers to the development of positive relationships with ethnic minority communities. Professionally qualified staff may not have acquired the requisite skills and capacities needed to establish effective links with local communities, or to engage communities in consultation about service needs, or to identify ethnically responsive service options, or to monitor and review services in an ethnically sensitive way. The specialist capacity within library services may also be under threat from reduced funding levels.

The Local Agenda

1. Few library services have developed specific objectives and targets relating to racial equality and ethnic diversity and, where these exist, such objectives and targets are often not measurable or are minimal in scope. Performance assessment and the measurement of the quality of library services have tended to operate in a colour-blind/ethnically biased way. Ethnic minorities have had few opportunities to input into the definition of quality standards.

2. Ethnic minority communities, far from being homogenous, are extremely diverse. Library needs are not always expressed in terms of ethnic identity; the needs of ethnic minorities continue to change, as do notions of ethnic identity.

3. There are few champions available to drive forward race equality in individual library authorities. Any withdrawal of special funding such as the Home Office Section 11 programme is likely to further restrict progress in this regard.

4. The ethnic composition, attitudes, skills and expertise of library staff may present a barrier to service effectiveness in ethnically diverse contexts. Ethnic minorities are under-represented amongst staff; few staff has the opportunity to engage in work with local community organisations; few staff has the experience of undertaking research and ethnic monitoring activities.

5. Current resource pressures on public library services have given rise to a new social distance between public libraries and the communities they exist to serve. Few library staff has the time and opportunity to engage in dialogue and networking activities outside the public library space. The current performance orientation within the public library service further militates against ethnically inclusive service provisions.

6. Public library services need to do more to understand the needs of citizens — especially within ethnically diverse contexts. Current approaches to service provision are modelled on a traditional paternalistic form of local government rather than on an effective dialogue and engagement with local people. As a result, the structure, form and content of public library services may not be appropriate within a culturally diverse and demographically fluid context.

7. Whilst a number of public library services are engaged in research, consultation and ethnic record keeping, much of this activity remains unfocused and piecemeal in approach.

8. Public library services are often working in isolation from other locally based agencies, which have been established to meet the specific needs of ethnic minority communities. The potential opportunities arising from collaborative working are not fully exploited. At the same time, many ethnic minority organisations are working in an unsupported and under-resourced fashion, and are not operating to their fullest potential.

9. Information technology solutions will become increasingly important within the context of public library service provision. For many groups of library users, including ethnic minority library users, information technology and remote access to public libraries will extend access and choice. At the same time, many ethnic minorities (particularly those who do not already access public libraries) and the community sector organizations, which support their needs, may not have access to the new technological media.

Action to combat racism

While there is no overall picture of a service relevant to Black communities emerging, it is true that a large number of initiatives are taking place throughout the country. *What's New*[431] regularly carries records of such initiatives. The LARRIE database carries over 12,500 local authority committee reports on race equality issues. While it is not possible to give details of such initiatives, some examples from the London Borough of Hackney of good practice are given below.

The Hackney experience

Hackney Library's Black & Ethnic Minorities Group was involved in many pioneering activities and policy initiatives. Perhaps its most significant contribution in

---

[431] What's New; LARRIE's Quarterly Update. Op. cit.

terms of policy was *Library Services for Black and Ethnic Minority Nationalities in the U.K. – A Report Prepared for the DNH Review of Public Libraries*.[432] This was a comprehensive Report submitted to the Department of National Heritage, which then had responsibilities for public libraries. The recommendations of the Report covered the following aspects as they affect Black staff and communities:

- Formation of Black workers and users/potential users groups;
- Staffing issues (levels and numbers);
- Service delivery, outreach, and community initiatives;
- Need for Annual Reports;
- Funding;
- Stock and materials policy;
- Education and training of information workers;
- New technology and service to Black communities.

The Report concluded with a plea for a library service "without walls":

> There is a tremendous potential in the Library service to provide an essential educational and cultural service to the whole population. BEM nationalities have missed out in many ways in the current form and content of library services. This is particularly true in inner-city areas of large cities where there are significant numbers of BEM people.
>
> A qualitatively different library service could become the centre of the social and cultural lives of BEM people in Britain. Information and education are their main requirements and appropriate library structures can provide these important inputs. For this to happen, it is necessary that a new, imaginative leap is made in the way library service is provided. Building-based services are essential, but they need to be supplemented by a new aspect of service that will serve BEM people in the best way possible. A service that reaches out from library buildings to where people are – in community centres, at street markets, at social, cultural and educational centres which are the basis of social lives of people. Such "libraries without walls" will provide a new type of library service, which is relevant to the needs of BEM people.
>
> It is also necessary to link up with the initiatives in education and cultural life already taken by BEM nationalities. These include a vast network of supplementary schools, nationality language classes, ESOL classes, social and cultural associations, publishing and book-selling services, etc. The organisation of Notting Hill Carnival and other cultural and social events is an indication of the creative and educational potential and achievements of BEM people.
>
> Libraries should harness all such local initiatives and reflect this life force. Active support in this direction by DNH can be the catalyst to encourage library services to become such centres.
>
> Finally, it is by making available relevant survival information to BEM communities through unconventional, non-traditional methods – i.e. community radio, outreach, word of mouth, etc. and making available liberating non-fiction and imaginative literature of their heritage, which will determine whether we as librarians are helping

---

[432] Black & Ethnic Minority Workers Group (Hackney) (1994) Library Services for Black and Ethnic Minority Nationalities in the U.K. – A Report Prepared for the DNH Review of Public Libraries.

(or not) to perpetuate the formation of an "underclass". The social cost of not providing relevant information services to BEM nationalities is too high to contemplate. The Comedia Report mentions some of these. It is a good sign that BEM nationalities are becoming increasingly more assertive about their rights to an adequate and relevant service.

It is therefore very important that the DNH defines a politically correct agenda for library/information services to BEM nationalities. This agenda should spell out compulsory policies and procedures so that libraries will no longer be part of the problem in marginalising BEM people through institutional racism, racist attitudes and behaviour. This agenda should also set up positive guidelines to help and enable librarians, and, if necessary, force them, to be part of the solution in making library/information services more acceptable and accessible to BEM people and thus empowering them.

It is a sign of institutional racism in Britain that the Review of Public Library for which this Report was written totally ignored this Report and its recommendations. It is ironic that the Stephen Lawrence Inquiry Report as well as recent initiatives on Social Exclusion by the Labour Government is returning to these issues — after almost five wasted years.

Many other significant changes took place in the service delivery of Hackney Libraries in 1995/96, again through the initiative of the Black Workers Group supported by a new committed leadership in Libraries as well as at Directorate-level. One of the most significant changes was the emphasis given to services to Black and Minority Ethnic communities which comprise almost 48 percent of Hackney's population (including the Turkish, Kurdish, Greek, Jewish and Irish communities which are included in the "White" category in the last population census). This proportion is bound to rise in the next generation as almost 75 percent of children in Hackney schools today are of Black and Minority Ethnic backgrounds.

In 1995/96, 25 percent of the total stock fund was allocated to Black and Other Minority Ethnic (BME) materials as a way of correcting an historical imbalance. This represented a significant increase on previous years.

But it was not enough to set aside an increased stockfund for Black material. An appropriate structure was needed to administer and monitor this increased spending. Discussion and consultation on these measures took place at all levels. In order to properly spend and monitor the 25 percent BME allocation, a BME Stock Steering Group (BSG) was established. The standards set by BSG and the experience gained from its work are examples of good practice, which can be used in other authorities as well. Details about the project are available in Durrani, Pateman, and Durrani.[433]

Another achievement in Hackney was the formation of the Three Continents Liberation Collection (TCLC) at the C.L.R. James Library. TCLC was initiated, planned, and implemented entirely by the grassroots staff in the library service with support from committed individuals from other Council Departments and the community. If ever there was a "people's project" TCLC is one, in the fullest sense.

The history of C.L.R. James Library itself is interesting. In common with black people's struggles nationally in the early 1980s, the people of Hackney took to the streets for various grievances, including the need to provide a library service that reflected the

---

[433] Durrani, Shiraz, Pateman, John, and Durrani, Naila (1999): The Black and Minority Ethnic Stock Group (BSG) in Hackney Libraries. Library Review. 48(1) pp. 18 – 25.

needs of Black and Other Ethnic minorities of Hackney. In response to this demand, the Council decided in 1985 to change the name of one of its libraries, Dalston Library, to C.L.R. James Library as a commitment that the library service would in future respond to the needs of these communities. Cyril Lionel Robert James has come to symbolise the struggle of Black people throughout the world for their basic rights.

But as is usual in such cases, the library's name change remained a mere cosmetic change. But the situation soon began to change. Around 1986, there developed within the library service a struggle between a Euro-centric group of librarians who questioned the very need of having any Black. In contrast, a group of librarians who believed in providing a service that the community really needed came together to form a core group who decided among other things that the name of the C.L.R. James Library needed a proper *content*. That, after all was what people had wanted rather than an empty gesture of a name change.

It was this TCLC Support Group that worked out the idea of the Collection, prepared detailed plans and reports, undertook feasibility studies, consulted communities and came up with final plans for TCLC.

Such positive examples are of course not embedded in the wider service, within individual authorities nor nationally. As long as there is a lack of committed Black managers in positions of power, and as long as Black communities have no say in local decisions, such experiments will remain just that — experiments to be discarded as soon as the pressure to maintain them is gone.

Perhaps what makes the situation worse is the lack of leadership from the professional body, which is supposed to take lead on such fundamental issues as racism. While almost every profession in Britain has addressed the issue of institutional racism following the publication of the Stephen Lawrence Inquiry Report, the Library Association remains totally silent on the issue. Its ostrich-like position is reinforced by delegating its race concerns to a sub-Committee with limited resources and almost no power. It is a matter of record that when a few members introduced resolutions at an AGM on race and class some years back, the Association was happy to allow a "democratic" vote among a white, middle-class membership to reject such concerns to the dustbins of its century-old history. It is no wonder that the Association's membership reflect an almost non-existent Black membership.

Some initiatives

Best Value

The government is set to become the guiding basis of local authority performance. Best Value can be characterised as a nationally prescribed performance management system. Performance measures and performance indicators will be fundamental to the best value regime. Best Value is one way in which the government plans to modernise and transform local government. It proposes that Best Value will deliver services to clear standards — covering both cost and quality by the most effective economic and efficient means available. In carrying this out local authorities will be accountable to local people and have a responsibility to the central government.

While the White Papers do not indicate equality as an integral part of Best Value, it is included as an aspect of quality. As the Local Government Management Board states:

> Unless a service's definition of quality includes making it accessible to and appropriate for all members of the community, and contributes to equal opportunities and social inclusion, then the definition of quality is limited. Best Value encourages councils to design, plan and deliver services, which are sensitive to the diverse needs of all residents and citizens… Equalities — that is equal access to services, anti-discriminatory policies, diversity of services, equal opportunities in employment — all need to be built in from the start.

Best Value emphasises consultation with local people on service aims and standards. If carried out in the spirit in which this policy has been set by the Government, the " focus on consulting local people and more open and accountable council should (ideally) contribute to equality".[434]

Equalities and Performance Indicators

Performance indicators provide a baseline for planning, targeting and measuring change in service provision. Targets for improvements in take-up by particular groups can be set in local performance plans, then measured again as part of the next service review to see if take-up actually has increased over time.

Equalities indicators are a vital way of demonstrating whether services are reaching everyone. The indicator can show who is benefiting from services and who has access to them, providing essential information to local residents, officers and members. Such indicators provide an accurate picture of current service use by different sectors of the population. This enables libraries to see which groups are using the service and check the level of under-use of the service among various sections of the local community.[435]

The Audit Commission introduced new performance indicators for collection in 1998/99, to be published in 1999. It requires each council to report whether they:
- publish a comprehensive equal opportunities policy;
- monitor how the policy is carried out;
- follow the CRE and EOC codes of practice on employment;
- monitor employees with respect to equal opportunities;
- indicate the level of the CRE Standard for Local Government they achieve in the provision of service to the community.

The Audit Commission is currently consulting on performance indicators for 1999/2000.

Equality and procurement strategy

Equality considerations need to be included as part of the Library procurement strategy. Equality in service delivery and employment should be built into any tendering and contracting process. Councils should consider ways in which they can support local businesses or community organisations to enable them to successfully apply to become service providers.

The Local Government Management Board lists three ways in which equalities considerations should be incorporated in the procurement strategy:

---

[434] Local Government Management Board (1998): Equality control. LGMB website: http://www.laria.gov.uk/content/newsletr/59/news13.htm [Accessed: 18 September 2007]
[435] Ibid.

- what impact will the choice of the provider arrangement have on equalities;
- how do the different providers being considered meet equalities considerations e.g. their response to questions in relation to their performance under Section 71 of the Race Relations Act 1976;
- what requirements can be written into the service agreements, requiring the provider to meet all the obligations under the Council's equalities policies.[436]

Equality and employment issues

Equality should be considered as an important aspect of delivering a Best Value service. The workforce needs to reflect the local and national ethnic make-up of the people if the staff are to deliver a relevant service. As the Local Government Management Board (LGMB) says, "A representative workforce is more likely to have the knowledge and skills to provide quality services which meet the needs of all the community".[437] It is thus important to collect data on the equality profile of the workforce, covering for example, proportion of ethnic minority staff, their grades, promotion history and prospects, and their training and work experience records.

Black & Other Minority Ethnic Managers

There is a growing awareness that business, as well as local authorities, need to reflect the cultural diversity of the community they serve. While this has been put into practice in many local authorities, BME staff has tended to remain at the lowest levels. Urgent action is now needed to ensure that such diversity is reflected in the higher decision and policy making levels of local authorities.

There can be no progress in providing an "equal" service for Black and Other Minority Ethnic (BME) communities without having committed senior managers from these communities. They need to be involved in decision and policy making positions so that the concerns of their communities are represented and given adequate representation at the highest levels, not only in the Library Services itself, but in local authority as a whole. No meaningful change in policy and practices can result if there is an inadequate proportion of BME managers.

As the Local Government Management Board says, "Black and Other Minority Ethnic managers can make a unique and valuable contribution to improving performance and service delivery to the diverse communities local councils serve."[438]

Black and Other Minority Ethnic people make up almost 6 percent of British population. Yet "only 1.4 percent of chief executives, chief officers and deputy chief officers come from black or other minority ethnic backgrounds". Overall, the local government in England and Wales employs over two million people. Of these, approximately 700,000 are involved in white-collar administrative and professional functions. The Local Government Management Board found that in a sample of 53 local authorities, for whom ethnic monitoring data was available, there were 6,000

---

[436] Ibid.
[437] op. cit.
[438] Local Government Management Board (1996): Evening the odds; research into management development for Black and other minority ethnic managers. Executive Summary. the quotations in the following section are all from this publication, unless otherwise stated).

BME employees in management positions at Senior Officer grades, i.e. SO1 and above.[439]

While serious action is necessary to redress this imbalance, it is not enough to aim merely at increasing the number of BME managers at the senior level. Two other issues are important. Essential criteria for all managers should include commitment to change and to improving the service to all marginalised communities, not merely in improving the personal professional development of managers. Ways also need to be found to enable minority communities to be actively involved in deciding how library resources are used and what services are provided.

Secondly, there should be organisational policies, structures and support mechanisms to enable BME managers to implement change. LGMB recommends that any schemes to support BME managers must be part of the mainstream and must not be seen as separate or marginal. In addition, LGMB says,

> Merely increasing the number of black and other minority ethnic managers in senior positions will not, by itself, improve organisational practices or services to the communities they serve. In development terms, black and other minority ethnic managers need to emphasise their capacity to transform their organisations. However, this must be matched by an organisational development framework, which links service enhancement with employees' development. It must be clearly supported by senior management.

Thus an essential ingredient for success of a programme to ensure that there are more BME managers in local authorities was highlighted by LGMB:

> Without the leadership and commitment from the very top of their organisations black and other minority ethnic managers fear that measures taken to develop them will not create a fast track for development and career progression in local government.

Such commitment from top leadership has had success in other management development programmes run by LGMB, such as the Top Managers Programme and the Women's Leadership Programme. A similar BME Managers Programmes need to be initiated as a matter of urgency.

The Survey's recommendations[440] should be essential reading for all working in or interested in local authorities. They are grouped under three sections: recommendations for The LGMB, for local authorities, and for BME individuals.

Role of Officers with Equalities Responsibility

Equalities officers and other officers responsible for equal opportunities have specialist skills and knowledge that they can bring to the best value process. This includes: knowledge and experience of working with and consulting different groups in the community and how to make services more responsive and accessible to them; knowledge of particular service needs of different groups and good contacts with voluntary groups.

Effective 'mainstreaming' of equalities should make it a day-to-day management responsibility. Officers with equalities responsibilities can play a number of roles:

- Ensure that at least one member of senior management has responsibilities and support to protect and promote equalities.

---

[439] Local Government Management Board. (1998) Equality control.
[440] Ibid.

- Make sure that equalities is a part of local priorities and objectives.
- Work with service managers to help them put in place the service outcomes and performance measures that will deliver equalities.

The CRE's Standards for Racial Equality

The Commission of Racial Equality, in its publication *Racial equality means quality*, "sets out the quality standards for local government in the pursuit of racial equality".[441]

The Racial Equality Standard sets up a common framework for the development of racial equality that can be used by all local authorities. It aims to bring racial equality into the mainstream of local government. The Standard is a mechanism for self-assessment and forward planning. The Standards are applicable in authorities with large as well as small ethnic minority populations.

CRE emphasises three elements needed to ensure that equal opportunity policies are working: commitment, action and outcome. These are crucial elements in any racial equal opportunity policy but often tend to be ignored in practice.

The CRE Standards are a major programme to achieving race equality in action. Not only does it set out the legal, quality and other justifications for implementing the Standards, it also sets out tools to measure outcomes. There are five levels of achievements that represent progress on racial equality in five areas. While the Standard is defined at a corporate level, it needs to be applied at departmental level, in this case in Libraries. The five areas are:

- Policy & planning
- Service delivery and customer care
- Community development
- Employment (Recruitment & selection)
- Employment (Developing and retaining staff)
- Marketing and corporate image

Within each area are set out five levels of achievements and planning processes that should make it possible to facilitate planned progress to a higher level of achievement.

Stephen Lawrence Inquiry

There are 24 recommendations in the Macpherson Inquiry report, which are relevant to local government either directly or indirectly. These recommendations encompass: employment; training and development; community safety; education; housing; consultation; community leadership and social exclusion.

For local authorities to avoid the charge of institutional racism, workforces and committee structures should represent the talents and abilities of all sections of the community; quality services, sensitive to the needs of different communities or groups, should be provided; an effective consultation practices and working relationships with black and other minority ethnic communities should be in place.[442]

---

[441] Commission for Racial Equality (CRE) 1995: Racial equality means quality; a standard for racial equality for local government in England and Wales. London: CRE.
[442] Stephen Lawrence Inquiry: Home Secretary's Action Plan (1999): op. cit.

Lessons for Public Libraries

In *Returning a stare; People's Struggles for Political and Social Inclusion*,[443] we looked at the struggles of people from different parts of the world—Chile, India, Kenya, Zapatistas, the Kurdish people, among others—to "return the stare" and resist various forms of social oppression and economic exploitation. There are various lessons for public libraries if they are to play a role in these struggles. These are recorded below:

Risk and danger in professional work

It is obvious that no public library will be able to document openly state oppression against its own people. Yet it is important that library workers do not use this as an excuse for not recording, preserving and making available, at a later stage, records of events taking place around them. The film crew in Chile managed to do this and there are obvious risks they faced. But if library workers are part of the people they seek to serve, they face similar risks anyway. If they cannot become activist-librarians, the least they could do is to join hands with activists to ensure that the library's functions are kept in the forefront of the struggle. Perhaps library and information workers need to study the examples of journalists who often risk their lives in the course of their professional work. The concept of risk and danger in professional work needs to be incorporated in the core values of the LIS profession if it is to be socially relevant.

Multi-media approach

Libraries need to pay more attention to forms other than printed books: radio broadcasts, sound recordings, photographs, video filming, recording and preserving oral histories should become important forms that they actively collect and promote.

Underground and alternative material

Public Libraries need to pay attention to underground and alternative material, which are essential for people struggling for change. The possibilities of cheap and easy means of communication that the Web and e-communications allow need to be harnessed by libraries to acquire, store and disseminate information that the struggling people consider relevant. Those who are active in the struggle have already adopted these technologies as tools for their struggles. If libraries are to be considered partners in the people's struggles, they will need to accept the new media, not to satisfy the business and other needs of the "already rich", but for the needs of the socially excluded.

Less Euro/U.S.A. Centric Approach

Public Libraries in Britain and other "developed" countries need to examine their work practices, outlook, and mission statements with a view to making them less Euro/U.S.A.-centric. There is an assumption in the profession that the "Western" model of public libraries is the best. This model has failed to stop the exclusion of perhaps a third or more of our populations from the informational world. It is time

---

[443] Durrani, Shiraz (1999): Returning a stare; People's Struggles for Political and Social Inclusion. Open to All? The Public library and social exclusion. (2000) Vol. 3: Working Paper, 6. op. cit.

we asked for some technical expertise from those majority world countries which have had more success than ourselves in providing a relevant educational and information service.

Library service for working class

We need to question and challenge the static role that public libraries have acquired in Britain. The class bias in public libraries is analysed by Pateman[444] who says:

> "There is plenty of evidence to suggest that, while public libraries are used by all social classes, they are predominantly middle class institutions...; the service is managed and operated by middle class people who share their middle class values with middle class library users".

Needs-led approach

LIS is a sanitised profession that wants to keep away from getting involved in people's struggles, that wants to remain "neutral" while those with power and wealth gobble up an ever-increasing proportion of library budgets. Again a comparison with another profession may help to understand our real situation: NHS doctors insist on the best medicine for their patients irrespective of their financial or social standing. What matters is the needs of the patients. The library profession needs to come up with a similar "needs-led" approach to satisfying the information needs of people.

A dynamic approach

Public libraries need to see themselves as part of the society as a whole. People's struggles for social justice and economic liberation are waged at various levels: political, economic, social, cultural and educational. Communications can be at the heart of these struggles, linking all the different struggles and providing a basic support mechanism. Any search for relevance will need to explore this dynamic role of libraries.

Library workers will need to become activists in the various struggles of the people. Only thus will they become relevant to the people they serve and avoid the one-dimensional approach that is the rule today. There needs to be a new debate about what being a "professional" means.

Links with people's struggles

Public Libraries need to become friends to all those who have *No friends but mountains*. This can happen only when they establish active relationships and communications links with people's struggles. The real solution would be to recruit people from these struggles as librarians and information workers. Perhaps then we can start making links at the national and international level with the struggles of different people. Perhaps then we can start breaking down the "what's it got to do with me" mentality among a large number of middle class library professionals.

---

[444] Pateman, John (1999): Open to all?. op. cit.

ICT to support people's struggles

The Zapatistas' ability to grasp, with enthusiasm, new communications technologies and use them actively for their struggles holds a lesson for libraries.

Conclusion

Public libraries are in danger of serving the needs of only a section of "the public". A large proportion of the population is not reached by the public library service. These include many working class people, as well as large proportions of Black and Other Minority Ethnic people who make up almost half the population in many boroughs. They are hit additionally in being excluded from the educational institutions as well. Public Libraries had they been "open" to Black people, can provide a way for such people to find a way to overcome the forces of exclusion surrounding them. But this is not the case and the excluded remain excluded from education, from information and from any possibilities of a meaningful change.

Too often, the blame for this exclusion is placed on the shoulders of the excluded. On the whole, racism can be eliminated but only when victims of racism are empowered or empower themselves to combat racism in libraries as in other spheres of life. In the final analysis, racism survives on the basis of the powerlessness of its victims. In the information field, power is held by members of the entrenched white middle class most of whom are not committed to equality. They do not personally, or as a class, suffer from effects of racism, and thus do not play an active part in combating it. Their narrow professional and social outlook ensures a blinkered approach in policy as well as in practice. Their power base ensures that any individual or group attempting to challenge racism is "put in their place". Thus the question of racism is closely related to the question of power and class. The resolution of racism is dependent on the elimination of exploitation and oppression generally from the society.

In the meantime, until Black communities possess power to eliminate racism, legal and structural frameworks are essential in order to combat racism. The recommendations from the research of Roach and Morrison, from the Lawrence Inquiry Report, the CRE's *Standard for racial equality for local government in England and Wales*, as well as the Government's initiatives on social exclusion and Annual Library Plans provides a basis for such a framework. In addition, a stronger Race Relation Act will also be necessary as there is little hope for a change without some compulsion.

Incorporating reflective learning ... in information management (2007)[445]

Incorporating Reflective Learning: rationale and initiatives in a programme on information management (2007)

While reflective learning has been recognised as an important pedagogical tool, a number of areas need development. These included the necessity for "integration between theory and practice".[446] The need to put theory into practice from a critical and informed perspective is of increasing significance in a rapidly globalised world requiring new skills among citizens. The development of transferable intellectual and study skills within a lifelong learning context is equally important.

Reflective learning is implicit in one of the four main purposes of higher education as seen by the Dearing Committee: "to inspire and enable individuals to develop their capabilities to the highest potential levels throughout life".[447]

The need for incorporating reflective learning has now been well accepted in pedagogical terms. Indeed, it is a course requirement set by the Quality and Assurance Agency:

> There should be integration between theory and practice by a variety of means according to the type of degree and mode of delivery... The strategy should make available opportunities for participants to reflect on their knowledge, experience and practice... A dissertation or project can be particularly important in this context.[448]

Bourner defines reflective learning as the "process of interrogating experience with searching questions" and provides a useful background to reflective learning, setting it within the context of lifelong learning which is then seen in its dual aspects, planned and unplanned learning. "Much learning across the lifespan is unplanned, experiential and emergent", he says, explaining that it is "reflection which turns experience into learning".[449]

The application of these ideas to teaching and learning has important practical implications. The first one is whether lecturers themselves are reflective, lifelong learners and whether they incorporate such learning in their teaching. As the UK Centre for Legal Education says, "it is extremely difficult to encourage students to

---

[445] Investigations. vol. 4 (i) Autumn 2006/07. ISSN 1740-5106. http://www.londonmet.ac.uk/capd/in-house-journal-investigations/home.cfm.
[446] Quality Assurance Agency (QAA, 2002): Masters Awards in business and management. Subject Benchmark Statements. Quality Assurance Agency for Higher Education. [online]. Available from: www.qaa.ac.uk/academicinfrastructure/benchmark/masters/mba.pdf . [Assessed: 14 May, 2006].
[447] Dearing (1997): National Committee of Inquiry into Higher Education. Available from: www.leeds.ac.uk/educol/ncihe/. [Accessed 15 May, 2006].
[448] Quality Assurance Agency (QAA, 2002): op. cit.
[449] Bourner, Tom (2003): Assessing reflective learning. Education + Training. Vol. 45(5) 267-272.

learn reflectively unless the lecturer embodies such an approach".[450] DASS has taken up this challenge seriously:

> ... For us to provide appropriate teaching and learning opportunities to the students, we ourselves need to be aware of the issues and also ensure that these are reflected in our curricula.[451]

Secondly, all modules need to be re-assessed critically to ensure they meet the reflective learning requirements. It will not be effective if only a few modules incorporate reflective learning. Further, it will give an incorrect impression to students as to what learning is all about.

Another aspect that needs to be addressed is that reflective and critical learning can take place only if students enjoy lectures and other aspects of the learning process. For their part, students are keen to learn from new ideas and experiences if delivered in a creative way. The challenge is whether such enjoyment and reflective learning can be embedded in all modules.

"Lack of a learning culture"

The information and library sector needs effective leaders who can regenerate the services in order to meet the needs in a rapidly changing world. Libraries, according to Leadbeater, are in "serious trouble".[452] He maintains that, "public service renewal requires strong political leadership...Libraries lack such leadership". One way of injecting leadership is a wider use of reflective learning.

MLA recognizes that "lack of a learning culture is the single most important barrier to developing the workforce". MLA, London expands on this:

> Learning is a process of active engagement with experience. It is what people do when they want to make sense of the world. It may involve the development or deepening of skills, knowledge, understanding, awareness, values, ideas and feelings, or an increase in the capacity to reflect. Effective learning leads to change, development and the desire to learn more.[453]

Thus the challenge for information management courses is to ensure that they inculcate reflective learning among students as a lifelong learning process. However, this is not always possible within the formal teaching environment. The limit on time, the need to cover large topic areas and meet complex learning outcomes often leave little time to ensure that effective reflective learning takes place.

Another area that has not been adequately addressed in the information sector is innovation. Mulgan and Albury define innovation as "the creation and implementation of new processes, products, services and methods of delivery which

---

[450] The UK Centre for Legal Education (UKCLE) (1995): Aiding reflective practice. Available from: http://www.ukcle.ac.uk/resources/assessment/guide/reflective.html. [Accessed 16 October, 2005].
[451] Ideas and Issues in Social Exclusion. No. 1 (October, 2006). Internal newsletter of the Department of Applied Social Sciences, London Metropolitan University.
[452] Leadbeater, Charles (2003): Overdue; how to create a modern public library service. Laser Foundation Report. London: Demos. Available from:
http://www.demos.co.uk/publications/overdue. [Accessed: 7 March 2006].
[453] Museums, Libraries and Archives Council, London (2006): ALM London Workforce Development Strategy. Creating skills, supporting development and championing diversity. Available at: http://www.mlalondon.org.uk/lmal/index.cfm?NavigationID=309. [Accessed: 30 December 2006].

result in significant improvements in outcomes, efficiency, effectiveness or quality".[454] Perhaps the best way of teaching "innovation skills" — as with leadership skills — is through reflective learning.

It is to meet the above requirements that Information Management Services (ISM) is developing an alternative approach to embed reflective learning in their work.

Information Services Management: Changes in Modules

A number of changes were made in 2006 to existing modules. One reason was to incorporate reflective learning in the teaching programmes.

The rationale given for the proposed modification was to "meet the changing needs in the workplace as expressed in various policy initiatives at national and international levels". Modification also reflected "the need to ensure reflective learning among students" and to ensure "workforce development to meet new challenges as an on-going process".[455]

This new approach included the production of *Ideas and Issues* for students. It is "an irregular current awareness service which alerts you to new ideas, experiences, reports and developments of relevance to the modules. It is meant to supplement the recommended readings and lecture notes for your modules. *Ideas & Issues* aims to give you a wider perspective and increase your awareness about current developments".[456]

Ideas and Issues highlights the need to keep up with new information during the course of the module, as well as when students return to work. At the same time, students are expected to reflect on matter included in *Ideas and Action* and to develop this new information in the weekly seminars and in assignments. Crucial part in this is played by the weekly seminars where "each student is expected to contribute to one debate on one issue". This activity is designed to:

> build up the skills necessary in presenting a persuasive argument... Active participation in seminars will enhance your learning and provide a greater depth and perspective to the issues raised in lectures.[457]

Short course

The "Leadership for innovation, equality and change; a two day 'Ideas into Action' Short Course" takes reflective learning a stage further. It includes some initial pre-course reading, a first day dealing with theoretical issue, and a follow-up day where the emphasis is on reflective learning through implementation of ideas and action plans developed on day one. The draft publicity explains:

> The second day will build on the work of the first day. It will use actual workplace situations to develop action plans based on ideas and experiences from the first day. Each participant will develop an "Ideas into Action" plan. These will be discussed to understand issues around leadership, roles and responsibilities.

---

[454] Mulgan, Geoff and Albury, David (2003): "Innovation in the public sector". Prime Minister's Strategy Unit, Strategy Unit, Cabinet Office. Discussion Paper. Available from: http://www.strategy.gov.uk/downloads/files/pubinov2.pdf. [Accessed 7 March, 2006].
[455] London Metropolitan University. Department of Applied Social Sciences (2006): "ISM. Minor modification proforma". (internal document, May 2006).
[456] Ideas & Issues, 2006. op. cit.
[457] Society, Information and Policy. Module Booklet CMP068N. 2006-2007. DASS.

> The Course offers a place to think, a place to be creative, a place to plan... and act...The Course will thus help you to become more aware of alternative ideas. It will provide opportunities for reflective learning from reports and journal articles and your and other people's experiences.[458]

Thus the approach is to move away from "traditional" training days, which stop at imparting new information. This normally means that the learning process is rather limited as participants are then caught up in daily workplace activities with the new things learnt being pushed to the background by pressures of work. The Short Course uses an active learning and reflection approach — which continues after the formal course — to overcome these shortcomings.

Conclusion

The above is only a beginning of a process of incorporating reflective learning in new and revised modules and projects. An "open" approach to learning from other experiences and ideas is used to ensure that the latest theories are being incorporated.

Learning by doing: lifelong learning through innovations projects at DASS (2007)[459]

The learning and teaching environment

Learning and teaching programmes, such as the Information Management ones housed at the Department of Applied Social Sciences (DASS) at the London Metropolitan University, have a particular responsibility in developing an appropriate learning culture among students even as they develop their knowledge, skills, and awareness. This is given greater seriousness by three linked challenges facing British society and the workplace today — at a social-economic, pedagogical, and workforce development level. This first section looks at these challenges, whilst the following sections examine two projects, which can be seen as a way of addressing the challenges — these are the Quality Leaders Project[460] and the Progressive African Library and Information Activists' Group (PALIAct).[461]

Globalisation and the Information Society

The first challenge facing British society, and its teaching institutions, is the process of globalisation influenced by, and in turn influencing, information technology. While it is not intended to explore this in depth in this paper, it is necessary to be clear about what the process means and what it implies for institutions such as ours.

Castells' explanation on globalisation is still valid. He saw it as:

---

[458] Unpublished Department of Applied Social Sciences (DASS) file.
[459] ASLIB Proceedings. Vol. 59(2) pp. 187 – 200. March 2007.
[460] For further details see: http://www.seapn.org.uk/qlp.html.
[461] For further details see: http://www.seapn.org.uk/PALIAct-new.html

> ... [a] technological revolution, centred around information (which) has transformed the way we think, we produce, we consume, we trade, we manage, we communicate, we live, we die, we make war, and we make love: a dynamic global economy has been constituted around the planet, linking up valuable people and activities from all over the world, while switching off from the networks of the power and wealth, people and territories dubbed as irrelevant from the perspectives of dominant interests.[462]

Sivanandan explored the wider impact of these changes:

> The technological revolution of the past three decades has resulted in a qualitative leap in the productive forces to the point where capital is no longer dependent on labour in the same way as before, to the same extent as before, in the same quantities as before and in the same place as before. Its assembly lines are global, its plant is movable, its workforce is flexible. It can produce ad hoc, just in time, and custom-build mass production, without stockpiling or wastage, laying off labour as and when it pleases. And, instead of importing cheap labour, it can move to the labour pools of the Third World, where labour is captive and plentiful and move from one labour pool to another, extracting maximum surplus value from each, abandoning each when done.[463]

Kundnani sees "the economic paradigms of the industrial age in the process of being replaced by new paradigms of the globalised, information age". He notes:

> Developments in information technology since the 1970s have made possible new forms of economic organisation in both manufacturing and also in media industries, which have undergone substantial changes in the last twenty years.[464]

The IBM Community Development Foundation report defines the term "Information Society" in terms of its economic contribution:

> ...the creation, distribution, and manipulation of information has become the most significant economic and cultural activity. An Information Society may be contrasted with societies in which the economic underpinning is primarily industrial or agricultural. The tools of the Information Society are computers and telecommunications. ... [Information Society is] characterised by a high level of information intensity in the everyday life of most citizens, in most organisations and workplaces, by the use of common or compatible technology for a wide range of personal, social, educational and business activities, and by the ability to transmit, receive and exchange digital data rapidly between places irrespective of distance.[465]

These developments in globalisation have a profound impact on the form and content of teaching and learning in all disciplines. However, this impact is the greatest in the information sector in particular as the developments affect the very core of the teaching programmes and affects the skills necessary for students to survive in an increasingly globalised world. It is the course content and the very process of learning, the how and the what, that need to be constantly re-examined and made more relevant to today's reality.

The constant examination and changing of the learning process is particularly necessary in all natural and social sciences as it is here that more rapid changes take

---

[462] Castells, Manuel (1998): The power of identity. Oxford, Blackwell.
[463] Sivanandan, S. (1999): Globalism and the Left. Race & Class, Vol. 40 No. 2/3, pp. 5-19.
[464] Kundnani, A. (1999): Where do you want to go today? The rise of information capital. Race & Class, Vol. 40 No. 2/3, pp. 49-71.
[465] IBM Community Development Foundation (1997): The Net Result — Report of the National Working Party for Social Inclusion, available at:
http://www.britishcouncil.org/ism-info@uk-glossary.htm (accessed 7 March 2006).

place in the context of globalisation. The laws of nature do not change as rapidly and are perhaps easier to quantify and teach. In contrast, social rules are more dynamic and need constant examining and codifying. It is in this dynamic context that the new approach to learning explored in DASS needs to be understood.

Reflective learning

The need for reflective learning for lifelong learning has now come to be recognised as an important tool in the teaching and learning field. Bourner sets reflective learning within the context of lifelong learning, which is then seen in its dual aspects: planned and unplanned learning. "Much learning across the lifespan is unplanned, experiential and emergent",[466] he says, explaining that it is "reflection which turns experience into learning". The key idea is that "developing students' capacity for reflective learning is part of developing their capacity to learn how to learn". Bourner concludes by looking at the need in universities to prepare students for lifelong learning "that will comprise reflective learning as well as planned learning".

This has particular application for public libraries, which according to Leadbeater, "are in serious trouble". Leadbeater maintains that, "public service renewal requires strong political leadership…Libraries lack such leadership".[467] One way of injecting leadership is wider use of reflective learning.

The Museums, Libraries and Archives Council (MLA) recognises that "lack of a learning culture is the single most important barrier to developing the workforce" and expands on this:

> Learning is a process of active engagement with experience. It is what people do when they want to make sense of the world. It may involve the development or deepening of skills, knowledge, understanding, awareness, values, ideas and feelings, or an increase in the capacity to reflect. Effective learning leads to change, development and the desire to learn more. The unique resources of museums, libraries and archives offer a range of learning opportunities and support for everyone to engage in learning activity.[468]

Thus the second challenge for information management courses is to ensure that they inculcate reflective learning among students as part of a lifelong learning process. However, this is not always possible within the formal learning and teaching environment at universities. The limit on time and the need to cover large learning outcomes, often leave little time to ensure that effective reflective learning takes place. It is for this reason that the approach taken by the innovations projects at DASS can provide an alternative approach to reflective learning.

Leadership, innovation and workforce development

---

[466] Bourner, T. (2003): Assessing reflective learning. Education + Training, Vol. 45 No. 5, pp. 267-272.
[467] Leadbeater, C. (2003): Overdue; how to create a modern public library service". Laser Foundation Report, Demos, London, available at:
http://www.demos.co.uk/publications/overdue (accessed 7 March 2006).
[468] Museums, Libraries and Archives Council, London (2006): ALM London Workforce Development Strategy. *Creating skills, supporting development and championing diversity.* Available at: http://www.mlalondon.org.uk/lmal/index.cfm?NavigationID=309[Accessed: 30 December 2006].

The final challenge is to ensure that personal and organisational development takes place on an on-going basis in keeping with an ever-changing social reality. This can be ensured through developing leadership skills in students who will be the future leaders in the information profession. The need to constantly innovate requires appropriate skills among students and this also needs to be part of the learning and teaching process at universities.

This is linked with the need for "workforce development". Thus, MLA's Workforce Development Strategy has four overarching strategic objectives as explained by Museums, Libraries and Archives Council:

1. A workforce fit for purpose: with the challenge of diversifying the workforce composition identified as the key priority.
2. Enhancing leadership and workforce skills: addressing skills, knowledge, attitudes and behaviour throughout the workforce; enabling museums, libraries and archives to adapt and respond to new and emerging modernizing agendas.
3. Empowering learning and change: with the biggest barrier to change identified as the lack of a learning culture in the sector and the organizations.
4. Research for action: with the challenge being the lack of robust, usable workforce data and in-depth research to enable museums, libraries and archives to make a strong case for investment to key funding bodies.[469]

If such strategies are to lead to meaningful action, information courses need to address issues raised in the above objectives. In addition, innovation is one area that has not been adequately addressed in the information sector. As Mulgan and Albury say:

> Innovation should be a core activity of the public sector: it helps public services to improve performance and increase public value; respond to the expectations of citizens and adapt to the needs of users; increase service efficiency and minimise costs.[470]

Mulgan and Albury also provide a useful definition of innovation:

> Successful innovation is the creation and implementation of new processes, products, services and methods of delivery, which result in significant improvements in outcomes efficiency, effectiveness or quality.[471]

Yet it is not easy to teach such "innovation" within the context of a modular learning environment.

It is in the above context that the rest of this paper looks at two projects run by the information management team in DASS. This does not imply that the projects are the only way in which the challenges mentioned above are addressed. Other initiatives

---

[469] Museums, Libraries and Archives Council (2004): Learning for Change: Workforce Development Strategy, London, available at: http://www.mla.gov.uk/resources/assets//W/wfd_learning_for_change_pdf_5661.pdf (accessed 15 October 2005).

[470] Mulgan, G. and Albury, D. (2003): Innovation in the Public Sector. Prime Minister's Strategy Unit, Cabinet Office. Discussion Paper, available at: http://www.strategy.gov.uk/downloads/files/pubinov2.pdf (accessed 7 March 2006).

[471] Ibid.

include the development of a short course, for example on "Leadership for innovation, equality and change" and the new Masters-level module entitled "Information for Development". Thus the projects below need to be seen as aspects of an on-going realignment of contents of various existing modules and the creation of new ones. Further discussions are also taking place within DASS to develop a Department-wide modular programme, which would offer all DASS modules on a pick-and-mix basis to meet varied learning needs among different organisations and individuals.

The Quality Leaders Project — Youth

The Quality Leaders Project—Youth (QLP-Y) is an externally funded project based in DASS, working closely with the University's Management Research Centre (MRC).

QLP is a work-based learning and developmental programme, which uses the approach "management development through service development". It requires joint work between relevant local authority departments and their local communities. It provides skills, support, and experience to "quality leaders" and their teams in participating authorities. It also develops innovative, relevant services for young people based on consultation. Each authority releases a Quality Leader (QL) for at least two days a week, as well as a diverse team working with the QL. In addition, the authority provides a mentor and a sponsor to support the QL. One of the roles of the mentor is establishing the learning needs of the Quality Leader. Actual learning, especially reflective learning, is then assessed by the QLP Steering Group when the mentors submit regular feedback forms for which "mentors' guidance notes" have been provided.

The project started in 1999. Its feasibility study and pilot phase were funded by the Museum, Libraries and Archives Council (MLA). QLP was "highly commended" in the Organisational Change category of the Diversity Awards by the Chartered Institute of Library and Information Professionals.[472] In 2005, the Mayor of London's Commission on African and Asian Heritage also acknowledged the contribution of QLP.[473]

QLP-Y produces *QLP News*, as well as an irregular newsletter, *Youth Ideas & Action*, which provide an update on the project as well as developments in youth work and staff development. Copies of these, together with other material such as the feasibility and pilot phase reports, conference presentations, and journal articles are available on the QLP website.[474]

QLP-Youth – the current strand

The current strand of QLP-Youth is in two phases. The first, six-month, phase was funded by the National Youth Agency. During this period, participants from youth

---

[472] CILIP (2003): CILIP Rewards Outstanding Achievement in Promoting Diversity and Challenging Inequality, CILIP, London, available from:
http://www.cilip.org.uk/aboutcilip/newsandpressreleases/archive2003/news031121e.htm (accessed 30 July 2006).
[473] Mayor of London (2005): Delivering Shared Heritage; the London Mayor's Commission on African and Asian Heritage. Mayor of London, London, p. 35, The QLP section available at: http://www.seapn.org.uk/qlp_extract.doc (accessed 7 March 2006).
[474] QLP website is at: http://www.seapn.org.uk/qlp.html.

and library authorities were given project management skills and they devised service development proposals in consultation with young people. The second phase lasts for two years during which the service development proposals will be put into practice. This phase is funded by the Paul Hamlyn Foundation and started with a Development Day on 13 October, 2005, at DASS. Youth and library services from Barnet, Haringey, Lincolnshire and Portsmouth are participating in the programme.

The programme places equal emphasis on developing staff as on developing services, as one is seen as strengthening the other. Skills being developed include the delivery of "audience development" workshops. These seek to increase the reach of libraries and youth services to meet the needs of all young people, particularly refugees and asylum seekers and those who have not been reached before. Audience development is a more inclusive term than "reader development". It allows for connecting people to a learning and "reading experience" through non-print media, such as arts, cinema, music, drama and other cultural activities. It involves all the senses. Thus, the Quality Leaders develop their skills in consultation, in project management, and in organising new services, which involves partnership work. Emphasis is placed on self-learning, particularly through reflective learning. At the service delivery level, the programme aims to provide regular workshop sessions for young people in activities such as the ones mentioned below, the final choice being made by the young people themselves through an intensive consultation process:

- presentations from writers, poets, film makers, media and other professionals;
- production of youth magazines by young people themselves;
- websites designed and maintained by young people;
- music workshops, book and newsletter production sessions, radio broadcast workshops, film and video making modules;
- podcasting;
- organising guest speakers (including young people themselves) from different fields so as to enable the young people to meet potential role models from diverse communities and different fields.

As part of the funding arrangements, each participating authority is provided with a small budget to run audience development workshops and for the purchase of basic equipment. Whereas a "normal" teaching course at universities would find it difficult to impart skills in such a diverse range of activities, it is an integral part of QLP-Y.

On a long-term basis, there is scope for research to develop the "management development through service development" concept further, assess its effectiveness, and extend the scope of the project. Publishing a "QLP Manual" to capture all management and service development ideas and experiences is already being actively considered. QLP, as a model, has the potential of developing its approach so that it can be offered to a larger number of authorities within Britain. There is also a possibility of extending the programme to other fields where it is felt there is a need for improvement in staff skills or service, for example skills in delivering health information. In the past it has been used for developing staff skills and services to Black and Ethnic Minority communities, while the current strand addresses youth services and skills and includes refugees and asylum seekers.

CILIP, MLA and the London Mayor's Commission are among organizations, which have expressed an interest in QLP. A group of librarians from Sweden came to

London in 2005 to learn more about the QLP approach to developing services to marginalised and excluded social groups.

Durrani and Bartlett explain the rational of the QLP approach:

> The Public Library Service in Britain needs a major shift in its very mindset. It is sometimes assumed that the role of the public library never changes and remains the same as it has done for over 150 years. Whether the current service is relevant to meet current needs is an issue that requires urgent resolve. Questions such as: "What are libraries for?" "Who do they serve?" "What services are needed?" "What is the best way of providing these services?"... are increasingly raised by policy makers and people on whose behalf services are provided. The questions have become even more urgent in the context of rapid changes in information and communications technologies and the tremendous rate of change in every aspect of our lives.[475]

Percival looks at the service development aspect of QLP-Y:

> I believe that QLP-Youth will make a significant contribution to our library service, by increasing levels of participation by young people, empowering them by giving them the confidence to air their views, and most importantly ensure that they are taken seriously. For far too long, public libraries in Britain have been run from above, with only the views of an extant readership taken into account. QLP-Y gives young people a real chance to affect change from below and I sincerely believe that a change in the way libraries deliver their services to young people and other socially excluded groups will help bring about the fundamental social changes in wider society that we all desire.[476]

However, such service development cannot take place unless there is development in staff skills and learning at the same time — and that is what QLP-Y is all about.

QLP-Y approaches staff and service development for young people within the context of national policy framework, both from library and youth services aspects. In order to make this possible, a dedicated post of "Lecturer in Youth Policy" has been established in the Department of Applied Social Sciences. It is the responsibility of this post-holder to ensure that all relevant youth policies are reflected in all aspects of QLP-Y work. She also researches on practices in youth services in libraries and youth services and prepares a "good practice" guide. Such policy and practical experiences are then circulated to all through the irregular *QLP Youth Ideas and Issues*, in the various presentations at Development Days and included in the draft "QLP Manual" as a way of embedding relevant ones in QLP-Y programmes.

QLP-Y is currently in the process of appointing external evaluators who will look at the real impact of this new approach to learning and skill development. Among the aspects examined reflective learning achieved by QLs will be included, as well as the overall impact of QLP-Y in changing services and cultures in local authorities. If funds allow, it will also include an analysis of learning achieved through QLP-Y as compared with other projects such as Mosside Powerhouse and Blackburn's Curve. DASS, by supporting initiatives such as QLP, is clearly exploring alternative methods of providing a new learning environment, which meets the needs in a changing environment. At the same time, the QLP approach combines the theories of learning and teaching and of service and project development with practice, thereby ensuring

---

[475] Durrani, Shiraz and Bartlett, Dean (2004): Young people in control. *Public Library Journal.* Autumn, No. 2, pp. 22-25.
[476] Percival, Dave (2005): Libraries, young people and QLP-Y". Bibliotek i Samhälle (BiS: Libraries in Society), available at: http://www.seapn.org.uk/dpercival_youthlibs0905.rtf (accessed 3 November 2005).

a longer-term, better embedded learning process which can be useful in other circumstances as well. Successful candidates also achieve a diploma in work-based learning, which requires evidence of new skills and learning acquired through participating in the programme.

One example of the QLP programme influencing other aspects of teaching is the module "Combating racism, managing equality". This was initially designed for the first phase of QLP-Y, but has since been incorporated in the MA module "Information and Social Exclusion". This places particular emphasis on reflective learning as it is built up over several months with discussions, relevant readings, and discussions relating to reality in workplaces.

Progressive African Library and Information Activists' Group (PALIAct)

The African Progressive Librarian and Information Activists' Group (PALIAct) is a DASS initiative in partnership with a group of progressive African librarians and information workers. DASS has played a crucial role to bring together a number of progressive information activists from Africa by providing a new vision based on experiences of progressive librarians and political activists in Africa, Europe and the U.S.A. It is part of the progressive librarians groups around the world, perhaps the most prominent one being the Progressive Librarians Guild in the U.S.A. with its publication *Progressive Librarian*. A brief history of PALIAct is available in Durrani.[477]

Just as QLP-Y is an attempt to develop relevant skills and competencies in staff to deliver a relevant service to young people, PALIAct is a similar attempt at an international level. It has not developed to the same extent as QLP-Y, but has attracted a great deal of interest as seen in press coverage in a short period of time. At the same time, a pilot project is being established in Kenya and this has already set some ambitious targets. It has not only developed new skills and provided valuable experiences to PALIAct staff, but the Kenya Centre, in partnership with the Network Institute for Global Democratization (NIGD) based in Helsinki and with the Kenya Library Association, has provided training to librarians in collecting and disseminating information from the World Social Forum, the next one taking place is in Nairobi in January 2007.

PALIAct aims to provide a new vision to help create a people-orientated information service that could meet the information needs of workers and peasants. It works towards providing an anti-imperialist and a Pan African world outlook among African librarians and information workers. It also seeks to set up an alternative information service in partnership with the potential users of the service as a way of showing what needs to be done. PALIAct aims to form partnerships with progressive information and other workers within Africa and overseas. One of its aims is to mainstream this new approach to service and staff development. It thus does not compete with existing service providers, but seeks to inject the spirit of innovation and risk-taking in a field, which remains rather conservative and isolated from social and political forces around it.

PALIAct recognises that there is a public library service in African countries and it does not claim to be the only initiative that seeks to provide a relevant service. For

---

[477] Durrani, Shiraz (2006): Progressive librarianship in Africa, the PALIAct story. *Focus on International Library and Information Work*. Vol. 37 No. 1, pp. 4-8, available at:
http://www.cilip.org.uk/specialinterestgroups/bysubject/international/publications/focus/currentissue.htm. [Accessed: 29 December 2006].

example, the recently concluded XVII Standing Conference of Eastern, Central, & Southern African Library & Information Professionals (SCECSAL XVII), in Dar es Salaam, Tanzania (10-14 July, 2006) attracted twenty-five papers from participants from a large number of countries.[478] At the same time, representatives from the Library Association gave details about the innovative services they offer. For example, the Kenya Country Report mentions some initiatives:

> KLA has over the last ten years been involved with projects aimed at promoting reading and literacy among the disadvantaged urban, peri-urban slums and rural grassroots communities in Kenya. This is in line with the principle of *"Education for All"* and the Millenium [sic] Development Goals, and the related global human rights covenants on access to information and education for all. KLA facilitated the reading promotion project in collaboration with the National Book Development Council of Kenya (NBDC-K) through the East African Book Development Association (EABDA), and the Ministry of Education. During this period, several Children Reading Tents (CRTs) were hosted in primary schools in identified needy rural districts/divisions in Kenya. The primary objective of the CRTs is to develop a desire for reading for children in their formative years for lifelong education, and to improve on their literacy and numeracy skills, thus enhancing their capacity for creative and life skills, and empowering them to cope with the different subjects for educational attainment.[479]

PALIAct does not aim to replace or challenge the existing library associations and services. It is seeking active partnerships with them and with other stakeholders, as the challenge of developing a relevant service requires close cooperation from all. In fact, PALIAct in Kenya worked in partnership in delivering a training programme for librarians from Kenya and Uganda to prepare them for the World Social Forum (WSF) taking place in Nairobi in January 2007. The purpose of the workshop was:

> ...to prepare and train librarians for participation in the World Social Forum 20-25 January 2007, and in the WSF process, both as citizens and in their role as information specialists. This particular workshop should also be useful for trainers, who will themselves prepare and train more librarians for participation in the WSF.[480]

This approach shows how PALIAct aims to develop an alternative model of information services to ensure development for working people. But such initiatives remain at the margin of policies and practices of current information services. While many information services are now looking at ways of meeting changed information needed in a fast changing world, they are incapable of bringing about the major changes in the way information services are provided. Their inability stems from a complex set of reasons, ranging from historical factors to lack of effective leadership skills among many current senior managers and decision makers. For various reasons,

---

[478] The Conference Proceedings are available at: http://www.tlatz.org/scecsal2006/Volume1.pdf. (Accessed 29 July 2006).
[479] Gitachu, R. (2006): Kenya Library Association (KLA): Kenya Country Report, 2004-2006. Presented during SCECSAL business meeting held on 14 JULY 2006 in Dar es Salaam, Tanzania, available at: http://www.tlatz.org/scecsal2006/COUNTRY%20REPORT.html (accessed 29 July 2006).
[480] The WSF goes to the library (2006). Available at: http://www.nigd.org/libraries/bamako-nairobi. The quoted text is written by Mikael Böök for the "Training the trainers, WSF Workshop for librarians" 3-5 July, Nairobi. The Workshop proceedings are available at: http://www.nigd.org/libraries/bamako-nairobi/tot-workshop/. [Accessed: 29 July, 2006].

they are not active in the one area that is an essential requirement for any meaningful change to take place: becoming politically involved in developing an information service that is based on creating and delivering a vision of service based on meeting the needs of the majority of people. This may sometimes require the profession to challenge those in power, which is difficult in any situation, but particularly so in an African context. It is this political aspect that PALIAct seeks to incorporate in its work. It is in this aspect, among others, that it hopes to provide an alternative model of information service.

Another important point, which distinguishes PALIAct, is that it seeks to develop a new, participative model that can be applied differently in different situations. It does not seek to impose a "universal model" in all countries or even in different parts of the same country. Local activists, working closely with communities, decide what services are relevant for meeting their local needs. In Kenya, for example, there are already two centres—one in Nairobi and one in Naivasha, each working out relevant services for their local communities.

A key point to be noted about PALIAct is the term "activists" which takes it away from a strong focus on "professionals" that is so important for current information services. Thus PALIAct works with activists from other fields, such as medicine and agriculture among others. Thus the Naivasha Centre in Kenya is planning to work with local artisans, architects, and designers in their proposals for developing a community information, education, and culture centre.

Further thoughts on ideas that have influenced the PALIAct approach in developing an alternative, anti-imperialist information service are provided by Durrani.[481] PALIAct puts into practice several ideas on reflective learning developed in the first part of the paper. Those involved in PALIAct do not attend any formal classes where they acquire new information, knowledge, or new skills. Their learning is almost entirely through a reflective process, aided by workshops, discussions, readings, and increased awareness of new ideas and practices (for example, through *PALIAct Ideas and Issues*, now renamed *Information Equality, Africa*). Weekly workshops, discussion and learning meetings are an integral learning process for the Naivasha Centre in Kenya. The WSF workshop mentioned earlier is yet another example of such reflective learning. In this case, the evidence for the actual learning is the group's input in the World Social Forum meeting in Nairobi in January 2007. In all cases, the evidence that any learning takes places is in the actual delivery of new services as judged by the communities served.

Some early experiences from the Kenya PALIAct Centre

Plans to establish a community library at Maua Primary School in Naivasha

PALIAct activists in Kenya visited the Maua Primary School in February 2006. The community in which the school stands is comprised largely of immigrant farm labourers who have moved to Naivasha from around the country to work in the

---

[481] Durrani, Shiraz (2006): Politics of Information and Knowledge in Africa; the struggle for an information inclusive society in a globalised world. Paper presented at the XVII Standing Conference of Eastern, Central, & Southern African Library & Information Professionals (SCECSAL XVII), Dar es Salaam, Tanzania, 10-14 July 2006, pp. 40-65, available at: http://www.tlatz.org/scecsal2006/Volume1.pdf (accessed 28 July 2006).

flower industry. It is the only school in the community that accommodates all children regardless of where their parents work.

The community and PALIAct agreed to set up a community school that would cater to all children and their parents. It was felt that the library should cater to the entire community. In such a situation, the children would improve their academic performance even more as the parents will also be informed and, one hopes, more receptive to new ideas. They discussed the long-term possibility of purchasing land and building a community educational and cultural centre with a library at the centre. In the meantime, setting up "reading tents" for children was considered as a possible activity that can start in the near future. Students of librarianship will be able to do their work experience in such initiatives and so become more aware of local conditions and needs while developing increased awareness about meeting people's needs.

The Kenya PALIAct Centre is also looking at the possibility of developing health information services among Nairobi slums.

Caterpillar Book Box Project

A meeting was held in London between John Lake and Shiraz Durrani on 20 January at DASS to discuss co-operation between PALIAct and IFLA Public Libraries Standing Committee (IFLA-PLS). Lake is the Secretary of Section 8 of IFLA Public Libraries Standing Committee and Division III, Libraries Serving the General Public. The discussion covered a wide range of areas of co-operation, including the possibility of PALIAct Kenya Centres being involved in the Caterpillar Book Box Project. Lake provides further details about the project:

> One of strategic plans for the next 2 years [for IFLA Public Libraries Section] is to assist with practical steps for librarians and information workers in Africa particularly in relation to the provision of HIV/Aids health information and to continue a pilot mobile library type project called the Caterpillar Book Box to provide books to rural communities in Africa.[482]
>
> The term "Caterpillar Project" was coined from an existing project in Kenya, which was tested in the North (Kenya) and South (rural South Africa) areas of Africa.
>
> The Caterpillar Book Box is a folding case which is 1.8m high on castors for ease of movement and the shelves accommodate approximately 100 books fuelled by a crate depot of approximately 500 books to replenish the stock in circulation... The pilot scheme is located in Koekenaap, which is a very poor farming area where 60 percent of the adults are illiterate and only 30 percent of nine year olds can read. They are too poor to travel the 20 miles to the nearest library. The adults are nomadic as they earn a living during the grape season, which lasts only three months a year before they move in search of other work.
>
> The Caterpillar Book Box is the only access that this community has to books. The children have been very excited by the existence of the first Caterpillar Book Box, which bears the IFLA logo.

---

[482] Lake, J. (2006), "The IFLA Caterpillar Book Box Project", *PALIAct Ideas & Action*, No. 1, pp.2-3, available at: http://www.seapn.org.uk/documents/PALIACTIdeasandActionNo.1Jan06.pdf (accessed 30 July 2006).

When finalised, this cooperation will add a new dimension to the work of PALIAct. It will connect a major international information organization with information and community activists in delivering a service with active participation of local communities. It has the potential of setting a new standard in delivering community-based information services, thereby providing an alternative model to suit African conditions. The real contribution that PALIAct can make to African development can be better seen in the context of the brain drain facing Africa. The Association of University Teachers explains the seriousness of the situation:

> ...roughly 30 percent of Africa's university trained professionals live beyond the continent's borders. Moreover, a recent estimate suggests that up to 50,000 Africans with PhDs are working outside the continent. All of this has occurred at a time in which demand for higher education in Africa is increasing.[483]

It is in this context that PALIAct is attempting to support African professionals in their own countries, helping them to develop their skills to solve their own problems. This will have the effect, it is hoped, not only to fill the gap created through the loss of trained professionals and academics as well as a way of discouraging persistence of brain drain.

Putting ideas into action

It is too early to judge how successful the two projects, QLP and PALIAct, will be in developing lifelong skills of participants. However, valuable lessons are being learnt on the process of learning as well as on issues around developing relevant information-related services.

That DASS has encouraged such projects is an indication of its commitment to innovation in the learning and teaching, and particularly in the information sector. The long-term significance of the two projects discussed above should be seen not only in the context of the specific aims of each project. A crucial aspect of such projects is how and to what extent they influence the "mainstream" learning and teaching programmes in information management. Some examples of how the projects have influenced the teaching programmes have been mentioned.

The first phase of a more fundamental shift in the teaching programme in Information Management was implemented in May 2006 when a number of changes were made in some of the modules taught by the current writer; this involved changing the module titles (and scope) of some modules, and starting a new module entitled "Information for Development."

It is noteworthy that the rational for these changes included the need for incorporating reflective learning in a more formal way. London Metropolitan University explains this further:

> There have been substantial social and technical developments since the modules were introduced. These changes need to be reflected in the learning and teaching environment so as to meet the changing needs in the workplace as expressed in various policy initiatives at national and international levels. Key developments can be summed up as:
>
> - Rapid globalisation and development of the Information Society
> - The need to ensure reflective learning among students

---

[483] Association of University Teachers (2006): Reversing Africa's brain drain". Available at: http://www.aut.org.uk/media/pdf/s/8/ReversingAfricasBrainDrain.pdf. (Accessed 8 March 2006).

- The need to develop effective leadership skills
- The need to innovate in order to meet changing needs
- Workforce development to meet new challenges as an on-going process.

It thus falls on Universities to have a long-term view and vision of the learning and teaching needs that a society faces in order to ensure national and personal well-being. It is their responsibility to meet the needs of the society through developing appropriate and relevant learning and teaching programmes. The proposals for modification and changes in these modules are one such attempt.[484]

One manifestation of changes envisaged in the above is evident in the short course on "Leadership for Innovation, Equality and Change." The learning outcome for this course indicates that reflective learning is an important aspect of the course. The first part of the course deals with the theoretical and policy aspects of the topic. The second part then aims to put the theories learnt into practice through an active reflective learning process. The publicity for the short course provides details of the course:

> The course will equip you with new ideas that you can take to your workplaces. It will help you challenge organisational habits that deaden. It will introduce you to new ideas for effective and creative leadership while enabling you to create your own solutions to your own challenges. It will help you to put your ideas into action. All this will take place in a friendly learning environment offering you opportunities for discussion, debate and reflection. The course offers a place to think, a place to be creative, a place to plan... and act.
>
> Each participant will produce an "Ideas and Action" plan based on their own experiences and real-life situations. You will have an opportunity to present and get feedback on your concerns and plans. In addition, there will be opportunities to set up peer support groups and a network to carry on a dialogue with participants and the course leader after the course so that you will be able to discuss concrete issues and challenges that emerge in your workplace over the coming months. This will be an opportunity to get support for putting into practice ideas developed during the course. A follow-up course can be set up if there is a need to review progress and challenges.
>
> The course will thus help you to become more aware of alternative ideas. It will provide opportunities for reflective learning from reports and journal articles and your and other people's experiences. It will help you become confident leaders taking control of your organisations and workplaces.

The short course itself will be evaluated internally both in terms of take up and in the learning that it enabled participants to achieve.[485]

Prospects

---

[484] London Metropolitan University. Department of Applied Social Sciences (2006): "ISM. Minor modification proforma". (Internal document, May 2006).

[485] London Metropolitan University. Department of Applied Social Sciences (2006). Draft publicity for the short course. It is now part of a new Module, "Innovation and development in Information Service" (Details available at: http://www.londonmet.ac.uk/depts/dass/research/informationsocietyandjustice/teachingandlearning.cfm [Accessed: 07 October 2007].

This paper set out to examine the learning and teaching programmes in information management at DASS. It looked at the changing needs in meeting learning needs in the context of a fast-changing world situation. We examined a number of projects and modules, which seek to address the need for incorporating reflective learning in university courses.

There remain a number of areas that require further research and implementation. Perhaps the key aspect is finding appropriate methods for assessing reflective learning in the projects as well as in modules and short courses. This aspect has been recognised by a number of authorities. For example, Kember et al. conclude that most courses (in the higher education) lack methods for reflective learning.[486] At the same time, the Quality Assurance Agency (QAA) mentions the following as course requirements:

- Benchmarking statement on reflective skills
- Mechanisms to monitor achievement[487]
- Responsive to reflective skills[488]

Similarly, Dearing[489] mentions the need for such learning as issues relevant for employability, lifelong learning and Masters requirements. The work mentioned here is part of an on-going process of change in curriculum development as well as in finding an appropriate method of enhancing the learning and teaching experience. The process includes further research and evaluation to see if the processes described in this article meet the needs of a changing learning and teaching environment.

---

[486] Kember, D; Leung, D.Y.P.; Jones, A. et al. (2000): Development of a questionnaire to measure the level of reflective thinking. *Assessment & Evaluation in Higher Education*, Vol. 25 (4) pp. 381-396.

[487] Quality Assurance Agency (QAA) (2002): Masters Awards in Business and Management. Subject Benchmark Statements, Quality Assurance Agency for Higher Education, available at: www.qaa.ac.uk/academicinfrastructure/benchmark/masters/mba.pdf (assessed 14 May 2006).

[488] Quality Assurance Agency (QAA) (2006): Code of Practice for the Assurance of Academic Quality and Standards in Higher Education. Section 6: Assessment of Students. Draft for Consultation, Quality Assurance Agency for Higher Education, available at: www.qaa.ac.uk/academicinfrastructure/codeOfPractice/section6/draft/COP%20Section%206%20draft.pdf (assessed 14 May 2006).

[489] Dearing (1997): National Committee of Inquiry into Higher Education. Available at: www.leeds.ac.uk/educol/ncihe/ (accessed 15 May 2006).

Changing course content to meet changing needs (2007)[490]

Social information modules and projects

The Department of Applied Social Sciences (DASS) offers a number of modules exploring the social aspects of information. They are offered as part of the Information Services Management (ISM) MA course. This also includes a number of related teaching and learning initiatives.

Rationale

There have been substantial social and technical developments in recent times. These changes need to be reflected in the learning and teaching environment so as to meet the changing needs in the workplace as expressed in various policy initiatives at national and international levels. Key developments can be summed up as:

- Rapid globalisation and development of the Information Society
- The need to ensure reflective learning among students
- The need to develop effective leadership skills
- The need to innovate in order to meet changing needs
- Workforce development to meet new challenges as an on-going process.

While developments in technological aspects of the information and knowledge development are generally well-developed; important social aspects may lag behind, unless teaching and learning programmes keep pace. As the need for skills in the market changes, University teaching is in danger of becoming less attractive if it does not provide the required skills.

At the national level, the Modernising Government White Paper, 1999 highlighted the central role of policies in translating political vision into programmes and actions to deliver 'outcomes' — "desired changes in the real world."[491]

Prof. Hepworth sees the need for change in the role of public libraries: "the emphasis [for public libraries] should shift to whether libraries help governments promote their wider health, educational and social objectives." [492]

Information services are expected to play a key role in this shift in society. This is underpinned by legislative requirements such as the Race Relations (Amendment) Act 2000, the Human Rights Act (1998) and the establishment of the Commission on Equality and Human Rights.

At the international level, the World Summit on the Information Society's (WSIS) Action Plan "sets time-bound targets to turn the vision of an inclusive and equitable Information Society into reality." At WSIS Geneva in December 2003, world leaders

---

[490] Prepared from unpublished Departmental files.
[491] See Policy Hub, available from: <http://www.policyhub.gov.uk/better_policy_making/>. Accessed 19 March, 2006.
[492] Quoted by Ezard, John (2005): "New challenges for libraries outlined". Monday July 4, Guardian. Available from: <http://books.guardian.co.uk/print/0,,5230449-99819,00.html>. Accessed: 19 March, 2006.

declared "our common desire and commitment to build a people-centred, inclusive and development-oriented Information Society, where everyone can create, access, utilize and share information and knowledge, enabling individuals, communities and peoples to achieve their full potential in promoting their sustainable development and improving their quality of life, premised on the purposes and principles of the Charter of the United Nations and respecting fully and upholding the Universal Declaration of Human Rights." [493]

At a wider, global level, recent change has seen the rapid economic and hence political, rise of the BRIC countries (Brazil, Russia, India and China). South and East Asia are fast becoming the engine rooms of the world, with China already having overtaken Britain as the fourth largest economy in the world. In such a rapidly changing situation, it is essential that Universities help Britain maintain its competitive edge in the world. This can be best done by developing a stronger information and knowledge society. Prof. Hepworth explains the role that libraries and information services need to play:

> But while there have been success stories such as the MLA-managed The People's Network... Hepworth thinks that the Internet is "not the same as knowledge. Knowledge is converting that information into something of economic or social value. That's what libraries are there to do and I think more can be built up around the web."
>
> ... Hepworth thinks that libraries, "should be a showcase for the global economy. I can't see another place that can do it." If only more people realised.[494]

These DASS initiatives also seek to address an important gap in the teaching and learning programmes in the information management sector. This is in relation to the fundamental question: "What is information for?" Too often this question is not even raised, or if raised, no coherent answers are explored. Different people with different interests and perspectives respond to this in different ways. The module "Information for Development" explores theories and practices in this area and will also include the aspect of social and human justice within its remit. A new module just introduced — "Innovation and development in information services" — examines the role of leadership and the need for introducing organisational change within the context of meeting "developmental" needs of individuals, communities, and countries. "Information and Social Exclusion" looks at issues of social justice in the context of exclusion from information.

Projects such as the Quality Leaders Project—Youth (QLP-Y)[495] and the Progressive African Library and Information Activists' Group (PALIAct)[496] help to bridge the gaps between theory and practice, between ideas and action, between the academic world and real workplaces.

---

[493] WSIS, Basic information (FAQ). Available from:
<http://www.itu.int/wsis/basic/faqs.asp>. Accessed on: 19 March, 2006.
[494] "Knowledge is an open book" Olav Bjortomt interviews Professor Mark Hepworth. March 29, 2005 . Timesonline. Available from:
<http://www.timesonline.co.uk/printFriendly/0,,1-8247-1544014,00.html>. [Accessed 17 March, 2006].
[495] Details about QLP-Y are available from: http://www.seapn.org.uk/qlp.html.
[496] Details about PALIAct are available from: http://www.seapn.org.uk/PALIAct-new.html

Students, and sometimes employers, may not always be fully aware of the changing needs in a changing world. Nor would they always be in a position to decide what steps are necessary to bring about the desired changes and outcomes.

It thus falls on Universities to have a long-term view and vision of the learning and teaching needs that a society faces in order to ensure national and personal well-being. It is their responsibility to meet the needs of the society through developing appropriate and relevant learning and teaching programmes.

Ideas into action

The facts behind the Three Continents Liberation Collection (1993)[497]

The Three Continents Liberation Collection (TCLC) is in the news once again as the Library Association mentions it in one of its publications. As the lead originator of the project and launch of the TCLC, I wish to take this opportunity to thank all those who belonged to the Core Group, which later expanded and became the TCLC Support Group. It was this Support Group which brought into being in October 1989 the TCLC, once a very vibrant community collection with potential for development in many directions, but today a mere shell of the original vision.

This Core Group consisted of myself, Mackenzie Frank, Ali Tahvildar, Phil Kennedy, Shellarie Nestor, Naila Durrani, S.Gunasingam and Hopeton Dunn. Amongst the many Hackney staff who actively supported the TCLC throughout were Chris Broadhead, Sarah Mosedale, Genny Fernandes, Ram Mittal, Alan Parello, Earl Bailey, Esther Bakari and many, many others. Later on, new staff such as Ayten Storry and Carolyn Hodgson, have given invaluable active support to TCLC. The efforts of all these people were beyond the call of duty and they worked entirely out of their commitment to the aims of the Collection, not because of any requirements in their job descriptions.

A few points about the development of the TCLC can be made here. TCLC is perhaps the only project in the library field in the country, which has been initiated, planned, and implemented entirely by the grassroots staff in the library service with support from committed individuals from other Council Departments and the community. If ever there was a "people's project" TCLC is one, in the fullest sense. Those who were behind the project will bear witness that the biggest challenge was to convince Library's Senior Management about the viability and necessity of the project. Many petty technicalities were raised time and again and had to be struggled against before the project finally took off. A full history will one day record how many good ideas, which were perfectly feasible, could not see the light of day because of the cynicism and total lack of interest and in fact active discouragement from some whose simple agreement could have allowed us to work miracles.

The history of C.L.R. James Library itself is interesting. In common with black people's struggles nationally in the early 1980s, the people of Hackney took to the streets for various grievances, including the need to provide a Library Service that reflected the needs of Black and Ethnic Minorities of Hackney. In response to this demand, the Council decided in 1985 to change the name of one of its Libraries, Dalston Library, to C.L.R. James Library as a commitment that the Library Service will in the future respond to the needs of these communities. Cyril Lionel Robert James has come to symbolise the struggle of Black people throughout the world for their basic rights. For example it was C.L.R. James who gave much publicity to the struggle of Mau Mau in Kenya against British colonialism. In Kenya the Mau Mau activists noted with satisfaction the support

---

[497] Hackney Libraries News. July 12, 1993.

their movement received from C.L.R. James. Thus it was an honour for Hackney that his name could be thus used in one of our Libraries.

But as is usual in such cases the Library's name change remained a mere cosmetic change. It was considered sufficient for black people that an empty shell be provided for them, without any meaningful content, for a dry bone to be thrown at them. But the situation soon began to change. Around 1986, there developed within the library service a struggle between a euro-centric group of librarians who questioned the very need of having any black collections and undermined the Council's Equal Opportunity policies by refusing to buy material or provide services of interest to BEM communities. In contrast, a group of librarians who believed in providing a service that the community really needed came together to form a Core Group who decided among other things that the name of the C.L.R. James Library needed a proper content. That after all, was what people had wanted rather than an empty gesture of a name-change.

It was this TCLC Support Group that worked out the idea of the Collection, prepared detailed plans and reports, undertook feasibility studies, consulted communities and came up with final plans for TCLC. The Group by now included supporters from other Council Departments, academicians, organised community groups such as Hackney African Organisation, Hackney Asian Association, Hackney Women's Centre, various local Turkish organisations, Jenako Arts, Institute of Race Relations as well as independent bodies such as Oxfam, Amnesty International, Hackney Commission for Racial Equality, etc. Many institutes were so impressed by what the Collection had done and by what it represented that many valuable donations of complete runs of back periodicals were made. These included an Index on Censorship, Africa Events, and publications from the World Association for Christian Communication. Other donations have included publications from Liberation, African Concord, as well as signed copies of publications by the well-known historian, Richard Hart. Features and news items about the Collection have appeared in the Hackney Gazette, The Voice, East London News, Library Association Record, Early Times, Spare Rib, and East African Standard (Nairobi). Planning meetings of the Support Group attracted people from all parts of London.

The greatest difficulty facing the Group was to get the approval from Library Senior Management. John Spence, then the Principal Librarian, Community Services gave total support to the project as did Angela Fletcher, then Principal Librarian, Operations. It took years of struggle for the proposal to be accepted. Finally a letter of support from the Chair of Community Services, Hajra Khote helped to turn the tide in our favour. The project was approved almost overnight. A sum of £4,000 for the Collection was suddenly made available. In itself this was an insignificant amount in comparison to the overall stockfund, but was a major victory for the TCLC. Although no additional full time staff could be found to set up or develop the Collection, it ran entirely on the enthusiasm of a large number of committed staff. The launch in October 1989 was a week-long event attracting important personalities including Richard Hart and Ngugi wa Thiong'o, with the Council represented by the Chair of Community Services, Hajra Khote whose speech was one of total commitment on the part of the Council to the Collection. Important personalities who have taken part in other activities organised by TCLC include Colin Prescod and Fatima Ibrahim.

TCLC had an immediate impact. Users came from all over Hackney and included students from Hackney College, teachers, parents, Council employees, community members, and Hackney-based activists from around the three continents. Students from other London Colleges such North London Polytechnic, Polytechnic of Central London found an easily accessible source of information in TCLC which they could not find anywhere locally. Over the first few years, visitors came from Germany, South Africa, and Tanzania. Important personalities who have visited the Collection include John La Rose, founder of the Black, Radical and Third World Bookfair, and G.Pande, President of the United Artists' Association, India. Regular visits were made by Library and Information Science, post-graduate students from Thames Valley University. All were totally impressed by the Collection and the commitment, enthusiasm and vision of the staff at C.L.R. James Library and members of the Support Group.

Just as the TCLC was being consolidated, there came restructuring of the Library Services. Little account was taken of the special needs of the TCLC although reports were again written about the dangers of a lack of support for the Collection. It has been suffering ever since. A shell remains, for how long and in what form remains to be seen. In the meantime library staff can take just pride in creating a socially relevant service where none existed before.

In recording my appreciation of the work of a large number of staff who, worked tirelessly in making TCLC a reality, I am reminded of Brecht's poem "Questions from a Worker." Let us not forget that a major achievement such as TCLC can succeed only on the basis of joint, united work of many people. It was truly a *harambee* (Kiswahili for "many people working together on a self-help basis") effort on a vast scale. Let us pay tribute to all those who contributed their labour to the Collection. They have achieved what remains unattainable for even large organisations on the basis of official edits and directives. This gives hope for the future. A project that can generate so much enthusiasm among Council staff, users, visitors and anyone who came in contact with it surely has a long future ahead.

The Black and Minority Ethnic Stock Group in Hackney Libraries (1999)[498]

Shiraz Durrani, John Pateman, and Naila Durrani

ACKNOWLEDGEMENT: The achievements recorded here are due entirely to all members of BSG whose hard work and commitment has made this experiment a success. Particularly crucial has been the 4-person administrative and coordination team, which has been at the heart of the whole system and has ensured that every aspect of work takes place like clockwork. Finally, the whole exercise was made possible by the support and vision of Gus John as the Director of Education and Leisure Services. The support of Ricci de Freitas, AD (LACE) has enabled BSG work to continue smoothly.

The national context

---

[498] Library Review 48(1) 1999. pp.18-25

Since the changes in Section 11 funding, [499] different local authorities have responded in different ways to provide a service to their Black communities. In general, there has been a *decline* in the quality and quantity of service provision to Black communities. At the same time, qualified and experienced Black staff have either been redeployed out of local authority service or have been offered lower level posts or jobs that have nothing to do with service to Black communities. The decision-making process has become even more dominated by non-Black staff. Years of experience and community links have been lost. The effect has also been felt in the Black book trade, which has suddenly seen a dramatic decline in funds made available for Black material.

It is in this context that the experience in Hackney should be seen. It reverses general national experience and sets new standards in the quality of service to Black communities. In addition, it has empowered Black staff at all levels to be active in fundholding, in making, implementing and monitoring stock policy.

Black and local suppliers have been used to supply all areas of stock, exposing the myth that Black suppliers are not able to supply material required by public libraries.

The model has been modified and improved over a period of over two years and is in the process of being formally structured into the new staffing structure following a comprehensive Library Review.

The Hackney factor

After years of decline, Hackney Libraries are undergoing a process of radical transformation. Library staff, in a well-planned series of consultations, came up with a number of vision statements. One of these deals with service to Black and Minority Ethnic communities. This has become the guiding principle of service to Black communities.

Many significant changes have taken place in service delivery of Hackney Libraries in the last few years. One of the most significant changes has been the emphasis given to services to Black and Minority Ethnic communities which comprise almost 48 percent of Hackney's population (including the Turkish, Kurdish, Greek, Jewish and Irish communities which are included in the "White" category in the last population census). This proportion is bound to rise in the next generation as almost 75 percent of children in Hackney schools today are of Black and Minority Ethnic backgrounds.

In 1995/96 twenty-five percent (£100,000) of the total stock fund (£400,000) was allocated to Black and Minority Ethnic (BME) materials (books, periodicals, Audio Visual etc.). The decision to increase the percentage spent on BME materials to 25 percent was intended to begin the process of correcting an historical imbalance. In other words, for many years not enough had been spent on BME materials in Hackney and we are now determined to ensure a fairer allocation for this community.

The 25 percent figure represents a significant increase on previous years. However, it is still short of the BME population in Hackney, which is nearer 50 percent. In future years we may need to increase the 25 percent BME allocation to

---

[499] "Section 11" was a special funding project initiated by the Government to support initiatives at local level to provide services to Black and Minority Ethnic (BME) communities who had traditionally missed out from the "normal" funding and services from Local Government. Thus a large number of BME Librarians were employed to initiate and provide services to their communities.

bring it more in line with this population. This redirection of resources did not have any adverse effect on other parts of the service because the total size of the stock fund remained the same. Stock purchased from the BME fund is available to all library users.

But it was not enough to set aside an increased stockfund for Black material. An appropriate structure was needed to administer and monitor this increased spending. Discussion and consultation on these measures took place at all levels. The initiative was driven by Gus John, the Director of Education and Leisure Services. The Libraries Senior Management Team put a number of measures into practice, including the involvement of Black Workers Group members at management meetings. This move recognised that Black staff were not well represented at senior levels of the service.

In order to properly spend and monitor the 25 percent BME allocation, a BME Stock Steering Group (BSSG) was established in 1995. This group was responsible for the selection of all BME materials—books, newspapers and periodicals, reference material, material in nationality languages spoken in Hackney, music, videos, etc. BSSG was a halfway house where part of the existing stock services section continued to provide administrative and financial support. Stock selection, was overseen by a five-member team of senior library staff and library assistants. Regular (monthly) stock approval meetings were held where material supplied by Black bookshops were looked at and purchased. In advance of such stock selection meetings, BME library assistants were encouraged to make purchase suggestions. The aim was to increase participation and responsibility; empower black staff; provide training opportunities; and involve the Black Workers Group in aspects of managing the service.

BSSG worked extremely hard to organise the purchase of over £100,000 worth of stock. This involved a regular programme of stock approvals supplemented by shop visits and ordering from lists prepared in consultation with community members. BSSG also liaised with the stock services team and individual suppliers. Keeping on track of this expenditure was time consuming and sometimes problematic. The work of BSSG was carried out by those staff, in addition to their day-to-day duties. It became clear by the end of 1995/96 that this situation could not go on and that a more formal and widespread system was required. Although BSSG had involved many staff at all levels (including library assistants and library attendants) in stock selection for the first time, this had created time tabling difficulties (for example, in releasing staff to attend the Black, Radical and Third World Bookfair).

The Formation of BSG

The Review of Hackney Libraries presented new opportunities for BME stock work. The stockfund was increased to £600,000 and the BME allocation of 25 percent now released £150,000 for expenditure in this area. The staffing structure was changed to reflect a reduction in Library sites from 14 to 7.

It was decided to make qualitative changes in BSSG in answer to the new challenges provided by an increased stockfund and to overcome weaknesses found in the BSSG structure. This was achieved by forming the BME Stock Group (BSG). The aim was to build the functions of BSSG into the new BSG but also to keep a degree of continuity from BSSG, whilst spreading the workload and allocating time for BSG duties. To this end a discussion paper was taken to the Library Review Implementation Steering Group (LSG) outlining how the new system would work. BSG will continue to function until the new staffing structure is in place. It will then be integrated into the new structure.

How BSG Works

BSG is made up of various component parts.

The administrative and coordinating unit

This is a complex unit which administers funds, and keeps its own financial records; places orders and passes invoices for payment; maintains links with suppliers, with community groups and with Library's Stock Services, as well as all Library staff who are involved in stock purchases; monitors that material is actually made available at sites, and does some publicity and promotional work.

The unit became functional in June 1996 and is made up of:

A Black Area Librarian who is the fund holder and coordinator of BEST (described below). It was proposed that senior management would delegate the running of BSG to the Area Librarian who would report to the Library Steering Group. The BME stockfund was placed in this officer's cost centre and he became the authorised fundholder and signatory.

A professional Black member of staff who had carried out the administrative and co-ordinating function almost single handedly under BSSG, now continued the work in BSG and provided professional, administrative and coordination support. Her other work involved establishing contacts and providing a strategy for Outreach, and this enabled BSG to actively involve local community groups in stock purchases. The work that she is carrying out for BSG is complex. It involves financial work (keeping accounts, monitoring expenditures, passing invoices), administrative work (facilitating approval meetings and shop visits), maintaining contact with, and supporting, the suppliers; delegating research work to suppliers and other staff; coordinating work with stock services; community outreach and publicity, and supervising the work of BSG staff.

Two Black Library Assistants spend 50 percent of their time (17.5 hours) on BSG work. Their work involves all day-to-day administrative work, checking and passing invoices for payment, carrying out research as and when required, preparing or helping to prepare orders, checking lists against computer records to avoid duplication, and ensuring the smooth running of approval meetings and general administrative duties.

The stock selection teams

The real strength of BSG is the active professional involvement of almost 30 staff who are being allocated time to help select BME stock. In all, 28 library assistants are involved in 33 tasks (selecting stock for adults and young persons, in books, music, videos, etc.) and some are working on more than one stock area. This compares with 35 library assistants who were on the mailing list of the Black Workers Group at the time. Under BSSG there were five members of staff in the main BME stock team and the involvement of library assistants was minimal, erratic, and involved only looking at approvals — making recommendations only — with limited empowerment. The new BSG structure has improved on this not only in terms of the quantity (number of staff involved) but also qualitatively (in the amount of decision making that they are involved in).

The selection of staff on different teams was made on the basis of their interest, commitment and expertise as shown in practice during the BSSG year (1995/96). It would be difficult, if not impossible, to find a similar exercise in library staff empowerment. For the first time, library attendants are involved in stock selection in their own right. In addition, hidden talents in many fields, including music and languages, have been discovered and given space to expand.

The stock teams are encouraged to get as many other staff as possible — Black and White — involved in suggesting new stock items for purchase. They have also been asked to get feedback from site supervisors and other senior staff so as to include as wide a range of suggestions into the stock acquisition process as possible.

These teams are the ones who go to stock approval meetings, which are held at the Black bookshops on a monthly basis — one for adult books, one for material for young people. They also go to other shops for other areas of stock.

An example of the positive achievements of the stock teams is the work of African, African-Caribbean and South Asian music teams which define BME music, decide on the breakdown of funds between different types of music (for example, Jungle, reggae, African music, gospel, etc.), how many copies to purchase, and which sites need how many copies. The work of the music team is crucial in monitoring the time taken for stock to physically appear on the shelves and in ensuring that the appropriate funds are allocated and spent on relevant furniture, publicity, etc. This has resulted in a realistic and passionate involvement in policymaking and implementation of issues related to BME music.

The BEST structure

This consists of three Team Librarians, each having responsibility for a specified stock area to facilitate and support the work of different stock teams: adult books; young persons books; special collections (reference; Three Continents Liberation collection; nationality languages); other areas (Jewish/Torah Collection; Irish; Islamic collection; combating racism); music and videos. The Team Librarians provide a link between the Library Service's staffing unit and the BSG administrative and coordinating unit. They go to stock approvals meetings to provide professional and training support to Library Assistants. They help to arrange shop visits and prepare final order lists from shop visits after checking the pickings lists against the Library's computer records to avoid duplication

Of the three Team Librarians, one professionally supports stock selection of all BME general music, Irish and the Three Continents Liberation collections, South Asian nationality language and approval meetings for adult books in English. The second Team Librarian supports adult stock selection at approvals meetings, while the third supports young persons stock selection and Jewish interest stock selection.

Not all members of BEST are Black and so ensure that the BSG structure does not become a marginalised Black group. Thus the integration of the BSG structure into the general structure will be easier as BEST already provides a basis for it.

Stock promotion

An important aspect of this new approach is to promote the new stock acquired under BSSG and BSG. The month of July 1996 was celebrated in all Hackney Libraries as Black Celebration month. All sites held displays of new Black and Minority Ethnic material. In addition, a series of book lists of material purchased in the year 1995/96 and 1996/97 was produced.

The production of these lists is making the new material more accessible to users — actual and potential. These and other services will be further promoted through the new Outreach Services planned to start in 1997.

As an additional development, an experiment to promote Black material is being tried at Stoke Newington Library to alert library users to new BME material. Users are encouraged to recommend items they consider suitable for purchase by the library. This addresses one of the key Council policies in empowering local residents. At the same time this enables users who find the reserve system too expensive, to influence the acquisition of stock. It is proposed to expand this system to other libraries if it proves to be useful and popular.

Democracy and Empowerment

The question of "democracy" in deciding the work of BSG needs to be addressed. This involves several issues. It should be understood that empowerment does not imply total democracy. The Library Service (as indeed the whole Council) is a hierarchical organisation, with officers appointed to carry out policies laid down by members. There cannot be total democracy in service delivery, nor can democracy, in this sense, ensure service delivery. The process of democracy takes place when residents elect councillors to represent them, not in service delivery, such as libraries.

A certain amount of management decision, direction, planning and coordination are essential in any work situation and in any project. This is particularly true in a new project; otherwise a lack of direction and support can kill it. This was true for BSSG and is true for BSG as well. Thus management had to take decisions about the overall scope of the project; who will run it, the fund breakdown, what is the expected outcome, etc. If such decisions are not taken by management the result can be chaos leading to failure and demoralisation of staff. This is particularly important in a sensitive area such as BME services.

The role of the BSG administrative unit is to ensure that this extremely complex structure works efficiently — without this unit the whole structure would collapse. In addition, it involves the spending of over £150,000 and requires efficient procedures to ensure that this takes place in line with Council procedures. Far from being cushy desk work, the four people involved in coordinating and administrative work have taken on a heavy burden, in order to ensure that BME staff and communities get the service they deserve.

Achievements

The standards set by BSG and the experience gained from its work are examples of good practice, which can be used by management to integrate BME work into the new structure. These are summarised as follows:

1. Allocating 25 percent of total stockfund for BME materials in 1995/96 and ensuring that this level of funding for BME stock was maintained in 1996/97. The new structure should ensure that this percentage is continued. Of this 25 percent, one third needs to be spent on nationality language materials.
2. Empowering many BME staff members in their own areas of interest and/or expertise in selecting stock.
3. Addressing all areas of BME stock, in consultation with the community through outreach work.
4. Processing by suppliers to get the stock to the shelves quickly and more efficiently.
5. Working with Stock Services on better cataloguing and processing of stock.

6. Using Black and local suppliers, especially for music, which has opened up a wider range for view and purchase. All the small suppliers have given an excellent stock and services.
7. Organising monthly BME approval meetings, separately for selection of adult materials and young persons' materials. These enable empowered staff to see and select new stock on a regular basis.
8. Setting up approval collections from two suppliers to cover a broad range of stock in a coordinated way to avoid duplication. The new experiment of going to shops for approval meetings has given library assistants the opportunity to meet the suppliers.
9. Supplementing the approval meetings for stock in English with shop visits for language materials and special collections, or order lists prepared on the basis of outreach, special requests/recommendations and catalogues. All these avenues for stock selection also function as training forums on stock work.
10. This complex approval mechanism set up by BSG has been made possible by an efficient administrative and logistics system, which ensures that different parts function in unison.
11. Monitoring of funds, stock purchases and accounting procedures on paper rather than relying on Dynix which is good for other things but is not to be completely relied upon for accounting purposes.
12. Enhancing the role of Team Librarians. The present BSG model (where Team Librarians have a much higher profile) is a bridge between last year's BSSG (where there was a limited Team Librarian presence) and the new structure, which will integrate fully all BME stock work and staff empowerment.
13. Ensuring the systematic and regular selection, processing, and classifying of material in South Asian languages through specialist suppliers and CILLA. Improving the transliteration and processing by suppliers of all other nationality language stock.
14. Widening the experience and training of library assistants by encouraging them to attend CILLA meetings on a rotating basis.
15. Recognising and empowering Black music expertise among BME staff,— something that had stayed invisible for so many years within the system and which became visible and active through BSG.
16. Promoting the stock purchased by BSSG and BSG—a good example is the production of 16 stock lists for all areas of BME stock during the Black Celebration month (July 1996).

All issues not yet resolved

It would not be correct to say that BSG has resolved all issues related to BME stock work. Nor can we claim that mistakes have not been made. Given ideal conditions, we would have achieved even more, with fewer mistakes. Important issues that need to be addressed more seriously in the future include:

- The need for language skills recognition;
- Continued and more formalised training in stock work;
- Further staff empowerment at the library assistant level;
- Adequate staff resources to enable all the functions to be carried out smoothly;
- Further stock development of special collections such as ESOL;
- Ensuring adequate senior/middle management support for BME stock work;

- Monitoring African Languages Collections to decide whether it can be maintained, given the difficulty of getting a steady supply of new material.

BSG represents a change of emphasis and practice to recognise historical under-funding and marginalisation. We are seeking to use the many skills, experiences and backgrounds of our culturally rich and diverse workforce. Any change can lead to resistance, especially when empowering one group of staff may be perceived as disempowering others. However, we are determined to continue the process, as part of our Library Review, to build a library service that is relevant to the needs of the people of Hackney.

Reasons for BSG success

The success of any social experience depends on the presence of positive forces at a particular time. A number of such positive factors, both external to the Library and internal, came together in Hackney around 1993 to bring about the concept and practice of BSG.

The most important factor was the incorporation of the Library Service in the new Directorate of Education and Leisure Services — DELS — in 1993. This in itself need not necessarily have been a particularly positive influence. But we were fortunate that the director was Gus John, a man who had vision, courage, and commitment to set in motion the forces that became almost a revolutionary change in the Library Service. Gus John was an intellectual who not only had ideas for bringing about positive change, but matched these with courage and hard work to implement the ideas — a rare combination indeed. He was ready to support any positive forces that sought social justice. He was totally committed to bringing *education* in the broadest and the best sense to the people of Hackney.

This total commitment of Gus John was no doubt the major reason why the marginalised service to Black communities was put at centre stage in the Library service. But this could not have been brought to fruition without forces *within* the Library, which could take advantage of this "external" support. The Black and Minority Ethnic Workers Group (BWG) at that time was a well organised, articulate body. It had fought a long, hard struggle to ensure that Black issues — service and staffing — were given appropriate attention. It had articulated its ideas and concerns in well-researched documents. It was well organised and had fought hard to win the right to exist as an independent body which met monthly. It had a strong, united and well-led and guided Central Committee, which charted its policies and strategies.

More important, the BWG was ready to grasp the new opportunities offered when Gus became the director. It did not merely articulate the grief of Black staff. It was ready with concrete plans to solve the problems that faced Black services and staff. It found ready support from the new senior management that took over the Library Service after the formation of DELS. It also received support from the new Assistant Director, Ricci de Freitas, whose remit included the Library Services.

It is not often that all these positive forces come together at the same time. The opportunity came for Hackney, and the Black staff, were ready to take advantage. By being ready to seize the time, they turned their ideas into action. Thus the concept of BSSG and BSG came from within Black staff and its hard work was carried out by a core of a committed, hard working unit with support from the broad sectors of Black workers.

A bright future?

It is of course not possible to foresee what the future will bring. But we can see signs — both positive and negative — that point to the likely outcome. The final result will depend on how these forces interact and what support senior management give to positive forces for continuing the recent changes. On the positive side the new staffing structure allows for *structured* ways of service delivery for Black communities. The senior management is positive about the issues that BSG has been dealing with.

But the negative forces are also evident. Not all the Library staff has been happy with BSG and what it represents. The support of the middle management can be crucial but there is no certainty that it will be forthcoming. The current restructuring will change the balance of forces on the ground and it remains to be seen if those who control power support the aims and work of BSG. While formal support is almost guaranteed, the practical and positive will to continue may not always be there. In addition, the BWG has been rendered ineffective by internal fights and has become a mere shadow of its former self. There are likely to be few, if any, senior Black managers in the new structure. The few committed ones who may survive may be outnumbered and not be in a position to influence policy or practices in the future. The chronic weakness of the "numbers game" may be allowed to win once again.

Whatever the future, the bright example of BSG remains as a model that can work. It has challenged in practice, the often held (though seldom openly stated) view that Black people cannot perform at the highest level, that services to Black communities are doomed to wither because of "lack of supplies," "shortage of suppliers," "bad services," etc. That in itself is a major victory.

Young people in control (SD-DB, 2004)[500]

The Quality Leaders Project — Youth strand is changing library services for young people with young people. SHIRAZ DURRANI and DEAN BARTLETT chart the progress.

The need to redefine library service

Public libraries in Britain need a major shift in its very mindset. It is sometimes assumed that the role of the public library never changes and remains the same as it has for over 150 years. Whether the current service is relevant to meet current needs is an issue that requires urgent resolve. Questions such as, "What are libraries for?" "Who do they serve?" "What services are needed?" "What is the best way of providing these services?" — are increasingly raised by policy makers and people on whose behalf services are provided. The questions have become even more urgent in the context of rapid changes in information and communications technologies and the tremendous rate of change in every aspect of our lives, pushed by forces of corporate capitalism and globalisation. The Secretary of State, Tessa Jowell, poses a number of challenges to the profession:

---

[500] Durrani, Shiraz and Bartlett, Dean Public Library Journal. Autumn 2004. pp. 22-25

This is a critical time for the future of public library services. Although for over 150 years, libraries have given pleasure and provided opportunities to learn, it is now time to ensure that libraries are relevant and inviting to future generations...the challenge is to generate new users...it is important to learn lessons about why people do not use libraries — only one third do, so how do libraries attract the other two thirds?[501]

The Secretary of State made it clear that she wants change in public libraries. She explained what needs to happen so that libraries "become, once again, central points in local communities":

> But they can only take back this role if they consult local people, and put them in the driving seat. Not just once, but as a continuous dialogue.[502]

There is also an increasing concern to improve services to young people of all classes, races, gender, and to address other factors, which have resulted in excluding young people from an "equal" share of public service. There has been a definite support from the government for improving public services, with an increasing focus on services to young people. These changes have affected education, youth service, health and social services. It is now reaching the public library field. Recent policy developments have placed new focus on providing services to young people with an active involvement of young people themselves. A recent MLA report sums up this changing environment:

> Library services to young people will have to be developed against a rapidly changing policy background. The relationship between local and central government is very different from ten years ago; there have been fundamental changes to political structures, planning regimes and methods of assessing performance.
>
> A rapidly changing policy scene challenges library services to re-examine their services for young people. *Every Child Matters* requires local authorities to work in quite different ways; *Learning to Listen* is emphasizing the importance of young people's participation in society. [503]

It is in this rapidly changing context that the Quality Leaders Project-Youth (QLP-Y)[504] needs to be assessed. QLP seeks to provide a relevant model of library service to meet the needs of people and thereby connect people to their libraries.

The QLP-Y approach

While most libraries provide a reasonably satisfactory service for children, many fail when it comes to providing imaginative and relevant services to those between the ages of 13-24. Boagey poses an important challenge to the profession: "Young people need to be at the heart of transforming libraries."[505]

This is the very area in which the QLP-Youth fills an important gap. The model provides a way of consulting young people to be active partners in developing a new service that meets their needs. In the process it ensures partnership working with youth and other services.

---

[501] Jowell, Tessa (2004): "DCMS public libraries seminar, 21 June, 2004". Quotes taken from notes by Alison Bramley for SCL members..
[502] Lend it like Peckham! (2004).
[503] Fulfilling their potential (2004).
[504] Further information about QLP is available at: http://www.seapn.org.uk/qlp.html
[505] Boagey (2003).

QLP is a programme of "management development through service development." It thus provides a balanced approach, which develops staff and improves their skills as part of developing services. The learning and service development aspects of the QLP are inherently intertwined in the structure of the QLP programme. This structure follows a fixed scheme consisting of six key areas in a specific order: QLP induction, project management, consultation, best value and performance, service design and service implementation planning.

Embedded within the formal learning structure are a number of new modules that bring awareness of essential requirements that often get ignored in other learning experiences. These are "combating racism/ managing equality" and "managing youth service." The former was developed specifically for the previous strand of QLP and aims at equipping participants with awareness of issues of racism and equality, both from a theoretical and legal point of view as well giving examples of practical approaches of mainstreaming equality in all aspects of local authority work. The latter—"managing youth service" was introduced for the youth strand of QLP. It brings the best aspects of youth work as required by the National Youth Agency and recent legislation on working with young people. Again, a practical approach is taken and example of creative partnership between libraries and youth service is used. Added to the above, are lessons and experiences of working with young refugees and asylum seekers.

A significant part of the underlying philosophy behind the QLP is that the person being developed would be exposed to a number of opportunities to interact with much more senior decision-makers within their organizations and would do so in a very visible way within both their own organisations and also within the socially excluded partnership communities with whom they work. This ensures a social identity approach to their development while at the same time drawing in local communities in the development of services for them.

The key propositions of QLP are that the meeting of unrecognised or under-recognised needs requires new or enhanced services, and new and enhanced services require new skills and know-how (including new management know-how). Acquisition of these new skills will create a level playing field for staff who have not been able to reach management positions, thereby enhance their ability to reach senior management positions.

The QLP approach involves consulting local communities, establishing what their new or unmet needs are and then developing proposals for a new service, which address these needs. Users and potential users are included in the consultation exercise.

The programme looks at providing services in new and different ways so as to attract and reach people not reached before. It emphasises the need to work in partnership with other Council departments as well as with community groups. QLP challenges important aspects of current public library ethos: *content* of library service, the *quality* of service provided, the *method of delivery* and *who* decides what services are needed. In essence, it redefines what a library service is all about and encourages organisational change in order to provide a new service in a new way.

QLP-Y targets young people

The QLP steering group decided at the start of the QLP-Y programme that any improvement in service to young people will need to take a partnership approach if the needs of young people are to be satisfied. The key partners they identified were

Youth and Library Services in the local authority context. It was realised that the government's programme for developing services to young people had much to offer to library authorities seeking development to services to young people. It was also necessary to explore innovative ways of service delivery, as the "traditional" approach has not met fully the needs of this segment of our society.

QLP-Y takes as its starting point the agenda set by two key initiatives that drive youth and library services today: on the one hand, the comprehensive programme provided by the National Youth Agency;[506] on the other hand, are the guidelines in Framework for the Future.[507] The latter has been strengthened recently with a very useful and important initiative for developing services to young people. This is the *Fulfilling their potential* programme.[508]

The funding for QLP-Y comes from two sources: the partners in Innovations programme (PIN) of the National Youth Agency fund phase one of the programme which involves developing skills of the participating Quality Leaders and their teams and leads to the production of a youth service development proposal. The second phase, which implements the project proposal, is funded by the Paul Hamlyn Foundation which supports innovation and change in the public library service for young people and also focuses on meeting the needs of excluded groups such as refugees and asylum seekers.

The driving force for QLP comes from the QLP Steering Group which initiated the programme and which provides the overall direction and ensures that the programmes meet the vision it set out with. QLP moves away from the "wants-driven" service, which guides many library services to a "needs-based" service[509] that takes on board new or unmet needs of local populations—in this case the needs of young people.

Phase one: management development

The development project is of six months duration and is located within a formal project management framework. The person in charge of managing this project is the Quality Leader, who is responsible for establishing, convening and leading a part-time project team, the Development Team, who are charged with the development of a new service based upon the results of a consultation process with the community. The role of the Development Team is to carry out such activities as may be specified by the Quality Leader in consultation with team members. In order for this process to work in the context of the pressured realities of organisational life and the demands being made upon potential members of the project team, it is essential that each Quality Leader is supported by two key people from within his or her organisation (a project sponsor and a mentor). In leading this team, the aim is to develop an idea for a new service which is based upon a thorough consultation with the community, and

---

[506] Some details are included in Durrani (2004). More details are available from the National Youth Agency website: www.nya.org.uk.
[507] "The DCMS has published a new strategic framework for the public library service: Framework for the Future. The policy document outlines the Government's long-term strategic vision for the role of public libraries. Its purpose is to help local and library authorities agree on the key objectives for the public library service with central government and local communities."
http://www.culture.gov.uk/global/publications/archive_2003/framework_future.htm.
[508] Fulfilling their potential (1994).
[509] See Smallwood (2002) for further details on a needs-based service.

which involves planning operational processes, resources and implementation steps and developing a formal proposal for the new service.

The first phase of the QLP-Y programme took place from January to July 2004. Six authorities are taking part: Birmingham, Gloucestershire, Haringey, Liverpool, Merton, and Swansea. Liverpool's Quality Leader is from their Youth Service, while the others are from Library Service. The Quality Leaders presented their proposals on 26 July, and successful ones will be awarded a University diploma in work-based learning.

Phase 2: Implementation stage

The next stage of QLP-Y is the implementation phase, which will last for two years and will start in September 2004. The QLP Steering group, under the QLP coordinator, will discuss with each participating authority how the service development proposal developed by the Quality Leaders will be implemented in their authority.

The final shape of what activities take place will depend on the outcome of consultation with young people and what the service development plans recommend. It is likely to take the form of various workshop activities that suit young people. These workshop sessions are perhaps the most innovative part of the application. The sessions are programmed to reflect the specific aspects that the young people themselves decide meet their needs. They thus will be flexible in order to be tailored to local requirements. They will also enable young people themselves to be the providers of such sessions, rather than being merely passive recipients of a service provided by an "outsider." At the same time, the programme will enable outside skills, ideas and expertise to be brought into the local youth communities, thereby injecting new and different ideas on the local scene.

Funding provided by the Paul Hamlyn Foundation will enable activities such as presentations from writers, poets, film makers, media and other professionals, music workshops, book and newsletter production sessions, broadcast workshops, film making modules, various informal learning experiences, audience development activities, ICT-related activities as well as guest speakers from different fields. In this way it will enable young people to meet potential role models from diverse communities and from different fields. Libraries will thus be able to reach young people in new ways which young people themselves help design.

QLP-Y service development proposals

While the final details of the plans developed by the Quality Leaders have still to be worked out, the following are likely projects for each authority:[510]

Birmingham

Quality Leader: Saleem Ayub
Project: *Multi-media Workshop. Birchfield Library. Birmingham.*

The workshop would have a project worker developing creative activities encompassing a variety of cultures, with importance given to activities that promote reading, creative writing, and the learning experience.

---

[510] This section has been provided by the Quality Leaders.

The new service would incorporate a reading club and other current library initiatives at Birchfield Library. It will promote local talent-creating opportunities for young people to express themselves in a variety of ways. Their writing would be catalogued and incorporated into the current service. A young person will be selected as a "library guide," and would support and assist the project worker in developing a newsletter that will act as a link with the local schools, the library, the workshop, and other partners. They will attend staff meetings and contribute to the shaping of the service provision for young people, in communicating the concerns and views of those they are representing. The "guides" would have rewards and some type of accreditation for their work.

The project worker will create opportunities for refugees and asylum seekers to make confident the use of libraries by having awareness days and selected creative activities which include: developing an archive of their lives and experiences to break barriers and create a better understanding between the different communities in Birmingham. The archive would again be incorporated into the current service provision at Birchfield Library/ Citywide, and will have links with other exciting initiatives such as Stories from the Web, Black History Month, Young Readers Birmingham Festival, as would the work of young people generally.

There will also be a variety of other creative activities for both young people, including refugees and asylum seekers, with some of the activities interlinked with other partners.

Gloucestershire

> Quality Leader: Ros Armstrong
> Project: *Youth work tool-kit and activities*

The service development proposal for Gloucestershire is a tool kit of strategies, events and activities using ICT to actively engage and encourage young people into the library. This is the main thrust of the service development but Ros is also proposing developments in relation to staff training: (1) how to exploit the tool kit and (2) customer care in relation to young people.

The involvement of young people in staff recruitment and a partnership to provide a space for young people in Gloucester city centre are also proposed.

Haringey

> Quality Leader: Nazma Parveen
> Project: *Citizen rights awareness programme for young people*
> Details are being finalised.

Liverpool

> Quality Leader: June Barron
> Project: *Social inclusion programmes*

The proposal is to develop a creative arts project supporting literacy and using library resources. It is a partnership programme involving Youth Service, Alternative Education, Social Inclusion and Leisure, ConneXions and Youth Offender Services — all of which are part of the Project Steering Group. Some aspects of the proposal had been planned before the QLP-Y programme started. The QLP-Y will introduce new and creative aspects to this proposal.

The targeted young people include those being referred to the Youth Service and are the most difficult to engage. The young people coming on the project are referred through the pupil provider panels of Liverpool Education. These young people are hard to reach, at risk of exclusion, absent from school with personal relationship and education difficulties. Many have fallen through a number of nets and education alternatives. It is accepted that it requires considerable skills to engage young people, to build relationships and to establish communication links with them. It is emphasised that the programme is a voluntary engagement in which young people choose to participate or not. A number of visits are made to their homes and links forged with parents.

Further consultations will be held to gauge and challenge the needs of young people. It is likely that a programme of activities for young people will be launched, and will include sessions as follows:

Team building/problem solving; introduction to healthy lifestyles; sports hall; music workshops; one to one work health sessions; diet—cook off preparation; healthy eating; introduction to communication; ready steady cook; mental health; pamper sessions.

Merton

Quality Leader: Anthony Hopkins
Project: *Creative Connections*

Merton Library and Heritage Service (MLHS) are looking to develop a program of creative writing workshops, entitled 'Creative Connections,' in each of their seven libraries within a 16-month period. This was identified as a need within the youth community from an extensive consultation with over 500 young people. The target audience is young people aged between 11 and 24 years old. Performance indicators will monitor participation in the workshops from all sections of the youth community. The project aims to:

- Increase library reach to those who have traditionally not used libraries.
- Promote social cohesion.
- Encourage informal learning, participation and teamwork within the youth community.
- Increase staff skills in working with young people through the provision of training.
- Bring in staff with new skills (eg. youth workers, creative writing experts) that add value to the service.
- Empower young people through the production of their work in magazines, displays, on the Internet and in book form.
- Promote literacy and assist with government targets to increase the levels of literacy amongst young people.

Swansea

Quality Leader: Emma Rees
Service Development Proposal: *Rethinking Gorseinon Library*

The service development proposal for The City and County of Swansea is a programme of events for young people, the target age being 13-19. The proposal is to make the library relevant for young people in the Gorseinon area and to get them into the library! Proposals include creating space for young people in Gorseinon Library, which will be designed by young people themselves. The space will be used to hold activities and events shaped by young people. This will be an approach never before tried locally and will cost several thousand pounds to maintain.

Change is an unchartered territory

Change is an unchartered territory, which frightens some people. But not changing will retard the much-needed development of public libraries in a new direction. QLP-Youth is an important way of achieving meaningful change. Jon Boagey makes an uncompromising demand for change:

> Their (young people's) active involvement in shaping the service will make their libraries into places where the customer leads, not the staff. If libraries want to find a place for young people that isn't just an awkward spot between the bean bags, there needs to be a radical shift in the way users are involved in the service. Now is the time to make it happen.[511]

QLP-Y offers a unique opportunity in actively involving young people to shape the service they need—and develops staff skills to ensure that new services are delivered in practice.

Quality Leaders Project—Youth: a search for a relevant information service (2005-06)[512]

One of the assignments given to students, as part of the "combating racism, managing equalities" module of the Quality Leaders Project-Youth (QLP-Y) is the following:

> Your authority has just got a large grant from Europe and now has resources to implement major changes in the service to ensure that it meets the needs of all its citizens. You are to design a new library service. Your task is to plan the new service, which meets all equality requirements. You are to design an integrated, relevant library service for young people. You should ensure that the new library service meets the needs of current and potential young users. Please ensure that you include refugees and asylum seekers in this exercise and address the needs of young members of Black and Ethnic Minority communities.[513]

---

[511] Jon Boagey (2003): op. cit.
[512] Black Caucus of the American Library Association (BCALA) Newsletter. Dec/Jan 2005-06
[513] QLP Manual. (unpublished).

This assignment sums up not only what the QLP-Y is all about, but also what is required if public library services are to meet the needs of local communities and remain relevant in a fast-changing world. In so doing, it points to a possible ideal information world where information services are open to all, in theory as well as in practice. Key requirements are effective leadership, creative thinking, a commitment to change, an understanding of the needs of communities, especially those marginalised — and the courage to give power to the people to direct services they need. The process of liberating a library service starts with liberating the mind of the librarian. The process is linked directly with the liberation of the society as a whole from forces of oppression and exploitation. QLP is a small step in this complex social struggle.

It is not possible in this short article to look in detail at all key propositions of the QLP-Y programme and indicate what key milestones have been set and met. QLP-Y has established its own website, produces a "QLP News" and issues "QLP-Y Youth Ideas and Action" as a way of disseminating information and networking. These can provide further details and are available, together with other documents, at the QLP website.[514] A "QLP Manual" is under preparation and will be published by Emerald next year.[515] This will carry all the rich ideas and experiences from QLP.

The key propositions of the QLP approach are that the meeting of unrecognised or under-recognised needs requires new or enhanced services, and new and enhanced services require new skills and know-how (including new management know-how). Thus the programme is one of "management development through service development."

The two phases of QLP-Y

QLP-Y is in two phases: the first six months give specific skills and experiences to "Quality Leaders" and their teams. This includes leadership, project management skills, consultation skills, budgeting and planning and preparing service development proposals. The key element of this phase is the module "combating racism/managing equality" as equality is key to a successful service. At the end of the six months, participants develop a service development proposal arrived at in active consultation with local young people.

The second phase then implements the service development proposals over a two-year period. It is noteworthy that the project is not funded from the mainstream funds of library and youth services, although they contribute in kind, mainly in terms of release time of their staff. The first phase was funded by the National Youth Service's Partners in Innovation programme; the two-year, second phase is funded by the Paul Hamlyn Foundation.

The project is managed by the Department of Applied Social Sciences of the London Metropolitan University and is run in partnership with the Management Research Centre. Participants come from five local authorities in England: London Boroughs of Barnet and Haringey, Lincolnshire, Liverpool, and Portsmouth.

QLP-Y is based on a belief that local authorities need to change and innovate in order to develop a relevant service. This requires organisational and cultural change. Authorities also need to address resource allocation and demonstrate commitment to developing services and staff.

---

[514] See: <http://www.seapn.org.uk/qlp.html>.
[515] The Manual will be published at the end of the programme in 2008.

A brief historical development of QLP

- 1999: QLP starts
- 2000: Feasibility Report (sponsored by the Museums, Library & Archives Council – MLA)[516]
- 2001: Pilot stage (participants were Birmingham and Merton)[517]
- 2002: QLP BME strand (sponsored by MLA)
- 2004: QLP-Youth – 2 phases (National Youth Agency; Paul Hamlyn Foundation)
- 2005: QLP moves to the Department of Applied Social Sciences of the London Metropolitan University (DASS) where it works in partnership with the Management Research Centre (MRC).

The key aspects of QLP-Y include the following:

Development of staff skills and experiences

Participating authorities select Quality Leaders (QL) from within their staff and also appoint a small team to work with the QL. The staff is provided a well-constructed training programme. The overall project management and coordination is provided by senior staff in DASS and MRC. They are supported by two key staff especially appointed for QLP-Y work: a Lecturer in Youth Policy who works with DASS and ensures that the national and local policy requirements on youth services are integrated in project proposals and are actually delivered. A Research Assistant is based at MRC and works exclusively on the project.

In addition to the above, QLs get the support of a mentor and a sponsor based in their own authorities. The former provides day-to-day support to ensure that the QLs and their teams meet project requirements. The sponsor is generally a senior Council official who provides a high-level support within the authority.

During the whole period of the project, the QLs receive theoretical knowledge as well as experience in developing and implementing services. They are also exposed to senior policy and decision makers. This helps to develop their self-confidence and awareness of policy work, as well as getting a better understanding of local communities and their needs.

Audience Development

The QLP approach identifies two aspects under the term "audience development." The first aspect is to increase the reach of libraries and youth services to meet the needs of all young people, particularly refugees and asylum seekers and those who have not been reached before. The second aspect expands on what has

---

[516] Quality Leaders Project for Black Library & Information Workers – Final Report of Research Findings, Feasibility Study, and Proposals. By Management Research Centre, University of North London. 6 April 2000. Commissioned by the Library and Heritage Services of the London Borough of Merton for a Project Supported by the L.I.C. Available from: <http://www.seapn.org.uk/reports/qlp.pdf>. Accessed: 18 December, 2005.

[517] An Evaluation of the Quality Leaders Pilot Project: A Pilot of Stage 2 of the Quality Leaders Project with London Borough Of Merton and Birmingham City Council. 5th July 2001. Dr. Dean Bartlett. Management Research Centre. University of North London . Available from: <http://www.seapn.org.uk/reports/qlp2.pdf>. Accessed: 18 December, 2005.

come to be known as "reader development." "Audience development" is a more inclusive term: it includes people who may have visual impairment and meets the needs of disabled people generally. It includes people who may not be literate either in English or in their own languages. It also allows for connecting people to the "reading experience" through non-print media, such as arts, cinema, music, drama and other cultural activities. It involves all the senses, rather than being restricted to the use of just one.

The "audience development" approach to library and youth work develops new areas of service provision, which a "traditional" library may not have provided as mainstream activities. Over a period of time, this approach will help to develop a new model of a joined-up library-youth service.

Audience development activities

Audience development workshop sessions are perhaps the most innovative part of QLP-Y. The sessions are programmed to reflect the specific aspects that the young people themselves decide meet their needs. They thus need to be flexible in order to be tailored to local requirements. They enable young people themselves to be the providers of such sessions, rather than being merely passive recipients of a service provided by an "outsider." At the same time, the programme enables outside skills, ideas and expertise to be brought into the local youth communities, thereby injecting new and different ideas on the local scene.

Audience development activities can include the following:

- Presentations from writers, poets, film makers, media and other professionals;
- Music workshops, book and newsletter production sessions, broadcast workshops, film making modules;
- Various informal learning experiences;
- ICT-related activities;
- Guest speakers from different fields as a way of enabling the young people to meet potential role models from diverse communities and from different fields.

It is expected that these sessions will attract those young people who may never have used library or youth services and become active participants in a new service which they themselves help design and deliver. The workshops approach is based on a belief that the learning and social needs of young people can be met more meaningfully as part of a cultural and social programme so as to avoid a feeling of "school out of school." The crucial element is the empowerment of young people so that it is they who decide on the type of activity they are comfortable with.

Audience development activities can help increase the reach of services and meet needs. In the long run, they can have a number of benefits:

- Mainstream new youth services which a "traditional" service may not provide.
- New model of joined-up, relevant library-youth service.
- Redefine service provision.
- Mainstream equality.
- Develop staff skills and experience.

- Change organisational culture.

QLP-Y addresses many challenges facing public library and youth services. In general, books are not the coolest service from a youth perspective when new technologies have taken over their thinking and perspective. Thus young people have whole-heartedly adopted the mobile phone, which they have used creatively to create their own communities of interest and solidarity. Local services have not managed to capture their imagination with the services they offer young people who want more activities associated with ICT, media, publishing, broadcast, drama, film-making, music, etc. –almost all absent from menus of local services offered to young people. In addition, most working-class young people are not traditional library users; they have suffered disproportionately as resources are focussed on current services often aimed at middle-class youth.

Within the youth services, there is perhaps a better approach to delivering a relevant service to young people, mostly driven by a stronger legislative framework. Yet here also, the impact has not been as significant as it could have been. For example, with huge resources available to youth services, as well as to organisations such as Connexions, there has not been a significant improvement in services to young people. An entirely different approach, based on a new vision and on principles of equality and justice for young people, which genuinely empower young people in reality, not on paper, is what is urgently required. While some of these are included in recent legislation and National Youth Service programmes (e.g. Quality matters), the reality is the opposite. QLP-Y seeks to address these challenges.

So does QLP-Y deliver an "ideal information world"?

That is the question that the editor of the *BCALA Newsletter* asked us to consider. To be honest, the answer has to be "no" – although a qualified "no". QLP-Y has the potential to deliver an ideal information world, but at present it is only a pilot project that needs to be mainstreamed, both in terms of funding and in being taken up by a larger number of local authorities. This is an area being currently explored by a number of organisations and key individuals and the QLP Steering Group, and will be one of the tasks of the proposed QLP Advisory Group.

At the same time, one cannot create a model of "excellence" in a vacuum. Unless the culture in the profession as a whole changes, a new effective leadership develops and accepts the principles and practices that underpin QLP, no significant change can take place. The profession has not fully accepted the need for change and is often in denial of the serious decline facing it unless drastic changes are made. But when that consciousness arises, as it surely must under increasing pressure from the government and forces of globalisation, QLP will be ready with a model that can develop relevant information services for all. An African saying goes, "there are no paths, traveller. Paths are made by walking." QLP takes this simple truth very seriously.

Progressive librarianship in Africa: The PALIAct story (2006)[518]

Introduction

The Progressive African Librarian and Information Activists' Group (PALIAct) is an initiative of the Department of Applied Social Sciences (DASS) at the London Metropolitan University. It is a partnership with a group of progressive African librarians and information workers. PALIAct has the support of the progressive librarians groups, including the Progressive Librarians Guild in the U.S.A. with its publication *Progressive Librarian*,[519] and Bibliotek i Samhälle in Sweden with its publication *bis*.[520]

PALIAct seeks to develop people-oriented information services decided upon by workers, peasants, pastoralists, fisher people and other marganilised individuals and groups whose information needs have not been met. It involves working in partnership with other professionals and service providers. PALIAct operates on principles of equality, democracy and social justice and encourages a Pan African world outlook among information and community activists. PALIACT sees the right to relevant information as a basic human right.

The idea for PALIAct has been under discussion over many years, but got a new lease on life during the International Federation of Library Associations (IFLA) meeting in Glasgow in 2002 when a number of participants agreed that a new approach to meeting Africa's information needs was needed. This was discussed at the Africa Regional Section meeting as well as in smaller, informal groups. The key idea that emerged from these discussions was that "African librarianship needs to liberate itself from the colonial-imperialist mould." These views were in keeping with the consensus that Issak found:

> The consensus of opinion seems to be that African librarians need to rethink what a public library is all about, in terms of what is needed, what will be used, and what is sustainable in Africa. Perhaps some new and more viable visions will result. In particular, public libraries in Africa need to start to be more aggressive and introduce services that are attractive to the users. Librarians must begin to know their potential users, and not only assume that they are school children. More dynamism and more involvement of the user community, extended to all users are required for the improvement of public library services.[521]

Those who showed an interest in the ideas discussed at IFLA came from Britain, Cameroon, Cuba, Ethiopia (including librarians from the Economic Commission for Africa, and the then OAU), Ghana, Kenya, Mexico, Nigeria and the U.S.A.

An informal network of those interested was set up, but no action was taken to formalise the organisation. It was felt that the first step was to spread the idea widely in Africa and to develop the organisation once there was sufficient grassroots support.

---

[518] Focus on International Library and Information Work. Vol. 37(1) 2006. pp. 4-8.
[519] See Progressive Librarians Guild website for further details: http://libr.org/plg/index.html.
[520] For details about bis, see: http://www.foreningenbis.org/index.html.
[521] Issak, Aissa (2000): Public libraries in Africa; a report and annotated bibliography. Oxford: International Network for the Availability of Scientific Publications (INASP).

The proposal was revived when a librarian from Ghana, George Obeng, visited Ethiopia and met some of those present at the Glasgow IFLA meetings. He wrote:

> I was in Addis Ababa for a UN documentation workshop last October... on the last day I had dinner with Petrina, the Librarian at the ECA. She talked extensively about how you tried to work on the progressive library association. You could see that it pains her that it couldn't work. Why don't you try to revive it?[522]

At the same time, there was renewed interest and support from the editor of the newsletter of the Black Caucus of the American Library Association,[523] Roland Barksdale-Hall, as well as from other committed individuals, including Del R. Hornbuckle.[524] Support also came from Al Kagan[525] who is active in IFLA as well as in the Social Responsibility Round Table of the American Library Association.[526]

It was then decided to launch a semi-formal "ideas forum" as the first stage of setting up a progressive organisation. A formal organisation could then be set up if and when the idea takes root. Thus was born PALIAct. Its first action was the mailing in February 2005 of its vision and proposals to those who had indicated an interest. The statement is available at the PALIAct website.[527] The great interest in the ideas was indicated by the fact that the statement got wide coverage in professional press.[528]

The PALIAct vision

PALIAct provides a vision for a people-orientated information service that could meet the information needs of workers and peasants. It works towards providing an anti-imperialist and a Pan African world outlook among African librarians and information workers. It also seeks to set up an alternative information service in partnership with the potential users of the service as a way of showing what needs to be done. PALIAct aims to form partnerships with progressive information and other workers within Africa and overseas.

---

[522] E-mail from George Obeng to Shiraz Durrani, 24 December, 2004.
[523] For further information about BCALA, see: http://www.bcala.org/.
[524] Del R. Hornbuckle manages the Academy of Educational Development (AED)'s Global Learning Portal in USA.
[525] Al Kagan is the African Studies Bibliographer and Professor of Library Administration African Studies Bibliographer and Professor of Library Administration at University of Illinois Library.
[526] Social Responsibilities Round Table (SRRT) is a unit within the American Library Association. It works to make ALA more democratic and to establish progressive priorities not only for the Association, but also for the entire profession. Concern for human and economic rights was an important element in the founding of SRRT and remains an urgent concern today. SRRT believes that libraries and librarians must recognize and help solve social problems and inequities in order to carry out their mandate to work for the common good and bolster democracy. SRRT's main Web site is hosted at http://libr.org/SRRT.
[527] PALIAct website: http://www.seapn.org.uk/PALIAct-new.html
[528] This included the following: Link-up March 17(1) 2005; Pambazuka News 22 June, 2006 — Pambazuka News (Pambazuka means arise or awaken in Kiswahili) is a "tool for progressive social change in Africa. Pambazuka News is produced by Fahamu, an organisation that uses information and communication technologies to serve the needs of organisations and social movements that aspire to progressive social change". It is available from: http://www.pambazuka.org/en/category//28705. Accessed 18 April, 2006; Newsletter of the Black Caucus of the American Library Association. August-September, 2005; Library & Information Update 4(9), September, 2005; IFLA Journal 31(3) October, 2005l Library & Information Gazette, December, 2006.

The World Summit on the Information Society recognised that "education, knowledge, information and communication are at the core of human progress, endeavour and well-being."[529] PALIAct seeks to contribute to this through a people-oriented information service run and managed by/on behalf of workers, peasants, pastoralists, fisher people and other marginalised individuals and groups whose information needs have not been met. It aims to develop new services based on equality for all.

An important principle that guides PALIAct is that there should be a strong partnership between information professionals, communities and groups. This is to ensure that librarians do not work in isolation as often happens now. At the same time, it is important that whatever new services are developed reflect the real needs of communities as decided by the communities themselves. For this to happen, it is essential that communities are active partners and decision-makers in planning and monitoring services.

As the name of the organisation suggests, PALIAct is made of *activists*, not those who talk but take no action. Active participation is essential if real change is to be achieved.

PALIACT recognises the right to relevant information as a basic human right. The struggle for a relevant information service, is intimately linked with the political struggles of the people in organising a society that ensures that the material, social, cultural and political needs of the people are met.

Progress and prospects

Following the distribution of the initial statement, a new publication was initiated — the *PALIAct Ideas and Action*, the first issue of which is available on the PALIAct website.

The response to these initiatives has been encouraging. Based on these, it was decided to pilot two country centres — in Kenya and Ghana. The Kenya Centre has elected an interim committee headed by Esther Obachi and has been working on a number of initiatives.

Discussions were held in London on March 24, 2006 with Samuel A. Zan, the Director of the Social Enterprise Development Foundation of West Africa, Ghana (SEND) and Marika Sherwood[530] to explore the possibility of setting up a Ghana PALIAct Centre.

At the same time, contacts were made with the Network Institute for Global Democratization (NIGD).[531] Mikael Böök[532], a member of NIGD wrote to PALIAct suggesting that, "NIGD can apply for financial support for one participant of PALIAct from the Finnish Foreign Ministry." The idea was that somebody from PALIAct participates in the library-related workshop at the World Social Forum in Bamako. The workshop was arranged by NIGD and took place during the World Social Forum (WSF) in Bamako, Mali in January 2006. In the event, Esther Obachi and Muthoni Wanjohi from the Kenya PALIAct Centre attended the Forum.

---

[529] World Summit on the Information Society (WSIS), Declaration of Principles. Available from: http://www.itu.int/wsis/docs/geneva/official/dop.html. Accessed: 14 April, 2006.
[530] Marika Sherwood is Senior Research Fellow, Institute of Commonwealth Studies, University of London and the Editor, Black & Asian Studies Association Newsletter.
[531] Details available from NIGD website at www.nigd.org.
[532] Details about the work of Mikael Böök can be found at: http://blogi.kaapeli.fi/book/. He can be contacted at <book@kaapeli.fi>.

The Kenya PALIAct Centre is now on the organising committee of the next WSF forum to be held in January 2007 in Nairobi. As a follow up to the discussion at Bamako, PALIAct has taken up the challenge and is organizing a training of trainers' workshop for librarians in Nairobi in preparation for the 2007 WSF conference. The plan is to train librarians on how various WSF activities during the conference can be covered so that the information collected from the forum can be disseminated through public libraries.

Some recent developments

A British PALIAct Support and Advisory Group has been formed to publicise PALIAct activities and to explore ways in which PALIAct centres in Africa can be supported. One of its activities will be to address a meeting of the International Library and Information Group of CILIP on May 17, 2006.[533]

Presentation on the theme, "Politics of information & knowledge in Africa; the struggle for an information inclusive society in a globalised world," at the XVII Standing Conference Of Eastern, Central, & Southern African Library & Information Professionals (SCECSAL XVII), Dar es Salaam, Tanzania, July 10-14, 2006. This will include a section on PALIAct. [534]

A proposal for greater cooperation between the Department of Applied Social Sciences and relevant Departments of African Universities is being prepared and will be further discussed in June-July, 2006. Central to this will be the PALIAct and QLP projects as well as joint delivery of a number of modules taught at the London Metropolitan University.

Challenges

In its short life, PALIAct has made much progress and has developed an impressive list of individual and organisational supporters. However, the organisation faces major challenges and it is by no means certain that it will develop as actively as it has done during its first year. Some of the challenges are summarised below.

Mainstreaming PALIAct vision in public libraries

Perhaps the greatest challenge facing PALIAct is that it does not have the active support of public library structures in Africa. These are not only rather marginalised themselves, but face major problems in keeping afloat. In this context, they have neither the vision, nor the resources and desire to take up the challenges posed to the sector by PALIAct.

PALIAct's greatest strength is the enthusiasm of those who are working actively for its programme. However, their involvement in the organisation is entirely on a voluntary basis, additional to their personal and work commitments. That activists have come forward to join the organisation is an indication of the great need for such an initiative – in libraries as well in communities. But long-term sustainability can be guaranteed only if its vision and activities are mainstreamed within the public library sector in Africa. The political will to do so needs to come from African governments and regional organisations, such as the Africa Union.

---

[533] Library & Information Gazette 7 April, 2006.
[534] Conference details are available from: http://www.tlatz.org/scecsal2006/.

Lack of material resources

PALIAct has no material resources. It has grown up on a very positive vision and the commitment of its supporters around the world, but no funds. It has tremendous support from communities, as witnessed by the new partnership between local communities, schools, community activists and professionals who came together in Naivasha, Kenya to set up a community information resource centre. Resources in terms of books, material, computers, software, etc., can hopefully be raised initially from supportive organisations and individuals. The key challenge at the moment is to set up strong organisations in African countries with a group of committed activities. This challenge is well met in Kenya.

ICT resources

Communications within Africa and with places outside of Africa pose another challenge for PALIAct. While easy access to the Internet and e-mail is now taken for granted in Europe and the U.S.A., this is not always the case in Africa. Yet activists there are taking advantage of whatever local resources are available in Universities and other places to ensure that information is regularly exchanged.

Effective leadership

An important challenge is the development of effective leadership to enable PALIAct to become sustainable. No country, organisation or profession can expect to achieve its vision without developing its members in areas such as appropriate ideological awareness and orientation, an understanding of historical and current contradictions facing the country or organisation, a clarity about who and what their allies are in terms of achieving their goals, and an understanding of organisational change brought about by innovation and creativity. The development of leadership requires that these theories are then reinforced by opportunities for practical work as a way of gaining experience which can give increased confidence to individuals as well as to organisations. It is only through such life-long learning programmes that there can be any hope of ensuring the sustainability required for long-term development.

DASS has teaching and learning programmes, resources and modules in this area, and will make these available to PALIAct.

While Africa faces a number of problems in developing its people and resources in a meaningful way, it faces large challenges too. PALIAct can be a small — but crucial — step in a long journey to sustainable development. Going by the commitment of those in Africa already working on the proposal, there is ample ground for optimism. The key question for people in Europe and the U.S.A. is whether they can work in partnership with the new generation of African information activists who are the PALIAct pioneers. The Department of Applied Social Sciences has shown its commitment to this process. Let the others take a stand too.

> You've got to change the whole culture, open up things that have previously appeared closed.
>
> - Sir Herman Ouseley (*The Guardian* October 2, 1997:17)

Quality Leaders Project (Youth): Report 4 to PHF (2006)[535]

A year is not a long time in the life of local government. But it is half the lifetime of the QLP-Y Project. The context of rapid changes at the global level and also in local authorities in the last 10 years or so provides opportunities as well as challenges to projects such as QLP-Y which seek to introduce innovation. Such innovation and change need to be seen in their context of almost annual local government restructures, often accompanied by budget and staff cuts.

The total overhaul of services to children and young people in recent years has seen a major restructure of all local authorities. Similarly, changes that have culminated in the introduction of the Framework of the Future in public libraries have themselves resulted in a major service re-think and a deep questioning of the very role of public library services. These developments need to be seen in the broader context of changes associated with corporate globalisation influencing and, in turn, influenced by revolutionary changes in information and communications technology. Changes in the economic and political power at the global level provide yet another major shift in world politics, economy, technologies, culture and in the world of ideas. The rapid rise of the BRIC countries (Brazil, Russia, India and China) has seen a shift in the relative power of the U.S.A. and Europe. Thus China has overtaken Britain as the fourth largest economy in the world.

Such changes are not mere background news for QLP-Y. They provide a very powerful message for change in services to young people if they are to meet the challenges of the 21st Century. They also provide tools and incentive for change, which makes innovative projects such as QLP-Y not only possible, but essential. Global changes provide a challenge for local services to meet new and unmet needs of young people. At the same time, they create conditions, which ensure that change, if relevant and implemented sensitively, will succeed.

An essential requirement for meeting these various challenges is the availability of effective leadership. Such leadership can provide a clear vision and strategy, which are essential if the public sector is to meet the rising expectation of citizens awakened to their rights. A key ingredient in bringing about required change is the active involvement of the very people on whose behalf services are provided. Their voice must inform policy decisions. An active partnership of all service providers and communities is yet another essential ingredient for success in local service.

The QLP-Y programme aims to meet these various challenges. It is a complex programme whose ramifications are not always easy to understand. It often demands shifts in thinking and requires acting outside local government boxes. The QLP-Y project was, in many ways, ahead of its time. It emerged in the last years of the 20th Century when perhaps its approach and vision were not fully appreciated by many. Yet in the rapidly changing world of today, it provides a useful model that has the potential to meet today's challenges. The QLP-Youth strand provides an important opportunity to test the theories of the "QLP vision" in the social context of four pioneering local authorities: Barnet and Haringey in London, Lincolnshire and Portsmouth. Taken as a whole, these four authorities provide a varied set of needs and conditions—both in terms of staff development and in developing relevant services to young people. They provide a tough challenge to QLP-Y.

---

[535] Report No. 4: The Paul Hamlyn Foundation. May 2006 – November 2006.

This, the fourth report to the Paul Hamlyn Foundation, provides a record of the achievements of QLP-Y in a relatively limited period of time since implementation started. The past year has seen a slow, but necessary, period of building a foundation for QLP-Y to take off. The period has, at times, been frustrating with its slow developments and apparent inactivity where small initiatives seem not to meet the challenges facing the project. The current period can be seen as one where QLP-Y starts taking off. It is a period where the small, quantitative changes of the previous period are now leading to important qualitative changes.

Whereas the key concerns in the previous period was internal processes, the key issues now are outcomes. The focus in the previous period was on internal library/youth service matters; this is now shifting to the wider areas of local authorities as a whole. The previous period was involved in providing skills, confidence and a new vision to Quality Leaders and their teams; it is now focused on young people in the communities. The previous period looked at the library or youth services internally; now the two services are increasingly marching ahead hand in hand and reaching out to other service providers and other Council Departments. New partnerships, formal and informal, are now the norm in all authorities. Small shoots of these significant changes are growing in each authority.

In some cases, young people themselves are providing leadership. This is people power at a very basic level. Such empowerment of young people (and their staff) is at the centre of QLP-Y thinking.

Some evidence of new services being introduced is provided in this report: Barnet with its youth promotional video; Haringey's creative writers' workshops and the Tottenham Carnival photo documentation project; Lincolnshire's artwork for comic book and Portsmouth's display of painting by young people.

But the QLP-Y is keen to let the evaluation of the QLP-Y be done by independent evaluators who will judge the project and assess its impact on young people, staff and services. Details of the start of this process are provided in this report.

A key development in the past year has been the visits to authorities by members of the QLP-Y Steering Group. The first round of visits was covered in the last report; this one provides details from the second round. This is a key mechanism to bring the authorities and QLP-Y together face to face, to see life from the other's point of view and to explore new ways of working, thinking and developing. The visits provide a human face to the often abstract and academic world of projects and management theories.

This report also reflects recent changes in the organisation of QLP-Y itself: a clearer vision and strategic approach, stronger management and performance management focus and a clearer implementation focus. An important change that is likely to come to fruition in the next reporting period is a new emphasis on policies driving practices. The organisation of this report itself reflects these important developments in the way chapters are organised. This indicates that the project itself is learning and developing even as it helps others to learn and develop.

Innovation and change require vision, commitment, resources, risk-taking and management support. By signing up to the QLP-Y programme, the four participating authorities committed themselves to the vision and requirements of the programme. It is to the credit of these authorities that they have maintained their support and commitment to the project. This report documents the achievement of these authorities, of their Quality Leaders and their QLP Teams.

QLP-Y on a journey of a thousand kilometres (2007)[536]

As the Quality Leaders Project (QLP-Y) reaches the final six months in three of the authorities, it is possible to get an initial indication of the effectiveness and the impact of the project. The fourth authority, Barnet, still has a year to completion as their start had been delayed due to restructuring, but even here, there are important developments as recorded in this report.

During this reporting period, there have been some significant developments both nationally and internally within QLP-Y. At the national level, both the aspects covered by the project—Library and Youth Services—have had important policy initiatives which provide useful benchmarks. The internal QLP-Y developments indicate a new confidence in meeting project targets.

National policy development

Library policy initiative

The Museum, Libraries and Archives Council (MLA) have started a consultation process under the title "A Blueprint for Excellence—Public Libraries 2008-2011." The outcome of this consultation is likely to influence the future role and function of public libraries. The document sets out to achieve a "shared universal understanding of the role of the modern public library and the core services the public and communities can expect." The consultation expects there to be a "universal entitlement for children, young people, families and communities to an accessible local library and place of resource, a service working in partnership to engage with communities, and a global, interactive information service." The Blueprint raises an important question, which has been at the centre of the work of QLP-Y. It states:

> A significant percentage of the population uses the library. But are they getting the service they need and want, and what about others who are not using the service? At a time of increasing pressure on local authority budgets...it is time for the public library service to take a hard look at both its role in society and the services it can and should be providing.[537]

These questions are at the core of QLP-Y and the final reports from the project (from QLP-Y itself as well as the Final Evaluation Report) will attempt to see the impact of the project from the above standpoint. The QLP model already seeks to meet new or unmet needs of local communities, especially those not already reached by the services. Again, its approach is to develop new services through active consultation and participation of young people.

---

[536] Quality Leaders Project – Youth. QLP-Y Report to Paul Hamlyn Foundation. No. 5. December 2006 – April 2007. Executive summary.

[537] MLA (2007a): A Blueprint for Excellence—Public Libraries 2008-2011. The consultation paper is available at: http://www.mla.gov.uk/resources/assets//B/blueprint_11126.pdf. [Accesssed 29 May 2007].

However, there is a worrying aspect of this MLA initiative. The consultation document seems to assume that public libraries are already delivering an acceptable level and quality of service and the need is for the "rest" to catch up with the best. This was also the approach of the previous policy initiative from MLA — "Framework for the Future."[538] This concern, was raised by the present author in a response to the consultation:

> There may be a danger of making assumptions about services before the consultation is concluded. For example, the document seems to assume that public libraries are already delivering an acceptable level and quality of service and the need is for the "rest" to catch up with the best. It says: "This approach to future improvement does not call for complete re-invention of public libraries as we know them today but makes an explicit commitment to ensuring the services of the best public libraries are supported and provided to every citizen, everywhere." What if the evidence indicates a need for a "complete re-invention"?[539]

As the QLP-Y experience shows, there is need for some fundamental shift in policies, organisational structures and cultures if the needs of young people are to be met in a meaningful way. The QLP-Y experience, together with some other material, has been submitted to MLA as part of the consultation response.

Out of the nine "key challenges" mentioned by the "Blueprint for Excellence," two are particularly relevant for QLP-Y. These are:

Staff — enabled and empowered to lead and deliver customer-focused services that meet the national entitlement.

Innovation — exploring new service models and new partnerships better to meet changing customer needs and offer new approaches to service delivery and evaluation.

Developing management and other staff skills are again areas in which QLP-Y has placed increasing emphasis, while innovation in service development and delivery are key areas that QLP-Y seek to develop, hence the "audience development" approach. Both these are summed up in our motto "management development through service development."

It would thus seem that QLP-Y is already pioneering the key areas that MLA has identified as requiring particular attention. The QLP-Y Evaluation is again another area where the approach we have taken sets new standards in managing evaluation. It is hoped that the final MLA report based on this consultation will incorporate the QLP-Y experience.

Youth service

There have been two key policy initiatives in service provision for young people. The first is the Ofsted Report, "Building on the best: overview of local authority youth

---

[538] MLA (2003): Framework for the future. Available at: http://www.mla.gov.uk/webdav/harmonise?Page/@id=73&Document/@id=18382&Section[@stateId_eq_left_hand_root]/@id=4332. [Accessed: 30 May 2007].

[539] Durrani, Shiraz (2007): Documents for developing an excellent & relevant public library service. Submission to MLA as part of the consultation on "A Blueprint for Excellence — Public Libraries 2008-2011". 29 May 2007.

services 2005/06."[540] It is not within the scope of this report to look at this important report in detail, but two areas need mention. First, one of its key findings is that "the quality of strategic and operational leadership and management is a key factor in bringing about improvement." Secondly, one of its recommendations is to "seek to build upon the managerial and relevant experience of youth service officers and engage them in key strategic developments."

As with the earlier MLA consultation, the Ofsted Report highlights the management development aspect that QLP-Y has pioneered. As sections in this report indicate, we place a greater emphasis during the period under review on this aspect (explained further below).

The second youth policy initiative is the Fulfilling Their Potential Conference held in February 2007,[541] where a new vision for library service for young people was the theme. Beverley Hughes, Minister for Children, Young People and Families, gave a keynote address at the conference. She urged local authorities to ensure libraries are treated as essential partners in helping young people achieve their full potential. Hughes underlined the role of public libraries in the context of social exclusion:

> Libraries are uniquely positioned to reach out those young people who typically find our services hard to access — young people in care, young people with disabilities or young people from traveller families, who the typical one-size-fits-all approach to public services will do little to help.[542]

While the approach that Fulfilling Their Potential is taking in meeting the needs of young people needs to be praised, perhaps it is rather limited in scope. MLA explains this role:

> At the heart of Fulfilling Their Potential is a commitment to involving young people in the process. From selecting books and other materials to training staff and designing library spaces, young people are getting actively involved in creating modern library and reading services, which meet their needs.[543]

The QLP-Y approach seeks a more fundamental role for young people by empowering them to inform policies in service development and resource allocation as far as services to young people are concerned. It also expects some structural reorganisation and culture shifts if the new services to young people are going to be sustainable and welcomed by young people themselves.

QLP-Y developments

There have been a number of key developments during this period within QLP-Y. Details are mentioned in the report, but some of these can be highlighted here:

QLP Evaluation Interim Report

---

[540] OFSTED (2007): Building on the best: overview of local authority youth services 2005/06. Available at: http://www.ofsted.gov.uk/publications/2706. [Accessed: 15 Feb 2006].
[541] MLA (2007): New vision for library services will help young people achieve their potential. 08 February. Available at:
http://www.mla.gov.uk/webdav/harmonise?Page/@id=82&Section[@stateId_eq_left_hand_root]/@id=4289&Document/@id=27142&Session/@id=D_bIfMPSPbdQ5eRp0afEYO. [Accessed: 29 May 2007].
[542] Ibid.
[543] Ibid.

The team carrying out an independent evaluation of QLP-Y issued its interim report in February 2007. The full report is attached to this report. Some highlights from the report can be mentioned here:

- The most important aspect of the QLP-Y initiative was seen by participants as responding to the needs and wants of young people, particularly those who have not traditionally been library users, and ensuring that they are much more involved in the delivery and design of services.
- Participating staff noted their personal development as a result of engaging in project activities at local level. The project has also raised the profile of work with young people in libraries.
- The QLP-Y initiative has started to involve young people who were previously non-library users in activities and drawn them into the library. Interest in continuing use of the libraries has also increased as a result of the activities. Young people participating in the project are also seen to have developed personally, for example, in terms of their levels of confidence.
- There has been some impact on service provision in some of the areas, although it is still too early to assess the impact of QLP-Y generally on services or on wider organisational cultures.

It would appear that QLP-Y is on its way to meeting the key requirements set out in our funding application—but the final report will give a fuller picture.

Focus on Quality Leader (QL) development

Following feedback from project visits and feedback from Quality Leaders during Development Days, it was decided to shift the focus of the project to the development of Quality Leaders (QL), although the service development aspect was not ignored. While a needs assessment exercise was carried out to assess the differing needs of QLs, it was decided that there needed to be a more proactive approach in supporting QLs. This need was further emphasised as mentors and sponsors were not able to support the development of their QLs in the way envisioned in the original application.

The approach taken was to support the development of QLs as strategic leaders and active agents of organisational change. For this to be meaningful, they needed to have the confidence that comes from clear awareness of their own contribution to service development and from an active involvement in policy making. Thus the emphasis was on moving away from purely operational work to a more strategic approach. In this context, it was felt, that QLs would further develop their ideas and experience even as they developed new skills.

This, however, proved not as easy as it may appear, as the contact time between the Project Team and QLs is rather limited and mainly confined to the rather infrequent Development Days. It was always difficult to organise Development Days as not all QLs could be released from their work on the same days. This was overcome, to a certain extent, by a more pro-active electronic contact, for example in the project to write the joint article for *Public Library Journal* where face-to-face meetings were supplemented by e-mail contacts. This new approach was more successful as the following examples indicate. This approach will be further developed in the next reporting period.

At the same time, QLP-Y staff, themselves, have developed through their participation in the project. This will be examined further in our Final Report.

The new approach to developing QLs is based on the following initiatives:

Journal article

It was decided to support interested QLs in writing articles on their experience in professional journals. The first outcome of this exercise is an article written by Durrani, S.; Ibrahim, S; Lusted, C.; Percival, D.; Sowter, E.; Stalker-Booth,C — who "put their heads and experience together to write about the role and impact of the QLP-Y." The title is "Filling the youth-shaped hole."[544]

Editing *QLP News*

Another way that QLs are being given confidence and new skills is in offering them the opportunity for editing *QLP News* where the content is decided entirely by them based on their own experiences of QLP-Y projects in their authority. The first such issue (No. 5); has been prepared by Catherine Lusted from Barnet. The issue is ready to go to print. It is anticipated that each authority will edit a future issue before the project ends.

Research experience

A Barnet case study is being conducted by some members of the QLP Project Team along with the Quality Leader and Mentor from Barnet. This is expected to be in two phases, the first one involves writing an article to be submitted to *Public Library Journal*, whose editor has already indicated interest in publishing it. A meeting has been held to plan the article, tasks have been assigned and further work will be carried out during the next reporting period.

The second phase will see an in-depth Barnet case study. However, whether this goes ahead will be decided on the basis of the availability of resources within the Department of Applied Social Sciences (DASS) to support such activities, as the QLP funds do not allow for this. Based on the availability of funding and interest from other authorities, similar case studies can be carried out for each participating authority, providing a wealth of insight and knowledge on the QLP-Y experience.

QLs take control

The Quality Leaders expressed their wish, at a Development Day, to organise a joint event under the general theme of "Liberation." They are now taking decisions and initiatives without PG support. This indicates their growing confidence in their own ability to organise and implement projects. The Project Group has offered each authority £2,000 to help organise the event expected to be held in London as an "altogether" event, as well as local events. QLs subsequently organised their own Development Day to progress the plan. A member of PG and Evaluators Team attended the Day as observers. This will be further reported in our next report.

Short course

---

[544] Durrani, S.; Ibrahim, S.; Lusted, C.; Percival, D.; Sowter, E.; Stalker-Booth, C (2007): Filling the youth shaped hole. Public Library Journal. Vol. 22 (2) Summer 2007, pp. 7-10.

Following the attendance by QLs at a DASS lecture during a Development Day, a number of Quality Leaders, Mentors and Sponsors have shown an interest in QLs attending a DASS Short Course on "Leadership for Innovation, Equality and Change." The details of these will be worked out during the next reporting period if funding can be found from within the QLP-Y budget. It is possible, given adequate funds, to give University accreditation for the short course.

"Information and Democracy"

This is an initiative within the Information Management Team at DASS. It involves setting up a new website and an electronic journal under the title "Information and Democracy."[545] The journal is aimed at the academic world, professionals as well as students — all of whom are offered an opportunity not only to contribute articles, but also to be involved in the production and editorial work. These opportunities are also being offered to QLs and their team members. Dave Percival, the Quality Leader from Portsmouth, is now a member of the Editorial Board.

The above developmental opportunities are expected to contribute to the long-term sustainability of the work already started under QLP-Y. The experience of developing library services for young people at the Sighthill Estate in Edinburgh highlights the central role that library staff, play in developing a "youth-friendly" library service. Frank Russell, commenting on the success of the initiative, said:

> This is a template any library could build on, but you would have to recruit staff who would fit the model. The librarians are the key — they connect with the young people and retain their respect.[546]

The Sighthill approach was to recruit staff from non-library backgrounds as a way of bringing in required skills to deliver a relevant youth library service. While this is a valid approach, it is not always available to all authorities. It is also necessary to develop "youth skills" among current staff. The QLP-Y approach is to combine both these aspects: the QLs themselves can come from staff delivering service from libraries or youth service, but the concept of the QLP Team allows less experienced staff and community members also to be involved in the programme, thus offering them developmental opportunities.

Service and Project development

Authorities have continued to develop services started in the previous period. However, different authorities have developed services at a different pace. There is also a variance in the quality of new services and new ideas developed and implemented, as is the case in the level of youth involvement and audience development activities. This is only natural as conditions in each authority differ and take different routes. Progress in each authority is highlighted in this report and strengths and challenges are outlined.

An important feature of QLP- Y work is the regular visits to authorities by members of the Project Team. These have provided valuable opportunities to assess progress response to challenges and provide new momentum to the project. This was not planned for in our original application and we have had to find resources (PG staff time as well as travel costs) from project and from DASS resources.

---

[545] Now renamed: "Information, Society and Justice".
[546] Chesshyre, Robert (2007): Turning the page. Telegraph Magazine. 14 April. pp. 42-46.

QLP publications — connecting theory with practice

As part of ensuring that QLP-Y meets national policy direction, we produced a new publication *Youth Policy Review*. It provides separate sections for Youth Work and for Libraries. The publication has proved popular with authorities as well as at the University. This is perhaps the key area which QLP-Y has sought to advance — to ensure that participants are aware of national policy developments, and that these guide QLP-Y project activities. A useful guide was necessary for this. We expect to bring out another issue of *Youth Policy Review* before the Project ends — as well as further issues of *QLP News*, and *Youth Ideas and Action*. At the same time, the development of QLP website has been strengthened with a new QLP site being developed within the Research page of the Department of Applied Social Sciences (DASS). This will remain as the main depository of all QLP material even after the Project ends.

The above will be supplemented by the production of the "QLP Manual" — subject to funding for PG time to develop this. External funding will also be sought for this.

What we have learnt

We have added a new section in the Report — "What we have learnt". This allows us to start evaluating the project and document lessons learnt. We expect to develop this section further for our final report.

All authorities have found QLP-Y a valuable Project. In many cases it has enabled organisational change to take place and respond more positively to national policy agenda. The feedback from John Pateman, Mentor at Lincolnshire, has lessons for the Project as a whole, as well as for the authorities. John says:

> 1. QLP has added value. Shortly after we signed up to QLP the Library Service and the Youth Service (which were in the same Department) were split into separate Directorates. Without the QLP program it is likely that Library and Youth Services would not have worked so closely together on joint projects.
>
> 2. QLP has led to culture change...there have been significant shifts in attitudes and behaviours, which are less easy to measure.
>
> 3. Selection of QLs — in retrospect it may have been more appropriate to have selected less experienced staff to assume the roles of QL's, as this may have given more scope for personal development. [One of the QLs], in particular, has taken on a completely new job role during QLP process.
>
> 4. The role of mentors should be reviewed — the line manager of the QLP could become the sponsor to ensure that expectations are clear and activity takes place within deadlines.[547]

Much hard work remains to be done before the end of the Project. Our main challenge, however, is to ensure that the gains made in the past are not lost, and that

---

[547] e-mail from John Pateman to Shiraz Durrani. 8 June 2007.

the Project continues to grow and develop in a sustainable way. Our next round of visits will look into this aspect.

Yet it would be incorrect to say that everything has worked out as we had planned. QLP-Y is involved in social aspects of organisations and service and there are no set guidelines that can guarantee that expected outcomes will, indeed, be the real outcomes. While a overall analysis of this aspect will be the subject of our Final Report, a few aspects have been mentioned in Section 7: "What we have learnt".

Pitcher, Eastwood-Krah and O'Neille[548] point to the real challenge facing QLP-Y, as well as service providers when they say "The challenge will be to mainstream these activities and to change the culture in the long term, so that young people are involved as a matter of course in developing services". An important contribution that the Project is already making is summed up by Durrani et. al.:

> It is interesting to see them [Quality Leaders] making the crucial connection between theory and practice and moving from operational to strategic issues. The Project has given them opportunities not only to understand the dynamics of organisational change but to become active agents of change. In this, the Project is helping to develop effective leadership skills".[549]

As the saying goes, "a journey of a thousand kilometres starts with the first step". QLP-Y is taking this first step with confidence.

The last word

The Project could not have developed as well as it has without the enthusiasm, hard work and commitment of Quality Leaders and their Teams in all authorities. This includes all the young people involved in the project. Finally the hard work, sometimes in difficult circumstance, by Emily and Michael need a special mention.

Filling the youth shaped hole (2007)[550]

Overview

Public libraries face major challenges in meeting the needs of young people. "Fulfilling their potential"[551] sees the need for "nothing less than a fundamental

---

[548] Pitcher, Jane and Eastwood-Krah, Mary with O'Neill Maggie
Evaluation of Quality Leaders Project (Youth) Initiative. Interim Report.
February 2007. Available at: http://www.seapn.org.uk/qlp.html. [Accessed: 22 September 2007].

[549] Durrani, Shiraz (2007): Documents for developing an excellent & relevant public library service. Submission to MLA as part of the consultation on "A Blueprint for Excellence — Public Libraries 2008-2011". 29 May 2007.

[550] Durrani, S.; Ibrahim, S.; Lusted, C.; Percival, D.; Sowter, E.; Stalker-Booth, C (2007): Filling the youth shaped hole. Public Library Journal. Vol. 22 (2) Summer 2007, pp. 7-10.
[551] Fulfilling their Potential: a national development programme for young people and libraries.(2004) Available at:
http://docs.google.com/View?docID=ddph8gnx_19gxpcqx&revision=_latest. [Accessed: 28 April 2007].

change in focus for libraries". That is precisely what the Quality Leaders Project – Youth (QLP-Y) [funded by the Paul Hamlyn Foundation] aims for.[552] Its central tenet is "management development through service development". Pitcher, Eastwood-Krah and O'Neill sum up its approach:

> The QLP-Y project is designed to address social exclusion of young people from libraries and other services, through developing partnership between library services, youth services and community groups. Its aim is to create opportunities for young people to participate in society and to develop their creativity, reading and life skills, through developing staff skills and innovative services responsive to the needs of young people.[553]

QLP (Y) Report to Paula Hamlyn Foundation provides background to QLP aims:

> The QLP-Y...demands shifts in thinking and requires acting outside local government boxes...in the rapidly changing world of today, it provides a useful model that has the potential to meet today's challenges.[554]

But the challenges are not easy to meet. Historical imbalance in services to young people is compounded by a lack of strategic approach to address the imbalance. This results in what a participant in QLP-Y describes as a "*youth shaped hole in most of our libraries*".[555] While there is no doubt that there are many examples of good practice in providing innovative services, these remain as pockets of excellence. An overall vision that includes the provision of relevant, creative and effective services to meet unmet and new needs of young people has not yet been developed and implemented. Pitcher, Eastwood-Krah and O'Neill sum up the real need:

> The challenge will be to mainstream these activities and to change the culture in the longer term, so that young people are involved as a matter of course in developing services.[556]

QLP-Y attempts to mainstream services to young people in an innovative way.

The contributors to this article are Quality Leaders working with the Project. They provide examples of service development and reflect on their own development. It is interesting to see them making the crucial connection between theory and practice and moving from operational to strategic issues. The project has provided them opportunities not only to understand the dynamics of organisational change but to become active agents of change. In this, the Project is helping to develop effective leadership skills.

The Project gains from being based in an academic institution. It is not an isolated project "doing its own thing" within the Department of Applied Social Sciences. It is linked closely with various Modules being taught within the School of Information Management. One issue addressed in the teaching programme is seen as:

> [D]eveloping an appropriate learning culture among students even as they develop their knowledge, skills, and awareness. This is given greater seriousness by three

---

[552] Further information about the Quality Leaders Project is available at: http://www.seapn.org.uk/qlp.html.
[553] Pitcher, Eastwood-Krah and O'Neill (2007): op. cit.
[554] Quality Leaders Project – Youth (2006): QLP-Y Report No. 4 [to PHF]. May 2006 – November 2006. Part 1: Main Report. Available at http://www.seapn.org.uk/qlp.html#reports [Accessed: 29 April 2007].
[555] Pitcher, Eastwood-Krah and O'Neill (2007).
[556] Pitcher, Eastwood-Krah and O'Neill (2007) op. cit.

linked challenges facing British society and the workplace today—at a social-economic, pedagogical, and workforce development level.[557]

Another issue is to incorporate reflective learning in modules and projects. This is done through "an 'open' approach to learning from other experiences and ideas is used to ensure that latest theories are being incorporated".[558]

Thus QLP-Y brings together ideas and experiences from teaching within the Department as well as from the Management Research Centre. The contributions below provide evidence of the achievement and challenges facing not only QLP-Y but public libraries as a whole in their attempt to find new social relevance in a fast changing, globalised world.

Those behind QLP-Y are aware that it is not their own assessment of the Project that matters. It will be the ultimate beneficiaries of the project who will decide on this. They are the young people themselves, as well as the Quality Leaders and their Teams. Thus independent, external evaluators will provide their own assessment of the project. Their final report is due in December 2007. In-depth insight will be provided by a case study of the Barnet experience which will examine the process of change and assess those aspects of the Projects that contribute to meaningful change.

However, it is possible to see initial results at this stage. Pitcher, Eastwood-Krah and O'Neill say:

> Although the evaluation is still part-way through, some impacts of the project are evident already. Participating staff noted their personal development as a result of engaging in project activities at local level ... The project has also raised the profile of work with young people in libraries.[559]

To varying degrees, the QLP-Y initiative has started to involve young people who were previously non-library users in activities and drawn them into the library. Interest in continuing use of the libraries has also increased as a result of the activities. Young people participating in the project are also seen to have developed personally, for example in terms of their levels of confidence.

There has been some impact on service provision in some of the areas, although it is still too early to assess the impact of QLP-Y generally on services or on wider organisational cultures.

The following reports by Quality Leaders are part of an on-going process of documenting and assessing the impact of activities on the ground. They should provide useful insight for planners, policy makers, managers and staff.

---

[557] Durrani, Shiraz (2007): Learning by doing; Lifelong learning through innovations projects at DASS. ASLIB Proceedings. Vol. 59(2) March. pp.187 – 200.
[558] Durrani, Shiraz (2006/07): Incorporating reflective learning: rationale and initiatives in a programme on information management. Investigations. vol. 4 (i) Autumn 2006/07. pp. 74-79. ISSN 1740-5106.
[559] Pitcher, Eastwood-Krah and O'Neill (2007): op. cit.

Book Reviews

Sturges, Paul and Neill, Richard (1990): The quiet struggle. London: Mansell. (1991)

...

The strength of the book is in the fact that it does not look at libraries in isolation from their overall information context. Far too many studies on libraries have looked at the library scene in such minute details that they fail to recognise the broader influences that affect the existence and development of libraries. ...

One of the shortcomings of the book is that it does not recognise the post-independence reality of African society. Africa today is sharply divided between different classes and there is a fierce class struggle going on. Failure to recognise this reality leads the authors to see Africa as a unified whole without seeing the wealth and poverty existing side by side. It is thus possible for authors to make such generalizations as Africa being "almost untouched by the technical complexities and expense of computer technology, or even by the diverse messages conveyed by books". Such generalizations are far from true, as the latest technologies exist side by side with centuries old traditional technologies.

Again in the authors' assertion that "a totally oral society was until very recent times the norm in virtually every part of Africa", it is difficult to understand what is meant by "very recent times". As early as the beginning of this century, for example, in Kenya there existed printed material including newspapers which were used by the African and Asian workers. Additionally, written forms of many African languages had developed before colonialism came to Africa.

As mentioned earlier, the authors have shown the correct path in not seeing library work in isolation but [within] the overall context of information in society. At the same time, the book stops at this *information* context, without seeing the information itself in its wider *political* context. The reasons why no relevant library and information services have emerged are to be found not in the failure of African librarians but because of imperialist exploitation of Africa, which has affected every aspect of life, including information.

For the authors, it is enough to accept the "inescapable reality of poverty" of Africa. It is not necessary for them to question why the richest continent in the world is at the same time the poorest. But unless this question is discussed, it will not be possible to understand why Africa produces only 1% of world's books. Nor will it be possible to devise a relevant information service.

The failure to understand the class contradictions in Africa leads to yet another shortcoming. The title of the book leads one to expect an analysis of the *struggle* in the information field. Nowhere in the book are we shown who is confronting whom and over what issues. It is merely implied that there is a struggle for information. The Introduction correctly mentions various struggles taking place in Africa and the

---

[560] African Book Publishing Record (1991).

"struggle for information, the struggle for knowledge" is seen in this context. But the dialectical nature of the struggle is not seen nor explored.

In spite of these shortcomings, "The Quiet Struggle" is one of the most important studies to examine the information scene in Africa in recent years. At the very least, it will open the eyes of non-African scholars and information workers to the basic facts well known by African library workers. The book can be a useful tool to guide one through some debates and practices taking place in Africa and a useful record of recent developments on the continent.

Foreword to Kinyatti, Maina wa: Mother Kenya (1995)[561]

Mother Kenya: London: Vita Books; New York: MMRC

It is 2 June, 1982. The underground circles in Kenya are flooded with news of the imminent arrest of various people who have taken a principled stand against the unpopular Moi-Kanu regime in Kenya. The previous day Moi had attacked them at a public meeting. Among the first names mentioned is that of Maina wa Kinyatti, the foremost historian in Kenya. Subsequent news items continue the story. Special Branch Police search Maina's house while he is out; Mumbi stands firm and demands a list of all the items the Police take away; Maina defies the Police who intensify search for him. The following day comes the news that Maina boldly walks to the Police Station, in his own time, having completed more important assignments first.

Maina is subsequently charged with "subversion" and jailed for six years. He does not even get any remission of the sentence and serves all six years. Most of this time was spent in solitary confinement. He was adopted by Amnesty International as a Prisoner of Conscience.

What was it in Maina that made him a particular target of the regime? What powerful force did he represent that the regime saw him as a danger to its very survival? An answer to these questions can be sought only in the context of the resistance movement that emerged in Kenya almost at the time of independence in 1963. The roots of this resistance can be traced in the economic, political and social conditions after independence. While the official KANU version glorifies the early years of independence, the resistance movement sees the situation differently:

> 'Independence' in Kenya has led to the looting and squandering of our resources, and the virtual silencing of our people. It has led to the increasing misery and impoverishment of the many. Aspirations for better lives under uhuru have been betrayed by predatory politicians who talk of "nation-building" while fattening on the nation's wealth and people's labour."[562]

These conditions then resulted in an intensified resistance movement of which Maina was a part. Mwakenya places this resistance in its historical context:

---

[561] Kinyatti, Maina Wa (1997): Mother Kenya: Letters from Prison, 1982 1988. London: Vita Books.
[562] Cheche Kenya: InDependent Kenya. 1982. London. Zed Press. p. xi. This is a reproduction of an underground book circulating in Kenya in the early 1980s.

> the most dramatic development...was the emergence of worker/peasant based underground groups. They began articulating an ideology that fully reflected the workers' struggle. The seventies saw the development of a vigorous underground press best symbolised by *Mwanguzi* which ran to more than twelve issues. Between 1974 and 1982, the underground groups and newspapers had become the real voice of the Kenyan people.[563]

As Ngugi wa Thiong'o, the Spokesperson for Mwakenya, explained:

> In the mid-1970s people began to organise underground, manifesting themselves in above ground publications, such as *Independent Kenya*, by the Cheche group. These culminated in the appearance of the December Twelve Movement and its publication *Pambana*, which was circulated widely in 1982. Mwakenya is an offshoot of the December Twelve Movement.[564]

The early 1980s was a time for major changes in Kenya. The repressive side of Moi-Kanu regime was obvious to all and the initial honeymoon period with the regime came to an end. Resistance was on the increase once again. The regime was becoming increasingly isolated from the people and gained stability by granting military concessions to the USA in return for military and political support.

In this situation, the resistance movement gained strength in various ways: active struggle in form of strikes, boycotts, demonstrations, attacks on police etc. This struggle was reinforced by resistance at political and ideological level. It is the coming together of these different levels of the people's struggle that resulted in a qualitatively different resistance movement in Kenya in the 1980s.

An important aspect of this new resistance was its strong, united organisation. Guided by an overall central authority, underground political groups soon began to emerge. They set out their ideological standpoint which opposed the capitalist road of Kanu. It is clear that the main thread running through the underground opposition in Kenya was a strong anti-imperialist ideology and a commitment to a socialist road to development. The commitment to the struggles of workers, peasants and other working people was what differentiated these movements from the practice of the Kanu regime.

The resistance movements were strengthened by having a stronger organisational network. They functioned in tight cells in response to the lack of opportunity for open political activities. Such study circle method complemented the traditional method of influencing and directing activities of open, democratic organisations. One such group was Cheche Kenya which was active in the early 1980s.

The underground movement brought about a qualitative change in the political situation in Kenya. It changed the economic struggles of the workers, peasants and other working people into a political struggle, thus posing a real threat to the Moi-Kanu regime. In the interview quoted above, Ngugi establishes this crucial role of the underground and also shows the links between the underground and the open resistance to the regime:

> It is the underground resistance which has linked the economic, political and social problems to the KANU political system. What has happened in 1990 is that what has often been debated underground has suddenly come to the fore and has been taken up by other forces, for instance, the clergy and the lawyers. Whereas before, workers

---

[563] Mwakenya: Draft Minimum Programme. 1987. Nairobi. p.13.
[564] Ngugi wa Thiong'o interviewed by William Acworth. Ufahamu; Journal of the African Activist Association. XVIII (2) 41-46 (1990).

were always on strike, peasants were uprooting trees, students were demonstrating, but there was a tendency to see these things in isolation. That is, the workers would see their problems as economic, or the peasants might see their problem as a wrong official in a co-operative. Now for the first time all these forces began to openly link their problems to the political system, as symbolised by Moi and KANU. They are saying that our problems have to do with the type of party KANU is and the type of leader Moi is.[565]

The role that Maina and other people played in linking the economic and political struggles is crucial in explaining the fierce repression unleashed by the regime in the 1980s. By late 1970s there developed a powerful underground alliance of workers, peasants, urban youth, students and committed intellectuals. It was this anti-imperialist alliance which changed the political map of Kenya for good. Its influence spread throughout the country and affected all aspects of life, ranging from social organisations, cultural and educational groups, trade unions, peasant and worker organisations, University circles and, of course, political movements. The open political manifestation of this national movement can be seen in the publications from this alliance, such as *InDependent Kenya, Pambana, Mzalendo Mwakenya, the Draft Minimum Programme of Mwakenya* and Mwakenya's *Register of Resistance*.

The political influence of this movement can be seen in many aspects of Kenyan life of this period. For example, the strength of the worker and peasant activities can be seen in the well co-ordinated strikes and peasant activities in the late 1970s and early 1980s as documented in the *Register of Resistance*. The struggle to organise a militant working class organisation was symbolised in the struggle around the University Workers' Union which became a major national movement and attracted the participation of workers throughout Nairobi.

The cultural movement was started by the University travelling theatre and was given a tremendous mass support with the production of Ngugi wa Thiong'o and Micere Mugo's *The Trial of Dedan Kimathi* in 1977. It reached its peak in the Kamiriithu Cultural Centre people building their largest open air theatre in Africa and with their productions of *Ngaahika Ndeenda* and *I will Marry When I Want*. Another aspect of this cultural struggle was the attempt to make the Kenya National Theatre really "national". Various progressive plays continued to be performed at the University of Nairobi theatre, including the militant version of *Kinjikitile* in 1984.

The struggle in the educational sector started with the struggle to change the English literature syllabus in schools and at the University of Nairobi. The regular public lectures at the University of Nairobi and other activities on the campus led to the birth of militant political organisation in schools and University campus.

The political manifestation of these resistance activities was the December Twelve Movement and the birth of its public paper, *Pambana*. By the time the first issue of *Pambana* was widely circulated in May 1982, the political situation in the country had reached a boiling point. This indirectly encouraged the coup of August, 1982 which almost overthrew the weakened Moi. But finding strength from British and US government support, Moi came back to power in a wave of killings.

The arrest of Maina in 1982 is linked very closely with these developments. Maina had come to be identified together with a number of other activists as one of the people behind the surge of activity directed towards challenging the regime in every field. A full history of the post-independence resistance movement will reveal that

---

[565] Ngugi wa Thiong'o, interview. Ibid. p.43.

Maina was one of the people behind the upsurge of the movement for change from the late 1970s.

Maina was part of the Cheche Kenya group which published the underground publication, *InDependent Kenya* which circulated widely in 1981 and was published in London by Zed Press in 1982. The Zed Press edition's author statement mentions that "the Kenyan authors of this book have to remain anonymous because they are still living in their country." While it is not the intention in this short Foreword to document the history of the underground movement of this period, it can certainly be revealed that Maina was one of this "anonymous" authors. But Maina was also active in distributing the book underground. This was no mean achievement, given not only its large size — the Zed Book edition runs to 119 pages — but the fact of the repression of the regime that made it extremely difficult to travel within the country without alerting Moi's vast army of informers. The circulation of the book had to be done in extreme secrecy.

InDependent Kenya marked a new period in the resistance movement in Kenya:

> The ongoing resistance of workers, peasants, and students had now been joined by committed intellectuals and professional people such as lecturers, doctors, lawyers, and teachers... The Cheche group brought together intellectuals and workers in an underground organisation. Gone were the days of individuals and small groups who brought out a single-page leaflet focusing on a single issue. The whole concept and approach of InDependent *Kenya* was different. The book was a study of Kenya's history and politics... *InDependent Kenya* represented an important ideological step in understanding the realities of neo- colonialism.[566]

Maina the historian of the working class in Kenya played an important part in *writing* the book, while Maina the political activist played an important part in its *distribution*, thus ensuring that the book reached its potential readers.

Maina was again a part of the December Twelve Movement which emerged from the Cheche Kenya group.

> The emergence of the December Twelve Movement was perhaps the most significant political event in Kenya since independence. It marked the end of the attempts by democratic forces to form legal opposition parties... It became the historical role of the Movement to articulate the new phase in Kenyan politics where it was possible to struggle for national democratic rights only at an underground level. What distinguished the December Twelve Movement from earlier underground movements was the fact that for the first time, a Programme which became an alternative to KANU's capitalism was presented nationally. The December Twelve Movement stood for a national democratic revolution which would unite all national forces opposed to imperialism.[567]

An important point to be noted about Maina was that he has never stood alone to seek personal gain or glorification. In a sense he merges with an advanced political organisation as one of many, equally taking up every challenge that the movement as a whole faces. His struggle is the struggle of the many. It is therefore difficult to see his contribution in isolation, for he has always worked in a disciplined way as part of a larger organised group. His high level of social commitment and dedication reflects the high political achievement of the resistance movement in Kenya.

---

[566] Durrani, Shiraz (1990) Voices of Resistance; Underground Publishing in Kenya after Independence, 1963-90. Internal document prepared for UKenya, London. pp. 9-10.
[567] Durrani, Shiraz: ibid. pp.12.

Maina has never given up hope for social justice and democracy in Kenya. Wherever people have organised and resisted, Maina always stands as a tower of strength. So he was there when the December Twelve Movement regrouped as Mwakenya after the repression of the early 1980s. He is present once again when Kenyan overseas joined hands with Mwakenya to form UKenya.

Every time I think of Maina in exile, I see him busy in his basement which he has converted into a study, surrounded by posters and books of struggles of people around the world, working at all hours of the night — busy not only documenting the past struggles of the people of Kenya but totally immersed in the current struggles for change and democracy. His is a life-time struggle which is a shining example to the new generations of Kenyans who are continuing the tradition of resistance.

One of Maina's great contribution to Kenya is his documentation of Kenya's history in works like *Thunder from the Mountains; Mau Mau Patriotic Songs*, *Kenya's Freedom Struggle* and *Mau Mau; A Revolution Betrayed*. Perhaps the greatest tribute that the peasants and workers of Kenya paid to Maina was the singing of Mau Mau resistance songs when hundreds of people gathered outside the courtroom when Maina was sentenced.

Mother Kenya is yet another critical look at the reality of repression in Kenya, at the reality of resistance that has reached right in the prison cells. At the same time it gives an insight into the life and mind of Maina. The book teaches and it sings as it records the daily struggle for a just society. As long as oppression and exploitation remain, Maina and other fighters for justice will continue to teach and sing songs of resistance. The struggle continues...

Libraries for all — A tool for change? (1999)[568]

This is indeed a welcome document which is well researched and presented. It correctly identifies problems of great social significance and identifies the means of resolving them. It is refreshing to see the government taking a leading role that the profession and local authorities should have taken, but had not — partly out of inertia and lack of interest, partly as a result of the policies of the previous government. The positive points in the Policy Guidance need to be supported and developed further at local, professional and community levels. Action is long overdue and the concern of this review is to ensure that effective action is taken.

The following points should thus be seen in the context of this overall positive perspective on the Policy Guidance. They are meant to strengthen the final document in order to ensure that the goals are achieved in practice, and not remain as one more document in the "busy" librarian's "to-do" pile.

General considerations

- Social and economic exclusion: the language that the government uses has an important influence on the actual policies and practices. The term "social inclusion/exclusion" shows only a partial picture and is likely to lead the

---

[568] A review of Libraries for All: Social Inclusion in Public Libraries; Policy Guidance for Local Authorities in England. October 1999. London: DCMS.

thinking of policy-makers to a partial solution of the real problem. A better term would be "Social and economic exclusion" as it takes on board not only the social *effects* of exclusion, but also the economic *causes* of exclusion. With this clarity of the problem and its effects, it will be easier to find appropriate resolutions to the problems. It also gives dignity to the excluded individuals and communities who are then seen not as responsible for their exclusion, but as victims of economic forces in an increasingly globalised world.

- Power relationship: there is no mention of who (in terms of class, race or other "excluded" categories of people) controls power in the library service — either at the level of elected councillors or of senior staff. Those who have power use it to reinforce the power of the social class or group they represent. They will go to any lengths to ensure their continued monopoly over the power they have. Exclusion cannot be eliminated unless the excluded have power to change the status quo. The report does not provide for a change of power relationship in the LIS. Thus all the good intentions will remain just that — intentions.

- Libraries seen in isolation: the social context in which English (and British) libraries exist is largely ignored in the Policy Guidance. The distribution of wealth and power in society as a whole influence the way public institutions such as libraries operate. The context of a society where private ownership of property and production for profit allow some to have excessive wealth, power and influence at the expense of the rest of the community needs to be taken into account. It is this reality which leads to a large number of people being excluded from social wealth and power. Libraries cannot be seen in isolation from social forces all around them, nor can solutions be found if this reality is not understood.

- A wish list: the Executive Summary is in danger of being seen as a wish list, devoid of any achievable means of combating or eliminating social and economic exclusion. It does not provide tools to measure where the libraries are at present, thus allowing libraries to claim that "we are already doing all this." One of the objectives of the informal discussion group was to "identify the means of achieving objectives." It remains to be seen if the means have been adequately identified. More thought needs to be given to this part of the Guidance.

- Creative environment of real empowerment: the "socially excluded" seem to be seen in the document as a passive group whose needs are to be met by goodwill and patronage from those in power. The real solution is to give them power and influence over policies, procedures and practices — not in an abstract, formal way by "engaging them" but in a new, creative environment of real empowerment. The good intentions of the Policy Guidance can be lost if the excluded themselves are not involved in finding a solution to their exclusion.

- Standards of Service: perhaps the greatest weakness of the Policy Guidance is that it fails to establish a guaranteed, minimum standard of service for the "excluded" which alone can change the situation. The CRE's *standard for racial equality for local government in England and Wales*[569] provide a model for ensuring that there is a criteria of achievement which can be measured in a scientific way and higher targets set year after year. No mention is made of such a system of standards and needs to be included in the final document. The forthcoming standards of public libraries will provide another opportunity to do this.

- Lack of connection with relevant reports and research: There is no reference to the Roach and Morrison's "Public Libraries, ethnic diversity and citizenship"[570] and the Macpherson Report.[571] This is surprising, especially as the government has committed to accept "all" recommendations from the Macpherson Report. Further discussion on the aspect of ethnic/race exclusion in the Policy Guidance is given in a separate paper.[572]

- Support structures of the "already included": another aspect of social exclusion missing from the Guidance is the existence of extensive support structure that sustains those who are "already included." Such support is backed by resources controlled by the group itself. Whether it is information, connections, or support structures, those who are already included get additional help from such support structures. Those excluded from this support cannot break into the support structures as there are subtle barriers built all around it. Any attempt to combat exclusion will need to address this "invisible" but very real barriers and to create new structures to support the excluded.

- Resource implications: while it may be possible to redirect some resources, and while it is also true that some services "aimed at the socially excluded people can also be used by other members of the community", the danger of increasing social conflicts from such redirection should not be minimised. Those who have benefited from library services for generations are not likely to give up some of the services in the interest of the "socially excluded" without a fight. There needs to be a ring-fenced additional funding arrangement from the government to enable local authorities to begin to address the problem. This can be on a similar basis as that used in cancelling foreign debts of the "least developed countries", provided the resources are then used to eliminating poverty. It remains to be seen if the government sees social and economic exclusion as worthy of the same support as the development of ICT.

---

[569] Commission for Racial Equality (CRE) 1995. Racial equality means quality; a standard for racial equality for local government in England and Wales.

[570] Roach, P. and Morrison, M. (1998) Public Libraries, ethnic diversity and citizenship. Centre for Research in Ethnic Relations, University of Warwick, Warwick.

[571] Stephen Lawrence Inquiry: Report of an inquiry by Sir William Macpherson of Cluny (1999). The Home Office. Cm 4252-1.

[572] Durrani, S. Public Library Policy and Racial Exclusion. Forthcoming Working Paper for the Public Library Policy and Social Exclusion. Public Library Policy and Racial Exclusion. See: http://www.lmu.ac.uk/ies/events/soc-excl.htm

- Training library staff: this is indeed an essential method of bringing about change. One of the greatest difficulties in implementing change and in eliminating exclusion is staff attitude and reluctance to change. To a large degree the majority of staff currently represent the class, race and other interests of the "included". It is therefore important to change the balance in staffing so that there is equal representation from the excluded groups, especially in the senior, decision-making levels of staff. It is important that the government reviews the various legal barriers to achieving proportionality in staffing. It is not enough to expect a natural, evolutionary process to redress the balance on its own. A legal requirement that over a fixed number of years, all levels in the library should reflect the proportion of the excluded community in the local as well as national context should be imposed. The experience of achieving religious equality in Northern Ireland should be creatively applied in Britain as a whole. To a certain extent the CRE Standards do address this need.

- In addition, there should be a special training budget, similar to New Opportunities Fund, to train and develop staff from excluded communities so that the authorities can achieve proportionality and parity. The LIC-funded feasibility study for the Quality Leaders Project[573] should provide some valuable lessons which can be applied to all excluded communities and groups.

...

Conclusion

The Policy Guidance is very good in terms of the universalities, but weak on particularities. Although this is a good approach for a guidance document, the experience of the "Equal Opportunity" shows that authorities can be very good in applying the "universalities" but when it comes to particularities, all sorts of institutional and personal problems creep in to negate the policy.

It is therefore important for this Guidance to be more specific and spell out the minimum standards required. Thus different types of exclusion need to be identified: class, race, disability, sex and sexual orientation, etc. In each type, a minimum level of achievement needs to be recommended over a period of say 5 years. The decision as to whether the levels have been achieved should not be an internal one, but be linked to the Annual Library Planning process and be assessed by independent assessors who should include the communities and classes currently excluded.

In any policy affecting social and economic exclusion, there is a need to address historical imbalance suffered by the excluded communities. An intensive period of

---

[573] The Quality Leaders Research Project for Black LIS workers is "a feasibility study to assess if Quality Leaders approach is appropriate to address the needs identified by Black communities and LIS workers. It aims to recommend a practical way of addressing shortcomings highlighted in several recent research and national reports in providing service to Black communities and in the position of Black LIS workers in the workplace. At the same time, it will address the government's concern about eliminating social exclusion and will take the lessons and recommendations from the Public Library Policy and Social Exclusion Project." — Quality Leaders Research Project for Black Library & Information Workers.

change to overcome the effects of such exclusion should be specified so as to create a level playing field.

There is an urgent need for an Equality Charter as part of basic human rights legislation, with redress provided through courts of law. Experiences in other countries and in other fields show that only such legal requirements can eliminate social and economic exclusion. The Policy Guidance can become a real engine for change if it adds such legal powers to its arsenal.

Stop talking, start doing! (2000)[574]

Reese, Gregory L and Hawkins, Ernestine L. *Stop talking, start doing! Attracting people of color to the library profession.* 1999. Chicago: American Library Association. xix, 136pp. ISBN 0-8389-0762-8.

A relevant book at an appropriate time

At a time when the elimination of racism is in focus in Britain following the Roach and Morrison Report and the Stephen Lawrence Inquiry Report, it seems appropriate to examine the experiences and solutions in another country – USA. *Stop Talking, Start Doing!* thus comes out at a relevant time. Its central message, "Stop Talking, Start Doing" is also timely in pointing out the need for action to address the problems identified in both the above reports. There has been much talk already. Time for action has now arrived. The concerns and possible solutions that Reese and Hawkins examine have a high relevance for us in Britain.

The strength of the book lies in the fact that it makes a well presented case for change. The authors look at the needs of a changing population which demand a change in the direction of library and information service. They look at actual experiences and make recommendations for the type of change needed. It is a "practical guide to finding, nurturing, retaining a diversified workforce for libraries that reflect and attract the communities they serve". At one level it is a manual of implementing change, presenting, in a simple way, solutions which have been tried out. The recommendations are simple and effective, based on a changing world.

A refreshing aspect of the book is that it looks at library and information services and professional concerns of ethnic minorities in all fields: public, school, colleges, universities, and business libraries. It thus avoids the trap that we in Britain often find ourselves in – that of looking at services in isolated packages of public libraries, or academic libraries, or school libraries. Thus the solutions that emerge address all aspects of service to ethnic minority communities.

Racism in library and information world mirror racism in society

It is to the credit of the authors that they do not see racism in isolation in LIS. They are aware that it is the racism in the society as a whole which is then also persistent in the information world. Another important aspect of racism in Reese and Hawkins' book is that they make a connection between economic deprivation and a

---

[574] Review article Library Management. 21(8) 2000.

poor deal for ethnic minority communities and professionals in libraries and information:

> While the U.S. standard of living is the highest in the world, the experience of millions of ethnic minority citizens is one of inadequate housing, poverty-level incomes (whether employed or unemployed), illiteracy, and low educational attainment. It is very unfortunate that our institutions of higher learning, library service, and the profession itself mirror the racism and limited access to economic and educational opportunities present in the larger society.

The book intends to "demonstrate the importance of having a racially and ethnically diverse workforce in the library profession".. The very fact that there is a need to demonstrate this is an indication of existence of racism. The books provide library educators and practitioners with "strategies that will assist in the recruitment of ethnic minorities to the field of library and information science." It is thus a manual of how to bring about change in a profession which is rather reluctant to change.

The book is based on the experiences of the African American library profession in the USA and provides many practical ways of increasing minority representation in the profession. The Preface make it clear that the scope of the book covers only the African American experience within the library profession where "the most glaring inequalities have come to light". The authors, however, are aware that "other minority groups have experienced many of the same difficulties." Their population breakdown, information needs and ways of addressing their needs are also discussed.

The need for change

Changing demographics

The urgent need for change in the profession is the central basis of the book. A number of reasons for change are identified. Perhaps the most powerful challenge to the profession is the changing demographics in the USA. The projections speak for themselves:

By 2010, 38 percent of Americans under the age of eighteen will belong to minority groups. By 2058, the "average" US resident will trace his or her descent to Africa, Asia, the Hispanic world, the Pacific islands, Arabia—almost anywhere but white Europe.

Reese and Hawkins point to the differing needs within the African American communities. "They differ by socio-economic class." Those in lower socio-economic classes are the "ones who usually take a direct hit from the burdens of injustice by whites within our racist society." At the same time, middle-class African Americans are able to adjust and handle the burden of racism and ongoing prejudice in a different manor.

The effects of these changes are substantial. "Educating, training, and managing this increased workforce diversity is already posing a tremendous challenge for educational institutions as well as other government, industrial, and major business organizations throughout the United States". At the same time, such changes pose new challenges in the information field as well. "Library administrators and employee trainers must develop new skills in order to work effectively with the many new types of employees, such as understanding how it feels to be different and establishing a common ground with minority employees."

As the composition of the population changes, so do the needs of this population. The time to prepare for this change is now. "Most library programs do not yet make mainstream library activities available to multicultural populations" say Reese and Hawkins. They identify two areas where the profession will need to prepare:

The library and information science profession must position itself for the developments being brought forth demographically within our society. If we plan to continue as forerunners in the information business, we must seriously evaluate *how* we will deliver effective library service in the immediate future and *who* will deliver it. [Emphases added].

Globalisation and diversity

Another major force that is driving change in USA as a whole as well as in the information field is globalisation. Reese and Hawkins say that "diversity became an issue when three powerfully significant trends reached their own critical points at about the same time". These trends are:

- The global market in which American corporations must now do business became intensely competitive.
- The makeup of the U.S. workforce began changing dramatically, becoming more diverse.
- Individuals increasingly began to celebrate their differences and become less amenable to compromising what makes them unique. This inclination represents a marked departure from previous times when predisposition was to "fit in".

Ethical considerations

The need for change is also driven by ethical consideration. The first reason is that in a society where ethnic minority populations make up about 26 percent of the population, they make up only 10.5 percent of library school graduates, despite years of "positive actions".

The authors are conscious of the central role that information plays in the new information world:

> Probably no other profession needs sensitivity to the issues of diversity more than that of the librarians. They have always been keepers of cultural wisdom, private histories, arguments, and debates. Librarians need to consider the value of having minorities in libraries today, for their benefit to the multicultural user populations as well as for the value of gaining new perspectives for the development of service, programmes, and collections.

It thus bases its case for change on ethical grounds. Yet this area is perhaps the weakest in the book. It should have been the strongest case for requiring the service to ethnic minorities to change, yet the authors emphasise other reasons for change such as population shifts, globalisation, and changing business needs. While the American Library Association (ALA) has achieved much more than its British equivalent, it appears that there is a long way to go before the ethnic minorities receive an "equal service". The authors see the ALA as the "largest library advocacy group and the moral center of the profession, is the logical leader for new initiatives to expand the ranks of ethnic knowledge navigators and to bring about cultural diversity in our libraries and digital communities."

Yet there needs to be more moral demands on the Association to respond quickly and effectively to the needs of a changing population. The authors, instead of making a strong ethical case for change, are satisfied with making mild pleas for faster change. For example they say, "The American Library Association has provided little support to effect changes until very recently, with the introduction of the Spectrum Initiative." When discussing the Spectrum Initiative, they are content to plead that the "ALA can expand this effort to address services to our diverse communities by initiating additional programmes that respond specifically to the under-representation of minority library and information professionals."

The time is right for urgent change now, not merely to make pleas for change. It is time to "move the Centre" so that the needs of ethnic minority services and professionals are no longer at the periphery of the information world, but at the very centre. The achievement of this is not a matter of goodwill of well-meaning people who are in position of power. It is a question of ethics which demands change, not sometime in the future, not in a piecemeal fashion, but as a revolutionary change, right now.

The reluctance of the authors to demand radical change is due not to a lack of awareness of a need for a radical solution, but in order to move with the establishment to bring about organic, albeit slow, change. One wonders whether we are being fair to our communities by making such time-delaying compromises with those in power on behalf of the ethnic minority communities. We are in danger of sacrificing the futures of the next generation of ethnic minority population by making such compromises which we may not have the right to do. Instead of representing their interests, we are in danger of taking on the position of those who oppose change.

Reese and Hawkins see the need and the potential for an "inclusive, all-color, professional cadre of expert knowledge navigators to provide new communities of new populations with quality library and information services." They thus see two aspects of the problem: the information needs of the "new populations" and those who have the potential to provide this need — the "inclusive, all-colour professional cadre." The book goes into details of these two aspects.

Facts about ethnic minorities

By the year 2000, 80 percent of the U.S. workforce will be minorities, women, and people from other countries. By the year 2010, white man will account for less than 40 percent of the total workforce.

Although the book addresses mainly the needs of African American communities and professionals, it keeps the needs of other ethnic minority groups in mind all the time. It is a welcome move to acknowledge that the "ethnic minority" populations are not homogeneous. Thus the profiles and ways of each ethnic minority groups are explained:

- African Americans: number about 30 million and account for more than 12 percent of the U.S. population and 14 percent of its workforce... we must clearly understand, respect, and accept the fact that many African American values differ from those of Caucasians. The authors give an interesting example of how a local health authority failed to reach the African American youth through the library, and in the end gained success by reaching them through the local community barbershop.
- Asian Americans: the 1990 census counted more than seven million Asian Americans or 3.5 percent of the U.S. population. Some researchers claim that the real figure is 10 million. They are the wealthiest of all minorities. We can

reach Asian Americans through their television programs and subcarrier radio channels. We can also effectively reach Asian Americans through events and community organisations. Supporting such festivals provides the relevant involvement necessary to reach any minority group.
- Hispanic Americans: The Hispanic American population is predicted to grow to 30 million by the year 2000 and 41.2 million by 2020. They share several characteristics. Two of the most important are language (Spanish) and religion (most are Catholic). Each segment of the Hispanic American population deserves individual attention. They may differ by country of origin, culture, beliefs, and opinions.
- Native Americans: It is extremely important that everyone construct positive images of present-day Native American people to prevent racial or cultural stereotypes from becoming part of their beliefs.

Resistance to change: "the whitest industry in America"

Having established the need for change, Reese and Hawkins look at what the situation in the library and information field is and at forces that resist change. Stating that "we simply must open the doors of our profession to ethnic minorities", the authors set the hostile scene in the world of information for ethnic minorities:

We hear too often that the library profession is simply inhospitable to anyone who does not fit the stereotypical librarian background: white, privileged, with cultural enthusiasm, tastes, and the habits of social interaction associated with an Ivy League background.

Many African American library professionals outwardly describe the library and information science profession as one with a "hostile climate for minorities" that prevents them from feeling welcome. This criticism ranges from outrage to wry lamentation; some have commented that the profession is the "whitest industry in America."

Many ethnic minorities describe a hostile climate during interviews and employment in libraries that prevents them from feeling welcome.

There is a set of assumptions about minorities and a tendency to underestimate minority employees...it is difficult to establish your credibility when there is a mindset in which many white library professionals choose to remain ignorant of the severity of issues dealing with recruiting minorities to the profession.

Too often minority librarian professionals find themselves facing obstacles that have restricted their ability to ascend to management and decision-making positions.

Minorities still struggle to make inroads in a historically inhospitable profession that has proven resistant to change.

Such experiences mirror in the USA as well what Gus John[575] says about Black experience in Britain: "There is too little recognition of the fact that this society validates white people automatically while constantly expecting Black people to be proving ourselves."

---

[575] John, Gus, Talk given at the Conference The Significance Of The Stephen Lawrence Inquiry For Public Libraries. London And Home Counties Branch: The Library Association In Association With The Association Of London Chief Librarians (ALCL). Executive Briefing: Monday 28 June 1999. Quoted in Durrani S, Struggle against racial exclusion in libraries; A fight for the rights of the people. Leeds: Leeds Metropolitan University. Public Library Policy and Social Exclusion. Working Paper No. 13.

Tools and experience for bringing about change

It is a major strength of the book that it does not merely highlight problems, but makes available tools that can help to defeat the problems identified. Among the many suggestions it makes are the following:

Management and diversity — *Moving from the "comfort zone"*

The authors highlight the fact that it is a management responsibility to ensure that diversity is "mainstreamed". This is a crucial issue that is too often ignored, resulting in what has become popular in Britain as "institutional racism"[576]... They go to the heart of the matter when they talk of moving beyond the "comfort zones":

> The executive levels and administrations of the library profession have for far too long not been required to venture beyond their comfort zones. However, it is no longer possible to ignore the diversity of library customers and the need to make library staffs more representative of the communities they serve, whether they are on a college campus or in a neighbourhood branch library.

Reese and Hawkins show a number of areas where management responsibility is crucial:

- Any type of effective management of diversity requires organisational change on at least three levels:
- cultural, involving changes that alter the organisation's basic assumptions, values, beliefs, and ideologies that define its view of itself and its environment;
- structural, involving changes in the grouping of positions and departments within the organisation;
- Behavioral, involving changes in behaviors, attitudes and perceptions among individuals and work groups.

Valuing diversity

Valuing diversity translates into enhanced productivity, profitability, and competitive advantage. Specifically:

- Library management must view diversity as a business issue that affects the library industry's ability to compete effectively.
- Library management must view diversity as top-down initiative that requires overhauls in the library's traditional culture
- Library management must create an environment that reflects this commitment.

The test of such an environment will be the library's ability to attract and retain managers who are dedicated to making diversity work. "The new litmus test of the progressive organizations of the future will be reflected not only by how well they

---

[576] "The collective failure of an organisation to provide an appropriate and professional service to people because of their colour, culture or ethnic origin. It can be seen or detected in processes, attitudes and behaviour which amount to discrimination through unwitting prejudice, ignorance, thoughtlessness and racist stereotyping which disadvantage minority ethnic people." Sir William Macpherson (Stephen Lawrence murder inquiry report, 1999).

recruit and attract minorities but also whether their corporate culture truly values diversity and views it as an asset".

Leaders of change

The authors see the main impetus for change coming from ethnic minority staff themselves, not some external "experts" and "advisers". "It is essential that we utilize our pool of talented ethnic minority library professionals to lead change in introducing the profession and services to the many ethnic minorities".

Stop talking, start doing

At the centre of Reese and Hawkins' book is the Stop Talking, Start Doing workshops. They explain the start of the movement:

> At the ALA's Annual Conference held in 1994, the Chapter Relations Committee introduced the first "Stop talking, Start Doing" ethnic minority recruitment workshop. This workshop has been conducted at each Midwinter and Annual ALA conference since that time. This truly invigorating workshop is the brainchild of Florence Simkins Brown.

The authors sum up the spirit of the workshops: "Stop talking about the issue of ethnic minority recruitment and start formulating some new and creative ways to address this extremely important issue." This spirit needs to inform the whole issue around institutional racism in the library and information sector. The "stop talking, start doing" spirit was taken a stage further at the 1996 workshop when Camila A. Alire delivered a "message regarding the state of Colorado's commitment to making both public and academic libraries attractive to the minority public". Alire and her Colorado Ethnic Populations Committee produced a document entitled *Walking the Walk: The Colorado Perspective*. This had five areas of emphasis that demonstrates the library service's commitment to change and service improvement:

- Library personnel training: recruitment, hire, retention of ethnic minority personnel; ethnic minority populations to be treated by library staff members with sensitivity, courtesy, and respect.
- Library services to meet the information needs of ethnic minorities and to reflect diverse cultural values.
- Collection development: to contain a wide variety of materials by, about, and in the language of the state's ethnic minority populations.
- Celebrations: celebrate the heritage and culture of Colorado's ethnic minority populations.
- Partnership: develop partnerships with community groups to better serve minority populations.

It is interesting to note that the document then did not remain in the files of the library service. The points from it were incorporated in a "Model statement for Public Libraries" with each of the above points being turned into principles which each Library in Colorado was expected to sign up to. In addition, they were expected to use these performance indicators to see if the desired outcomes with time limits, were achieved. The following are just a few of the eleven indicators used in Colorado:

...

A number of interesting comments can be made on the above. First, there is not a strict division between public, academic and school libraries as is the case in UK. This enables the service to ethnic minority populations to be a seamless whole and not compartmentalised. The needs of communities are seen as central and the programme of needs assessment, as well as providing services to "targeted ethnic minority population" are areas in which British librarianship have much to learn. Similarly, including "appropriate ethnic minority representation" on boards of trustees is an area which needs to be given serious consideration.

It is also important to note that achievement of the desired results was not left to goodwill of managers. It became a requirement which then forced managers to move from their "comfort zones" to achieve the targeted results in the specified time.

Spectrum initiative

The Spectrum Initiative comes from the American Library Association. It is a "strategically planned and organized effort to recruit ethnic minorities to the library profession." It is important to note that the ALA concerns itself with recruitment and training issues relating to ethnic minorities. "The Spectrum Initiative has done more to recruit ethnic minorities to library schools within a very limited span of time than has taken place ever before," say Reese and Hawkins. In essence, the Initiative is a three-year programme designed to invite schools of library and information science to form a consortium for the purpose of educating a total of 50 students per year representing the four largest ethnic minority populations—African Americans, Asian/Pacific Islanders, Latino/Hispanics, and Native Americans.

The authors explain how the project works and how it is financed, with matching funds from library and information schools and ALA:

> Students receive scholarships of no less than $5,000 per year to attend a master's degree program at one of the consortium schools. Each consortium school receives $30,000 per year to carry out a variety of enrichment activities for the students. An annual leadership institute is held for graduates and midcareer minority librarians to meet and discuss issues of diversity and library leaders. The Spectrum Initiative is being funded with $1.5 million from the ALA Future Fund.

It is not clear from the book whether the programme led to the graduates of the Spectrum Initiative then managed to get decision-making position in libraries. In another context, the authors say, "Too often minority librarian professionals find themselves facing obstacles that have restricted their ability to ascend to management and decision-making positions." The lack of advancement opportunities has been taken into account by the Quality Leaders Project for Black Library and Information Workers in Britain[577].

Support groups

It is necessary for any oppressed group to have an association and a structure where the members can meet and discuss their problems and work out strategic solutions to their problems. This is a fundamental right to organise that is often denied to ethnic minority staff.

---

[577] See: Time to make a difference. Library Association Record. 102(5) May 2000, p. 246.

The authors address this need in the USA. "It is important that once minority candidates are brought into the profession or into the library schools they are allowed to express themselves as individuals and get support from faculty, colleagues, and management that allows them to flourish."

Reese and Hawkins' solution to this challenge is exactly what Black library workers in Britain have been struggling for over a long period:

Support groups must be formed within library institutions to give minority employees a forum within which to voice their concerns and to discuss their contributions to the organisation, as well as to serve as an outlet for cultural and social support.

The authors link the provision of networks with a system of mentoring as a possible solution of the many problems facing the information services:

In larger library organisations, it may be helpful to organize African, Hispanic, Asian, and Native American networks by granting them official recognition and providing a senior manager to act as a mentor. These groups help new employees adjust and provide direct feedback to management on problems that concern the groups. Combining mentoring with the issue of increasing diversity in a profession only makes good sense.

Reaching out to people of color – outreach services

Reese and Hawkins recommend that if we are to promote the profession to American minorities, "we must use techniques that marketers and advertisers have already begun to use".

The authors place particular importance on the information services moving out of buildings to reach the people they are supposed to serve. Their message is clear on what information workers need to do:

If your goal is to successfully provide a service or deliver a message to the African American community, you must *go to* and become *involved in* the African American community. You must take the time to learn the culture and lifestyle of the minority population with which you are attempting to make contact. [Emphases in the original].

One often hears librarians in Britain lamenting the fact that when they call community consultation meetings, few members attend. One wonders how many of them follow the advice given above by Reese and Hawkins. However, the authors are conscious that outreach does not "happen" in a vacuum. ...

While in Britain, we are still struggling with understanding what "social exclusion" is and how to eliminate it, the U.S. has moved ahead by instituting mechanism to address the social problems associated with such exclusion. While the British Library Association resists the very formation of a Black Workers Group, ALA recognises and supports the following caucuses as affiliates:

ALA Ethnic Caucuses
Asian/pacific American Librarians Association
Black Caucus of the American Library Association
National Association to promote library services to the Spanish speaking
Chinese-American Librarians Association
American Indian Library Association

Reese and Hawkins provide details of the purpose of these and examine how they operate. Their experience is essential reading for black library workers and communities.

Conclusion: Power is the key link

Stop Talking, start doing! is full of exciting ideas and experiences which are well presented and explained. That the experiences are so very applicable to the British situation makes them all the more relevant.

The authors explore the need for change and make a convincing case why changes are necessary. They also provide a large number of ideas which can help to eliminate racism in the library and information sector. What they fail to do, however, is to explore reasons why racism persists and the possibilities of eliminating it. They do not study the question of power in the society. While ethnic minorities increase as a proportion of the total population; while they make increasing contribution to the production of national wealth, they remain powerless victims of racism and class exploitation. The imbalance of economic power beneath the surface of social life in the U.S. is well explained by Reese and Hawkins:

> While minorities make up only 25 per cent of the U.S. population, they will contribute 70 percent of growth during this decade.

Yet they do not control 70 percent of economic power. The authors do not address the reasons behind this disparity between major economic contribution by people of colour and their lack of power to influence the direction of their lives as well as that of their country. This is where perhaps one weakness of the book lies: it does not see the connection between capitalism and the resultant poverty and powerlessness of people of colour and working people. If this connection is not seen, then a correct solution to racism so well documented in the book can also not be found. Earlier on, we noted the authors' contention that racism in the society finds its way into libraries. Yet this understanding then does not inform their methods of eliminating racism. Its elimination from the society as a whole is a prerequisite for its elimination from the information sector.

Another element which is important, but which perhaps falls outside the scope of the book, is the socio-economic context in which libraries operate. Racial oppression is an important aspect of capitalism where social exclusion, social oppression and economic exploitation are the basis of organised life. The prevailing free market system ensures that economic activity satisfies the profit motives of the few, leaving the material, educational and cultural needs of the majority of people unfulfilled. In this context, the issues of racial oppression and class exploitation are intertwined and cannot be considered in isolation. This essential connection between race and class should be kept in mind in any attempts to combat racism.

The distribution of wealth and power in society as a whole influence the way public institutions such as libraries operate. The context of a society where private ownership of property and production for profit allow some to have excessive wealth, power and influence at the expense of the rest of the community needs to be taken into account. It is this reality which leads to a large number of people being excluded from social wealth and power. Libraries cannot be seen in isolation from social forces all around them, nor can solutions be found if this reality is not understood. Perhaps the second edition of the book (there certainly is a need to review the situation in perhaps five years) can add such a context as the background to "Stop talking."

Black[578] quotes Lowell Martin: "The public library [in USA] remains a mainstream agency, serving a middle level of user groups, both in terms of financial and educational background. If this is the 'people's university,' less than half of the people are enrolled, and there are few additional applicants".

These points, however, should not detract from the significance of the book. It needs to be read not only in the U.S. but wherever people of colour are struggling for their rights. People of colour in Britain, as well as managers and decision makers in particular in the information field can benefit by reading this book. This is not only because of a lack of such studies in Britain; it is also because many of the experiences in the U.S. are applicable to Britain. Similarly, many of the solutions suggested are also applicable. Without exposure to such ideas, our solutions will remain incomplete. It is only on the basis of a wide range of ideas that a relevant British solution can be found.

Black perspective on history of libraries; a review article (2000)[579]

Tucker, John Mark (Editor): *Untold Stories; Civil Rights, Libraries, and Black Librarianship.* Graduate School of Library and Information Science, University of Illinois. Champaign, IL, USA. 1998. 210pp. ISBN 0-87845-104-8. $27.

History, it is said, has so far been written from the point of view of the ruling classes. The struggles of working class, *and from a working class point of view*, has yet to be fully written, popularised and accepted as the real history. Brecht raised the question of the worker's point of view of history. Just as the working class point of view is suppressed, so is the struggle of Black people in general, not only in Europe and Americas, but the world over. This one-sided interpretation of social life is reinforced daily by a distorted coverage of *present* events in the trans-national controlled media. This then will become tomorrow's history. Thus the cycle of distortion of working class and Black histories continues growing at even greater rate aided by the increasing powers of new information and communications technologies which seek to control the whole world in a globalised search for ever accelerating profits.

In this context, it is not surprising that the working class, Black and anti-imperialist struggles of the people remain untold. This is true in all fields, but particularly so in the library and information field, especially in Britain today. Yet the forces that seek to suppress this history also create conditions for the story to be told in one form or another, in one country or another, in one period or another. It is the black library workers in North America who are in the forefront of documenting their struggles. An enterprising group of people in mid-nineties used the new tools

---

[578] Black, Alistair (2000), Skeleton in the cupboard: social class and the public library in Britain through 150 years. [Written for Library History, May 2000].
[579] New Library World 101 Vol. (1155) April 2000.

provided by the Internet to document the struggle of "colored" librarians "in our own voices".[580] Another group towards the end of the millennium used local library resources to research the past struggles of black communities and librarians to tell the "Untold Stories."

Untold Stories is a collection of essays exploring the "relationship between books, libraries, and the great social movement of our times, the American civil rights movement." The book examines the struggles of Black communities and librarians in USA as well as in Canada for a relevant and "equal" service. This is done in the context of the Black civil rights movement. The underlying assumption is that library services reflect contradictions in a society at a given time and that to understand libraries, one needs to understand the social context and contradictions and struggles in the society at the time. "Democracy is not an institution but a process of emancipation," says a discussion paper from the Communist Party of Britain. *Untold Stories* documents this process in a particular historical period.

The process of emancipation by Black people in North America years ago is obviously of interest to historians, but does it have any relevance to British librarians today? The relevance of this book to British readers is shown in two statements made by two people in the context of two different continents, at different times, but connected by the same social and political issue: institutional racism in the library field. The first statement is made by one of the contributors in the book, Musmann (pp. 78-92).

> Many libraries in the South [US] remained segregated institutions until well into the 1960s. The American Library Association made few attempts to enforce equal treatments for its African-American members nor did the Association make any collective efforts to assist in improving library services to such a large group of unserved individuals. As MacCann stated so eloquently, African-Americans "were to be treated as permanent American underclass and the library history shows the library profession's culpability in sustaining that status" (p.91).

Is the library profession in Britain equally culpable? The answer is hinted at in the other statement which was made by Bob McKee, the Chief Executive of the British Library Association at the conference, "Institutional Racism; stamping it out in Libraries" at the LA on 12th November, 1999. Acknowledging that "institutional racism does exist in our profession", McKee exposed the extent of the problem by saying that out of over 20,000 personal members of the LA, only 1.2% — i.e. 286 individual members — were of African, Caribbean or Asian background. Even more worrying, Bob revealed that only 3 Black members earned over £27,000.[581] This implies an almost total powerlessness of Black library workers and communities. This is perhaps the first such acknowledgement from the professional organisation in Britain.

Another important issue raised by the book which is equally applicable to the British scene is to explore the reasons why such "unequal" treatment is tolerated for so long and what conditions suddenly force organisations to admit the existence of racism? In the British case, racism has existed in the library field for as long as there are Black people in Britain. As Gerry German said at the LA Conference, Black people

---

[580] Neely, Teresa Y. and Abif, Khafre K. (1996) In Our Own Voices; the changing face of librarianship. 1996. Lanham, Md, The Scarecrow Press.
[581] Khan, Ayub (2000): Stamping out institutional racism. Library Association Record 102(1) pp. 38-39.

do not need to be convinced that they are victims of racism—they live the effects of daily racism as made obvious at the discussions at the workshops and in the "Case studies".[582] The recent focus on "institutional racism" by the Government following the community struggle surrounding the murder of Stephen Lawrence[583] and the Macpherson Report provides the reasons why the existence of racism has come to be accepted by the white establishment in almost all fields in Britain. It is no longer possible *not* to acknowledge its existence in our profession.

The papers included in the book are divided into 3 sections: "Legacies of Black Librarianship", "Chronicles from the Civil Rights Movement" and "Resources for Library Personnel, Services, & Collections". They were prepared for the American Library Association's conference at Miami Beach in June 1994 and were prepared by the Library History Round Table, in co-operation with ALA's Black Caucus, Library Research Round Table, and Social Responsibility Round Table. It was this initiative that enabled the "untold stories" of Black library struggles to be told.

The fact that such pioneering research was conducted under the umbrella of the professional body in itself has lessons for Britain. The British Library Association has up to now resisted the formation of a Black caucus-type organisation and has paid no more than lip service to the needs of Black library workers and Black communities. The prospects of promoting research and conference papers on history of the struggle of Black librarianship are not even on the table yet.

The book looks at factors that "stimulate social change" and the role that books and progressive ideas and individuals play in this process of change. The "interwoven threat" that tie these essays together include the central belief in the social role that libraries can play in the liberation process. As Tucker (pp. 1-9) says in the Preface:

> What might be achievable in the growth and development of an individual, a group of students, a community, a race, or a society, could take root in the ability to read and be nourished in the opportunity to use a neighbourhood library. (p.4).

The experience from Canada reinforces the positive role that librarians can play in the liberation of black people. Kester quotes Rolfe[584] on the role of the public library as having "an important role to play in providing resources to counteract past derogatory and biased stereotypes in published materials that have contributed to racism in Canadian society." Kester own views on the role of the library provide another model for British libraries and librarians:

> Public libraries have done much to encourage diversity and alleviate racism in our society. Our work as librarians has empowered and "liberated", and we need to see each other as liberators of mind, both personally and politically. The minority librarian as liberator has done much in the self-assigned role of working with the African/Caribbean Canadian community, and in disseminating and developing the diverse literary, musical, and other artistic works of the black artist and writer...The

---

[582] Case Studies (1999): Case Studies & Comments. Anonymous comments about experiences of institutional racism in libraries from 9 Black librarians. Circulated at the Library Association conference Institutional Racism; stamping it out in libraries. Library Association 12 Nov. 1999.

[583] The Stephen Lawrence Inquiry; report of an inquiry by Sir William Macpherson. presented to Parliament by the Secretary of State for the Home Department. 1999. London. The Stationary Office. CM 4262-I.

[584] Rolfe, R (1984) North York Public Library: Collections and services for black and Caribbean community. North York, Ontario, Canada: North York Public Library.

development of black special collections in public libraries in Canada has been the story of the development of black people's self-affirmation and self-determination.

The first section "Legacies of Black Librarianship" carries four important areas of black librarianship whose history dates back to early Sunday schools in 1799. It covers Sunday schools movement, African-American social libraries, Black academic libraries, and the first Black public libraries.

In the nineteenth-century USA, Sunday schools became the "window for personal and legal emancipation because they taught reading, writing, geography, account-keeping, sewing, and knitting to girls between five and twelve years of age. Though the Bible was the cornerstone, Sabbath or Sunday schools taught children and young people, then adults, to read and write, and African-Americans were, from the beginning, a central constituency of New York City's Sunday schools." (Pettit, p.10). For many Black parents in Britain today, supplementary schools provides an important way of providing a relevant education for their children.

A theme that runs through the essays is that it is not only Black people who received poor library service: working class and women also suffered. Thus Black working class women suffered from the triple oppression. This was reflected, for instance, in the New York City's inauguration of Sunday schools as early as 1803 for "the poorest and most vulnerable residents of the city, white and African-Caribbean female children." (Petit, pp. 10-11).

Albritton (pp. 23-46) records the rise of African-American literacy and library societies with its "self-improvement" movement. Thus while white Americans were "setting up reading rooms, literary and debating societies, church literary groups, and early libraries before the Civil War," African-Americans were prohibited from using libraries, attending lectures, or participating in debates. But they did not wait for such facilities to be provided by others: they founded over fifty counterpart literary and library societies, and formed their own cultural, improvement, and education societies. Thus the "founding of these libraries as a type of social library was characteristic of the self-improvement movement in early American history" (p.36).

Hooper (pp. 47-61) looks at how significant political and economic changes influenced the development of black academic libraries—something alien to British experience—between the two World Wars. Thus "libraries of our traditionally black colleges and universities became monuments to human hope. The dedicated work and sacrifice of individual blacks and whites overcame inadequate resources, prejudice, hatred, and the fear of one's enemies, as well as ignorance, authoritarianism, and the condescension of one's friends." Most Black LIS workers in Britain will indeed be familiar with all these day-to-day problems even today. Circumstances have not allowed similar achievements in Britain as the ones noted in the essay by Hooper.

Williams (pp.62-77) tells the story of a "library of a particular type—the black public library scratching out a meagre existence in separate, unequal, hostile circumstances." (Tucker, p.5). It records the experience of the Holland Library, a racially segregated institution. Segregation of African-Americans in the United States "affected all aspects of Southern Black-White relations, including activities of real or imagined intimacy." Williams notes a truth which deserves to be taken seriously in Britain too when she says "Even libraries, frequently viewed as benign institutions, reflected the prevailing social realities."

There has obviously much change in library provision for black communities over the period covered in this book. It is interesting to note the reasons for this change.

Kester (pp.167-181) mentions perhaps the most important factor that has forced the pace of change. This is the struggle of the black communities:

> In the New York Public Library experience, according to Rob Rolfe, it wasn't until "increasing pressure generated from within the community as well as government studies and the programs and the collection initiated at the York Woods Library" that a climate was created for the library to look seriously at enhancing library service to the African/Caribbean Canadians within the entire library system. (p.170).

Lee says, "Quite often the advances made for blacks were brought about through the efforts of non-government agencies or concerned citizens with state and local agencies offering minimal support." (p. 93). Davis and Malone (pp. 110-125) record the proud achievements of the Freedom Libraries:

> Freedom libraries alone did not change attitudes, but they enabled the project to liberate African Americans from white domination. In the end the establishment of Freedom Libraries constituted a form of direct action, an attack on the 'Closed Society' where ideas and information represented a genuine threat to vested interests of the status quo. Freedom Summer Libraries simply did what the libraries are supposed to do — with their typically immeasurable but nevertheless real, impact on the individual human mind." (pp. 122-3).

It is not possible in a short review to cover wealth of experiences covered in the book. The following sections pick out important themes that may be of interest to British readers.

Black or people of color?

One issue of interest is that of the names that are used to describe Black communities. Tucker raises the matter of "diversity in the nomenclature adopted by contributors":

> Words and phrases frequently used include blacks, Blacks, negroes, Negroes, African Americans, African-Americans, Afro-Americans, and people of color. These terms reflect the dynamic nature of the subject in a context that ranges from personal reminiscences to historical scholarship... a fluidity of usage is perhaps something of a commentary on black life in America. (p.7).

Tucker's quote from Powledge[585] points to a possible "way forward" for us in Britain in deciding what "Black and Other Ethnic Minority" communities call themselves and what the rest of the people call them:

> I respect the desire of any group, particularly those who are oppressed, to choose the name by which they prefer to be known. I also respect the need of oppressed groups to choose new names from time to time, to mark the stations along their march out of oppression.

Lack of documentation of Black library struggle

Kester mentions an important fact about the lack of documentation of black library struggle which is relevant to the British scene as well.[586]

---

[585] The only criticism of the book in terms of its otherwise excellent references and bibliography is that the apparently important work by Powledge is not listed anywhere in the references. It appears to be an interesting reference and is also quoted at the beginning of the Preface by Tucker.

Although black librarians, and more specifically black women librarians, have only recently organised a professional forum and associations in Toronto for dealing with issues of mutual concern, the pressing information needs of the African/Caribbean Canadians as well as workplace discrimination have resulted in little in documentation about the experience of African/Caribbean Canadians as professional librarians.

Lee (pp.93-109) quotes Rice Estes who wrote in 1960 that Black librarians of South (US) "cannot speak out because of fear of reprisals and political retaliation" — sentiments heard today in Britain among Black librarians.

The lessons of the black struggle

Throughout the book, there are important lessons learnt about what needs to happen if services to oppressed communities are to improve. A few are listed below:

- *The need for developing links with the community.* Kester's research found that "Social and other services have not been able to respond adequately in meeting residents' defined needs. Many in working class and racially marginalised communities have felt that the "system" has been working against them. Residents have felt victimised by professional and other local social agencies in the community. Establishing trust with the community has thus been an important aim of many social service agencies including libraries."
- *Outreach as an essential means of developing links with the community.* Kester provides a good model of what outreach means: "Outreach to the nonuser would need to be personalised. Hard-to-reach populations might also be interested in non-print media and products of popular culture — such as rap music — as an alternative to traditional literature. Key to developing good relationships with community residents and users has been the need to be seen as 'approachable.' Thus, successful outreach has meant planning programmes with schools, grassroots community organisations, 'moms and tots' groups, or literacy groups, and youth associations."
- Davis and Malone provide the outreach aspect of Freedom Libraries in 1964: They served "civil rights goals in at least two ways: (1) by delivering books to people who had no other access to them, and (2) by instilling an appreciation of information in people who then demanded service at their local public libraries…they gave hope to the next generation." "That winter people would march to the library to stage a sit-in or picket. Such activity eventually forced public libraries in Mississippi to comply with the Civil Rights Act of 1964."
- *Collection development.* Issues discussed include the "adding of nonprint materials to the adult West Indian/Black Heritage Collection"; "buying trips to Third World Bookstores and Crafts and other book and music stores which deal with Caribbean and black heritage material"; promoting and encouraging black publishers, booksellers, and authors and of aiding, through financial and moral support, the production of black material; "Librarians make selection bureaucratically, hence, many small press materials, especially materials depicting the African/Caribbean experience may be missed when

---

[586] This point is also addressed in: Durrani, S. Black communities and information workers in search of social justice. New Library World Vol. 100 (1151) October, 1999. pp. 265-278.

selection has not included coverage of these presses". (Kester, pp. 173-4).
- *Role of African/Caribbean Librarians*. The importance of library users being able to see a minority librarian with the ability to understand their culture. It is important "to let the members of the community know that they have representation. We are there for them. We are a link. We are the broker for the community between the institution and the community" (Kester). Other aspects: Black librarians can make libraries "warm, inviting, and accepting" for the community, provide positive role models, act as "publishing watchdog" as well as play the "scrutinising role" as librarians have a social duty to select materials which portray cultural minorities in a positive light"; black librarians have a special responsibility to see that black heritage is passed on.
- *Confronting and challenging racism and effecting social change.* "We need to acknowledge the existence of systemic racism in our working and institutional environment and design approaches for confronting it directly" (Kester, p. 179).

"*Untold Stories*" contains a rare wealth of information on the black struggle in North America. It explores a whole range of issues surrounding the need for basic change in search for a fair and just society. It documents the valuable experiences from one part of the world. Its lessons need to be learnt by all societies seeking social justice and the elimination of "social exclusion". It needs to be read by all black LIS workers in Britain. It also needs to be read by all library managers and librarianship students.

Review: Framework of lost opportunities (2003)[587]

Framework for the Future: Libraries, learning and information in the next decade[588]
DCMS, 2003. A brief review published in "Library & Information Update" (March 2003)

The key question which history will ask the "Framework" (whatever happened to the "strategy"?) is whether it enabled public libraries to become, *in practice*, more open, relevant, and responsive to the needs of the people they are supposed to serve. I think it will fail this crucial test. The Framework is not a "blueprint with detailed targets", but aims to provide libraries with a "shared sense of purpose". An opportunity has thus been lost to make the necessary fundamental changes in libraries. It fails to give urgency to the need for change and implies that by making small changes, all will be well. "Evolution" is the catch word, when 150 years' of evolution has led to 17% less visits, and a fall of almost a quarter in visits from

---

[587] Library & Information Update, vol. 2(3) March 2003, p. 18.
[588] The word "public" is missing from the title of the document which is not about all libraries, only public libraries.

1992/93. It is a dangerous document that lulls us into complacency that a major surgery is not required, that the use of a few bandages will cure the patient. Carrying the seal of DCMS makes it even more damaging. It is not even a consultation document—it is The Final Word.

Public libraries need a stronger planning process through a strengthened Annual Library Plan. Instead, the Framework advocates a dumbing down of the Plans. We need a stronger regime of Public Library Standards. The Framework offers: "We now believe the time is right to move away from this mechanism". We need more outreach more monitoring, performance management and target setting. Instead we get a "strategy" for local authorities to "consider how they might translate these policies into a set of programmes". *Consider*, and then what?

Libraries will need to "demonstrate how they intend to deliver their services in…promoting reading and informal learning; access to digital skills and services; and tackling social exclusion", proclaims the Framework. Given the vagueness of this statement, all libraries can easily demonstrate that they are doing this already. So where is the change and development needed for the Next Decade?

In its long history, public libraries have not managed to reach the whole population. *Open to All?*[589] which was commended by the then Cabinet Minister, painted a very gloomy picture of the current situation. The Audit Commission documents a declining service. Vast numbers of people are "socially excluded", as the government is at pains to point out. Will following the examples of the "groundbreaking libraries" mentioned in the Framework enable public libraries to become open to all? There is nothing in the Framework that will change the situation in the next decade—or the one after.

Focus on buildings and technologies will not stop the decline of British public libraries. A clear vision, imaginative thinking, strong pressure for change, innovation, and effective leadership will—but where are they in the Framework?

---

[589] Open to All?: op. cit

Organize, do not agonise

Here ends this search for social justice, resistance, taking stands, putting ideas into action, information activism. What, if anything, has been achieved as a result of this journey? The information services have not shifted much ground, working people do not have information services that meet their needs, those with political and economic power still decide the direction of information (and other) services: taking the "public" out of the library and moving towards more and yet more privatisation of public services. Social and community aspects of libraries are in danger of getting lost. The tremendous potential for informal learning, skill development, increasing awareness and widening horizons, qualities that libraries have, is being eroded. The neoliberal vision of a public library service promotes the emergence of libraries as McDonald type outlets or loanshops[590] on the march to privatisation. The current leadership is certainly not creating a new, socially-relevant model of public library service. Hendrix asks some important questions:

> What is the brave new world for public libraries when all around us [are] changing at breakneck speed... so what is the 10-year plan for libraries? Is there one? The blueprint seems more like an out of date grey print, lacking in so much, very short on real vision...where is the leadership, the high profile, the support, the long term and national strategic plan?[591]

An article in this book asks the question: "How much dictatorship and how much democracy is there in the library field in Kenya?"[592] The same question needs to be asked about British libraries. It is this dictatorship at the local level which is killing creativity and innovation, demoralizing staff and depriving communities of the services they need and deserve. A few selected "future leaders" are in turn nurtured to carry on the same traditions of the current post-holders. No wonder libraries are "sleepwalking to disaster". Further damage is done by the severance of the information sector from its political base which thus ensures that the real questions of relevance and social role of libraries are not even raised, let alone resolved.

And yet this is precisely what gives this collection its relevance today. The articles are a search for alternative voices and models of relevant library services. It does not matter that most of the projects mentioned here have not survived until now because the dominant powerbrokers have reasserted their "right" to close down services which they do not approve of, however much people need and approve of them. At best, most of the projects have been episodes in a long-running guerrilla warfare. A liberated territory of an alternative library service is established for a time, lessons learnt, minds influenced and then the backlash of "traditionalism" sweeps away the innovative services. Their aim is not only to sweep away the experience and skills of those who participated in them, but to rub out the very experience from the "mainstream" of library literature. It is thus a matter of satisfaction that records of many projects and activities have been preserved in these articles. They provide a

---

[590] The term "loanshop" was introduced by Naila Durrani (personal communication).
[591] Hendrix, Frances (2007): Is our long term vision impaired? Gazette (CILIP) 15-28 June, p.7.
[592] Lessons in Kenyan librarianship: leadership, management and the library worker (1984). See the Section "Society and information: a South perspective".

fuller picture of the possibilities and the potential that exists among library workers to innovate, experiment and seek out more relevant ways of providing a public library service. They indicate that the library publics and communities welcome, indeed demand, such new services as without their support, none of the projects could have been established or survived as long as they did.

It is a matter of concern that even the current Quality Leaders Project (Youth) was made possible by funding from a chartable organisation—the Paul Hamlyn Foundation and not from public funds. It is a matter of regret that at a time when "Britain's public libraries are in serious trouble",[593] there is no official support for radical alternatives to meet the working person's needs in a changing world. The reality of public library services in Britain today is shown by Leadbeater who also looks at the possible consequences for public libraries if no effective action is taken:

> Public service renewal requires strong political leadership to challenge complacency, set ambitious goals and legitimise innovation. Libraries lack such leadership.
>
> If they fail to rise to this challenge, public libraries may decline so far that they cannot be resuscitated. A hugely valuable public network, which should play a critical role in promoting equality of opportunity in an increasingly knowledge-driven economy, could be lost. The public library system could be sleepwalking to disaster.[594]

Five years after Leadbeater's report, no real action has been taken. Instead we have more surveys, more Parliamentary inquiries, more consultations and more "frameworks", none of which tackle the fundamental questions that Leadbeater and others have tabled.

Perhaps African librarians have given a better lead in questioning the role and social functions of their public libraries. Mcharazo sums up this search:

> Over the past three decades, library and information science professionals in the East, Central and Southern African region have been pre-occupied with the process of re-evaluating the new roles of libraries and information centres in addressing challenges in the continent. Specifically, they have debated modalities of making our libraries and information centres more Afro-centric, people centred institutions, geared towards stimulating the region's socio-economic and cultural development processes and national transformation.[595]

It appears that this time round it is Britain who needs to look to Africa, China and South Asia for technical assistance in running public libraries as "people-centred institutions" having regressed from its past glorious library service.

But can it kill ideas?

An interesting political poster circulating in Eastern and Southern Africa during the struggles against apartheid showed a Western arms merchant demonstrating the "benefits" of the latest gun to agents of the apartheid regime. The apartheid agents

---

[593] Leadbeater, Charles (2003): Overdue; How to create a modern public library service. Laser Foundation Report. London: Demos. Available at:
http://www.demos.co.uk/files/overdue.pdf. [accessed 02 June 2007].
[594] Ibid.
[595] Mcharazo, Alli (2007): Preface in Mcharazo, Alli and Koopman, Sjoerd (2007): Librarianship as a bridge to an information and knowledge society in Africa. [International Federation of Library Associations and Institutions, Publication 124]. Munchen: K.G. Saur.

knew exactly what they needed to fight the liberation forces and ask, "But can it kill ideas?".

It is alternative ideas, information, knowledge, visions and experiences that are urgently needed in the world today. Projects can be closed down; activists can be marginalised and disempowered — even imprisoned and killed in some countries; misinformation and "created truths" can be used to misrepresent and discredit progressive leaders and organisations. Countries such as Cuba can be victims of economic sanctions and assassinations. Chaos and massacres can be used in countries such as Iraq and Somalia on false information to justify new imperialism.

All the above can happen and yet ideas and experiences of resistance and liberation live on to guide the present and future generations. They live on in the oral traditions of people and in the minds of those who were involved in developing them. They remain in the pages of books and in web pages. No longer is it possible to say that there is only one model of public library service, the one approved by global capitalism. People everywhere are reclaiming the age of reason. They are part of a new global consciousness, a consciousness based on ideas of justice, of equality, of rights for working people. Their creation of a new world is based on the free flow of ideas.

It is worth remembering that social revolutions start with small sparks. But these sparks do not come from the sky. They are created by the spread of alternative ideas, vision and experiences that can ignite the imagination of people who move forward to force change in societies. A new world is possible, as the World Social Forum teaches us. Alternative ideas have the power to give birth to this new world. The Pan African Movement urges — "organise, do not agonise". And relevant information can be the spark that leads to real liberation. Mau Mau activists in Kenya urged people "never to be silent"". That, in the final analysis, is also the call of progressive librarians and information workers everywhere.

Index

African Caribbean Library Association (ACLA), 171, 216 (footnote)
Agricultural information, 3, 11, 13, 20-24, 26-27
Agricultural librarians, 21-22, 25, 27
Alternative information, xxxiv, 131, 215, 228, 262
American Library Association (ALA), 105, 324, 329
Asian Librarians and Arts Officers Group (ALAG), 171, 173, 216 (footnote)
Black Caucus of the American Library Association (BCALA), 295
BME (Black & Minority Ethnic communities), 91, 109, 114, 166, 178, 181, 219, 243, 275-
British Council, 55, 56
British Library Association (LA), xxx, 85, 86, 90, 93, 105, 110, 171-3, 216-7, 230, 236, 244, 262, 272, 330, 333, 334
BWG (Black and Ethnic Minority Workers Group, Hackney), 86, 236, 281
C. L. R. James Library, Hackney, 97, 243-244, 273-244
Capitalism, xxvii-xxiv, 9, 29, 48, 56, 95, 99, 101, 142, 143-148, 152, 156, 197, 199-200, 227, 238, 282, 317, 331, 342
Censorship, 30, 39, 42-43, 50, 183, 194
CILIP, xxx, 219, 261, 297
Class, xxix, 14, 29, 39, 46, 50, 53, 57, 60, 62, 71, 73, 79, 83, 92, 96, 99, 104, 124, 126, 134, 139, 147, 153, 160, 181, 193, 199, 216, 224, 230, 237, 251, 293, 313, 317, 332
Class struggle/s, 35, 44, 57, 59-60, 62, 71, 84, 92, 125, 141, 162, 313
Commitment, 8, 16-17, 19, 31,34, 54, 95, 122, 129-130, 139, 160, 165, 168, 170, 173-134, 181, 187, 206, 218, 235, 247, 248, 266, 272, 277, 290, 300, 308, 315
Communication, 7, 12, 14-18, 23-24, 27-28, 30, 33-34, 48, 51, 53, 58, 63, 74, 76, 79, 86, 100, 125, 148, 150-151, 153, 169, 171, 189-195, 198, 224, 227-228, 249, 288
Community librarianship, 126, 175-77, 182

Creativity, 8, 14, 17, 20, 105, 113, 129, 131, 170, 208, 211, 298, 340
Cuban Library Association, 73
Cultural change, 138, 290
Cultural revolution, xxxi, 157
Democracy, xxxi, 9, 16, 37, 43-53, 69, 84, 94, 124, 135, 146, 160, 181, 187, 197, 205, 211, 224, 279, 306, 318, 340
Diversity, 23, 92, 104, 121, 123, 132, 173, 179-80, 218-219, 240, 245-246, 324, 327-328, 330, 336
Diversity Council, 219
Diversity Group, 216, 219
Effective leadership,xxxii, 122, 125, 130-131, 170, 208, 264, 269, 2290, 293, 298, 299, 309, 339
Empowerment, 91, 130, 173, 182, 184, 277-279, 292, 300, 319
Equality, xxviii, 41, 56, 60, 66, 83, 90, 92, 103, 110, 113, 114, 119, 131, 138, 160, 166, 179, 181, 205, 218, 234, 240, 246, 251, 292, 294
Eurocentric; Euro-centric, 45, 55, 87, 97, 233, 244, 273
Films, 3,19,63,209
Freedom of information, 38-39, 43, 45-49, 52, 72, 80
Globalisation, xxvii, 84, 123-124, 128, 143-148, 158-60, 164, 196, 199-200, 205, 209, 217, 220, 229, 255-257, 267, 282, 293, 299,324
Hackney Libraries News, 86, 87 (footnote), 90, 237
Hackney, London Borough, 86, 87, 91, 97, 102, 174, 219, 232, 241-244, 272-278, 281
Hearts and minds, 122, 181
Human rights, xxviii, 35-36, 38-41, 114, 135-136, 187, 192, 218, 322
ICT, xxvii, xxix, 133, 138-139, 167-169, 183, 186, 220, 227-229, 251, 286, 293, 298, 321
Ideological struggle, 57, 58
IMF/International Monetary Fund, xxvii, 45, 143, 150, 198
Imperialism, xxviii, 5, 6, 9, 45, 48050, 58, 60, 67, 70, 76, 101, 142, 190-199, 210, 225-226, 228-229, 236, 317, 342
Information communication, xxvii 13, 18, 24

Information dissemination, 23, 24, 227
Information Equality, Africa, 207, 264
Information kiosks, 18-19
Information policy, 52, 186
Information Society, 187, 200, 255, 267, 270
Information system, xxviii, 13, 15-17, 20, 23, 26-29, 31, 33-34, 58, 60, 143
Innovation, 113, 119-121, 129, 131, 170, 253-254,299
John, Gus, 274, 276, 281
Justice, xviii, 56, 117, 85, 93, 113-114, 135-140, 148, 150-153, 187, 192-3, 197, 205-206, 219, 250, 270-271, 281, 293-294, 318, 338, 340, 342
Kabete Campus, University of Nairobi, 3,4, 6, 224
Kenya National Library Service, 11, 28
Larby, Patricia, 55-56
Leadership
  See Effective leadership
Liberation, xxxiii, 3, 13, 15, 18, 46, 51, 53, 58, 60, 73, 97, 100, 142, 148, 153, 157, 162, 183, 188, 198, 208, 226, 290, 334, 342
Libraries without walls, 125, 162, 223,
Library Association
  See British Library Association
Library management, 59, 87, 112, 185, 327
LIS (library & Information service/science), 62, 66, 85, 87, 89, 91, 93, 106, 107, 253, 171, 183, 217, 249, 250, 319, 323, 335, 338
Literature, 52, 56, 59, 71-72, 80, 84, 191, 316, 337
Loanshops, 340
London Metropolitan University, 165, 205, 215, 255, 266, 290-191, 294, 297
Mainstreaming, 112, 115, 118, 165-167, 216, 247, 284
Marketisation, xxxi
Merton, London Borough, 110, 113-122, 129-131, 164-165, 167-170, 232, 286, 288
Multiculturalism, 136
National Book Development Council (Kenya), 186
Ndegwa, John, 55
Needs based service, 116-117, 164, 222
Neo-colonialism, 48, 49, 57, 69, 76, 142
Neutrality, xxxii, 62, 88, 159, 160. 164, 204
Newspapers, 10, 15, 28-30, 33-34, 39, 153, 187, 193-195, 198, 227, 276
Oral, 3, 11-15, 18-19, 22-23, 25, 29-33, 53, 58, 77, 123, 150, 209, 228, 249, 342

Orature, 58, 77, 154, 191, 227
Organisational change, 170, 208, 259, 270, 284, 298, 304, 307, 309
Outreach, 87-88, 91, 114-120, 166, 177, 232, 277,330, 339
PALIAct, xxiii, 187, 196, 205, 210, 255, 262, 271, 294-298
Pambana, 34, 50, 60, 67, 73, 76, 224, 226, 316
Passion, 122
Paul Hamlyn Foundation, 115, 121, 220, 260, 285-286, 290, 300, 309, 341
Peasant information system, 13
Performance management, xxxi, 115, 132, 164-166, 244, 300, 339
Photo documentation, 227, 300
Policy and practice, 97, 124, 187, 209
Political struggle/s, xviii,28, 41, 60, 196, 205, 226, 296, 315, 316
Politics of information, 66-67, 134, 141, 164, 196, 225
Privatisation, 143, 340
Protest, 28, 53, 150, 154
Publishing, 29, 59, 63, 74-76, 90, 154, 168-169, 194-196, 224-226, 293
QLP News, 259, 307
Racism, xxii, 85, 89, 98, 103, 139, 162, 171, 179, 183, 209, 217, 234, 236, 239, 241, 251, 278, 289, 322, 334
Radio, 12, 17-19, 23-24, 28-30, 33, 65, 210, 227-218, 249, 260, 326
Reflective learning, 252-254, 257, 259-64, 310
Relevant information, xxviii, 13, 27, 34, 60, 143, 186, 197, 205, 228, 266, 289
Relevant service, xxi, 14, 28, 32, 87, 129, 139, 164, 206, 246, 262, 274, 290, 293
Resistance, xxvii, xxxiv, 6, 39, 53, 58, 67, 71, 74, 78, 89, 100, 136, 141, 147, 149, 165, 180, 190, 224, 226, 314, 340
Resistance literature, 52
Rural development, 4, 12, 15, 226
Sauti ya Wakutubi, xxx, 4 (footnote), 7 (footnote), 31
SCOLMA, 55
Social exclusion, 88, 93, 98, 113, 119, 127, 143, 151, 162, 171, 175, 184, 200, 216, 219, 231, 238, 248, 251, 303, 320, 330, 338
Social struggle/s, 10, 15, 20, 28,29, 42, 53, 56, 57, 60, 65-66, 124, 159, 160, 196, 227, 290
Socialism, 44-45, 58, 141-142, 146, 148, 226

Songs, 15, 19, 29, 52, 58, 73, 75, 77, 186, 191, 227, 318
Spectrum initiative, 325, 329
Struggle, 53, 57, 94
    See also Class struggle/s, Ideological struggle, Political struggle/s, Social struggle/s
Technology, xxvii, 7, 18, 23-27, 31, 48, 58, 61, 69, 90-91, 151, 191, 194-197, 220-221, 241, 255, 299, 313
Theatre, 32, 50, 58-59, 75, 224, 316
Three Continents Liberation Collection (TCLC), 243, 272-274
Training, xxix, 3-4, 9, 14, 21-22, 31, 43, 65, 91, 112, 117, 159-60, 217-218, 222, 246, 248, 255, 276, 291, 297, 321, 329
TRIPS, 123
Underground press, 39, 50-52, 72, 74-75, 77
Underground publications, xxx, 18, 34, 40-41, 50, 60, 71-72, 76, 78-79
UNESCO 137, 154, 187, 207
University of Nairobi, xxx, 3, 7, 31, 188, 224, 316
Video, 16, 149-150, 228, 249, 260, 300
Vision, xxviii, 50, 87, 92, 94, 96, 123, 126, 129-131, 134, 138, 196, 208, 222-3, 228, 272, 293, 295, 299
World Bank, xxvii, 45-46, 68, 143, 150
World Social Forum, xxvii, 192, 204, 209-210, 215, 262-264, 296, 342
World Summit on Information Society (WSIS), 137-138, 270
WTO, 130, 198, 217
Youth Ideas and Action, 290, 307
Youth Policy Review, 307
Zambia Library Association, 4

About Shiraz Durrani

Shiraz graduated from the University of East Africa in 1968 and got his library qualifications from the University of Wales. He is a Fellow of the Chartered Institute of Library and Information Professionals (CILIP). He worked at the University of Nairobi Library from 1968 to 1984. Shiraz was an active member of the then underground December Twelve Movement in the late 1970s and 1980s. Following the publication of his articles on the history of Kenyan anti-imperialist, liberation struggle in national press, Shiraz had to leave Kenya and move to Britain in September 1984. Here, he worked at Hackney and Merton public libraries before taking up the post of Senior Lecturer in Information Management in the Department of Applied Social Sciences at the London Metropolitan University.

Shiraz's main interest is politics of information. His book, *Never be silent: publishing and imperialism in Kenya, 1884-1963*, was published in 2006 (London: Vita Books). His earlier short book, *Kimaathi, Mau Mau's first Prime Minister of Kenya* (1986, London: Vita Books) remains an important resource for political activists in Kenya today.

LaVergne, TN USA
26 January 2010
171049LV00002B/2/P